Critical Analysis of International Debts on National Policies

Written & Compiled
by
Ashok M. Gadkari

GYAN

Published, 2020

Published by

Gyan Publishing House
5, Ansari Road
Daryaganj, New Delhi-110002
Phone: 011-47034999, 9811692060
www.gyanbooks.com
E-mail: books@gyanbooks.com

Printed at: G. Print Process, Delhi.

Cataloging in Publication Data—DK
Courtesy: D.K. Agencies (P) Ltd. <docinfo@dkagencies.com>

Gadkari, Ashok M., author.
Critical analysis of international debts on national policies / Mr. Ashok M Gadkari.
pages cm
ISBN 9788121219716

1. Debts, External. 2. Debts, Public. 3. Economic history. 4. Economic policy. I. Title.

LCC HC51.G33 2019 | DDC 330.9 23

Contents

Foreword

I have read this book. It consists of three parts and gives profound knowledge of Basic economic theory. In this, Classification of Competative Markets has introduced two new markets. .Exchange risk on FCNR interest part is very well explained and it also explains how dealing in foreign exchange is concluded and swap cost mechanism. Bank scam which took place in 1991 has been explained in details which common man will understand fully this complicated issue. Many corporate debtors have made default in repaying their loans. Author has studied this problem well and has given the reason for defaulters which are well acceptable.

Part II explains in details the economy of (1) India, (2) USA, (3) China, (4) Russia and other 8 countries. Critical Observations on these countries economy shows the deep knowledge and research qualities of the author. Author has also analyzed critically economy of these countries and has given pros and cons of the economy and explanation.

Part III consists of International debt and Domestic loans, loan servicing problems and other matters connected with external debt mechanism which shows author's detailed knowledge of this subject.

This book is worth reading by all people and especially by the students of graduation degree as study for their degree examination. The book is worth for prescribing as a textbook for B.A. standard by University of Bombay and other Universities in India.

Mr. Vaibhav S. Bedekar,
M.B.A. in Finance

I read this book completely. Author has divided the book in three Parts. Part I gives the economic theory in a simplified form which is easily understandable. Adam Smith Micro economic theory and Keynes's Macro economy is simplified and easily understandable. Dealing in foreign exchange, Bank's scam are written in details. In fact, I understood both these issues in this book.

Part II is very informative and written in details. Economy of 12 countries have been nicely described. I like the Critical Observations of economy of every country very interested and acquired good knowledge on this matter.

Author took great pain in giving detailed economy of each country. Critical observations are of research nature.

Part III shows the author's profound knowledge on various processes of the external debts and domestic loans, their optimal utilization and managing of the Loan servicing.

Book is certainly readable by everybody and I recommend that everybody should read it. Book is worth for prescribing for study by students appearing for Graduation Degree examination in Economics by University of Mumbai and other Universities in India.

Dr. Tanuja P. Korde,
M. D. (Pharmacologist)

PART - I

BASIC FUNDAMENTAL THEORY OF ECONOMICS

Introduction: This part consists of 13 chapters. Chapter 1 consists of definitions and explanations of basic economic terms and concepts. At the end of the chapter, Marginal Diminishing Utility has been explained with illustrations.

Chapters 2, 3 and 4 give information of Basic elements of Supply & Demand, Elasticity of Demand & Supply and Demand & Supply Behaviour respectively. Chapter 5 consists of Production, Business Organizations and ingredients of Labour Productivity while chapter 6 explains Marx's Communism theory in comparison with Liberal economy. Chapter 7 studies Macro & Micro economy of Keynes and Adam Smith. Chapter 8 explains Market Mechanism while Chapter 9 classifies Competative Markets. Chapter 10 mentions International Markets in details while Chapter 11. describes Capital, Interest & Profit. Chapter 12 speaks about Government Controls while Chapter 13 studies Efficiency and Inequality.

Chapter - 1

Economic Theory

1 . Definition of Basic Economic Terms & Concepts

(1) Economics

Definition: Economics is the study of how societies use scarce resources to produce variety of goods and services and distribute them among different individuals.

Explanation

It will appear from the above definition that in any society there is ascarcily of resources and the scare resources are utilized to produce goods to distribute to different individuals.

In economics, the societies have no plentiful resources which are to be distributed to all individuals. Economics, in that sense is a science to manage scarce resources for optimum production of the goods and services to satisfy needs of maximum individuals of the society.

(2) Market

Definition

Market place is a place where buyers and sellers come together to negotiate price of the goods either physically or through telephonic conversion or though internet connection. In this market, seller aims to make maximum profit while buyer aims to get maximum satisfaction by buying the goods.

Explanation

Fisherwomen in the Fish Market know the economic better than common man in pricing her fish product and make profit in the fish market. Details about the fish market and determination of price therein will be seen later.

Common man also must know basic economic concept. If he has Rs.100000- to invest, he will find out which financial institution is giving highest rate of return. There are three following options for him to choose.

(1) There are banks which quote the rate for 2 years deposit Rs.100000-@7% p.a. 8% p.a. and co-operative banks offering 8.5% p.a. interest for 2 years deposit for Rs.100000-

(2) There is also a financial credit institution such as Shreeram Transport Financial Institute which offers interest @ 9% p.a. This credit institution has been awarded by the International Credit Rating Agencies the credit Rating "AAA+".

(3)There is another newly established financial institute which advertises to give 25% p.a. as interest. This institution is not assessed by the Credit Rating Agency and has not awarded any credit rating to this institute.

If the person invests in the new financial institute offering interest @25% p.a. and the institute goes into liquidation, he will lose the interest and principal amount of Rs. 100000- The person will be reasonable in investing Rs.100000- for 2 years in the 2nd.option with interest @ 9% p.a.

Under the last half-century, the study of economics expanded to include a vast range of topics. Major subjects are:

Micro economy

Definition

Micro economy is the branch of economy which studies beheviours of individual entities such as market, firms, and households and market mechanism.

Explanation

Adam Smith is usually considered as the founder of micro economics, the branch of economics which today is concerned with the behavior of individual entities such as market, firms, and households. In the Wealth of National (1776), Smith considered how individual prices are set, studied the determination of prices of land, labour and capital, and inquired into strength and weakness of the market mechanism. He identified the remarkable efficient properties of markets and explained how self-interest of individuals working through the competitive market can produce a social economic benefit. Microeconomics now have moved beyond the early concerns to include the study of monopoly, the role of international trade, finance, and many other vital subjects.

Macro Economy

Definition

In contrast to micro economy, macro economy studies the overall performance of the economy and is based on changes in business cycles that affect the recession and hyoperinflation.

Explanation

Macroeconomics is concerned with the overall performance of the economy. Concept of Macroeconomics came in modern form from 1936 when John Maynard Kenyes published his revolutionary General Theory of Employment, Interest & Money. In 1930s, England and USA struck in the Great Depression with one fourth of one quarter of the American labour force was unemployed. Kenyes developed an analysis of what causes business cycles, which spell out high unemployment and high inflation. Today Macroeconomics examines a wide variety of areas such as how total investment and consumption are determined, how Central Banks manage money and interest rates, which causes international financial crisis and why some countries rapidly grow while others are stagnant.

Demand & Supply

Definition

In any market, there are buyers and sellers. Buyers need the goods and seller sell the goods. Buyers buy the goods which give most satisfaction and sellers sell the goods which give maximum profit.

Explanation

Economic life is an enormously complicated with hive of activities with people buying, selling, bargaining, investing and persuading.

Economics use the scientific approach to understand economic life. This involves observing economic affairs and drawing upon statistics and the historical record. For the complex phenomenonlike the impacts of budget deficits a cause of inflation, historical research has provided a rich mine of insights.

There is always competition between buyer and seller in fixing price at various level of production. If the price is high, seller tends to increase production while buyer will reduce the purchase of the goods whose prices are rising. But in this there is variation in demand fluctuations of buyers in purchasing goods on price basis.

Equilibrium of Price

Definition

Price is determined on the intersecting of demand and supply.

Explanation

When demand is high, the prices rise and supply of goods increase. On the other hand, when price decreases, the demand increase and supply decreases. Lower price gives lower profit and therefore manufacturers have no incentive to produce.

Elasticity of Demand on impact of price

Definition

Price fluctuations do not affect demand level on equal basis.

Explanation

If demand for any essential commodity is high, price fluctuation of that commodity does not change demand for that commodity on proportionate basis.

If price of food is increased, the demand for food does not reduce but the individual spends entire income on food and demand for other commodities are drastically reduced irrespective of the price changes in other commodities. This is known as elasticity of demand. If price increases but demand is not affected, the demand is said to be inelastic. This happens in case of essential commodities like food which are bare necessities. This is paradox of elastically of demand principle.

On the other hand, if the price of luxurious goods increase, the demand is sharply reduced for substitute goods known as high elasticity of goods. If the demand for the commodity is fluctuated on the proportion of price fluctuation, the demand elasticity is known to be normal.

Positive Economy

Definition

Positive economy considers facts of economy.

Explanation

Positive economics deal with questions such as why do doctors earn more than Janitors. Did the North American Free Trade Agreement (NAFTA) raise or lower the income of most Americans? Will small pension amount to farmers in recent Union Budget will improve their financial conditions? These questions can be resolved by reference to analysis and empirical evidence. This puts them on the realm of positive economics.

Normative conomics

Defintion

Normative economy involves value judgement such as ethical problems and fairness.

Explanation

Normative Economics involve ethical problems and norms of fairness. Should unemployment be raised to ensure that price inflation does not become so rapid? Should USA negotiate further agreements to lower tariffs on imports? There is no right or wrong answers to these questions because they involve ethics and values rather than facts.

Cool Heads

Definition

Economics relies on analysis and theories. Cool heads weigh the cost and benefits of different approach.

Explanation

Cool heads impartially studies practicability the economy of the country and makes broad generations such as benefits of international trade, opening of economy by liberation etc.

Warm Heads

Definition

Goal of economic science is to improve the living conditions of people in their every lives such as good food, safe drinking water and good houses. If this is done on ethical basis, it is known as warm heads.

Explanation

Society cannot long operate solely on the utopian principle such as "from each according to his ability, to each according to each need...

Society can support the unemployment for a while, but when employment insurance pays too much for too long, people will come to depend upon the government and stop looking for work. If they began to believe that the government owes them a living, this may dull the cutting edge of the enterprise.

Market

Definition

Market economy is one in which individuals and private firms make the major decisions about production and consumption.

Explanation

A system of prices, of markets, of profit and losses, of incentives and rewards determine what, how much, and for whom. Firms produce the commodities that yield the higher profit(what) by techniques of production that are least costly (how). Consumption is determined by individuals' decision about how to spend and property incomes generated by their labour and property ownership (for whom).The extreme case of a market economy, in which the government keeps its hands off economic decisions, is called a laissez faire economy.

Market Mechanism

Definition

Market mechanism is a process/mechanism for coordinating people, activities and businesses through a system of prices and markets.

Explanation

It is a Communication device for pooling the knowledge and actions of billions unknown variables and relations, problems that are far behind the reach of even today's fastest supercomputers.Nobody designs the market, yet it works remarkably well. In market economy, no single individual or organisations is responsible for production, construction, distribution or pricing.

In the physical market like fish market, buyers and sellers engage in face to face bargaining. In rural areas, open markets are familiar where farmers bring the goods for sale.

Market equilibrium

Definition

Some people are buying while others are selling, firms are inventing new products while government are passing laws to regulate old ones. Markets are finding equilibrium of supply and demand by determination of price of the goods.

Explanation

In market mechanism, demand and supply play an important part. Producers produce the goods in anticipation of the demand for goods. Producers take into account the elasticity of demand for goods and bring the goods in the market for sale. Price is determined and there is equalization of demand and supply known as market equilibrium.

Command Economy

Definition

When the government makes most economic decisions by giving economic commands from top of hierarchy to those further down the ladder, we say that process as command economy.

Explanation

In command economy, the individuals have no authority to influence the market. All decisions are taken by the government. Government decides whether capital goods are to be produced or consumer goods. It decides how much to be produced and what should be distribution machinery. This happens in Communist countries like Soviet Russia and China.

Mixed economy

Definition

When the economy is controlled by the individuals/ private sector with the interference at each stage from a large bureaucracy, it is called a "mixed economy".

Explanation

In mixed economy. There is no complete control of private sector or government. Both act together with boundaries demarkated to each sector.

India is a mixed economy. In the years that followed independence, India opted for a mixture of socialism and capitalism. A Soviet style planning was developed. The state wanted to have control over controlling heights of economy i.e. sectors that were views as critical for supplying inputs to other sectors e.g. steel. But state never managed to such complete control. Private sector was allowed to operate.

No contemporary Society falls completely into either of Command economy or Market free economy. Rather all Societies are mixed economics, with element of market and command.

Production Possibility Frontier (PPP)

Definition

Production possibility Front means the maximum quantity of goods that can be efficiently produced, given the technological knowledge and quantity of available inputs.

Explanation

When limited resources are used to produce quantity of one product in lieu of other, we say that there is possibility of production frontier. We can illustrate by following example.

Possibilities	*Butter (Millions of Pounds)*	*Guns (Thousands)*
A	0	15
B	1	14
C	2	13
D	3	12
E	5	0

Production Possibility occurs when an economy cannot produce more of one goods without producing less of another goods. It implies that economy is on Production Possibility Frontier.

In debating whether the United States should evade Iraq in 2003, people wanted to know how much the war will cost. The administration said it would cost only $50 billion while some economists said the war might cost as much as $2 trillion. Actually, it is reported that war costed $ 8 trillion.

These were not just mountains of dollar bills but also number represent resources diverted from other purchases. When output is devoted to military tasks, there is less available for civilian consumption and investment. .

Opportunity cost

Definition

In a world of scarcity, choosing one thing means giving up something else. The opportunity cost of a decision is the value of goods and services foregone.

Explanation

When Robert Frost wrote of the road not taken, he pointed to one of the deepest concepts of economics, opportunity cost. Since our resources are limited, we must decide how to allocate our incomes or time. When we buy a car or go to college, there will be forgone opportunity.

When the country decides to increase its gun purchases from 9000 to 12000, what is opportunity cost of this decision? You might calculate the cost in dollar terms but in economics, we always need to "pierce the vell" of money to examine the real impacts of alternative decision. Opportunity in the above example is that, we must give up butter to produce extra guns. In the above case, opportunity cost of 3000 extra guns is GBP 1million of butter foregone.

Inputs & Outputs

Definition of Input

Inputs are commodities or services that are used to produce goods and services.

Explanation

Inputs are factors of production. These are Capital, labour, raw materials and land. For production of finished goods, these resources are essential. Capital can be brought by the producer. Producer may charge interest on capital which becomes producer's income in addition to the profit. Cost of raw material, machinery, labour cost and land given by the land owner for rent are other costs of factors of production.

Outputs

Definition

Outputs are various useful goods or services that result from the production process and either consumed or employed in further production.

Explanation

Output are finished goods which are brought in the market place for selling. Buyers and sellers negotiate for the finished goods. Buyer gets maximum satisfaction from purchasing the goods at the price determined and seller gets optimum profit by selling the said finished goods.

Efficiency

Definition

Efficiency means the economic resources are being used as optimal as possible to satisfy people desires.

Explanation

One important aspect of overall economic efficiency is productive efficiency. That requires that machinery should be modern, labour should know how efficiently machine should be used for maximum productivity. Labour should be skilled and possess the technical knowhow. There should be good air in the factory where workers are working. Workers should get good food in the canteen and their residence should be clean and near the factory. If there is a distance from workers' residence and factory, there should be good transport facilities.

These will increase the productivity and optimum production will be taken to maximize profit. Welfare of labour is very important for this purpose.

General Aspects of Economics

Often, economics relies upon analysis and theories. Theoretical approaches allow economists to make broad generations, such as those concerning the advantages of international trade and specialization or disadvantages of tariff and quotas.

Economists have also developed a special technique known as econometrics, which applies the tools of statistics to economic problems. Using econometrics, economists use the enormous data to abstract simple relationships.

Budding economists should also be alert to common fallacies in economic reason.

(1) Post hoc policy: occurs when we assume that because one event occurred before another event, the first event caused the second event.

In the Great Depression of 1930s, some people had observed that the periods of business expansions were preceded or accompanied by the rising prices. From this, they concluded that the appropriate remedy for depression was to raise wages and prices. This led to host of legislations and regulations to prop up wages and prices in an efficient manner. They probably slowed recovery, which did not occur until total spending began to rise as government increased military spending in preparation of World War II.

(2) Second fallacy is failure to hold other things constant. A second pitfall is failure to hold other things constant when thinking about the issue.We may want to know that rising tax rates will raise or lower tax revenues. Cutting the tax rates will at the same time raise government revenues and lower the budget deficit. They point to the Kennedy-Jonson tax cuts of 1964 which lowered the tax sharply and were followed by an increase in government revenues in 1965. Lower tax rates produce higher revenues. This is fallacious statement. It overlooked the growth in the overall economy from 1964 to 1965.

(2) Fallacy of Composition: What hold true for one part of the system is also holds true for to whole. This is fallacious. True Statements:

(a) When one farmer has a bumper crop, he has a higher income. If all farmers produce a record crop, farm income will fall.

(b) If one person receives a great deal more money, that person will be better off, if everyone receives a great deal more money, the Society is likely to be worse off.

(c) If high tariff levied on a product such as shoes or steel, producers in that industry are likely to get more profit. If high tariff is levied on all products, the economic welfare of the nation is likely to be worse off.

Economic problems of What, for Whom and How much

Three problems of Economic Organisations are what, how and to whom.

(1) What commodities are produced and in what quantities.

(2) How the goods are produced. Society must determine who will do productions, with what resources, and what production techniques.

(3) For whom are goods produced? Is distribution of income and wealth fair and equitable?

Production of various Goods by the Indian Economy

Products	*2005-6*	*2006-7*	*Growth rate %*
Sugar (mn t)	18.5	24.2	30.81
Coffee(ooo t)	274.0	280.0	02.81
Cloth(bn. Sq.m)	48.1	52.1	10.39
Motor Cycle & Scooters (000's)	7601	8444	15.09

What: What the economy produces depends upon available technology and knowledge as well as demand pattern. Black and White TVs have been replaced by Colour TVs which are being substituted by flat screen TVs. The Old type monitors are being replaced by TFT monitors.

How: The production of energy illustrates very clearly the "now" choices available to an economy.

Energy Generated (Gross in billion kWh)

Year	*Hydro Wind*	*Thermal NCES*	*Nuclear*	*Total*	*Non utilities*	*Total*
1980-81	45.5	56.3	2.9	104.7	8.2	112.9
2000-01	74.5	408.1	16.9	499.5	55.00	554.5
2008-9	114.1	617.8	14.7	746.6	95.9	842.4

Next Table shows in percentage terms the contribution of different combinations of different sources of energy generation to the total

Year	*Hydro wind*	*Thermal NCES*	*Nuclear*
1980-81	43.4	53.8	2.8
2000-01	14.9	81.7	3.4
2008-09	15.3	82.7	2.00

For Whom: Goods and services produced in the economy are only available to those who have income to buy them. In most countries, incomes are distributed unequally – a relatively small proportion of the population has income sufficient to enable them to buy the most of the things they want. While a much larger proportion has income that may not enable them to buy even the bare necessities of life.

A measure of income inequality that is widely used is the GINI coefficient. It is a commonplace to describe Indian economic inequality to be relatively low since the GINI coefficient for India calculated on the basis of National Sample Survey (NSS) consumption data has been found to be quite low. For example, the GINI coefficient in 2004-5 was 0.325, and is indeed lower than in many developing countries, including China.

GINI coefficient often refers to India's distribution of Consumption expenditure as NSS does not collect income distribution. In other countries GINI coefficient refers to income distribution.

Chapter - 2

Basic Elements of Supply & Demand

Modern economy relies primarily on a system of markets and prices to solve the three main problems. Economy is built up on dual monarchy of tastes and technology. Consumer Sovereignty operating through money determines what gets produced and where the goods go, but technologies influence costs, prices and what goods are available. We shall consider in the Chapter how this process works to a market economy.

Markets are always changing. Yet a careful study of markets will reveal certain forces underlying the apparently random movements. We must first master the analysis of demand and supply to forecast prices and output in the individual market. Demand for gasoline and other oil products rose sharply after World War II as real gasoline prices fell and people moved increasingly to the suburbs. Then, in 1970s, supply restrictions, wars among producers, and political revolutions reduced production, with the corresponding prices spikes seen after 1973 and 1979. In the years that followed a combination of energy conservation, small cars, the growth of the information economy, and expanded production around the world led to falling oil prices. War of Iraq and growing world demand for petroleum after 2002 produced a further turmoil in oil markets. Real oil price of gasoline (in 2008 prices) fell from USD 3.50 in 1980 to around USD.1.50 per gallon in the 1990 and then rose to USD 4per gallon by the summer of 2008.

What lay behind these dramatic shifts? The theory of demand and supply shows how consumer preferences determine customer demand for commodities, while business costs are and foundation of the supply of commodities. Price of any commodity increases because demand for that commodity increases or supply of that commodity decreases. This is true for each market from Internet stocks to diamond or land. Changes in demand and supply drive changes in output and prices.

Demand Schedule

From the careful scientific analysis, it shows that demand for commodity depends on its price. The higher the price of an article, the fewer unit consumers are willing to buy. In the Kenyes theory of Employment in 1930, Kenyes proved that there is one exception for this. When price of bread increases, the customer will spend his/her income on purchase of bread and demand for other things will be reduced significantly irrespective of their prices. Except the above exception, however, lower is the market price, the more units of it are bought.

	(1) Price (USD per Box)	*(2) Quantity demanded Millions of boxes per year*	*Remarks*
A	5	9	Initial demand
B	4	10	Increase of 1 over A
C	3	12	Increase of 2 over B
D	2	15	Increase of 3 over C
E	1	20	Increase of 5 over D

Illustration: Demand Schedule

The graphical representation of the demand schedule is the demand curve. Demand curve in the above example graphs the quantity of the product demanded on the horizontal axis and the price of that product on vertical axis. Quantity and price are inversely related; That is, Q goes up when P goes down. Curve slopes downward, going from northwest to southeast. This important property is called law of downward sloping demand. It is based on commonsense as well as economic theory and has been empirically tested and verified for practically all commodities – cornflakes, gasoline, college education, and illegal drugs being a few examples.

Law of Downward Sloping Demand

When the price of a commodity is raised (and other things are held constant), buyers tend to buy less of the commodity. Similarly, when the price is lower, other things being constant, quantity demanded increases.

Quantity demanded tends to fall as price rises for two reasons:

1. First is the substitution effect, which occurs because a good becomes more expensive when the price rises. When the price of good A rises, I will generally substitute goods B, C, D,———
2. A higher price generally also reduces quantity demanded through the income effect. This comes into play because when a price goes up, I find myself somewhat poorer than I was before. If gasoline prices double, I have in effect less real income, so I will naturally curb on consumption of gasoline and other products.

Market Demand

The fundamental building block for demand is individual preferences. However, we shall focus on the Market demand, which represents the sum total of all individual demands. The market demand is what is observable in the real world.

The market demand curve is found by adding together the quantities demanded by all individuals at each price. Does the market demand curve obey the law of downward-sloping curve? It certainly does. If prices drop, for example, the lower prices attract new customers through the substitution effect. In addition, a price reduction will induce extra purchases of goods by existing customers through both the income and the substitution effects. Conversely, a rise in the price of a good will cause some of us to buy less.

Forces Behind The Demand Curve

A whole array of factors influences how much will be demanded at a given price: average level of income, the size of the population, the prices and availability of related goods and social tastes, and special influences.

The average income of consumers is a key determinant of demand. As people incomes rise, individuals tend to buy more of almost everything, even if the prices do not change. Automobiles prices tend to rise sharply with higher levels of income.

The size of the market - measured say, by the population- clearly affects the market demand curve. California's 40 million people tend to buy 40 times more apples and cars than do Rhode Island 1 million people.

The prices and availability of related goods influence the demand for a community. A particularly important connection exists among substitute goods – ones that end to perform the same function, such as cornflakes and oatmeal, pen and pencils, small cars and large cars, or oil and natural gas. Demand for good A tends to be low if the price of the substitute product B is low. For example the computer prices fell, demand for typewriters will fall and that of computers will rise.

There is set of objective elements i.e. tastes or preferences. Tastes represent a variety of cultural and historical influences. They may reflect genuine artificially psychological or physiological needs like liquid, love, excitement and habit like smoking cigarettes. They may include tradition or religion.

Finally special influences will affect the demand for particular goods. The demand for umbrellas is high on rainy season but low in sunny. This is called seasonal demand.

Shifts in Demand

Many factors affect the demand curve:

(1) Annual income: As income rises, people increase car purchases.

(2) Population: A growth in population increases car purchases.

(3) Prices of related goods: Lower gasoline prices raise the demand for cars.

(4) Tastes: Having a new car becomes a status symbol.

(5) Special influences: Special influences include availability of Alternative transportation, safety of automobiles, expectation of future price increases etc.

Shift in Demand

As economic life evolves, demand changes incessantly. Demand curves sit only in textbooks.

When does the demand curve shift? Because influences other than the good's price change. Let us work through an example of how a change in a nonprice variable shifts the demand curve. We know that the average income of Americans rose sharply during the long economic boom of the 1990s. Because there is a powerful income effect on the demand of the automobiles, this means that the quantity of automobiles demanded at each price will rise. For example, if the average income rose by 10 percent, the quantity demanded at a price of USD 10000- might rise from 10 million to 12 million units. This would be shift in the demand curve because the increase in quantity demanded reflects factors other than the good's own price.

The net effect of the changes in underlying influences is what we call an increase in demand. An increase in the demand for automobiles makes rightward shift in the demand curve. Shift means more cars will be bought at every price.

The Supply Schedule

The Supply side of the market typically involves the terms on which businesses produce and sell their products. The supply of tomatoes tells us the quantity of tomatoes that shall be sold at each tomato price. More precisely, the supply schedule relates the quantity supplied of a good to its market prices, prices of related rules and government policies.

The supply schedule for a commodity shows the relation between the market price and the amount of that commodity that producers are willing to produce and sell, other things remain constant.

Supply Curve

Hypothetical Supply Schedule for cornflakes shows that at a cornflakes price of USD 1 per box, no cornflakes will be produced. At such a low price, breakfast cereal manufacturers might want to devote their factories to producing other types of cereal, like bran flakes, that earn them more profit than cornflakes. As price of cornflakes increases, even more cornflakes will be produced. At even higher cornflakes prices, cereal makers will find it profitable to add more workers and to buy more automated cornflakes-stiffing machines and even more cornflakes factories. All these will increase the output of cornflakes at the higher market prices. This will result in upward-sloping supply curve for an individual commodity. One important reason for the upward slope is the "law of diminishing returns". Wine will illustrate this important law. If Society wants more wine, then additional labour will have to be added to the limited land sites suitable for producing wine grapes. Each new worker will be adding less and less extra product. The price needed to coax out additional wine output is higher. By raising the price of wine, society can persuade wine producers to produce and sell more wine; the supply curve for wine is therefore upward sloping, this applies to more other goods as well.

Supply Schedule Relates Quantity Supplied to Price

	(1) Price ($ per Box) P	*(2) Quantity supplied (millions of boxes per year) Q*
A	5	18
B	4	16
C	3	12
D	2	7
E	1	0

In examining the forces determining the supply curve, the fundamental point to grasp is that producers supply commodities for profit and not for fun or charity.

Production costs are primarily determined by the prices of inputs and technical advances. The prices of input such as labour, energy, or machinery obviously are very important influence on the cost of producing given level of output. When oil prices rose sharply in 2007, the increase raised the price of energy for manufacturers, increased their production costs, and lower their supply. By contrast, as computer prices fell over the last three decades, businesses increasingly substituted computerized processes for other inputs, as for example in payroll accounting operations; this increased supply.

An equally important determinant of production costs of technical advances, which consist of changes that lower the quantity of inputs needed to produce the same quantity of output. Such advances include everything from scientific breakthroughs to better application of existing technology or simple reorganization of the flow of work. For example, manufacturers have become much more efficient in recent years. It takes fewer hours of labour to produce an automobile today than it did just 10 years ago. This advance enables car makers to produce more automobiles at the same cost.

But Production costs are not only ingredient that goes in the supply curve. Supply is also influenced by the price of related goods, particularly goods that are alternative outputs of the production process. If the price of one production substitute rises, the supply of another substitute will decrease. An interesting example occurred in U. S. farming. The government has raised the subsidy on automotive ethanol to reduce imports of foreign oil. Ethanol is today primarily made from the corn. The increase demand for corn (a shift in the demand curve for the corn) increased the corn price. As a result, farmers planted corn instead of soybeans. The net result was that the supply of soybeans declined and soybean price rose. All of this occurred because of a subsidy to reduce oil imports.

Government policy also has an important impact on the supply curve. Environmental and health considerations determine what technologies can be used, while taxes and minimum-wage laws can significantly affect input prices. Government trade policies have a major impact upon the supply. For example, when a free-trade agreement opens up the U.S. market to Mexico footwear, the total supply of footwear in the United States increases.

The weather exerts an important influence on farming and on the sky industry. The computer industry has been marked by a keen spirit of innovation, which has led to a continuous flow of new products. Market structure will alter the supply, and expectations about future prices often have an important impact upon supply decisions.

Shift in Supply

Business and constantly changing the mix of products and services they provide. What is behind these changes in supply behavior?

When changes in factors other than a good's own price affect the quantity supplied, we call these changes shifts in supply. Supply increases (or decreases) when the amount supplied increases (or decreases) at each market price.

Technology: Computer manufacturing lowers the production cost and increases production.

Prices of relative goods: If truck prices fall, supply of cars rises.

Input prices: A reduction in the wage paid to autoworkers lowers the production cost and increases supply.

Government Policy: removing quotas and tariffs on imported automobiles increases total automobiles.

Special influences: Internet shopping and auctions allows customers to compare the prices of different dealers more easily and drive high cost sellers out of business.

When automobile prices change, producers change their production and quantity supplied, but the supply and the supply curve do not shift. By contrast, when other influences affecting supply change, supply changes and supply curve shifts.

Equilibrium of Supply and Demand

We have seen that consumers demand different amounts of cornflakes, cars, and computers as a function of these goods' prices. Similarly, producers willingly supply different amounts of these and other goods' prices. But how can we put both sides of the market together? The answer is that supply and demand interact to produce an equilibrium price and quantity, or a market equilibrium. The Market equilibrium comes at that price and quantity where the forces of demand and supply are in balance. At the equilibrium price, the amount that buyers want to buy is just equal to the amount that sellers want to sell. The reason we call this an equilibrium is that, when the forces of demand and supply are in balance, there is no reason for price to rise or fall, as long as other things remain unchanged.

A Market equilibrium comes at the price at which quantity demanded equals quantity supplied. At that equilibrium, there is no tendency for price to rise or fall. The equilibrium price is also called the market-clearing price.

This denotes that all supply and demand orders are filled, the books are "cleared" of orders and demands and supplies are satisfied.

Equilibrium Price Comes Where Quantity Demanded Equals Quantity Supplied

	(1) Possible Price ($ per Box)	*(2) Quantity Demanded (Millions of boxes per year)*	*(3) Quantity Supplied (millions of boxes per year)*	*(4) State of Market*	*(5) Pressure on price*
A	5	9	18	Surplus	Downward
B	4	10	16	Surplus	Downward
C	3	12	12	Equilibrium	Neutral
D	2	15	7	Shortage	Upward
E	0	20	0	Shortage	Upward

Effect of a shift in supply or Demand can be used to predict the impact of changes in economic conditions on prices and quantities.

CHAPTER - 3

ELASTICITY AND APPLICATIONS OF DEMAND & SUPPLY

Supply and demand can often tell us whether certain forces increase or decrease quantities. But for these tools, to be truly useful, we need to know how much supply and demand respond to changes in price. Some purchases, like those for vacation travel, are luxuries that are very sensitive to price change. Others, like food or electricity, are necessities for which consumer quantities respond very little to price changes. The quantitative relationship between price and quantity purchased is analyzed using the crucial concept of elasticity. The price elasticity of demand (sometimes simply called the price-elasticity) measures how much the quantity demanded of a good changes when its price changes. When the price elasticity of a good is low, it is "inelastic" and its quantity demanded responds little to the price changes. The precise definition of price elasticity is percentage change in quantity demanded divided by percentage change in price.

Price elasticity of demand = E*

= percentage change in quantity demanded/Percentage change in price.

Different categories of price elasticity:

(1) When 1 percent change in price calls forth more than a 1 percentage change in quantity demanded, the good has price-elastic demand. For example, if a 1 percent increase in price yields a 5 percent decrease in quantity demanded, the commodity has a highly price-elastic demand.

(2) When a 1 percent change in price produces less than a 1 percent change in quantity demanded, the good has price-inelastic demand. This case occurs, for example, when a 1 percent increase in price yields only 0.2 percent decrease in demand.

(3) One important special case is unit-elastic- demand, which occurs when the percentage change in quantity is exactly the same as the percentage change in price. In this case, a 1 percent increase in price

yields a 1 percent decrease in demand. This condition implies that total expenditures on a commodity stay the same even when the price changes.

While calculating price elasticity, we take into account the relation between the percentage increases of price with the percentage increase of demand. For example, Quantity demanded was 240 when price was Rs. 90-. Price increased to Rs. 110- and the quantity demanded was 160. When price increased by 20 percent, the resulting quantity decreased by 40 percent. Price elasticity is therefore E/p i.e. 40/20 = 2. The price elasticity is greater than 1. Observations are:

(1) All elasticities are written as positive numbers, even though prices and quantities demanded move in opposite directions for down-sloping demand curve.

(2) The definition of elasticity uses percentage changes in price and demand rather than absolute changes. A change in the units of measurement does not affect the elasticity. So whether we measure price in pennies or dollars, the price elasticity stays the same.

(3) The use of averaging to calculate percentage changes in price and quantity. Change is clearly 20=100-90.

Elasticity and Revenue

Many businesses want to know whether raising prices will raise or lower revenues. This question is of strategic importance for businesses like airlines, baseball teams, and the magazines, which must decide whether it is worthwhile to raise prices and whether the higher prices make up the lower demand.

Total revenue is by definition equal to price times quantity (or P*Q). If consumers buy 5 units at $3- each, total revenue is $15-. If you know the price elasticity of demand, you know what will happen to total revenue when the price changes.

1. When demand is price-inelastic, a price decrease reduces total revenue.
2. When demand is price-elastic, a price decrease increases total revenue.
3. In the borderline case of unit-elastic demand, a price decrease leads to no change in total revenue.

The concept of price elasticity is widely used today as businesses attempt to separate customers into groups with different elasticities. This technique has been extensively pioneered by the airlines. Another example is software companies, which have a wide range of different prices for their products in an attempt to exploit different elasticities. For example, if you are desperate about buying new operating system immediately, your elasticity is low and the seller will profit from charging you a relatively high price. On the other hand, if you are not in a hurry for an upgrade, you can search around for the best price and your elasticity is high. In this case, the seller will try to find a way to make the sale by charging a relatively low price.

The Paradox of the Bumper Harvest

When there is good harvest and production food grain is bumper, total income of all farmers fails.

Food grain is necessity and therefore demand for basic necessary food products such as wheat and corn tend to be inelastic. Therefore if the food products production is increased, the price falls and the demand does not increase resulting in lower income for each farmer and total farm income for all farmers. Similarly, if the production of essential and basic farm products is lowered, the price of such products rises but the demand does not lower resulting in increasing agriculture income of individual farmer and total agricultural income of all farmers.

Price Elasticity of Supply

Consumption is not only the thing that changes when prices go up or down. Businesses also respond to price in their decisions about how much to produce. Economists define the price elasticity of supply as the responsiveness of the quantity supplies of a good to its market price.

More precisely, the price elasticity of supply is the percentage change in quantity supplied divided by the percentage change in price.

If the amount supplied is completely fixed as in the case of perishable fish brought to marker to be sold at whatever price they will fetch. This is the limited case of zero elasticity, or completely inelastic supply, which is a vertical supply curve.

At the other extremes, say that tiny cut in price will cause the amount supplied to fall to zero, while the slightest rise in price will coax out an indefinitely large supply. Here, the ratio of percentage change in quantity supplied to the percentage change of price is extremely large and gives rise to a horizontal supply curve. This is a polar case of infinitely elastic supply.

Between these extremes, we call supply elastic or inelastic depending upon whether the percentage change in the quantity is larger or smaller than the percentage change in price. In the borderline unit-elastic case, where price elasticity of supply 1, the percentage increase of quantity supplied is exactly equal to the percentage increase in price.

Definitions of Price elasticities of supply are exactly the same as those for price elasticities of demand. The only difference is that for supply the quantity response to price is positive, while for demand the response is negative.

Definition of the price elasticity of supply, E/s is as follows:

E/s= percentage change in quantity supplied

Percentage change in price

Impact of A Tax on Price and Quantity

Government tax a wide variety of commodities – cigarettes, alcohol, imported goods and telephone services and so on. We are often interested in determining who actually bears the burden of the tax, and here is where supply and demand are essential.

Take the example of gasoline tax. In 2008, the average tax on gasoline in the United States was around 30 cents per gallon. Many economists and environmentalists advocate much higher gasoline taxes for the United States. They pointed out that higher tax would curb consumption, and thereby reduce global warming as well as lower our impendence on insecure foreign sources of oil. Some advocate raising gasoline taxes by $1 or $2 per gallon. What would be the impact of such a change?

For concreteness, suppose that the government decides to discourage oil consumption by levying a gasoline tax of $2 per gallon. Prudent legislators would of course be reluctant to raise gasoline taxes so sharply without a firm understanding of the consequences of such a move. They would want to know the incidence of the tax. By incidence we mean the ultimate economic effect of a tax on the real incomes of products and consumers. Just because oil companies write a cheque for the taxes does not mean that the taxes in fact reduce their profits. By using supply and demand, we can analyze the exact incidence of the tax.

It would be that the burden of the tax is shifted forward to the consumers, which would occur if the retail price of gasoline goes up by full $2 of the tax. Or perhaps consumers cut back so sharply on gasoline purchases that the burden of tax is shifted back completely onto the oil companies. Where the actual impact lies between these extremes can be determined only from supply-and-demand analysis. When the demand curve is inelastic, pretax price of gasoline will demand 100 billion gasoline annually. Imposition of tax $2 does not affect the quantity of gasoline demanded annually i. e. 100 billion. The demand curve does not shift because the quantity demanded at each retail price is unchanged by the gasoline-tax- increase.

By contrast, the supply curve definitely does shift upward by $2. The reason is that producers are willing to sell a given quantity (say 100 gallons) only if they receive the same net price as before. That is, at each quantity supplied, the market price must rise by exactly the amount of the tax. If producers had originally been willing to sell 80 billion gallons at $1.80 per gallon, they would still be willing to sell the same amount at a retail price of #3.80 (which after subtracting the tax, yields the producers the same $1.80 per gallon).

What is the new equilibrium price? We find that new equilibrium price has risen from $2 to about $3.80. The new equilibrium output, at which supply and demand are in equilibrium, has fallen from 100 billion to 80 billion gallon.

Subsidies

If taxes are used to discourage consumption of a commodity, subsidies are used to encourage production. One pervasive example of subsidies comes in agriculture. General rules for subsidies are exactly parallel to those for taxes.

General Rule on Tax shifting

The key issue in determining the incidence of a tax is the relative elasticities of supply and demand. If supply is inelastic relative to demand, as is the case of the land, then most of the tax is shifted to the suppliers.

The incidence of a tax denotes the impact of the tax on the income of producers and consumers. In general, the incidence depends upon the relative elasticities of demand and supply. (1) A tax is shifted forward in consumers if the demand is inelastic relative to supply. (2) A tax is shifted backward to producers if supply is inelastic relative to demand.

Minium Floors and Maximum Ceilings

Sometimes, rather than taxing or subsidizing a commodity, the government legislates maximise or maximise prices. Governments have limited the interest rates that lenders can charge. In wartime, governments often impose wage and price controls to prevent spiraling inflation. During the energy crisis of the 1970, there were controls to prevent gasoline prices. There are increasingly stringent limitations on the prices that doctors or hospitals can charge under federal health programs such as Medicare. Sometimes there are price floors, as in the case of the minimum wage.

These kinds of interferences with the laws of supply and demand are genuinely different from those in which the government imposes a tax and then lets the market act through supply and demand. Although political pressures always exist to keep prices down and wages up, experience has taught that sector-by-sector price and wage controls tend to create major economic distortions. Adam Smith knew when he protested against mercantilist policies of an earlier age, most economic systems are plagued by inefficiencies stemming from well-meaning but inexpert interference interferences with the mechanisms of supply and demand. Setting maximum or minimum prices in a market tends to produce surprising and sometimes perverse economic effects.

The Minimum wage controversy

The minimum wage sets a minimum hourly rate that employers are allowed to pay workers. In the United States, the federal minimum wage began in

1938 when the government required that covered workers be paid at least 25 cents an hour. By 1947, the minimum wage was fully 65 percent of the average rate paid to manufacturing workers. The most recent law increased the minimum wage $7.25 per hour in 2009.

This is an issue that divides even most eminent economists. For example, Nobel laureate Gary Becker stated flatly, 'Hike the minimum wage, and you put people out of work." Another group of Nobel Prize winners countered, "We believe that federal minimum wage can be increased by a moderate amount without significantly jeopardizing employment opportunities."

These types of debate are issues of interpretations rather than fundamental disagreements on empirical findings. Such issues are personal value judgements.

Rationing By Queue, By Coupons or Bu Purse

Enter the government, which passes a law setting maximum price for gasoline at the old level of $2 a gallon.

At the legal ceiling price, quantities supplied and demanded do not match. The market does not "clear" because it is against the law for sellers to charge the equilibrium price. Consumers want more gasoline than producers are willing to supply at the controlled price. This follows a period of frustration and shortage – a game of musical chairs in which somebody is left without gasoline when the pump runs dry.

The inadequate supply of gasoline must somehow be rationed. Initially, this may be done through first-come, first-served approach. People wait in line – this is rationing by queue. Because people's time is valuable, the length of the line will serve as a kind of price that limits demand. We see rationing by the queue today in markets like health care, where price of medical care is subsidized. This is wasteful system because much valuable time is spent waiting in line just as a way of preventing prices from reaching equilibrium. Sometimes, particularly during the large wars such as World War II, governments design a more efficient system of nonprice rationing based on formal allocation of coupon rationing. Perhaps people get a gasoline ration that is distributed on the basis of the number of automobiles. Under coupon rationing, each customer must have a coupon as well as money to buy the goods-in effect, there are two kinds of money. When rationing is adopted, shortages disappear because demand is limited by the allocation of the coupons.

There is a profound lesson here: Goods are always scarce. Society can never fulfil everyone's desires. In normal times, price itself rations the scarce supplies. When governments step in to interfere with supply and demand, prices no longer fill the role of rations. Waste, inefficiency, and aggravation are likely companions of such interference.

CHAPTER - 4

DEMAND & CONSUMER BEHAVIOUR

Choice and Utility Theory

In explaining consumer behavior, economics relies on the fundamental premise that people choose those goods and services they value most highly. To describe the way consumers choose among different consumption possibilities, economists a century ago developed the notion of utility. From the notion of utility, they were able to derive the demand curve and explain its properties.

Marginal Utility and The Law of Diminishing Marginal Utility

Consuming the first unit of ice cream gives you a certain level of satisfaction or utility. Now imagine the consuming a second unit. Your total utility goes up because the second unit of the good gives you some additional utility.

Market demands or demand curves are explained as stemming from the process of individuals' choosing their most preferred bundle of consumption goods and services. What about adding a third and fourth unit of the same good? Eventually, if you eat enough ice cream, instead of adding to your satisfaction or utility, it makes you sick!

This leads us to the fundamental economic concept of marginal utility. When you eat an additional unit of ice cream, you will get some additional satisfaction or utility. The increment to your utility is called marginal utility.

The expression "marginal" is a key term in economics and always means "additional" or "extra". Marginal utility you get from consumption for the consumption of an additional unit of a commodity.

Law of diminishing marginal utility is the law which states that the amount of extra or marginal utility declines as a person consumes more and more of a good.

The law of marginal utility states that, as the amount of a good consumed increases, the marginal utility of that good tends to decline.

Example

(1) Quantity of a good consumed Q	(1) (2) Total utility U	(3) Marginal Utility MU
0	0	
1	4	4
2	7	3
3	9	2
4	10	1
5	10	0

We will see that additional unit at each stage gives total utility increases upto 4 units to 10 total units. Marginal utility at each additional consumption of unit however reduces the marginal utility. At 1st unit, it is 4, second unit, 3 and so on.

Economists explain consumer demand by concept of utility which denotes the relative satisfaction that a consumer obtains from using different commodities. The additional satisfaction obtained from committing an additional unit of a good is termed as marginal utility, where "marginal" means the extra or incremental utility. The law of diminishing marginal utility states that as the amount of a commodity consumed increases, the marginal utility of the last unit consumed tends to decrease.

Economists assume that consumers allocate their limited incomes so as to obtain the greatest satisfaction or utility. To maximize utility consumer must satisfy the equimarginal principle that the marginal utilities of the last dollar spent on each and every good must be equal.

Only when the marginal utility per dollar is equal for apples, bacon, coffee, and everything, consumer will attain the greatest satisfaction from a limited dollar income. But be careful that to note that the marginal utility of a $50-per-cent bottle of perfume is not equal to the marginal utility of $50-per-cent glass of cola. Rather, their marginal utilities divided by price per unit are all equal in the consumer's optimal allocation. That is, their marginal utilities per last dollar, MU/P are equalized.

Equal marginal utility or benefit per unit of resource is a fundamental rule of choice. Take any scarce resource, such as time. If you want to maximize the value or utility of that resource, make sure that the marginal benefit per unit of the resource is equalized in all uses.

The market demand curve for all consumers is derived by adding horizontally the separate demand curves of each consumer. A demand curve can shift for many reasons. For example, a rise in income will normally shift DD rightward, thus increasing demand; a rise in the price of a substitute good (e.g. chicken or beef) will also create a similar upward shift in demand; a rise in the price of a complementary good will turn cause the DD curve to shift downward and leftward. Still other factors such as changing demand, population or expectations – can affect demand.

We can gain added insight into the factors that cause downward-slopping demand by separately the effect of a price rise into substitution and income effect. (a) The substitution effect occurs when a higher price leads to substitution of other goods to meet satisfaction. (b) The income effect means that a price increase lowers real income and thereby reduces the desired consumption of most commodities. For most goods, substitution and income effects of a price increase reinforce one another and lead to the downward – sloping demand. We measure the quantitative responsiveness of demand to income by the income elasticity, which is the percentage change in quantity demanded divided by the percentage change in income. Marginal utility wags the market price. This point is emphasized by the concept of consumer surplus. We pay the same price for the last quarter of milk as for the first. But, because of the law of diminishing marginal utility, marginal utilities of earlier units are greater than that of the last unit. This means that we would have been willing to pay more than the market for each of the earlier units.

The excess of total value over marginal value is called consumer surplus. Consumer surplus reflects the benefit we gain from being able to buy all units at the same low price. In the simplified cases, we can measure consumer surplus as the area between the demand curve and the price line. It is a concept relevant for many public decisions – such as deciding when the commodity should incur the heavy expenses of a road or bridge or set aside land for a wilderness area.

Chapter - 5

Production, Business Organization and Production Costs & Ingredients of Labour Productivity

Before we can get bread, someone must bake it. Similarly, the economy's ability to build cars, generate electricity, write computer programs, and deliver the multitude of goods and services that are in our gross domestic product depends upon our productive capacity Productive capacity is determined by the size and quality of the labour force, by the quantity and quality of the capital stock., by the nation's technical knowledge along with the ability to use that knowledge, and by the nature of public and private institutions. Why are living standards high in North America? Low in tropical Africa? For answers, we should look to how well the machine of production is running.

Our goal to understand how market forces determine the supply of goods and services.

Theory of Production and Marginal Products Basic Concepts

A modern economy has an enormously varied set of productive activities. A farm takes fertilizer, seed, land and labour and turns them into wheat or corn. Modern factories take inputs such energy, raw materials, computerized machinery and labour and use them to produce tractors, DVDs or tubes of toothpaste. An airline takes airplanes, fuel, labour and computerized reservation systems and provides passengers with an ability to travel quickly through its network of routes.

The Production Function

Given the available technical knowledge, land, and machinery and so on, only a certain quantity of tractors or toothpaste can be obtained from a given amount of labour. The relationship between the amount of input required and the amount of output that can be obtained is called the Production function.

The production function specifies the maximum output that can be produced with the given quantity of inputs. It is defined for a given state of engineering and the technical knowledge.

The relationship between the quantity of output (such as wheat, steel or automobiles) and the quantity of inputs (of labour, land and capital) is called the production function. Total product is the total output divided by the total quantity of inputs. We can calculate the marginal product of a factor as an extra output added for each additional unit of input while holding all other input constant.

According to the law of diminishing returns, the marginal product of each input will generally decline as the amount of that input increases, when all other inputs are held constant.

The returns of scale reflect the impact on output of a balanced increase in all inputs. A technology in which doubling all inputs leads to an exact doubling of outputs displays constant returns of scale. When doubling inputs leads to less than double (more than double) the quantity of output, the situation is one of decreasing (increasing) returns to scale.

Because decisions take time to implement, and because capital and other factors are often very long-lived, the reaction of production may change over different time periods. The short run is a period in which variable factors, such as labour or material inputs, can be easily changed but fixed factors cannot. In the long run, the capital stock (a firm's machinery and factories) can depreciate and be replaced. In the long run, all inputs, fixed and variable, can be adjusted.

Technological change refers to a change in the underlying techniques of production, as occurs when a new product or process of production is invented or an old product or process of production is invented or old product or process is improved. In such situations, the same output is produced with fewer inputs or more output is produced with the same inputs. Technology change shifts the production function upward.

Attempts to measure an aggregate production function for the American economy tend to corroborate theories of production and marginal products. In the twentieth century, technological change increased the productivity of both labour and capital. Total factor productivity (measuring the total output to total inputs) grew at round 1 ½ percentage per year over the twentieth century, although from 1970s to the mid-1990s the rate of productivity growth slowed markedly and real wages stopped growing. But underestimating the importance of new and improved products may lead to a significant underestimate of productivity growth.

Business Organizations

Business firms are specialized organizations devoted to managing the process of production.

Firms come in tiny one-person proprietorships, some in partnerships, and the bulk in corporations. Each kind of enterprise has advantages and disadvantages. Small businesses are flexible, can market new products, and can disappear quickly. But they suffer from fundamental disadvantage of being unable to accumulate large amounts of capital from a dispersed group of investors. Today's large corporation, granted limited liability by the state, is able to amass billions of dollars of capital by borrowing from banks, bondholders, and stock markets.

In a modern economy, business corporations produce most goods and services because economies of mass production necessitate that output be produced at high volumes, the technology of production requires much more capital than a single individual would willingly out at risk, and efficient production requires careful management and coordination of tasks by a centrally directed entity.

The modern corporation may involve divided incentives because of the divorce of ownership from control, which has produced the vast gulf between executive compensation and average wades.

Economic Analyss of Costs

Total cost (TC) can be broken into fixed cost (FC) and variable cost (VC). Fixed cost are unaffected by any production decisions, while variable costs are incurred on items like labour or materials which increase as production levels rise.

Material cost (MC) is the extra total cost resulting from 1 extra unit of output. Average total cost (AC) is the sum of every decline fixed cost (AFC) and average variable cost (AVC). Short-run average cost is generally represented by a U-shaped curve that is always intersected at the minimum point by the rising MC curve. Useful rules to remember are:

TC = FC+ VC. AC= TC/q AC= AFC=AVC

At the bottom of U-shaped AC, MC=AC= minimum AC.

Costs and productivity are like mirror images. When the law of diminishing returns holds, the marginal product falls and the MC curve rises. When there is an initial stage of increasing returns, MC initially fails.

We may apply cost and production concepts to a firm choice of the best combination of factors of production. Firms that desire to maximize profits will want to minimize the cost of producing a given level of output. In this case, the firm will follow the least-cost rule: different factors will be chosen so that the marginal product per dollar of input is equalized for all inputs. This implies that MP1 /P1 = MPA/ PA=.....

Economic Costs and Business Accounting

To understand accounting, the most important relationships are:

(1) The character of income statement (or Profit & Loss account); the residual nature of profits; and depreciation of fixed assets.

(2) The fundamental balance sheet relationship between assets, liabilities and net worth; the breakdown of each of these into financial and fixed assets; and residual nature of net worth.

Opportunities Costs

The economist's definition of costs is broader than the accountant's. Economic cost includes not only the obvious out-of- pocket purchases or monetary transactions but also more subtle opportunity cost, such as the return to labour supplied by the owner of a firm. These opportunity costs are rightly constrained by the bids and offers in competitive markets, so price is close to opportunity cost for marketed goods and services.

The most important application of opportunity cost arises for nonmarket goods- which may be highly valuable even though they are not bought and sold in markets.

Ingredients of Labour Productivity

Every enterpreneurs concentrates on reducing cost of product and produce the qualities product. For this purpose, in addition to modern machinery, he must have labour productivity. Entrepreneur should concentrate on labour productivity. Main ingredients of labour productivity are as under:

(1) Industry must have new modern advanced technology machinery and equipment at production site.

(2) Workers should be fully trained in operating these modern machines and equipments.

(3) Skilled workers should be hired. Raw materials should be ample and should be available at production site all the times.

(4) Autmosphere in production site/factory area should be peaceful and calm.

(5) There should be air-conditiong in office premises to increase productivity of workers and managing staff.

(6) Factory premises should be clean, and airy.

(7) Separate bathrooms arrangements for man and ladies should be provided. Special attention of cleaness of these sanitary facilities in the premises should be constantly monitored and maintained.

(8) Workers should be paid high salaries to manage financial needs of their families.

(9) Transport system should be up-to date so that workers from their residential areas will be brought to the factory premises and will be returned to their residential houses.

(10) Medical Insurance facility should be provided to the workers and their families free of cost or at concessional rates. Cashless medical facilities should be available for hospitalization and major operations.

(11) There should constructive workers Union with whom the management should discuss, understand the workers' problems for sympathetic resolution at the earliest.

(12) Workers should be provided with standard food/lunch/dinner all the times regularly at concessional rats.

(13) Depreciation Fund should be properly maintained and utilized for which it was established to replace old machinery with highly technical modern new machinery and equipments. Proper attention should be maintained by upper management to strictly comply with financial discipline. Otherwise, precarious condi-tions like Mumbai textile mills will prevail by utilizing depreciation fund for other purposes than to replace old machines with modern new machines and new equipments.

(14) If all these ingredients are fulfilled strictly, efficiently of the worker/labour will be improved and more production will be obtained from members/labour resulting in optimal productivity of the labourers.

CHAPTER - 6

THEORY OF KARL MARX'S COMMUNISM &THEORY OF LIBERALIZATION ADOPTED BY DEMOCRATIC COUNTRIES

Communism

In his book 'Das Capitol", Karl Marx has laid down the theory of Communism stating that in the communism, issues in financial conditions of farmers and workers will be satisfactorily resolved and they will administer the country and the state will "wither away". But any country which adopted the above theory such as Russia and China have not 'withered away." Even the issue of improving the financial condition of farmers and workers is complied with partially. Czecosalvika which adopted communism with the President Marshal Tito as the ruler has a different experience. Marshal Tito became the richest person in the world. This is the tragedy of communism.

In China, Mau Se Tong took over as a President of China.in 1970s. In China, ruling Party head is supreme and he ensures that there are no rival for him. Communist country does not believe in liberalization of economy. China had more than 135 crores as the population. Industries were producing low cost products which were used to be exported to other countries. But China's economy was not opened and therefore many countries impose restrictions on China's trade. In order to come out of it, China's leader Mau Se Tung opened the economy. This give boost to China's economy. Economic growth of China started rising to 7.5% p.a. at an average and China became second largest country after US. China took many US and UK companies under merger and acquisition but was not successful. It opened their companies in US and started dominating US in trade. Trade surplus of China was $350 billion. This resulted in country becoming financially strong. With its strong financial conditions, China, however, started dominating other countries by acquiring ownership of South China Sea area which belongs to Philippines, Japan and other countries. Present President Xi Jinping has become so supreme that he not only shows supremacy on political, military and economic sectors but also religious sector and instruct the people to follow what region he will instruct them to follow. Under "one Belt one Road" policy, China is dominating surrounding countries by financial assistance. India has refused to join the China's one road policy and US President has waged trade war on China by rising heavy customs duty on various items that US imports. This has slowed down China's economic growth to 6.3% in 2019.

Under the present leadership, China is developing spy activities to compete US but has not yet succeeded.

Situation in Russia is not very different. Putin is President who wants to dominate the world by the military strength. In order to come out of sanctions imposed upon them, China and Russia are engaged in introducing another international currency but are not yet successful at initial stage.

Though Communism does not believe in liberation of economy, Chinese economy and Russian economy has grown considerably only after adopting liberal economic principles to limited extent.

Liberal Economy

In liberal economy which is followed by US, UK and other democratic countries, goods are produced by the countries which are specialized and earn maximum profit. Such countries do not produce commodities whose cost of production is high and are not much profitable. These commodities are imported from the other countries.

Prior to 1991, Indian economy was not opened and there were exchange control regulations in force in India. In 1991, India's foreign exchange position was very bad and the country had foreign exchange reserves which were sufficient for maximum 2 weeks. External debt service was acute problem. Debt servicing rate was 34% and in order to repay interest and principal of external debt, India had to apply to IMF for bail-out package of $1.8 billion. IMF approved Indian application on the condition that India will liberate its economy. Indian economy was mixed economy that time. Under the leadership of Narsingh Rao, India introduced liberal economic policy which was most successful. External debt servicing rate drastically came down from 34% to 4% and India's foreign exchange reserves increased sizable to meet international liabilities for more than 6 months. India's financial growth rate is at present the highest in the world with 7.5% p.a.

In Liberation, the country who has opened its markets internationally for any outside country will get the financial assistance in foreign exchange to make development in its country by way of improving infrastructural facilities, constructing roads for easy transportation, installation of capital goods industry, heavy machinery, growth under industrial policy to enhance the industrial production and making development for merchandised agriculture, improved fertilizers, water supply to the farms etc. at very low interest rates from IMF or World Bank. Financial assistance received from other foreign countries will be at very high interest rates and with stringent conditions. Generally, if there is default in debt servicing, the Loan repayment is restructured but with austerity measures to be implemented by defaulting country such as increase in rising taxation to increase government revenue and reduction in public welfare expenditure to improve defaulting country's debt servicing ability in future. But there are countries like China which does not believe in restructuring of loan in case of default for the defaulting country but will capture any port or earning business of that sovereign country to get forcefully the repayment of its principal amount of loan and interest. Many countries are therefore afraid of taking external loans from China for "One Belt One Road" policy. China has therefore became most unreliable country as a lender of external debt. In case of default by the debtor country, London Club or Paris Club makes negotiation with lead bank to finalise the debt servicing issue which is binding on other associated banks giving loan to the debtor country. Debtor country should make a careful plan to utilize the amount of the external debt effectively for the development of the country within the stipulated time and ensured that the project is implemented successfully without delay in accomplishing its goals. In case of delay, the debt servicing problem occurs and can be resolved by bail out arrangement.

Under the theory of liberation, both countries open their markets for merger & acquisition permitting each other to provide capital in the foreign company as per the rules and regulation of that company. This results in capturing the market of the other country. This policy was adopted by China who acquired/ purchased stake in American countries thereby dominating the export market but China never opened their merger & acquitisation market fully. This tactics has been identified by US and US imposed Trade War against China. China's growth rate is expected to slow down to .6.5% in 2019.

Study of the annual growth rate reveals an important fact that no country can permanently have constant growth rate. It is volatile and widely fluctuates on year to year basis.

In Liberal country, tariffs are imposed to protect their own economy. On the other hand, Communist country cannot expand its economy without liberalization.

No country is therefore fully liberal or fully communist but every country is the mixture of both.

CHAPTER - 7

STUDY AND ANALYSIS OF ECONOMICS

Micro Economic theory of Adam Smith & Kenyes Theory of Macro economics

Micro Economics Theory

In his book, "Wealth of Nations", 1976 Adam Smith sponsored the economic theory known as Micro Economy. It studies small factors of economics in order to understand how the economy is built up. This branch of economy considers the behaviour of individual entities such as market, firms, and households. Smith considers how individual prices are set, studies determination of factors of production i.e. land, capital, raw materials and labour. His theory is based on Market mechanism of how prices are determined.

There are mainly two types of markets: (1) Physical market where Buyers and sellers meet physically and do the financial transactions by negotiating and fixing the price of goods. While seller is concerned with maximum profit by sale of product, buyer is interested in getting maximum satisfaction by purchasing goods. He wants maximum value for his money. Is other invisible market where buyers and sellers do not physically meet but prices are determined by demand and supply equilibrium of the goods. Government passes the laws to control price in the monopoly market. When essential commodities are in scarcity, Government acts as a market force and provides the citizens the essential goods at controlled price.

There is nothing like complete liberal market and government controlled market. It is a combination of both.

Having studied the market mechanism, we must look for factors of production i.e. capital which is provided by the producer. He gets interest income for the capital invested in the business. Land is purchased and production machines are bought. Raw material to convert in finished goods is bought. Producer also hires labour force to work on machines. Productivity of labour is essential which includes technique knowhow, knowledge of operating machine at optimal level and good atmosphere in the factory and sufficient wages to the workers are essential ingredients of labour productivity. All these cost will determine price of the product after taking profit into account.

Relating to Market Mechanism, Adam Smith writes as follows in his Wealth of Nation, 1776.

"Every individual endeavours to employ his capital so that its produce may be of greatest value. He generally neither intends to promote the public interest, nor knows how much he is promoting it. He intends only his own security, only his own gain. And he is in this led by the invisible hand to promote an end which was no part of his intention. By pursuing his own interest he frequently promotes that of Society more effectually than when he really intends."

Microeconomics now have moved beyond the early concerns to include the study of monopoly, the role of international trade, finance and many other vital subject. Monopoly of the producer will enable him to fix price at slightly upper level to make profit. If there is demand for his product in international market, he will increase his production in spite of lower demand in domestic market. If finance is available at cheaper rate, he will increase production and if interest rates for borrowing are high, he will reduce production. These will have impact on Recession or Inflection leading to the Business cycles.

Macro-Economic Theory

Macroeconomics is concerned with the overall performance of the economy. Concept of Macroeconomics came in the modern form in 1936 when John Maynard Kenyes published his revolutionary General Theory of Employment, Interest & Money. In 1930s, England and USA struck in the Great Depression with one fourth or one quarter of the American labour force was unemployed. Kenyes developed an analysis of what causes business cycles which spell out high unemployment and high inflation. Macroeconomics thus examines a wide variety of areas such as how total investment and consumption are determined, how Central Banks manage money and interest rates, which causes international financial crisis and why some countries rapidly grow while others are stagnant.

Economic life is an enormously complicated with hive of activities with people buying, selling, bargaining, investing and persuading.

Business cycle works as follows

If interest rates are reduced, more and more money is available for expanding economic activities. This will boost production, money supply, employment etc. When it crosses optimum limit, inflation and hyperinflation start. This results in rising the interest rate and reducing money supply by the Central Bank of the Country. This will reduce employment and production and economic activity will be weaken. If it crosses limit, there will be recession and whole business cycle will again start operating.

In order to control business cycles, Central Bank uses two instruments: (10 Money supply and (2) interest rate.

In India, Reserve Bank of India as a central bank, operates both these instruments. RBI has credit policy committee which reviews the economic condition quarterly and announces its credit policy for next three months. One year back, it kept interest rates constant without any change in Repo rate in order to regulate inflation. But when it saw that industries activities are sluggish, the Bank has been reducing its interest rate (repo rate) by 0.25% every quarter for last three consecutive quarterly period from 6.25% repo rate to existing 5.75% p.a. this will boost industrial and financial actives and employment will be rising reducing unemployment. In housing and car market prosperity, it instructs all banks to reduce vehicle loan and Housing loan interest rate to pass on benefits of reduction of repo rates to the Indian citizens.

Both these above theories aim at improving living conditions of people in their everyday lives, increasing the Gross Domestic Product and Gross National Income known as GDP and GNI respectively. This will rise individual income. Higher incomes mean good food, warm houses and hot water which means safe drinking water. These are bare necessities of individuals. By satisfying these needs, human life will be happy and pleasant...

CHAPTER - 8

MARKET MECHANISM

"Every induvial endeavors to employ his capital so that its produce may be of greatest value. He generally neither intends to promote the public interest, nor knows how much he is promoting it. He intends only his own security, only his own gain. And he is in this led by an invisible hand to promote an end which was no part of his intention. By pursuing his own interest he frequently promotes that of Society more effectually than when he really intends. - Adam Smith

-The Wealth of Nations (1776)

Market Mechanism

Most economic activity in most high income countries takes place in private markets - through the market mechanism. Who is responsible for making decisions in the market economy? No single individual or orgnisation or government is responsible for solving the economic problems in a market economy. Instead, millions of businesses and consumers engage in voluntary trade, intending to improve their own economic situations, and their actions are invisibly coordinated by a system of prices and markets.

Without constant flow of goods into and out of the city, customers will be on the verge of starvations within a week. But consumers actually do very well economically.The reason is that goods travel for days and weeks from the surrounding countries, into USA from 50 states and from the far corners of the world, with New York as their destination without coercion or centralized direction by anyone. These economic activities are coordinated through the market.

The market looks like mixed group of sellers and buyers. Food is produced in suitable quantities, get transported to the right place, and arrives in a palatable form at the dinner table. This shows that a market system is neither chaos nor miracle. It is a system with its own internal logic and it works.

A Market economy is an elaborate mechanism for coordinating people, activities, and businesses through a system of prices and markets. It is a Communication device for pooling the knowledge and actions of billions of unknown variables and relations, problems that are far beyond the reach of even today's fastest supercomputers. Nobody designs the market, yet it works remarkably well. In market economy, no single individual or organization is responsible for production, construction, and distribution or pricing.

In the fish market, buyers and sellers engage in face to face bargaining. Marketplace used to be a familiar sight in many villages and towns, where farmers bring their goods to sell.

Definition: Market is mechanism through which buyers and sellers interact to determine prices and exchange goods, services and assets.

Central role of markets is to determine the price. A price is the value of goods in terms of money. At a deeper level, prices represent he terms on which different items can be exchanged. The Market price of furniture may be Rs. 10000- while that of cricket bat may be Rs.1000- In essence, the market is saying that cricket bat and furniture trade on a 10 to 1 basis.

Prices serve as a signal to producers and consumers. If consumers want more of any goods, the price will rise. Sending signal to the producers that more supply is needed. Higher prices encourage the farmers to increase their production of goods which has more demand and also encourages consumers to substitute other foods than those whose price is increased.

Market Equilibrium: At every moment, some people are buying while others are selling, firms are inventing new products while governments are passing laws to regulate old ones. Foreign companies are opening plants in America while American firms are selling their products abroad. Yet in the midst of all this turmoil, markets are finding market equilibrium of supply and demand.

Definition of Prices: Prices coordinate the decision of producers and consumers in a market. Higher prices tend to reduce Consumer purchases and encourage production. Lower prices encourage consumption and discourage production. Prices are the balance wheel of the market mechanism.

How Markets Solve the Three Economic Problems?

There are three problems which market solves. (1) What goods will be produced? (2) How the goods will be produced? (3) To whom the goods will be produced?

(1) What Goods and Services will be produced is determined by the income of the consumers in their daily purchase decisions.

    Firms are motived by the desire to maximize profits. Profits are not revenues but the difference between the total sales proceeds and total costs.

(2) How things are produced is determined by the competition among the different producers. The best way for producers to meet the price

competition and maximize profits is to keep the costs at a minimum by adopting the most efficient methods of production. Sometimes change is incremental and advantage. Modern and latest technology will be used to produce efficiently the goods which have minimum cost and superior quality.

(3) For whom things are produced depends in large part on the supply and demand in the markets. For factor of production. Factor markets i.e.(market for factors of production) determine wage rates, land rate interest rate and profits. Such prices are called factor prices. The same person may receive wages from a job, dividends from stocks. Interest on bonds and rent from a piece of property. By adding of all the revenues from the factors, we can calculate the person's market income. The distribution of income among the population is determined by the quality of factor services (person – hours, acre etc.) and price of the factors. (Wagerates, land rates, interest rates etc.).

The Dual Monarchy

Who are the rulers in the Market economy? Major forces affecting the shape of the economy are dual monarchs of taste and technology. One fundamental determinant is the tastes of the population. It results in consumer's ability to purchase those goods i.e. demand. They pick up the point of the production possibility frontier (PPF).

Other major factor is the resources and technology available to a Society. Economic cannot go outside PPF. You can go to Hong Kong but you cannot go to Mars because there are no flights to Mar.

The products which are produced but have no demand are useless products.

Like a farmer using a caret and stick to coax a donkey forward, the market system deals out profits and losses to induce firms to produce desired goods

Efficiently. Consumers buy goods and sell factors of production, businesses sell goods and buy factors of production.

There is harmony between private profit and public interest.

Under the perfect competition and no market failures, marker will squeeze as many useful goods and services out of the available resources as is possible. But where the monopolies or pollution or similar market failures become pervasive, the remarkable efficiency properties of the invisible hand may be destroyed.

Distinguishing features of modern economy are three:

(1) An advanced economy is characterized by an elaborate network of trade that depends on specialization and an intricate division of members.

(2) Makes extensive use of money, which provides the yardstick for measurement of economic values and is the means of payment.

(3) Modern industrial technologies rest on the use of vast stocks of capital. Capital leverages human labour into a much more efficient factor of production and allows productivity many time greater than that possible in an earlier age.

Trade, Specialization & Division of Labour

As compared to the economics of 1700, today economics depend heavily on the specialization of individuals and firms, connected by extensive network of trade. Modern economies have enjoyed rapid economic growth as increasing specialization has allowed workers to become highly productive in particular occupations and to trade their output for the communities they need. Specialization occurs when people and countries concentrate their efforts on a particular set of tasks – it permits each person and country to use to best advantage the specific skills and resources in a mediocre way, it is better to establish a division of labour- dividing production into a number of people to teach, and persuade people to sell cars. It is usually 4 postgraduate years to become a certified neurosurgeon.

Specialization and trade are two keys in high living standards. By specializing, people can become highly productive in a very narrow field of expertise. People can then trade their specialized goods for other products, vesting increasing the range of quality of consumption and having the potential to raise everyone's living standards.

Trade, Money and Capital

1. As economics develop, they become more specialized. Division of Labour allows a task to be broken into a number of smaller choices that can each be mastered and performed more quickly by a single worker. Specialization arises from the increasing tendency to use roundabout methods of production that required many specialized skills. As individual and countries becoming increasing specialized, they tend to concentrate on particular commodities and trade their surplus output for goods produced by others. Voluntary trade, based on specialization, benefit all.
2. Trade in specialized goods and services today relies on money to lubricate its wheels. Money is a universally acceptable medium of exchange – including primarily currency and checking deposits. It is used to pay for everything from apple tarts to zebra skins. By accepting money, people and nations can specialize in producing a few goods and can then trade them for others;without money. We would waste much time negotiating and bargaining.
3. Capital Goods produced inputs such as machines, structures and inventories of goods in process – permit roundabout methods of production that add much to a nation's output. These roundabout

methods take time and resources to get started and therefore require a temporary sacrifice of present consumption. The rules that define how capital and other assets can be brought, sold and used are the system of property rights. In no economic system are private rights unlimited.

Visible Hand of Government

1. Although the market mechanism is an admirable way of producing and allocating goods, sometimes market failures lead to deficiencies in the economic outcomes. The government may step in to correct these failures. Its role in a modern economy is to ensure efficiency, to correct an unfair distribution of income, and to promote economic growth and stability.
2. Markets fail to provide an efficient allocation of resources in the presence of imperfect competition or externalities. Imperfect Competition, such as monopoly, produces high prices and low level of output. To combat these conditions, government regulate business or put legal antitrust constraints on business behavior. Externalities arise when activities impose costs or bestow benefits that are not paid for in the market place.
3. The government may decide to step in and regulate these spillover or provide for public goods.

Markets do not necessarily produce a fair distribution of income; they may spin off unacceptably high inequality of income and consumption. In response, governments can alter the pattern of incomes (for whom) generated by the market wages, rents, interest and dividends. Modern governments use taxation to raise revenues for transfer or income support programs that place a financial safety net under the needy.

4. Since the development of macroeconomics in the 1930s, the government has undertaken a third role, using fiscal powers (of taxing and spending) and monetary policy (affecting credit and interest rates) to pro.
5. Promote long run economic growth and productivity and to tame the business cycle's excessive inflation and unemployment.
6. Drawing the right boundary between an efficient market and government is an enduring problem for Societies. Economics is indispensable in finding the golden mean between an efficient market and publicity decided regulation and redistribution. An efficient and human society requires both halves of the mixed system – market & government.

CHAPTER - 9

CLASSIFICATION OF COMPETATIVE MARKETS INTO 5 CATEGORIES

Supply Behaviour of the Competitive Firm

A perfectly competitive firms produces a homogeneous product and is too small to affect the market price. Competitive firms are assumed to maximize their profits. Therefore competitive firm will choose that output level at which price equals the marginal cost of production, that is P = MC. Diagrammatically, the competitive firm's equilibrium will come where the rising MC supply curve intersects its horizontal demand curve.

Variable cost must be taken into consideration in determining a firm's short-run shutdown point. Below the shutdown point, the firm loses more than its fixed costs. It will therefore produce nothing when price falls below shutdown price.

A competitive industry's long-run supply curve, must take into account the entry of new firms and the exodus of old ones. In the long run, all of firm's commitments expire. It will stay in business only if price is at least as high as long-run average costs. These costs include out-of-pocket payments to labour, lenders, material suppliers or landlords and opportunity costs such as returns on property assets owner by the firm.

Supply Behavior in Competitive Industries

Each firm's rising MC curve is its supply curve. To obtain the supply curve of group of competitive firms, we add horizontally their separate supply curves. The supply curve of the industry hence represents the marginal cost curve for the competitive industry as a whole.

Because firms can adjust production over time, we distinguish two different time periods: (a) short-term equilibrium, when variable factors like labour can change but fixed factors like capital and the number of firms cannot, and (b) long-run equilibrium, when the number of firms and plants, and all other conditions, adjust completely to new demand conditions.

In the long-run, when firms are free to enter and leave the industry and no one firm has any particular advantage of skill or location, competition will eliminate any excess profit s earned by any existing firms in the industry. So, just as free exit implies that price cannot fall below the zero-profit point, free entry implies that price cannot exceed long-run average cost at long-run equilibrium.

When an industry can expand its production without pushing up the prices of its factor of production, the resulting long-run supply curve will be horizontal. When industry uses factors specific to it, such as scarce beachfront property, its long-run supply curve will slope upward.

Special Cases of Competitive Market

Under the demand rule, a demand for a commodity will generally raise the price of the commodity and also increase the quantity demanded. A decrease in demand will have the opposite effects.

Under the supply rule, an increase in supply of the commodity will generally lower the price and increase the quantity sold. A decrease in supply has the opposite effects.

Important special cases include constant and increasing costs, completely inelastic supply and backward-bending supply. These special cases will explain many important phenomena found in the markets.

Efficiency and Equity of Competitive Markets

The analysis of competitive markets focus light on the efficient organization of a society. Allocative efficiency occurs when there is no way of reorganizing production and distribution such that everyone's satisfaction can be improved.

Under ideal conditions, competitive economy attains allocative efficiency. Efficiency requires that all firms are perfect competitors and there are no externalities like pollution or imperfect information. Efficiency implies that economic surplus is maximized, where economic surplus equals consumer surplus plus producer surplus.

Efficiency comes because (a) when consumers maximize satisfaction, the marginal utility just equals the price; (b) when competitive producers supply goods, they choose output so that marginal cost just equals price; (c) since MU=P and MC=P, it follows that MU=MC.

There are exacting limits on the social optimality of competitive markets.

a. Efficiency requires perfect competition, complete information and no externalities. When all three conditions are met, this will lead to the important efficiency condition.

   Price ratio= marginal cost ratio

   = marginal utility ratio

b. The mostly perfect competitive markets may not produce a fair distribution of income and consumption. Societies may therefore decide to modify the laisser-faire market outcomes. Economics has the important role of analyzing the relative costs and benefits of alternative kinds of interventions.

Marginal cost is a fundamental concept for attaining any goal, not just for profits. Efficiency requires that the marginal cost of attaining the goal be equal in every activity.

After introduction of the Perfect Market mechanism, we shall now see the various categories of market. There are six markets as follows:

Perfect Market

Where buyers and sellers have full knowledge and information of the market. Generally there are identical products with many producers. Financial Markets and agriculture products are main ingredient of this market. No firm or organization can have control over price of the product. Marketing is based on market exchanging or auction. Government generally does not make interference in the fixing of price but make legislations to control the price for public interest in case of price inflation in the market for any reason. Government has thus invisible hand in case of emergencies.

Imperfect Market

Prices are higher and outputs are lower under imperfect market. But imperfect competitors have virtues along with vices. Large firms exploit economies of large-scale production and are responsible for much of the innovation that propels long-term economic growth.

A perfectly competitive market is one in which no firm is large enough to affect the market price, By strict definition, few markets in the U.S. economy are perfectly competitive. Aircraft, aluminum, automobiles computer software, refrigerators, electricity distribution are imperfect markets. Even today, the four largest U. S. firms produce three-quarters of U. S. aluminum output. The world commercial aircraft market is dominated by only two firms, Boeing and Airbus. In the automobiles industry, too, the top five automakers including Toyota and Honda have almost 80 percent of U. S. car and light-truck market.

Imperfect competition prevails in an industry where individual sellers can affect the price of their output. The major kinds of imperfect competition are monopoly, oligopoly and monopolistic competition.

Imperfect competition does not imply that a firm has absolute control over the price of the product. Imperfect competitor has some but not complete discretion over its price. Moreover, the amount of discretion over price will differ from industry to industry.

(1) Imperfect Competition has been divided into three categories: (1) Monopoly (2) Monopolistic Competition & (3) Oligopoly. In

Monopoly

There is a single producer. Product has no close substitute. Franchise monopolies (electricity, water) Microsoft Windows, patented drugs are some of the products of the Monopoly market. Firm's degree of control over price is substantial, considerable. Advertising is the method of marketing in monopoly market. Government has invisible hand in controlling unreasonable price rise.

Monopolistic Competition

There are many producers. There are many real or perceived differences in product. Economy for such market prevails in retail trade like pizzas, beer and personal computers. There is some degree of control over price in this market. Advertising and quality rivalry, administered prices.

Oligopoly

Appropriate example of this market is Fish market. There is visible fish market where number of fish selling women sell their fish. The price is determined by the direct negotiation with the purchaser/consumer. Product differential and quality are two ingredients in direct negotiation of price. If price is agreed by both sides, the transaction is completed. It looks like perfect competition but here the seller has some control over fixing price of her product by direct negotiation with physical buyers. Advertising is by way of direct negotiation only. Steel, chemicals are other two example of products in Oligopoly.

(2) Completely Controlled Market By the Government

Government of any country take charge of collecting and distributing very essential commodities like food-grains, medicine which are very short in supply or there is serious famine in the country. Every citizen of the country will be given a limited food-grains at each week through Government recognised ration shops and each citizen will be issued a ration card. Government of India used to import wheat from U. S. under PL480 after independence when there was acute shortage of essential commodities like food-grains. There were restrictions/prohibitions in celebrating any social programme with lunch or diners to public. Prices of the commodities were controlled by the government and Government used to distribute the commodities through government recognised rationing shops at control prices with limited quantity for each citizen.

(3) Market Where Government of Any Country has Completely Collapsed and Local Currency of the Country has Zero Value

Recent example of this situation is Venezuela. Local currency has been tremendously inflated by 13.5 lacs times. One Ice-cream is costly USD 25 per cup. There are no distribution centers for essential commodities. Some people sell some commodities but there are very long ques with each person having numerous bundles of currency notes to get small quantity.In 1918, same pathetic financial situation occurred in Germany. German currency value was zero that time.

CHAPTER - 10

INTERNATIONAL TRADE & INTERNATIONAL MARKETS

In the above pages, we discussed the domestic trade and domestic markets where buyers and sellers were both in the same country and have the same currency into which they are doing their transactions.

In international trade, however, the buyer and seller are from different countries having their different currencies in which they will pay for their goods, services provided by the seller in the other country.

Value of each currency in determined by the purchasing parity capacity of the currency in terms of other currency. For example, U. S. Dollar will be able to purchase the goods of Rs. 70- per dollar in terms of rupee currency which means that one dollar can purchase goods worth Rs. 70- Exchange rate between dollar and rupee is therefore USD1= Rs.70-

Exchange Rate is defined as, "Rate at which one currency is exchanged with other currency. It is called purchasing power parity of one currency against others for payment of dues for goods purchased by Indian from US. The rate is fixed or floating daily."

Fixed rate is one which is fixed between two currencies and generally does not change. While floating rate is one which changes daily as per the demand and supply of that currency in terms of other currency.

We shall take one example of how the international trade is carried out:

If we purchase the machinery of U. S. @ USD100000-and sell them steel worth Rs. 500000-, we have to pay Rs. $ 70 lacs against US paying India Rs. 500000-i.e. net payment from India to USA is Rs. 65 lacs.This net payment or gap is known as trade deficit. We can say that India has the trade deficit with US Rs. 65 lacs or $ 6500000/70 when USD and Rupee exchange rate is Rs. 70 per USD.

Each country needs foreign currency to make transactions in the International market.

USD is the international currency. Nations therefore keep their foreign exchange reserves in USD, Euro currencies. Most of the countries invest heavily in gold as alternative to foreign currency reserves as gold is accepted by all countries in payment of international liability.

Specialization, division of labour, and trade increase productivity and consumption possibilities. The gains from trade hold among nations as well as within a nation. Engaging in international exchange is more efficient than relying only on domestic production. International trade differs from domestic trade because it broadens the market, because trade takes place among sovereign nations, and because countries usually have their own monies which must be converted using foreign exchange rates.

Diversity is the fundamental reason that nations engage in international trade. Within this general principle, we see that trade occurs (a) because of differences in the conditions of production, (b) because of decreasing costs (or economies of scale), and (c) because of diversity in tastes.

Comparative Advantage Amount Nations

Recall that trade occurs because of differences in the conditions of production or diversity in tastes. The fundamental of international trade is Ricardian principle of comparative advantage. The principle of comparative advantage holds that each country will benefit if it specializes in the production and export of those goods that it can produce at relatively low cost. Conversely, each country will also benefit if it imports those goods which it produces at relatively high cost. This principle holds even if one region is absolutely more or less productive than another in all commodities. As long as there are differences in relative or comparative efficiencies among countries, every country must enjoy a comparative advantage or comparative disadvantage in the production of some goods.

The law of comparative advantage predicts more than just the geographical pattern of specialization and direction of trade. It also demonstrates that countries are made better off and real wages or more generally total national income are improved by trade and the resulting enlarged world production. Quotas and tariffs, designed to protect workers or industries, will lower a nation's total income and consumption possibilities.

Even with many goods or many countries, the same principles of comparative advantage apply. With many commodities, we can arrange products along a continuum of comparative advantage, from relatively more efficient to relatively less efficient. With many countries, the trade may be triangular or multilateral, with countries having large bilateral or two sided surplus or deficits with other individual countries.

Protectionism

Completely free trade equalizes prices of tradeable goods at home with those in world markets. Under trade, goods flow uphill from low-price to high-price markets.

Tariff rates/customs rates on imported goods will increase prices and will discourage import.The domestic prices of imported goods will increase leading to a decline in consumption. Quotas have very similar effects and may, in addition, lower government revenues.

A tariff causes economic waste. The economy suffers losses from decreased domestic consumption and from the wasting of resources on goods lacking comparative advantage. The losses generally exceed government revenues from tariff.

Most argument for tariffs simply rationalize special benefits to particular pressure groups and cannot withstand economic analysis. Three arguments that can stand up to careful scrutiny are the following: (a) the terms-of trade or optimal tariff can in principle raise real income of a large country at the expenses of its trading partners. (b) In a situation of less-than- full employment, tariffs might push an economy toward fuller employment, but monetary or fiscal policies could attain the same employment goal with fewer inefficiencies than this beggar-thy-neighbour policy. (c) Sometimes, infant industries may need temporary protection in order to realise their true long-run comparative advantages.

The principle of comparative advantage must be qualified if markets malfunction because of unemployment or exchange market disturbances. Moreover, individual sectors or factors may be injured by trade if imports lower their returns. Opening up to trade may hurt the factors that are most embodied in imported goods.

Protectionism has two coins. If one country initiates tariff policy or damping of goods, the other country will retaliate and there will be Trade war between two or more countries as it has been at present between U.S. and China and U.S. and European countries which may lead to reduction of world production resulting in Recession.

Under the Exchange Control Act and Rules therein which were in force in India till recently, Individual citizens were not allowed to hold foreign currency. If in any transaction, a citizen will get foreign exchange, it will have to surrender it to the Government and government will pay local currency in exchange of the foreign currency. Even Banks which are Authorised Dealers in foreign exchange were used to surrender that FCNR deposits in FCY to the RBI and RBI used to pay them rupee currency in exchange. We shall illustrate this by following example.

Bank A gets FCNR fixed deposits of USD 100000- from its non- resident customer for one year @ 8% p.a. interest rate, Bank has to surrender this deposit to RBI on the date of receipt and RBI shall pay the Bank rupee deposit Rs. @ 33- per USD which was Base rate/notional rate that time. As per term of Deposit, the Bank has to pay USD 800- as interest on Deposit on expiry of FCNR deposit. But this amount was not covered by RBI and the bank accepting FCNR deposits has to pay interest in USD. This exposes the Bank foe exchange risk.

As per Banking Act Regulations, the Bank has to deposit 10% deposit amount as cash reserves and 30% of deposit in SLR investment. This means Rs. 330000- will be kept as cash reserves @4% p.a. and Rs.990000- as SLR deposits where the bank will earn the interest @6% p. a. Balance amount Rs. 19, 80, 0000- the Bank is free to lend to the borrower customers as Loan approximately at the rate of @14% p.a.

Thus the Bank has earned 4% p. a. on cash reserves Rs.330000-@6%p.a.on SLR investments for RS. 990000- And 14% p.a. on Rs. 1980000- total interest will be Rs. 3,49,800- Our liability of paying interest is USD 8000- and we have RS.3,49,800- as interest earned on rupee deposits. If exchange rate on payment of interest is USD 8000- is 43.7250- per USD, there will be break through. If it is less than 43.725 per USD, there will be exchange profit but if the exchange rate is over Rs. 43.7250 the bank will lose on interest front. This will be likely situation because the exchange rates were very volatiles during Exchange Control Regulations that time. There was thus exchange risk on interest liability on FCNR for banks because the interest amount in USD used to remain uncovered in the FCNR Scheme.

One way to crystalize exchange risk is to book forward contract at the forward contract rate prevailing on date of annual interest date of the FCNR Deposits. A detailed paper on this issue to enable the bank to avoid interest risk on FCNR deposits was prepared by some bank officials but it was not implemented on the ground that the exchange loss is casual on account of interest rate differential between local currency rate and foreign currency rate.

This leads to the another issue of how the exchange rate for swap transactions are set up. We shall explain this with following example:

Interest rate on Rupees are @!2% p.a. and USD @ 6% p.a. then the currency with higher rate is said to be at discount compared with the currency whose interest rate is lower. Currency with lower interest is called premium currency.

Swap cost is nothing but interest cost. Dealing in the banks is done as follows:

If spot rate is 1.4285 i.e. Rs. 100= USD 1.4285 and local currency is at discount to foreign currency, the market will quote S/B as 12/19 which means that dealer will sell @ 1.4285-.0012= 1.4273 and in other case the dealer will purchase @ 1.4285-.0019=1.4266 Difference is the Swap cost to the dealer.

In case of B/S Market will quote as 12/14 which means the dealer will buy @ 1.4285- 0.0012 = 1.4273 and in other case, the dealer will sell @ 1.4285-0.001= 1.427. Thus in this transaction, difference is the swap gain to the dealer.

Please remember that this is a market quotation and therefore it is favorable to the market and not to the person who trades. Most of the times, the students at Bourse Course forget this and therefore has to reverse the transaction if caught by the Accountant/ Bourse Instructor or Director.

Banks are authorised dealers in the foreign exchange and therefore are authorised to deal in foreign exchange for covering customers exchange transaction. In the market, however, Odd amount cannot be covered fully and there remains Gap between Purchases and Sales in say USD pad which is exposed to exchange risk and exchange loss. There are sometimes Forward Exchange Contracts booked with the customers which are not fully covered and there remains the gap in the forward contract month. This is done intentionally on the future forecast view of the Exchange Dealer that forward margins will be lower in future. In such case, Exchange Dealer covers the transaction by spot transaction and crystalize forward margin for the forward booking. If he can cover the said forward transaction with less forward margin that is crystalized, he will earn the exchange profit for the Bank on this forward transaction.

Countries with huge trade deficit has to collect foreign currency to meet the deficit. Countries therefore keep their huge foreign exchange reserves or gold in their Central Banks. If there is still shortage in meeting their foreign exchange commitments, they will borrow foreign exchange from IMF or London/France club. It attracts interest which alongwith principal instalments of international borrowing will be required to be repaid regularly by the borrowing country known as "debt servicing". If not repaid on time, there will be restructuring of the borrowing by the lending bank sometimes on stringent conditions looking at financial position of the defaulted country at the time of default. Most of the times, IMF views such reconstructing or bail out as short term financial difficulties of the defaulting country.

Chapter - 11

Capital, Interest & Profits

Basic Concepts of Interest and Capital

Major Concepts

Capital: durable produced items used for further production.

Rentals: net annual dollar returns on capital goods.

Rate of return on investment: net annual receipts on capital divided by dollar value of capital measured as percentage per year.

Interest rate: yield on financial assets, measured as percent per year.

Real interest rate: yield on funds corrected for inflation, also measured as percent per year.

Present value: value today of an asset's stream of future returns.

1. Interest rates are the rate of return on financial assets, measured in percent per year. People willingly pay interest because borrowed funds allow them to buy goods and services to satisfy current consumption needs or make profitable investments.
2. We observe a wide variety of interest rates. These rates very because of many factors such as the term or maturity of loans, the risk and liquidity of investments, and the tax treatment of their interest.
3. Nominal or money interest rates generally rise during inflationary periods; reflecting the fact that that the purchasing power of money declines as prices rise.To calculate the interest yield in terms of real goods and services, we use the real interest rate, which equals the nominal interest rate minus the rate of inflation.
4. Assets generate streams of income in future periods. By calculating the present value of the asset, we can convert the stream of future returns into a single value today. This is done by asking what sum today will generate the total value of all future returns when invested at market interest rate.

5. The exact present value formula is as follows: Each dollar payable/ years from now has a present value (V) of \$1/(1+i)'.For any net receipt stream (N1,N2 ———N1), where N1 is the dollar value of receipt of t years in the future, we have

V= N1 + N2 N1

1-i (1+i) (1+i)

6. The Theory of Capital, Profits and Interest

   The third factor of production is capital, a produced durable item that is used in further production. In the most general sense, investing in capital represents deferred consumption today and instead producing buildings or equipment, society increases consumption in future, it is an economic fact that roundabout production yields a positive rate of return.

7. Interest is a device that serves two functions in economy, as a motivating device, it provides the incentive for people to save and accumulate wealth. As a rationing device, interest allows the society to select only those investment projects with the highest rates of return. However, as more and more capital is accumulated, and as the law of diminishing returns sets in, the rate of return on capital and the interest rate will be beaten down by competition. Falling interest rates are a signal to society to adopt more capital-intensive projects with lower rates of return.

8. Saving and investing involve waiting for future consumption rather than consuming today. Such thrift interacts with the net productivity of capital to determine interest rates, the rate of return on capital, and the capital stock. The funds or financial assets needed to purchase capital are provided by households that are willing to sacrifice consumption today in return for larger consumption tomorrow. The demand for capital comes from firms that have variety of roundabout investment projects. In the long run equilibrium, the interest rate is thus determined by the interaction between the net productivity of capital and willingness of the households to sacrifice consumption today for consumption tomorrow.

9. Profits are revenues minus costs. Economic profits differ from those measured by accountants. Economics distinguishes between three categories of profits: (a) an important source is profit as implicit returns. Firms generally own many of their nonlabour factors of production-capital, natural resources, and patents. In these cases, the implicit return on owned inputs is part of the profits. (b) Another source of profits is uninsured or uninsurable risk, particularly, that associated with business cycle. (c) Finally, innovational profits will be earned by entrepreneurs who introduce new product or innovations.

Capital, labour, raw materials, building, heavy machinery and advanced technology are all factors of production. In proprietary firm, if the proprietor owns the land, he will donate to the firm.Funds will be provided by the proprietor and labour will be hired.

In such cases, all factors of production except labour will be owned by the firm. Cost of production invariable terms will be of labour wages while all are fixed cost.

In case of large company, promoters float the company and issue the shares to the public. Share capital is used to purchase all factors of production except the labour. Company has to pay dividends on the share capital which is cost of production to the company. Wages are paid as variable cost of production.

In any company, the owner may lend his/her land and lent funds to acquire other factors of production. In such cases, the owner will, in addition to profit in business, will receive interest on land provided as well as the funds lent to the business as interest on funds.

Interest is the price paid by the enterpriser to the lender who postpone current consumption for future bigger consumption by lending money today. Lender will not lend money until he/she is satisfied with the rate of interest paid by the borrower on borrowed funds. If money is lent for five years and inflation is expected to rise 2 percent per year, interest rate @ 10% p.a. will be break-through rate. If the lender gets 12% p.a. interest on his funds, he will invest his fund for five years. This is how the rates are fixed in the market. Enterpriser will, of course, will be willing to pay 12% p.a. interest if he makes profit over all costs including interest payment in the business.

For certain essential industries, the government give incentives by way of tax holidays for five initial years to stabilize the business.

CHAPTER - 12

GOVERNMENT CONTROL OF THE ECONOMY

The economic role of government has increased sharply over the last century. The government influences and controls private economic activity by using taxes, expenditures, and direct regulation.

A modern welfare state performs four economic functions: (a) It remedies market failures; (b) it redistributes income and resources; (c) it establishes fiscal and monetary policies to stabilize business cycle and promote long-term economy growth; and (d) it manages international economic affairs.

Public choice theory analyses how governments actually behave. Just as the invisible hand can break down, so there are government failures, in which government interventions lead to waste or redistribute income in an undesirable fashion.

Government Expenditures

The American system of public finance is one of fiscal federalism. The federal government concentrates its spending on issues of national concern-on national public goods like defence and space exploration. States and localities generally focus on local public goods – those where benefits are largely confined within state or city boundaries.

Government spending and taxation today take approximately one-third of total national output. Of this total, about 55 percent is spent on federal level, and the balance is divided between state and local governments. Only a small fraction of government outlays is devoted to traditional functions like police and courts.

Economic Aspects of Taxation

Nations of "benefits" and "ability to pay" are two principal theories of taxation. A tax is progressive, proportional or regressive as it takes a larger, equal or smaller fraction of income from rich families than it does from poor families. Direct and progressive taxes on incomes are in contrast to indirect and regressive sales and excise taxes.

More than half of federal revenues come from personal and corporate income taxes. The rest comes from taxes on payrolls or consumptions goods. Local governments raise most of their revenue from property taxes, while sales taxes are important for states.

The individual income tax is levied on "income from whatever source derived" less certain exemptions and deductions. The marginal tax rate, denoting the fraction paid in taxes for every dollar of additional income, is the key to determining the impact of taxes on incentives to work and save.

The fastest growing federal tax is the payroll tax, used to finance social security. This is an "earmarked"levy, which funds going to provide public pensions and health and disability benefits. Because these are visible benefits the end of stream of payments, payroll tax has elements of benefit tax.

Economists point to the Ramsey tax rule, which emphasizes that efficiency will be promoted when taxes are levied more heavily on those activities that are relatively price-inelastic. A new approach is green taxes, which levy fees on environmental externalities, reducing harmful activities while raising revenues that would otherwise be imposed on goods or productive inputs. But in all taxes, equity and political acceptability are severe constraints.

CHAPTER - 13

EFFECIENCY OR INEQUILITY; THE BIG TRADEOFF SOURCES OF INEQUILITY

In the previous century, the classical economists believed that inequality was a universal constant, unchangeable by public policy. This view does not stand up to scrutiny. Poverty made a glacial retreat over the early part of the twentieth century, and absolute incomes for those in the bottom part of income distribution rose sharply. Since around 1980, this trend has reversed, and inequality has increased.

The Lorenzcurve is a convenient device for measuring the spreads or inequalities of income distribution. It shows what percentage of total income goes to the poorest 1 percent of the population, to the poorest 10 percent, to the poorest 95 percent, and so forth. The Gini coefficient is a quantitative measure of inequality.

Poverty is relatively a relative notion. In the United States, poverty was defined in terms of the adequacy of incomes in the early 1960s. By this standard of measured income, little progress in reducing inequality has been made in the last decade.

Income inequality declined markedly over most of the twentieth century. Then, beginning around 1975, the gap between rich and poor began to widen. The largest income gains have gone to very top of income distribution, to the richest 0.1 percent of people. Analysts believe that the "rich man's crash" of 2007-2009 will narrow income gaps at the very top, wealth is even more unequally distributed than the income, both in United States and in other capitalist economies.

Antipoverty Policies

Political philosophers write of three types of equality: (a) equality of political rights, such as right to vote (b) equality of opportunity, providing equal access to jobs, education and other social systems; and (c) equality of outcomes, whereby people are guaranteed equal incomes or consumptions.

Whereas the first two types of equality are increasingly accepted in most advanced democracies like the United States, quality of outcomes is generally rejected as impractical and too harmful to economic efficiency.

Equality has costs as well as benefits, the costs show up as drains from Okun's "leaky bucket". That is attempts to reduce income inequality by progressive taxation or transfer payments may harm the economic incentives to work or save and may thereby reduce the size of national output.

Major programs to alleviate poverty are welfare payments, food stamps, Medicaid, and group of smaller or less targeted programs. As a whole, these programs are criticized because they impose high benefit-reduction rates on low-income families when families begin to earn wages or other income.

Part - II
Economy of Countries with Critical Observations

Introduction: We shall now see the Economies of some countries in details and then make critical observations on various categories of economy of that country.

Economy of any country gives information about the Gross national GDP with details of its agriculture production, trade, transportation and communication, tourism, banking, mining and so on. In the financial field, it also gives details about its external borrowing, size of its budget plan, fiscal deficit, import and export trade volumes, Balance of trade and trade deficit, population, percentage of unemployment ratio to total population etc.

In critical observations, we shall see whether the country has defaulted in foreign exchange payments to the exported countries, and restructuring of external debt was made and financial restrictions imposed on the country at the time of restructuring of external debt, percentage of external debt to gross domestic product(GDP), per capita GDP and external and public debt created and outstanding of the country, productivity of the labour, present percentage of young workforce to total workforce, technical skills acquired by the labour force, future percentage of young labour force and technical knowhow and percentage of skilled workers to total workforce, computer knowledge and skill attained by the workforce, module of productivity tools, labour and factor costs of production etc. and natural climate of the country as well as the climate in the factory to induce higher productivity.

Chapter - 14

Economy of India

Indian economy has been developed into its present stage by four main following Periods.

(1) Mughal Rule from 1526-1797

(2) British Rule from 1797-1947

(3) Pre- Liberation 1947-1991

(4) Liberation 1997 to date.

Mughal Rule (1526 – 1797)

Indian economy was large and prosperous under the Mughal Empire upto 18th century. India and China may have accounted for 60-% -70% of world GDP in the 17th century. Mughal economy functioned on an elaborate system of coined currency, land revenue and trade. Gold, silver and copper coins were issued by the royal mints, which functioned on the basis of free coinage. The political stability and uniform revenue policy resulting from a centralized administration under the Mughals, coupled with a well-developed internal trade network, ensured that India before the arrival of the British was a large extent economically unified though 64% workforce was in agriculture (primary sector) and 36% workforce in secondary sector. This was higher than in Europe where 90% of the workforce was in agriculture in 1700 and 75% in 1750. Indian agriculture was advanced compared to Europe at that time with higher per capita agricultural output and standards of consumption.

The Mughal Empire had a thriving manufacturing economy, with India producing about 25% of the world's industrial output until 1750 making it the most important manufacturing center in international trade. Manufactured goods and cash crops had a relatively high degree of urbanization during this period with 15% of the population living in urban centres, higher than percentage of urban population in contemporary Europe that time and higher than that of British India in the 19th century.

In the early modern Europe, there was significant demand for production from Mughal India, particularly cotton textiles, as well as goods such as spices, peppers, indigo, silk and saltpeter. European fashion increasingly dependent on Mughal India textiles and silks. From the late 17th century to early 18th century, Mughal India accounted for 95% of British imports from Asia. Bengal Subah province alone accounted for 40% of Dutch imports from Asia. In contrast, there was little demand for European goods in Mughal India which was largely self- sufficient. Indian goods, especially, from those of Bengal were also exported in large quantities in other Asian markets, such as Indonesia and Japan. At the time, Mughal Bengal was the most important center of cotton textile production and shipping.

It is to be noted that Mughal came from the different countries and conquered the Indian Territory. They concentrated on Indian economic growth but unlike British they did not transfer that wealth into their home country. They stayed here and enjoyed that prosperity.

In the early 18th century, the Mughal Empire declined, as it lost western, Central and parts of South and North India to the Maratha Empire, which integrated and continued to administer those regions. The decline of Mughal Empire led to decreased agricultural productivity, which in turn, negatively affected the textile industry. Marathas were defeated in Panipat third battle, Maratha Empire disintegrated into several confederate states resulting political instability and armed conflict severally affected economic life in several parts of the country.

By the eighteen century, the British East India Company entered the Indian politics and established its dominance over other European powers. This marked a determinative shift in India's trade, and a less powerful impact on the rest of the economy.

British Rule (1797 – 1947)

During the British Empire, India's share of world income collapsed from 22.6% in 1700, almost equal to the European share of 23.3% at that time, to a low of 3.8% in 1952.

From the beginning of 19th century, the British East India Company's gradual expansion and consolidation of power brought a major change in taxation and agricultural policies which tended to promote commercialization of agriculture with a focus on trade resulting in decreased production of food crops. Mass impoverishment and destitution of farmers led to numerous famines and epidemic which were ruthlessly and cruelly handled by the Britishers resulting in killing lacs of people in famines and epidemics. The economic policies of the British Raj caused a severe decline in the handicrafts and handloom sectors intentionally which resulted in reduction of demand and widespread unemployment. After the removal of restrictions by the Charter of 1813, Indian trade expanded substantially with steady growth. The result was significant transfer of capital from India to England which was due to the colonial intentional policy of making England rich country at the cost of Indian disastrous economy. This led to a massive drain of revenue rather than any systematic effort of modernization of the domestic economy.

Under the British Rule, India's share of World economy declined from 24.8% in 1700 to 4.2% in 1950.India's share of global industrial output was 25% during 1750 to 1770. The British East India Company, following their conquest of Bengal in 1757 had forced open the large Indian Market to British goods, which could be sold in India without tariffs or duties, compared to local Indian producers who were heavily taxed under the British protective policies such as bans and high tariffs implemented to restrict Indian textile from being sold in Indian Market. Indian cotton was imported to England and textile manufactures were exported from England to India. Indian economy was thus completely intentionally ruined by Britishers for their selfish motives. They were the worst rulers of the Indian colony.

British territorial expansion in India In 1893, 91.3% of the Indian Territorywas occupied by the Britishers who encouraged free trade, and created a single currency with fixed exchange rates, standardized weights and measures and capital markets within the Company held territories. It also established a railways and telegraphs, a civil service that claimed to be free from political interference which was adopted by Indians after independence as IAS free from the political interference. Home Minister Mr. Vallabh Bhai Patel made lot of efforts for making IAS services free from any interference from political influence. British introduced the common law and adversarial legal system. British contribution to the introduction of improved education system with encouragement to learn English language was remarkable as many Indian students took improved education system and learnt English language. These educated young students got government jobs in the government offices.

Legislation to abolish Sati custom was another contribution of the British rulers.

Britishers also tried to reduce the gap between savarn Hindus and backward classes i.e. social inequality by casteism. But in that they converted Harigans to the Christen region and expanded their region. British defeated Peshvas with the help of army of the backward classes on 1st January. This is celebrated every year by the backward classes as their glorious success/ triumpt and clashes occur on this subject every year between two communities known as Koregaon Bhimas conflict.

In order to expand their rule over the independent states in India, Britishers introduced a legislation that those rulers who have no legitimate children cannot adopt sons/daughters of other families to qualify them as the next ruler as heredetary. This created agitation among the independent states which was one of the reason of 1857 coup of Indians with British army.

In 1872, agriculture was predominant sector and 91.3% of the Indian population was residing in villages. Urbanization generally remain sluggish in British India.

Second World War affected British economy in London tremendously with dispersal of industries, encouraging rural-urban migration, and in particular the large port of Bombay, Calcutta and Madras grew rapidly. Despite this, only one-sixth of India's population lived in cities by 1951.Developments like railways and road transports were used by British Raj for promoting their trade. While common law was adopted, this gave little comfort to Indians as the common law was favourable to Britain and therefore judgements were seen partial and not sound. Leaders of Indian Independence movement and economic historians have blamed colonial rule for the dismal state of Indian economy in its aftermath and argued that financial strength from wealth was taken from India by Britishers.

On 13-04-1919, Jalianawala Baug black event occurred. Independent Leaders had arranged the Meeting in the Baug. About 5000 people attended the meeting. General Dyer with his solders came to the Baug and gave ruthless firing orders to his soldiers without giving any chance to the people attending the meeting. For survival in order that people should not escape from firing, he closed all doors of the Baug and ordered his soldiers not to observe any rules of firing. This resulted in killing thousands of people in the Baug for that meeting. 1200 people were injured seriously. There was an enquiry of General Dyer thereafter but he was removed from his posting in India but no capital punishment was given to him. After some years, it was reported that he died in serious disease. Jalianawala baug episode shows the hatred and ruthless action of the Britishers. Britishers treated Indians as slaves. After 100 years from this incidence, British Government or Queen of England in Royal family have not expressed apology for such event but on the occasion of century completion from this event, Prime Minister and British Embassy Commissioner in India have expressed only regret for such incidence.

In World Wars I & II, Britishers tremendously lost their military manpower and the wealth with dispersal of industries, British ruthless behavior in handling Indian Independent agitations were published by USA regularly. US pressurized Britishers to give independent to India. There was also demand from Indians to give independence forthwith. British also realized that they have to grant Independence to this colony, they made efforts to divide the India into India and Pakistan. In their India Account, there were GBP130 million which were to be distributed into both countries. Generally, as per the principles of distribution of such fund, Population and area of each country are the criteria but Mahatma Gandhi insisted that Pakistan should be given half of this amount. Thus India and Pakistan got each GBP 55 million to start their countries in 1947.

Economy of Independent India During Pre-liberalization Period (1947 –1991)

Indian economic policy after independence was influenced by the colonial experience which was seen as exploitive by Indian leaders exposed to British social democracy. Indian rulers were impressed by the effective planning system of the Soviet Russia economy which was protectionist. Domestic policy tended towards protectionism, with a strong emphasis on import substitution industrialization, economic interventionism, a large government- run public sector business regulations and central planning, while trade and foreign investment policies were relatively liberal. Five year plans of India resembled central planning in the Soviet Union. Steel, mining, machine tools, telecommunications, insurance and power plants among the other industries were effectively nationalized in the mid1950s.

India's first Prime Minister, Nehru who adopted Fabian socialism inspired to Industrialist J.R.D. Tata, when Tata suggested state-owned companies will be profitable.

Jawarlal Nehru alongwith the statician Prasanta Chandra Mahalanobis formulated and oversaw economic policy during the initial years of the country's independence. Finance Minister Mr. C. D. Deshmukh also assisted them in designing and implementing the planning. Plans were mainly designed to improve agricultural production and industrial policy was to boost industrial production by installing capital goods industries, infrastructural development including transport and railways facilities. Heavy industries were planned to be set up by private and public sectors together and based on direct and indirect state intervention rather than more extreme Soviet styled central command system. The policy of concentrating simultaneously on capital and technology intensive heavy industry and subsidizing manual loco-skill cottage industries was criticized by home economists.

Industrial expansion required construction of large capital goods industries. To finance Fcy expenses for the same, heavy amount of external debt was taken from IMF on long term basis. However, interest payment in Fcy needed to be made on yearly basis. In order to repay interest liability, the government has to take fresh loan in fcy which piled the fcy external debt.Debt servicing ratio was also piling. After dissolution of Soviet Russia, India was in financial difficulties. Its foreign currency reserves were very migre to meet fcy needs of the country only for two weeks. India therefore approached IMF for bail-out package for $1.8 billion in 1991which was approved by IMF with the condition that India will liberized its market to the foreign investors. Prime Minister Mr.Narsiha Rao and Finance Minister Mr. Manmohan Singh agreed and successfully implemented the libersation which increased foreign exchange reserves of India and reduced its Debt Servicing Ratio from 36% in 1991 to 4% in 1995 which was reasonable. Heavy industries projrcts were also completed which started giving yields on investment, thus further improving financial condition of India.

Since 1965, the use of high yielding varieties of seeds, increased fertilizers and improved irrigation facilities collectively contributed to the Green Revolution in India, which improved the condition of agriculture by increasing crop productivity, improving crop patterns and strengthening forward and backward linkages between agriculture and industry. This resulted in the growth of capitalistic farming, ignoring industrial reforms and widening income disparities.

Subsequently, the emergency and Garibi Hatao concepts under which income tax levels at one point rose to a maximum of 97.5% – a world record for the communist economies started diluting the entire efforts.

In the late 1970s, the government led by Morarji Desai eased restrictions on capacity expansion by removing price controls, reduced corporate taxes and protected the creation of small scale industries in large numbers.

Post – Liberalization Period (Since 1991)

The Collapse of the Soviet Union, which was India's major partner, and Gulf War, which caused a spike in oil prices, resulted in a major balance of payments crisis for India, which found itself facing the prospect of defaulting on its loans. India asked for $1.8 billion bailout loan from the International Monetary Fund which in turn demanded de-regulation.

In response, Narsinnha Rao government including Finance Minister Manmohan Singh, initiated economic reforms in 1991. The reforms did away with the Licence Raj, reduced tariffs and interest rates and ended many public monopolies sectors, allowing automatic approval of foreign direct investment in many sectors. Since then, overall trust of liberalization remained the same, although no government has tried to take on powerful lobbies such as trade unions and farmers, on contentious issues such as reforming labour laws and reducing the agricultural subsidies. By the turn of 21st century, India has progressed towards a free market economy, with a substantial reduction in state control of economy, and increased financial liberalization. This has been accompanied by increase in life expectancy, literacy rates and food security, although urban residents are benefited more than rural residents.

While the credit rating of India was hit by nuclear weapons tests in 1996, it has since been raised to investments levels in 2003 by Standards & Poor's and Moody's.

We studied the Indian Economy at Macro levels upto this point. Let us now study the Indian economy at micro levels.

On micro level, Indian economy has been classified into three main sectors:

(1) Agriculture
(2) Industry
(3) Services.

Agriculture

Agriculture in India includes Animal husbandry, fishing and natural resources in India.

India ranks second worldwide in farm output. Agriculture in allied sectors like forestry and fishing accounted for 17% of the GDP. The sector employed 49% of its total workforce in 2014. This raised to agriculture accounting for 23% of GDP and 59% of total workforce in 2014.

Indian economy has diversified and grown with agriculture's contribution to GDP has steadily declined from 1951-2011. It is still the country's most important employment source and significant piece of its overall socio-economic development. Since the Green Revolution, special emphasis was placed in the Five Year Plans on agriculture and improvement of irrigation technology with application of modern agriculture practices and provision of agricultural credit, subsidiary and waiver of farmers' outstanding loans during famine. This resulted in yield growth of crop per unit area of all crops since 1950.

States of Uttar Pradesh, Punjab, Hariyana, Madhya Pradesh, Andhra Pradesh, Telangana, Bihar, West Bengal, Gujarat and Maharashtra are key contributors to the Indian agriculture. Foodgrains production which was 80 million metric tons in 1965 has now increased to 252 million in 2017 and 277 million metric tons in 2018. In comparison, US has foodgrains production 347 million metric tons and China has 302 million metric tons of foodgrains production. Russia has foodgrains production 75 million metric tons, with UK 10 million, France 20 million metric tons. Total foodgrains world production is estimated to 1.7 billion metric tons with total world population of 7 billion.

India receives the average annual rainfall of 1708 mm (47.6 inches) and a total annual participation of 4 billion cubic meters with the total utilization water 1.123 trillion cubic meters. 546820 sq. kilometers (211130 sq.miles) of the land or 39% of the total cultivated area is irrigated. India's inland water resources and marine resources provide employment to nearly 6 million people in Fisheries sector in 2010. India's fishing industry is the sixth largest in the world.

India is the largest producer of milk, jute and pulses, and has the world's second largest of cattle population with 170 million animals in 2011. It is the second largest producer of rice, wheat, sugar-cane, cotton and ground-nuts as well as fruits and vegetables. Fruits and vegetables account for 10.9% and 8% of the world's fruit and vegetable production respectively. India is the second largest producer and consumer of silk producing 1700 tons in 2005. India is the largest exporter of cashew kernels and cashew nut-shell liquid. Foreign exchange earned by the country by export of cashew kernels during 2011-12 reached $43.90 billion. 131000 tons of kernels were exported during 2011-12. There are about 600 cashew processing units in Kolam, Kerala.

Due to uncertain rainfall and sometimes untimely rainfall or no rainfall i.e. vagaries of rainfall, India's agricultural productivity is low and stagnant. It has however made tremendous progress in foodgrains production through technological improvement in cultivation and improved fertilizers. India exports Basmati rice, wheat, serials and fresh fruits.

When agricultural production is low or there is famines, India has to waive outstanding agricultural loans of the farmers which amounts to Rs. billions loss to the states and Central Government. To stop this, irrigation facilities should be improved and water conservation should be fully introduced so that there will be adequate water for land cultivation throughout the year and the agriculture will not entirely depend on rainfall.

Agriculture is an important part of the Indian economy. At around 153000 sq. kilometers (956 sq. miles), India has second largest amount of arable land after the US with 52% of the total land is under cultivation. Although the total land area of the country is slightly more than China or US, India's arable land is marginally smaller than that of US and marginally larger than that of China. However, agriculture output lags far behind in potential. The low productivity in India is a result of several factors. India's large agricultural subsidies are distorting what farmers grow and hampering productivity, enhancing investment, over - regulation of agriculture has increased the costs, price risks and uncertainty, and government intervention in labour land and credit are hurting the market. Infrastructure such as roads, electricity, ports, food shortage, retail markets and services remain inadequate. Average size of the land holding is very small with 70% of the holdings are being less than 1 hectare (2.5 acres) in size. Irrigation facilities are inadequate, as revealed by the fact that only 46% of the total cultivable land was irrigated in 2016, resulting in the farm being dependent on rainfall specifically the monsoon season, across the country. In order to bring additional 2 crores hectares (20 million hectares) i.e. 50 million acres of land under irrigation, various schemes have been attempted including additional irrigation Benefits programme which was provided Rs. 800 billion in Union budget. Farming incomes are also affected by the lack of food shortage and distribution infrastructure, a third of India's agricultural production is lost from spoilage.

Manufacturing & Industry

Manufacturing accounts for 26% of GDP and employs 22% of the total workforce. According to the World Bank, India's industrial manufacturing GDP output in 2015 was 6th largest in the world on current US dollar basis ($559 billion), and 9th largest on inflation-adjusted constant 2005 US dollar basis ($197.1 billion).The industrial sector underwent significant changes due to the 1991 economic reforms, which removed import restrictions, brought in foreign competition, led to the privatization of certain government-owned public-sector industries, liberalized the foreign direct investment (FDI) regime, improved infrastructure and led to an expansion in the production of fast-moving consumer goods.Post-liberalization, the Indian private sector was faced with increasing domestic and foreign competition, including the threat of cheaper Chinese imports. It has since handled the change by squeezing costs, revamping management, and relying on cheap labour and new technology. However, this has also reduced employment generation, even among smaller manufacturers who previously relied on labour-intensive processes.

Petroleum Products & chemicals

Petroleum products and chemicals are major contributors to the Indus's industrial GDP and together they contribute over 34% of its export earnings. India hosts many of the refineries and petrochemicals operations including world's largest refinery in Jamnagar that processes 1.24 million barrels of crude per day. India is third largest producer of chemical industry which contributes 5% of the country's GDP. India is also five largest producers of agrochemicals.

Chemical manufacturing industry contributed $141 billion (6% of GDP) and employs 17.33 million i.e. 4% of the workforce in 2011.

Pharmaceuticals

The Indian pharmaceutical industry has grown in recent years to become a major manufacturer of heath care products in the world. India produced about 8% of the global pharmaceutical supply in 2011 by value, including over 60000 generic brands of medicines. The industry grew from $6 billion in 2005 to $36.7 billion in 2016 and is expected to grow by 15.92% to reach $55 billion in 2020.

Engineering

Engineering is the largest sub-sector of India's industrial sector and third largest by exports. It includes transportation equipment, machine tools, capital goods transformers, switchgears, furnaces and cart and forged parts for turbines, automobiles and railways. Industry employ about 4 million workers. On value-added basis, Indus's engineering exported $6.7 billion worth of engineering goods in 2013-14 fiscal year and served part of the domestic demand for engineering goods.

The engineering industry of India includes its growing car, motorcycle and scooters industry, and productivity machinery such as tractors. India manufactured and assembled about 18 million passenger and utility vehicles in 2011 of which 2.3 million were exported. India is the largest producer and the 7th largest consumer of machine tools.

The automotive manufacturing industry contributed $79 billion (4% of GDP) and employed 6.76 million (2% of the workforce) in 2016).

Gems and jewellery

India is one of the largest centres for polishing diamonds and gems and manufacturing jewellery; it is also one of the two largest consumers of gold. After crude oil and petroleum products, the export and import of gold, precious metals, precious stones, gems and jewellery account for the largest portion of India's global trade. The industry contributes about 7% of India's GDP, employs millions, and is a major source of its foreign-exchange earnings. The gems and jewellery industry created $60 billion in economic output on value-added basis in 2017, and is projected to grow to $110 billion by 2022.

South Africa and Australia are major sources of diamonds and precious metals, but alongwith Antewerp, New York and Ramal Gan, India' cities such as Surat and Mumbai are hubs of the world's jewellery. Polishing, cutting, precision finishing, supply and trade. It is primarily artisan-driven in India which is manual, highly fragmented and almost entirely served by the family owned operations.

Eleven out of 12 diamonds set in any jewellery in the world are out and polished in India. It is also a hub of gold and other precious metal – based jewellery. Domestic diamond for gold and jewellery products is another driver of Indus's GDP.

Textile

Textile industry contributes about 4 per cent to the country's GDP, 14 per cent of the industrial production and 17% of export earnings. India's textile industry has transformed in recent years from a decline sector to a rapidly developing one. After freeing the industry in 2004-2005 from the number of limitations, primary financial the government permitted massive investment inflows, both domestic and foreign. From 2004 to 2008, total investment into the textile sector increased by $ 27 billion. Ludhiana produces 90% of woolens in India and is known as Manchester of India. Tripura is well known for hosiery and Itachakarnji is known for cotton textile looms.

Defence

With strength of 1.3 million active personnel, India has third military force and largest voluntary army. Total budget sanctioned to the Indian military for financial year 2017 was $53.5 billion which is expected to rise to $62 billion by 2022. The April 2019 Stockholm International Peace Research (SIPRI) Report states that compared with 2017 and 2018, in 2018 there was growth of about 2.6% growth in purchases of the international military weapons. Last year purchases of weapons was highest at $1.82 trillion in the world. America bought weapon worth $649 billion i.e. 36% of the world's purchases, followed by China at $250 billion, Saudi Arabia $67.6 billion, India $ 66.5 billion and Russia $61.4 billion. China has increased its military weapon purchases by 10 times compared to 1994 and China and America together have spent 50% of the total world's weapons purchases in 2018. On account of Yemen, Saudi Arabia has made surge in the purchases and India has done 3.1% rise in purchases due to constant threat from Pakistan and China on boarder areas.

India has China and Pakistan as their enemies on the Indian borders. In order to defend the attacks from both of them simultaneously, our army is i.e. military, naval and air force are constantly alert to face such attacks. We have built up our military, naval and air preparations and infrastructure facilities on the disputed territories have been developed. We have nuclear bombs and we recently purchased AS400 defence military aircrafts from USSR to combat any military attacks from our enemies. We have also become fourth "Space Force" recently after US, Russia and China.Recently1 'Chinuk" aircraft has been received from USA as a part delivery of 8 such aircrafts to be delivered by US to India as per the Agreement. We have also bought 46 Rafael aircrafts from France to increase our Air Force defence. India got first Rafael in October 2019.

Pulp & Paper

The pulp and paper industry in India is one of the major producers of paper in the world and has adopted new manufacturing technology.

Services

The Services sector has the largest share of India's GDP, accounting for 57% in 2012 up from 15% in 1950. It is the seventh largest services sector by nominal GDP, and third largest as per GDP PPP. It provides employment to 27% of the workforce. Information technology and business process outsourcing are among the fastest growing sectors having a stimulative growth rate of revenue 33.6% between fiscal year 1997-98 and 2002-03, and contributing 25% of the country's total exports in 2007-08.

Aviation

India is the fourth largest aviation market in the world recording an air traffic of 158 million passengers in 2017.The market is estimated to have 800 aircrafts by 2020 which would account for 4.3% of global volume, and is expected to record annual passenger traffic of 520 million by 2037. IATA estimated that aviation contributed $30 billion to India's GDP in 2017 and supported 7.5 million jobs – 39000 directly, 57000 in value chain and 6.2 million through tourists.

In March1953, India nationalized the then existing privately owned eight domestic airlines into Indian Airlines for domestic services and Tata group-owned Air India for international services. International Airport Authority of India (IAAI) was constituted in 1972 while the National Airport Authority was constituted in 1986. The Bureau of Civil Aviation Security was established in 1987following the crash of Air India flight 182.

The government deregulated the Civil Aviation sector in 1991 when the government allowed private airlines to operate. The aviation experienced a rapid transformation following deregulation. Several low-cost carriers entered the Indian market. Major entrants included Air Deccan, Air Sahara, Kingfisher

Airlines, Spice Jet, Go Air, Paramount Airlines and Indigo. Kingfisher Airlines became the Indian air carrier on 15-06-2005 to order Airbus A 380 aircraft worth $3 billion. However, Indian Aviation would struggle due to an economic slowdown and rising fuel and operation costs. This led to consolidation buy outs and discontinuation in 2007. Air Sahara and Air Deccan were acquired by Jet Airlines and Kingfisher Airlines respectively. Paramount Airlines ceased operations in 2010 and Kingfisher shut down in 2012. Now Naresh Goel's Jet has stopped operations in April 2019. In fact Elinad acquired the Jet's 24% capital but Jet could not survive due to lack of management and extravagant personal spending by Goel and Mallya who were both British citizens Both of them did not try to save their companies and Banks who financed them lost their money. Air Asia India, a low cost carrier operating as a joint Venture between Air Asia and Tata Sons launched in 2014. As of 2013-14, Indigo and Go Air were generating profits. The average domestic passenger air fare dropped by 70% between 2005 and 2014 after adjusting for inflation. Aviation industry has serious financial crisis. Recently, due to the Jet's failure 18000 people lost the jobs though some will be accommodated in some existing Airlines companies. Indian Airline was merged with Air India and is incurring tremendous financial losses since Mr. Praful Patel was Aviation minister in 2009.

Banking & Financial Institutions

Financial Services industry contributed $809 billion,37% of GDP and employed 14.17 million (3% of the workforce) in 2016, and the banking sector $407billion (19% of GDP) and employed 5.5 million people (1% of the workforce) in 2016. Indian money market is classified into the organized sector, comprising private, public and foreign-owned commercial banks and co-operative banks, together known as "Scheduled Banks" and unorganized sector which includes individual family owned indigenous bank or money lenders and non-banking financial companies.

Prime Minister Indira Gandhi nationalized 14 banks in 1969 followed by 6 other banks in 1980, and made it mandatory for banks to provide 40% of their net credit to priority sectors including agriculture, small-scale industries, retail trade and small business, to ensure that the bank fulfils their social and economic goals. Since then the number of bank branches has increased from 8260 in 1969 to 72170 in 2007 and the population covered by a branch decreased from 63800 to 15000 during the same period. Total bank deposits increased from Rs. 59.1 billion in 1970-71 to Rs. 38309.22 billion in 2008-09. Despite the increase of rural branches from 1860 or 22% of the total in 1969 of the total in 1969 to 30590 or 42% in 2007. Only 32270 of 500000 villages are served by a schedule bank.

India's Gross Domestic savings in 2006-07 as a percentage of GDP stood at a high 32.8%. More than half of the personal savings are invested in physical assets such as land, houses, cattle and gold.

Financial Technology

According to the report of the National association Software and Services Companies (NASSCOM), India has a presence of around 400 companies in the financial space with an investment of about $420 million in 2015. The NASSCOM report also estimated the fine tech software and services market to grow 17 times by 2020, marking worth of $8billion. The Indian fine tech landscape is segmented into 34% in payment processing, 32% in banking and 12% in the trading public and private markets.

Information Technology

The information technology industry in India consists of two major components. ItsServices and Business Process Outsourcing (BPO). Sector have increased its contribution to India's GDP from 1.2% in 1998 to 7.5% in 2012. The Sector aggregated revenue of $147 billion in 2015, when export revenue stood at $199 billion and domestic revenue at $48 billion growing by over 13%.

This growth is attributed to increased specialization and an availability of a large pool of low-cost highly skilled, fluent English speaking workers – matched by increased demand from foreign customers interested in India's service exports, or looking to outsource their operations.

About 2.8 million people worked in outsourcing sector as of 2012, earning annual revenue around $11 billion i.e. 1% of GDP. Around 2.5 million people graduate in India every year, wages are rising by 10-15 per cent as a result of skill shortage.

Insurance

India became the tenth largest Insurance market in the world in 2013 rising from 15th in 2011. At a total market size of $66.4 billion in 2013. It remains small compared to world's major economies, and the Indian Insurance market accounts to 2% of the World's Insurance business. India's life and non-life insurance industry has been growing @20% and double digit growth is expected to continue through 2021. The market remains about 360 million active life insurance policies, the most in the world of 52 insurance companies in India, 24 are active in life insurance business. Life Insurance Companies in India were nationalized in 1950.

Electricity

Primary energy consumption of India is the third largest after China and US with 5.3% global share in 2015. Coal and crude together account for 85% of the primary energy consumption of India. India's oil reserves meet 25% of the country's domestic oil demand. India's total proven crude oil reserves are 763.476 million metric tons while gap reserves stood at 1490 billion (1.49 trillion) cubic metres (53 trillion cubic feet). Oil and natural gas fields are located offshore at Bombay High, Krishna Godavari Basin and Cavery Delta and onshore in the state of Assam, Gujrat and Rajasthan. India is the fourth largest consumer of oil and net oil imports were nearly Rs. 820000- crores ($110 billion) in 2014-15. Which had adverse effect on the country's current Account trade deficit. The petroleum industry in India mostly consists of Public Sector Companies such as Oil & Natural Gas Corporation (ONGC), Hindustan Petroleum Corporation (HPCL), Bharat Petroleum Corporation Ltd. (BPCL) and Indian Oil Corporation (IOC). There are some major private Indian Companies in the oil sector such as Reliance industries Ltd. (RIL) which operates the world's largest oil refining complex.

India became the world's third largest producer of electricity in 2013 with a 4.8% global share in electricity generation, surpassing Japan and Russia.

Infrastructure

Indus's infrastructure and transport sector contributes about 5% of its GDP. India has a road network of over 5,472,144 kilometres (3,400, 233 miles) as at 31st March 2015, the third largest road network in the world behind US and China. At 1.66 km of roads per square kilometres of land (2.66 miles per sq. mile) the qualitative density of India's road network is higher than that of Japan (0.91) and US (0.67) and far higher than China (o...46), Brazil (0.18) or Russia (0.18). Qualitatively, Indian roads are mixed of modern highways and narrow unpaved and are being improved. As of 31st March 2015, 61.05% of Indian roads were paved. India has the lowest kilometer –line road density per 100000 people amount G-27 countries, leading to traffic congestion. It is upgrading in infrastructure. As of May 2014, India had completed over 22600 kilometres (14000miles) of 4 -or- 6 - lane highways, connecting most of its major manufacturing, commercial and cultural centres. India's roads infrastructure carries 60% of fright and 87% of passenger tariff.

Indian Railways is the fourth largest rail network in the world, with a track length of 114500 kilometres (71000 miles) and 7172 stations. This government owned and operated railway network carried an average of 23 million passengers a day, and over a billion tons of freight in 2013. India has a coastline of 7500 kilometres (4700 miles) with 13 major port and 60 operational non-major ports; which together handle 95% of the country's external trade by volume and 70% by value (most of the remaining handled by air). Nhava Shiva, or Mumbai is the largest public port while Mundra is the largest private sea port. The airport infrastructure of India includes 125 airports of which 66 airports are licensed to handle both passengers and cargo.

Retail

The rental industry contributed $ 484 billion (22% of GDP) 249.94 million (57% of workforce) in 2016. The industry is the second largest employer in India, after agriculture. The Indian retail market is estimated to be $ 600 billion and one of the top – five retail markets in the world by economic value. India has one of the fastest growing retail market in the world and is projected to reach $1.3 trillion by 2030.

India's retail industry mostly consists of local Mont and pop stores.Owner-manned shops and street vendors. Retail Supermarkets are expanding, with a market share of 4% in 2008. In 2012, the government permitted 51% FDI in multibrand retail and 100% FDI in single-brand retail However, a lack of back-end warehouse infrastructure and state level permit and red tape continue to limit growth of organized retail compliance with over thirty regulations such as "Signboard Licences" and "anti-hoarding measures" must be made before a store can operate to business. There are taxes for moving goods from state to state, and even within the states. According to the Wall Street Journal. The lack of infrastructure and efficient rent retail network cause a third of India's agriculture produce to be lost from spoiling.

Tourism

The World Travel & Tourism Council calculated that tourism generated Rs. 15.24 trillion ($210 billion) or 9.4% of the Nation's GDP in 2017 and supported 41.622million jobs, 8% of its total employment. The sector is predicted to grow at an annual rate of 6.9% to Rs.32.05 Trillian($450 billion) by 2028 (9.9% of GDP). Over 10 million foreign tourists arrived in India in 2017 compared to 8.89 million in 2016, recording a growth of 15.6%. India earned $21.07 billion in foreign exchange from tourism receipts in 2015. The US is the largest source of international tourists to India, while European Union and Japan are other major sources of international tourists. Less than 10% of international tourists visit Taj Mahal, with the majority visiting other cultural, thematic and holiday circuits. Over 12 million Indian citizens take internationaltrips each year for tourism, while domestic tourism within India adds about 740 million Indian travelers.

India has a fast - growing medical tourism sector of its health care economy, offering low – cost health services and long term Care. In October 2015, the medical tourism sector was estimated to be $3 billion, it is projected to grow to $7.8 billion by 2020. In 2014, 184298 foreign patients travelled to India to seek medical treatment.

Telecommunication

The telecommunication sector generated Rs.2.20 trillion ($31 billion)in revenue in 2014-15 accounting to 1.94% of total GDP. India is the second highest largest market in the world of telephone users (both fixed and mobile phones) with 1.53 billion subscribers as at August 2016. It has one of the lowest call tariffs in the world, due to fierce competition among telecom operators. There were 342.65 million internet subscribers in the country which is third largest internet user-base.

Industry estimates indicate that there are over 554 million TV consumers in India in 2012. India is the largest direct to home (DTH) television market in the world by number of subscribers.

Mining

Mining contributed $ 63 billion (3% of GDP) and employed 201.14 million people (5% of the workforce) in 2016. India's mining industry was the 4th largest producer of minerals in the world by volume and the 8th producer by value in 2009. It mined the processed 89 minerals of which four were fuel, three were automic energy minerals and 80 non-fuel. The government owned public sector accounted for 68% of mineral production by volume in 2011-12. Nearly 50% of India's mining industry, by output value, is concentrated in eight states: Odisha, Rajasthan, Chhattisgarh, Madhya Pradesh, Andhra Pradesh, Telangana, Jharkhand and Karnataka. Another 25% of the output by value comes from off-shore oil and gas resources. India operated about 300 mines in 2000, half of rich are coal, limestone and iron ore. On output value basis, India was one of the five largest global producers of mica, chromite, coal, lignite, and iron ore. Bauxite, barite zinc and manganese.

India is the fourth largest producer of steel and seventh largest producer of alunimium in 2013.

Indus's minerals resources contributed 23% of GDP in 2010 compare to 35 on 2000 and employed 29 million people – "decreasing percentage to total labour force. India is a net importer of many minerals including coal. India's mining sector declined because of complex permit, regulatory and administrative procedures, inadequate infrastructure, and shortage of capital resources and slow adoption of environmentally sustainable technology.

Iron & Steel

In fiscal year 2014-15, India was the third largest producer of raw steel and the largest producer of sponge iron. The industry produced 91.45 million tons of finished steel and 9.7 million tons of pig iron. Most iron and steel in India is produced from iron ore.

Construction

The construction industry contributed $288 billion (13% of GDP) and employed 60.42 million people (14% of the workforce) in 2016.

Foreign Trade

Until the linearization in 1991, India was largely and internationally isolated from the world markets to protect its economy and to achieve self-reliance. Foreign trade was subject to import tariffs, export taxes and quantitative restrictions.While foreign direct investment (FDI) was restricted by upper limit equity participation, restrictions on technology transfer, export obligations and government approvals. These approvals were needed for nearly 60% of new FDI in the industrial sector. The restrictions ensured that FDI averaged only around $200 million annually, between 1985and 1991, the large percentage of capital flows consisted foreign aid, commercial borrowings and deposits from non-resident Indians. India's exports were stagnant for the first 15 years after independence, due to general neglect of trade policy by the government of that period, imports in the same period with early industrialization, consisted predominantly of machinery, raw materials and consumer goods.

Since liberation, the value of India's international trade has increasing sharply, with the contribution of total trade in goods and services to the GDP rising from 16% in 1990-91 to 47% in 2009-10. Foreign trade accounted for 48.8% of India's GDP in 2015. Globally, India accounts for 1.44% of exports and 2.12% of imports of merchandise trade and 3.34% of exports and 3.31% of imports for commercial services trade. India's major trading partners are European Union, China, USA and UAE. In 2006-07, major export commodities included engineering goods, petroleum products, chemicals and pharmaceuticals, germs and jewellery, textiles and garments, agricultural products, iron ore and other minerals. Major import commodities included crude oil and related products, machinery, electric goods and silver. In November 2010, exports increased 22.3% year-on-year to Rs.850.63 billion ($12 billion) with imports were up 7.5% at Rs.1251.33 billion($17 billion). The trade deficit for some month dropped from Rs.468.65 billion ($6.5 billion) in 2009 to Rs. 400.7 billion ($5.6 billion) in 2010.

India is the founding member of General Agreement on Tariff & Trade (GATT) and its successor the WTO. While participating activity in its general council meetings, India has been crucial in voicing concerns of the developing world. For Instance, India has continued its opposition to the inclusion of labour, environment issues and the non-tariff barriers to trade in WTO policies.

Balance of Payments

Since independence, India's balance of payments on its current account has been negative. Since economic liberalization in the 1990s, precipitated by a balance of payment crisis, India's exports rose consistently covering 80.3% of its imports in 2002-03, up from 66.2% in 1990-91. However, the global economic slump followed by a general deceleration in world trade saw the exports as a percentage of imports dropped to 61.4% in 2008-09. India's growing import bill is seen as the main driver behind the large current account deficit, which rose to $118.7 billion or 11.11% of GDP in 2008-09. Between January and October 2010, India imported $821 billion worth of crude oil. Indian economy has run a trade deficit every year from 2002 to 2012, with a merchandise trade deficit $189 billion in 2011-12. Its trade with China has the largest deficit about $31 billion in 2013.

India's reliance on external assistance and concessional debt has decreased since liberalization of the economy and the debt service ratio decreased from 35.3% in 1990-91 to 4.4% in 2008-09. In India, external commercial borrowings (ECB) or commercial loans from non-residential lenders, are being permitted by the government for providing additional source of funds to Indian Corporations. The Ministry of Finance monitors and regulates them through ECB policy guidelines issued by RBI under the Foreign Exchange Management Act of 1999. India's foreign exchange reserves have steadily risen from $5.8 billion in March 1991 to $420 billion in April 2018. In 2012, UK announced an end to all financial aid to India, citing the growth and robustness of Indian economy.

India's current account deficit increased all-time high in 2013. India has historically funded its current account deficit through borrowings through companies in the overseas markets or remittances by non-resident Indians and portfolio inflows. The Economic Times noted that the development a 'sign of rising confidence among long-term investors in Prime Minister Narendra Moody's ability to strengthen the country's economic foundation for sustained growth.

Foreign Direct Investment

As the third largest economy in the World in GDP PPP terms, India has attracted foreign direct investment (FDI). During the year 2011, FDI flow into India stood at 36.5 billion, 51.1% higher than the 2010 figure of $24.15 billion. India has strengthened in telecommunication, information technology and other significant area such as components, chemicals, apparels, pharmaceuticals and jewellery. Despite a surge in foreign investments, rigid FDI policies were a significant hindrance over time for which India adopted a number of FDI reforms. India has a large pool of skilled managerial and technical expertise. The size of middle class population stands at 300 million and represents a growing consumer market.

India liberized its FDI policy and allowed 100% FDI in construction projects comprising housing, commercial premises, hospitals education institutions incremental facilities and city and regional level infrastructure. Between 2012 and 2014, India extended these reforms to defence, telecommunication, oil, retail, aviation and other sectors.

From 2000 to 2010, the country attracted $ 178 billion as FDI. Inordinately high investment from Mauritius is due to routing of international funds through the country given significant tax advantage – double tax is avoided due to a tax treaty between India and Mauritius, and Mauritius has capital gain tax haven, effectively creating a zero taxation FDI channel.FDI accounted for 2.1% of India's GDP in 2015.

As the government has eased 87 foreign investment direct rules across 21 sectors in the last three years, FDI inflows hit $60.1 billion between 2011 and 2017 in India.

Inflows

Rank	Country	in millions USD	Inflow%
1.	Mauritius	50,164	42%
2.	Singapore	11,275	9%
3.	USA	8,914	7%
4.	UK	6158	5%
5.	Netherland	4968	4%
		81, 476	67%

Outflows

Since 2000, Indian Companies have expanded overseas, investing FDI and creating jobs outside India from 2006 to 2010, FDI by Indian companies have deployed FDI and started operations in US, Europe and Asia. The Indian Company Tata is UK's largest manufacturer and private sector employer.

Remittance

In 2015, a total of $68.91 billion was made in remittances in India from other countries and a total of 8.476 billion was made in remittance by foreign workers in India.to their home countries. UAE, US and Saudi Arabia were the top sources of remittances to India, while Bangladesh, Pakistan and Nepal were top recipients of remittances from India. Remittances in India accounted for 3.32% of the country's GDP in 2015. In 2018, it was $ 80 billion.

Merger & Actuations

Between 1985and 2018, 20846 deals have been announced in, into (inbond) and out of (outbond) India. This amounts to a value of $618 billion in terms of value. 2010 has been most active year with almost $ 60 billion. Most of the deals were conducted in 2007.

Currency

Indian rupee is only the legal tender in India, and is also accepted as legal tender in neighbouring Nepal and Bhutan, both of them peg their currency to that of Indian rupee. India's monetary system is managed by RBI established on 01-04-1935 and nationalized in 1949. RBI is India's monetary authority. The benchmark interest rates are set by the RBI's Monetary Policy Committee.

The Rupee was linked to the British Pound from 1927 to 1946 and then to US dollar until 1975 through a fixed exchange rate. It was devalued in September 1975 and the system of a fixed par rate was placed with basket of currencies such as British Pound, US dollar, Japanese yen and Deusche mark. In 1991, after collapse of the largest trading partner, Soviet Russia, India faced the major international foreign exchange crisis and the Rupee was devalued by around 19% in 2 stages on 1st July & 2nd July 1992, a liberalized Exchange Rate Mechanism (LERM) was introduced. Under LERM, exporters had to surrender 40 per cent of their foreign exchange earnings to RBI and the RBI determined exchange rate. The remaining 60% could be converted at the market determined exchange value. In 1994, the Rupee was convertible on the current account with some capital controls.

After the sharp devaluation in 1991 and transaction to current account convertibility in 1994, the value of rupee has been largely determined by market forces. The rupee has been fairly stable during the decade 2000-2010.In September 2013, the rupee touched all time low Rs. 68.27 to the US dollar.

Year	*INR per US Dollar*
1975	9.4058
1980	7.8800
1985	12.3640
1990	17.4992
1995	32.4198
2000	44.9401
2005	44.1000
2010	45.7593
2015	64.05
2016	67.09
2017	64.14

In 2018 and 2019, the exchange rate remained between Rs.68-69 per $1.

Income & Consumption

Though India's Gross National Income per capita increased by 13.7% per annual from 2002-03 to 2010-11 to Rs. 53433-, the growth in inflation adjusted per capita income of the nation showed to 5.8% in 2010-11 down from 6.4% in the previous year. These consumption levels are all on individual basis. The average family income in India was $6671- per household in 2011.

According to 2011 census data, India has about 330 million houses and 247 million households. 50% of the households have four or fewer members with an average of 4.8 member per household. Thus the household produced a GDP of about $ 1.7 trillion. 67% of household use firewood, crop-residue or cow dug for cooking purposes. 53% have no sanitation facilities on premises. 83% have water supply within their premises or 100 metres (330 ft) from their house in urban area and 500 metres (1600 ft) from the houses in rural area, 67% of households have access to electricity 63% have landline or mobile telephones services, 43% have Televisions and 26% have two or four wheeler motor cycles.

According to New World Wealth Report, India's total wealth increased from \$3.165 Billion in 2007 to \$8.230 billion in 2017, a growth of 160%. India's total wealth rose by 25% from \$6.2 trillion in 2016 to \$8.23 trillion in 2017, making it the sixth wealthiest nation in the world. There are 20730 multimillionaires (7th largest in the World) and 118 billionaires in India (3rd largest in the World). With 330,400 high net worth individuals, India is home of 9th highest number of HNWIs in the world. Mumbai is the wealthiest Indian city and 12th wealthiest city in the World with a total net worth of \$950 billion in 2017. Twenty- eight billionaires.

Poverty

People below poverty line in India: 19% of the World population reside in India as per 2006 figures. India had about 61 million children in 2010. Between 1990 and 2010, India achieved 9.45% reduction in poverty under age 5. Since 1960, Poverty Eradication Schemes have been implemented by Indian Government with central planning which reduced the poverty in rural area in sizeable extent.

Employment

Agriculture and allied sectors accounted for 52.1% in 2009-10. Largest employed in organized sector was 20.7% in 2013-14.

Unemployment level is high @ 8.1% in 2018-19 of the total labour force 552 million i.e. 44.7 million are unemployed.

India made good progress in agriculture and the country has transformed from grain importer to net exporter of food today.

Corruption

Corruption has been a pervasive problem in India. Paying a bribe or padding influence to get job done in the public office was common with bureaucracy, licence raj till recently. But now Central & States Vigilance Commissions have been set up and Right to Information set up in 2005 have considerably reduced corruption and opened avenues to redress grievances.

Economic Disparities

India's average annual per capita income was \$1410- was poorest of the World's middle income group countries. It was just \$436- in UP and \$294- in Bihar.

Five Year Plans especially during pre-liberalization period attempted to reduce poverty on regional basis. More advanced states have been better placed, however, after liberalization.

Security Market

The development of security market began with the launch of Bombay Exchange Market in July 1875 and Ahmedabad Market in 1894. Since then 22 Stock Markets traded in Indian cities. Indian Stock Exchange Market became the tenth largest market in the world by market capitalization, just above those of South Korea and Australia. India's two major stock Exchanges, BSE and National Stock Market of India had capitalization of $1.71 trillion and $1.68 trillion as of February 2015. According to the World federation of Exchanges.

The initial public offering (IPO) market in India has been small compared to NYSE and NASDAQ raising $300 million in 2003 and $1.4 billion in 2012.

Present Status of Indian Economy at a Glance

(1) Economy of India is social democratic developing economy. It is the world's 6th largest economy by GDP Nominal and 3rd by GDP PPP.

(2) Its GDP Nominal is $ 2.848 trillion and GDP PPP $10.385 trillion as at 2018.

(3) Its population is 125 crores which is second highest after China's population of 140 crores.

(4) GDP Nominal per capita is $2134 and GDP PPP is $ 7738 as per 2018 figures. It ranks per capita GDP Nominal at 139th and GDP PPP at 122$^{nd.}$

(5) GDP by Sector is agriculture 17.32%, Industry 29.02% and services 53.66%.

(6) Labour force is 520.2 million which41.76% of total population.

(7) Labour force by occupation is as follows: Agriculture 47%, Industry 22% and services 31%.

(8) Unemployment is above 8.8% and average net salary is Rs. 113000-($ 1600-) as per 2017-18 figures.

(9) Main industries are textiles, chemicals, food processing, steel, cement, mining, petroleum, machinery, software, transport equipment and pharmaceuticals.

(10) In external trade, exports are $303.4 billion and Imports $ 465.6 billion with net trade deficit $ 162.4 billion due mainly to crude oil imports which is 30% of total imports. It is 5.70% of GDP.

(11) FDI stock inward is $377.68 and outward $ 155.24 resulting in FDI inwards $ 222.44 billion as per figures of 2017.

(12) $80 billion comes as inward remittances from Indians working abroad in countries like US, UAE, Saudi Arabia and others.

(13) Net internal investment is $ 391.9 billion.

(14) Public Finance

(15) Public Debt: 69.91% of GDP i.e.$1.99 trllion (2018)

(16) Budgetary deficit is Rs.12.25 trillion $ 170 billion which is 6% of GDP made up by revenue Rs.39.86 trillion ($550 billion) and Expenses Rs. 52.11 trillion ($730 billion) - 2018.

(17) External debt is $529 billion which is 17.6% of GDP Nominal. Public debt is 69.91% of GDP. According to standard norms, Public debt should be 60% of GDP and budgetary deficit is 4% of GDP.

(18) Before liberation of economy in 1991, India's debt servicing was 36% which after liberation came down drastically to 4%

(19) International Credit Agencies like S & P, T & C and Moody's have granted India's credit rating as BBB- for Domestic and Foreign and outlook as "Stable" which helps to attract foreign investments into India without any difficulties.

Critical Observations of Indian Economy

(1) It is surprising to note that the Indian Economy was large and prosperous under the Mughal Empire with 64% of the workforce in primary sector (including agriculture) and 36% of the workforce in Secondary and tertiary sector, higher than in Europe where 65.90% of the workers in agriculture in 1700 and 65.75% were in agriculture in 1750. During the Mughal Empire, India was producing about 25% of the world's output until 1750 and there was a significant demand for products of Mughal India from Europe especially cotton textiles and goods such as spice, pepper. Indigo, etc. Decline of the Mughal Empire led to the substantially fall in agricultural productivity which in turn negatively affected the textile industry.

(2) In contrast to Mughal India, British India ruling from 19th century through East India Company treated Indians as slaves and dumped their products into India, it commercialized agriculture resulting in considerable fall in production of food crops, mass impoverishment and destitution of farmers. Economic policy of the British Raj caused a severe decline in the handicrafts and handloom sectors, due to reduced demand and dipping unemployment. There was significant transfer of capital from India to England which led to a massive drain of revenue.

(3) Under the British Rule, India's share of the World economy declined from 24.4% in 1700 to 4.2% in 1950. India's GDP (PPP) was stagnant during Mughal Empire and began to decline in the British Raj. India's share of global industrial output declined from 25% in 1750 down to 2% in 1900. At the same time, UK's share of world economy increased from 2.9% in 1700 to 9% in 1870. East

India Company of UK forced open the large Indian Market to British goods. Thus in many fields, British ruined Indian economy at the cost of the British economy. There were famines in India and rich country like India became importers of foodgrains in British India. British India ruthlessly treated the Indians in epidemics which killed thousands of people residing especially in rural areas. British made laws and rules which were favourable for them and were proud of ruling the country as per these oppressive laws. In fact, these laws and rules were damaging Indian interest on all fields and there were injustice in the judgement of British India courts. Communication development made in India was only to make transfer of cotton easy from India to UK.by rail/ roads and make textile cloth for which large Indian Market was available. All prosperity of Britain was at the cost of India under the name of 'Industrial Revolution. Late Subhash Chandra Bose harassed British during the Second World War which crippled the British Economy and they were unable to manage large country like India post war which compelled UK to give Independence to India on 15th August 1947.

(4) Recently, under the trade policy, President Donand Trump has made trade ban and trade restrictions by imposing 25% tariff on Iron & Steel on China and European countries. While doing so, he remarked that no doubt, China is a bad trade partner but the European countries are worse than China as a trade partners who intentionally prohibited entry of American cars into their countries but freely exporting cars in America and thereby the U.S. A. has to incur the adverse trade balance of USD 150 billion to the European countries.

(5) Though India was oppressed by Britishers ruthlessly, Britishers introduced some good changes in Indian continent like education system encouraging Indian students to learn English language, abolition of Sati practice, introduction of ICS examination to select capable civil administrative officers and reduction of inequality in casteism.

(6) India made the tremendous development in the field of agriculture and other sectors by way of ion of Five Years Plans under the leadership of Prime Minister Jawarlal Nehru and Finance Minister C. D. Deshmukh who implemented these five years plans for tremendous industrial development and improvement of agriculture. Various heavy industries were set up for capital goods production and heavy dams were constructed for conservation of water and creating large quantity of electricity for rural development and agricultural development.

(7) Agricultural production which was about 80 million foodgrains in 1965 has been now increased to 277 million in 2018 by way of improved and modern latest cultivation methods, improved irrigation facilities and improved fertilizers.

(8) Large heavy industries under the full control of Central Government like ammunition, car manufacturing, and textiles.Capital goods were installed in implementation of long term planning which helped in increased productivity in every field. Infrastructural industries were set up.

(9) Indian youth skilled force resulted in tremendous progress in Computer industries, which has set up the Indian GDP in 2018 at USD 2. 5 trillion with external borrowing of India @ USD 500 billion resulting the ratio of external debt to GDP @ 20% which is reasonable for debt servicing. Since 1991, liberalization policy was introduced by Prime Minister Narsinvaha Rao and Finance Minister Manmohan Singh which resulted in further expanding the economy of India in various fields. India's export and imports increased during this period but India's trade deficit stands @ USD 160 billion in 2018 out of which trade deficit with China is USD 63 billion which needs to be reduced substantially by levying heavy customs duty on imported products from China. India's trade deficit comes largely from heavy import of petroleum products.India has developed as economy of 3rd rank in the world after USA and China.

(10) In diplomatic field, India has new outlook as" Look East and Act East "which expanded its relationship in trade with Hong-kong, Malaysia Singapore China and other eastern countries. India is successful in proving Pakistan vulnerable in Territories activities. It has good relation in defence field with Russia and USA. It has strategic partnership with USA in defence and other fields.

(11) Manmohan Singh has signed Automation Agreement with USA after explosion of nuclear bomb and has cordial relationship with all countries including USA. This Agreement was unfortunately not implemented but India had the advantage of removal of opposition by USA on Nuclear bomb possession by India.

Present Prime Minister Mr. Narendra Modi's claim that he has made progress in last 5 years which India has not made for 55 years in Congress rule is therefore not sustainable.He has definitely made progress but not to the extent he claims.

(12) In 1992, the government securities trading for Repo transactions resulted in financial crisis for the banks. Normally Government securities were traded in Repo market with the margin of profit paise 2 per Rs. 100- Suddenly, however, in 1991 onwards, these reverse Repo Government securities started trading with paisa 50- or Re, 1- profit for Rs.100-

which was susceptible. Like multiple credit creation of money by the banks on their public deposits, the dealers started trading in securities with multiple creation of securities. Large transactions such as Rs.50-100 crores per deal were done resulting in large profits. Security operations Heads of some banks tried to caution to the Bank Chief Executives about this abnormal transactions but since heavy profit was earned by the Banks in these dealing,internal controls were intentionally ignored which resulted in crisis. While purchasing or selling securities, actual physical securities were not exchanged but instead of this, Bank Receipts were exchanged as legal tender. Was this done to meet SLR requirements and government Securities were in scarcity? BR transaction were made through brokers with Bank of Cochin and Bank of Karad for Rs. 100 crores which banks were not credit worthy for such transactions. Harshad Mehta was main broker inventing such dealings along with the Bank's Dealers. In the non-existence of such Securities, such transactions were artificial and therefore crisis occurred which resulted in some banks making the financial loss more than RS.500-Crores. CBI teams were appointed to investigate this losses. Large number of junior officers were caught and punished. CBI came to the conclusion that internal controls were not implemented but this was true partially as internal controls were in existence but intentionally ignored and not implemented due to large profit creation from such dealing transactions. Limits to approve large amount of financial transactions of Bank top executives were substantially curtailed and dealings in Securities were completely stopped for at least one year.

(13) Presently Indian Banks are suffering from failure by the debtors corporations to repay their loans and bank's NPA is raised dangerously to 12 to 15% of total loans granted by the banks individually or by Syndicate/Consortium loan by various banks and in some cases about 20% which resulted in big financial loses to the banks. Some defaulters are definitely willful defaulters like Mallya and Nirav Modi while other like Videocon, Heads or other companies are defaulters but not willful but they are victims of substantial decline in industrial progress which is scaled at zero. This resulted in failure of industries in the aviation field which are making huge losses. Syndicate loans given by Lead Banker does not appear to have taken sufficient care and vigilance in monitoring such loans or there was pressure from the ministries to sanction these loans on top bank management. RBI also failed to monitor and detect the irregularities in repayment on time. Also Government has not made proper controls over the movement of the defaulters like Nirav Modi and Mallya who migrated to other countries and thereby escaped from paying loan dues to the banks. Decline in industrial growth has resulted in increasing unemployment to very hazardous level with unemployment added by demone-tarization

unemployment by at least 1crore. Unless the industrial growth will take place at high level, unemployment issue will be widen in the Indian economy. The issue needs to be urgently addressed and resolved satisfactory.

(14) Currency Demonetization was announced by Prime Minister Mr. Narendra Mody on 8 November 2016 has added fuel to the fire. No Black money was detected in the currency notes denomination and the efforts to detect black unaccountable money was completely failed. Because of cash transactions were completely stopped, it is reported that at least 3crore people lost their jobs permanently.

(15) In 2017, Government of India introduced one level tax country wide for all commodities at different rates as GST. This was a centralized tax. This policy has also not seen visible positive result in the collection of volume of revenue on GST (Goods and Sale Tax).

(16) During the USA President Mr. Regan who is famous for excessively spending money on Star War, Dr. Kissinger was his Defence Secretary. Dr. Kissinger, Jew born American, is well known for his diplomacy and he is known as best diplomat in USA. But if we observe his diplomatic policy, we find that his policy looked satisfactory in the short run but in the long term, repurcations of his policies showed adverse results. For example, He announced China as the most favourable nation for trading in order to get dissolution of USSR in 1991 at the earliest and he does not want the China to assist USSR to postpone this dissolution. This happened well but the China who was the financial Backward country far away from USA started compitition with USA and showed supremacy over USA in all fields. In International trade, China exports with USA was USD 500 billion and imports $150 billion resulting in the trade deficit USD 350- billion annually. This compelled present President Denord Trump to wage trade war with China by imposing 25% Customs duty on Steel and alunimium which affected the international trade of China seriously and his annual growth rate came to 6.7% from continuous 8% growth in the last three years. Industrial production slowed down in China and domestic demand for goods reduced with fall in constructive activities. China is now trying to negotiate with USA President Mr. Trump on trading terms but Mr. Trump is very tuff/firm and will agree to the trade terms which will arrive at equilibrium on balance of payment i.e. American Imports will be equal to American Exports which China will difficult to agree and accept .

(17) Defence Secretary Dr. Kissinger brought 7th Fleet of America in 1971 when India helped Bangladesh in its War with Pakistan for separation of the Bangladesh nation from Pakistan but helped in giving military aid to Pakistan in that war. This also failed as Pakistan became a terrorist country. His diplomacy was not successful here also. Even

though, Dr. Kissinger policy to keep China away from Russia also did not become successful as China is with Soviet Russia to fight against USA on all fronts including acceptance of USD as currency for international trade and defence competition.

(18) During the initial stage of Independence, India found it difficult to pay the external debt servicing payment of loan to IMF on time and many times had to reschedule the external debt servicing for interest and principal payment. This was on account of long term construction projects undertaken by India which will give earnings on long term basis. Since liberalization process initiated in 1991, the external debt servicing payment rate has been considerably reduced from 36% to 4% which is manageable.

(19) India is second largest country in the world after China with population 1.22 Billion againstthe World population of 7 Billion (17.42%) India's population in 2025 will surpass China's population. India will have a great asset of young population of about 600 + million workforce by 2050. India has at present no natural resources like USA but with 520 million young work force. India can produce largest in the world. For this purpose, India has to initiate a vigorous plan to train her workforce with computer skills and other most advanced productive skills in other industries. This will lead to increase productivity in agriculture and other advanced industries and make India the most prosperous country in the World. Necessary infrastructure and factories accommodating 600 million workforce should be provided on priority basis so that there will be no migration of labour force from India to other countries.

(20) With the assistance of Russia, India developed five years plans and achieved the industrial and agricultural growth through their implementation. Bokaro steel Industry in Bihar is a huge capital industry was set up by Russia in India. Russia also erected IIT Institution in India to give advanced technical knowledge to Indian youth to enhance their productivity.

(21) Foreign exchange earnings from Indian Residents working abroad has been continuously increasing from USD 66 billion in 1916 to USD 80 billion in 2018.

(22) National Fiscal budget for 2019-20 has many new provisions. Farmers for the first time will be given financial assistance of Rs. 6000- per year under this budget which is new facility and should be appreciated. This will result in expenditure of RS, 75000 crores annually. Then, unorganized labour will be given the monthly pension at the rare of Rs. 750- per month. This will result in expenditure of Rs. 3000 crores. Defence Budget also has been substantially raised to Rs. 3 trillion which is necessary to protect the country from external aggression from Terrorists in Pakistan and dual attack on India from Pakistan and

China. Off Course our military, air and naval forces are ready to face any such eventualities. Recent Punawala attack by Jai-Sai Mohamed where forty Indian Jawans were killed has been counterattacked heavily by India in which Terrorist bases and about 300 Terrorists killed in Pakistan is apt response to terrorists. Prime Minister Mr. Mody has rightly shown confidence and given military freedom/powers to the Defence authorities for counterattacking Pakistan's terrorists.

(23) Indian has maintained good relationship with other countries which assisted India in getting foreign financial assistance and military partnership with many countries to boost Indian economy and defence capacity.

(24) External debt $510 billion compared with GDP $2.848 Trillion works out to 18.92% which is reasonable.

(25) Domestic debt in local currency is 69.91% of GDP $ 2.848 trillion which works out to $1.9910 trillion. Generally interest rate are high for domestic debt which works out to 8..5% p. a. Debt servicing at this cost will compel the Government to take fresh loan for debt servicing which is not a satisfactory situation. It should be ensured that loan amount is fully utilized efficiently to infrastructural projects which will give positive protective returns above 8.5% p.a. to the Government to repay these loans without restructuring arrangements.

(26) Fiscal deficit Rs.12.25 trillion on fiscal revenue Rs. 39.86 trillion and fiscal expenditure Rs. 52.11 trillion works out to 6% excess expenditure to revenue collection which is manageable.

(27) Work force in India is 52 crores and unemployment rate works out to 8.8% which shows that 4.576 crores workforce is unemployed. New jobs should be createdby industrial growth which is slagging to enable the expansion of industries to accommodate all workforce and thereby enhanced the produc-tivity. Lot of efforts will have to be made to eradicate unemploy-ment.

(28) India has manufactured Brahos missile which is in great demand in many countries. India exports the missile to Vietnam. India has made good defence preparation. It has developed the art of preparing Sukhai 30 MKI defence aircrafts as per our requirements and recently made defence agreement with France under which France will supply 36 Rafael military aircrafts to India which will be included in the Air Force. This will tremen-dously increase the air defence capacity of India and India will be able to face Pakistan & China attacks easily jointly made by them.

(29) India has made Defence Agreement with USA's Boeing Company in 2015 to get 15 "Chinuk" helicopters. Out of these 4 "Chinuk" Helicopters were received by India recently in March 2019. These Helicopters are able to carry approximately 9.5 tons heavy military transport equipments. This will facilitate and enhance the Indian

Airforce capacity to make military transpor-tation of heavy equipments speedily.India has made rise of 3.1% on purchases of its defence equipment amounting to $66.5 billion on account of constant threats from China and Pakistan on Boarder areas.

(30) India has also made a good progress in space research and is sending their instruments on multiple basis for space research.

(31) On Wednesday 27-03-2019, India with the help of anti A- Sat Missile shot down/destroy LEO satellite which wasat an altitude of almost 300 kilometerwithin three minutes, jettisoning its long-standing reluctance to flex military missile in space. In the process, it joined an exclusive club of US, Russia and China that possess this deadly capacity. This is a great achievement of Indian Scientists. India became forth Space Power after America, Russia and China.Indian scientists and Chief of DRDO are congratulated for the same by Prime Minister and President of India. "It is a completely desi baby" said DRDO Chief, Mr. Chetan Kumar. Weare pride of the Scientists' valuable achieve-ment.

(32) Russia provided Nuclear Reactors to India for manufacturing nuclear bomb for explosion even there was a great opposition from USA. This gradually made India the major Nuclear power.

(33) In Retaliation of terrorism attack in Pulvama, India counter attacked terrorists in Balasore of Pakistan occupied Kashmir region and destroyed terrorism military bases in that area. It is reported that about 250-300 terrorists. For Territories activities of Jaish Leader Masood Azahar, Pakistan and China support him and China denies him to declare the international terrorist. Financial Action Task Force (FATF) has imposed restrictions on Pakistan for supplying financial assistance to Terrorists and have placed Pakistan on "grey List". This results in ban on international foreign financial assistance by any country to Pakistan.

(34) Indian goods export which was $ 303billion will rise substantially to $330billion in 2019. Indian imports is about $435 billion in 2017-2018. Foreign trade gap between Imports and Exports is bound to be narrowed by this rise in exports in 2019.

(35) India has completed negotiation with Airbus Defence to purchase 62 "C-295" Defence Aircrafts. Airbus Defence will have collaboration with Tata Advance System Ltd. (TASL). These aircrafts will be provided to Air Force and Border Line Force in the proportionate of 56 and 6 respectively.

(36) China being an aggressive country wanted Doklama of Bhutan to annex to his country. But India under an agreement with Bhutan has guaranteed Doklama's protection. India therefore prevented China to withdraw from making roads and other infrastructural facilities in that area. This resulted in conflict between India and China or about 3 months long period from June –August 2017. Ultimately China withdrew but now in March - April 2019, China has again tried to

intrude this territory again but Indian Army has been cautiously watching China's movement and will defend his territory by fighting with China tooth and nail on this issue.

(37) Prime Minister Nehru did not handle the Kashmir issue as an able and capable administrator. In case of any dispute, the statesman is expected to take appropriate decision. Faruq Abdallah was head of the Kashmir. Nehru tried to satisfy him and resolved the Kashmir issue as per his demands. Kashmir was an integral part of India and therefore special status to Kashmir was unwarranted. But Nehru utterly failed in resolving the issue and gave it a special status under Article 370 of the Indian constitution. This resulted in bringing this territory isolated by the industrialists. There were no industry and no jobs created in such situation. When Kashmiri boys become young, they had no jobs and they are attracted to terrorism and this rresulted in constant unrest in the valley. Unfortunately Mehbuba, Farooq Khan and his son do not understand this situation and makes this as a false prestige issue but government should firmly took decision to abolish Arkle 370 for the betterment of Kashmiri youth.

(38) Nehru also totally neglected the Pak Occupied Kashmir and did nothing to capture it like China who captured Tibet by military attacking India, fought war and won and annex Tibet to its country by its horrible ambition. Nehru should have taken military action against Pakistan and should have freed the Kashmir part occupied by Pakistan.Any country should meticulously defend its borders to avoid the disastroussituation like India. In 1961, Indian Young soldiers were ruthlessly culled by China.

(39) In order to resolve this long outstanding issue, Kashmir special status should be abolished by abolition of Article 370 of the Constitution. Industrialists should be permitted and encouraged to set up factories in that area and local labour force in Kashmir should be employed therein. Government should give full military protection to the industries for smooth working. This will gradually stop the terrorist activities and the Kashmir will be a wealthy state of India.

(40) Corruption has been a pervasive problem in India. Bribe or pedding influence to get a job done in the public office was usual and routine. In 2011, Transparency International ranked India at 95th place among 183 countries. By 2016, India saw a reduction in corruption and was ranked to 79th place. Bureau-cracy, licence raj excess regulations and approval procedures are main causes of corruption. Computerization of services, various central and state vigilance commission and the 2005 Right to Information Act have considerably reduced corruption and open avenues to redress grievances. India topped the worldwide list for black money with almost $1.456 trillion in Swiss Bank. This would amount to half of the country's total Nominal GDP.

(41) Pak Occupied Kashmir should be militarily attacked and Pakistan should be compelled to accept defeat in the war. This part of the Kashmir should then be annexured to India.

(42) China has giant and horrible ambition of becoming the world ruler under "One Rule One Nation' principle. Tibet was not the part of China before 1960. Tibet was a separate country practicing Buddha region and Priest Dalai Lama was their religiousGuru. Tibet was infavour of India. China was aware that India has not made any military preparation after independence in 1947. They demanded that India should accept that Tibet is China's integral part. Dalai Lama who was ousted from Tibet sought asylum in India. India gave him the asylum which Chinese opposed. Seeing that India will be easily defeated in war, China militarily attacked India in 1960 and defeated. There was tremendous loss of human life. As expected, China easily annaxured Tibet to its country. China has eye on Nepal and Bhutan but Indian army is now well prepared and China does not dare to attack militarily India as had happened in 1960. But we should constantly exercise vigilance in this area. China also wants to dominate Phillipines by surrounding some places owned by Phillipines by military fleets. America will help Philippines in war and this will be Third World War in which countries like Russia, Europe, Saria, Yemen,and Iran will be involved and will be threatening to mankind. China also does not accept the International Court judgement in favour of Philippines on South China territory issue. China should be timely controlled by USA and European countries including India to keep all countries peaceful In future. India should effectively implement its "look and act East" policy.

(43) Unlike South China Sea, Asian Pacific Ocean has been kept free to allow all countries to stay their fleets therein without domination of nay country in opposition of situation in South China Sea where China is dominating and threatening any other country to stay its fleets including USA. China has established very strong Naval Base in South China Sea. China is trying to dominate Indian Pacific Ocean but strong naval fleets of USA, Australia, Japan and India are prohibiting strictly China to do so. There is a Strategic Military and Naval Agreement between India, Japan. Australia and USA who have determined to stop China's naval aggression in this area.

44. Thought British rulers were ruthless when ruling Indian Empire from 1957 to 1947, it has improved its relationship with India after Independence. It now assists India to build up naval base in Indian Dockyard and has sent its War Ship "Elisabeth" in India for the same. It also supports India on POK and Jammu and Kashmir issue in security Council. It gives full supports to India against Pakistan on terrorism funding and for eradication of continuous terrorism attacks by Pakistan on India and Afghanistan.

Chapter - 15

Economy of the USA

Introduction

The Economy of the United States is a highly developed mixed economy. It is the world's largest economy by nominal GDP and the second highest economy by Purchasing Power Parity (PPP) GDP. It is the seventh highest per capita GDP (nominal) and the eleventh highest per capita (PPP) GDP in 2016. The US has highly diversified industrial sector. It is also high technology innovator with the second largest industrial output in the world. US has US dollar as its currency which is worldwide accepted and has become international currency. It is also foremost reserve currency backed by its science and technology, its military, the full faith of the US government to reimburse its external debt $21 trillion, its Central role in a range of international institutions since World War II, and the petrodollar system. It is the largest trading partner of China, Canada, Mexico, Japan, European Union, South Korea and Taiwan.

The nation's economy is fueled by abundant resources, a well-developed infrastructure, and a high productivity. Its estimated value of natural resources are 45 trillion in 2016. Americans have the highest average household and employer income among OECD nations. In 2010, they had the fourth largest median household income, down from second in 2007.The United States has held the world's largest economy since at least the 1890s. It is the largest producer of oil and natural gas and in 2016, it was the world's largest trading nation as well as the second highest manufacturer, representing fifth of the global manufacturing output. US has both the largest economy and the largest industrial sector at 2005 prices according to the UNCAD. It has the largest internal market for goods and it also dominates the trade in services. US total trade amounted to $4.92 trillion in 2016. Of the world's 500 largest companies, 134 have headquarters in the US.

The US has one of the largest and most influential financial markets. The New York Stock Exchange is by far the World's largest stock exchange by largest capitalization. Foreign investments made in the US total almost $2.4 trillion. While American investments in foreign countries total $3.3 trillion.

US economy is ranked first in international ranking on venture capital and global Research and development funding. Consumer spending comprised 71% of the USA economy in 2013. The US has the largest consumer market, with a household consumption expenditure five times higher than that of Japan. The nation's labour market has attracted immigrants from all over the world and its net migration rate is among the highest in the world. The US is one of the top-performing economies in studies such as Ease of Doing Business Index, Global competitiveness Report and others.

The US economy experienced a serious economic down turn during the Great Recession which technically lasted from December 2007 –June 2009. However, the real GDP regained its pre-crisis (late2007) peak by 2011, household net worth by Quarter 2, 2012, non-farm payroll jobs by May 2014 and the unemployment rate by September 2015. Each of these variables continued into post-recession record territory following these dates with the US recovery becoming the second longest on record of April 2018. Debt had by the public, a measure of national debt, was approximately 77% of GDP in 2017 ranked among the highest in income inequality to other western nations.

History of US

Colonial Era & 18th Century

It should be first noted that the US is a nation of immigrants. For hard work, labour from South Africa were brought known as "Red Indians". They toiled hard on agriculture and industries which resulted in US economically becoming strong. But these African labours were treated as slaves. Slavery continued till 19th century. The economic history of the US began with American Settlements in the 17thGeorge Washington was the first President of liberal USA in 1776.

19th Century

In 180 years, US grew to a huge, integrated industrialized economy that made up around one-fifth of the world economy. As a result, the US GDP per capita converged on and eventually surpassed that of the UK as well as other nations that it previously trailed economically. The economy maintained high wages, attracting immigrants by the millions from all over the world.

In the early 1800s, the US was largely agricultural with more than 80% of the population were engaged in farming. Most of the manufacturing centered on the first stages of transformation of raw material with limber and saw mills, textiles and boots and shoes leading in way. The rich resource endowments contributed to the rapid economic expansion during the nineteenth century. Ample land availability allowed the number of farmers to keep growing, but activity in manufacturing services, transportation and also other sectors grew at a much faster pace. By 1860, the share of the farm population in the US had fallen from over 80% to roughly 50%.

In the 19th century, recessions frequently coincided with financial crisis. The panic of 1837 was followed by a five year depression, with the failure of banks and then-record-high unemployment levels. Because of great changes in the economy over the centuries, it is difficult to compare the severity of modern recessions to early recessions. Recessions after World War II appear to have been less severe than earlier recession, but the reasons for this are unclear.

20th Century

At the beginning of the century, new innovations and improvements in existing innovations opened the door for improvements in the standard of living among American Consumers. Many firms grew large by taking advantage of economies of scale and before communication to run nationwide operations. Concentration in these industries raised fears of monopoly that would drive the prices higher and output lower, but many of these firms were cutting costs so fast that trends were towards lower price and more output in these industries. Lots of workers shared the success of these large firms, which typically offered the highest wages in the world.

The US has been the world's largest national economy in terms of GDP since at least the 1920s. For many years following the Great Depression of the 1930s, the danger of recession appeared most serious, the government strengthened the economy by spending itself and cutting the taxes or by growth of money supply. These measures encouraged spending and stabilized economy between1930s.and 1980s. From the New Deal era that began in 1933, the Great Society initiatives of the 1960s, national policy makers relied principally on fiscal policy to influence the economy.

During the World Wars of twentieth century, the US fared better than rest of the combatants because World War I and relatively little of the Second World War was rarely fought on American territory. Yet, War means sacrifice during the Wars activity, nearly 40% of US GDP was devoted to the war production. Decisions about large swaths of the economy were largely made for military purposes and nearly all relevant inputs were allocated to War efforts. Many goods were rationed, price and wages controlled and many durable consumers goods were no longer produced. Large numbers of workforces were inducted into military paid half wages, and roughly half of these were also sent into harm's way.

Few elevated officers were playing the role of directing the economy since spending and taxes were controlled by the US President and Congress. Baby boom occurred during 1970s.

US economy grew by average 3.5% from 1946-1973.but real median household income surged by 2.1% during the same period.

The worst recession in recent decades occurred during the financial year 2007-08 when GDP fell from 5% from the spring of 2008 to the spring of

2009. In recession of 1957-58, GDP fell by 3.7%. During oil crisis in 1973, it fell to 3.1%.

Since 1970s, several emerging countries have begun to close the economic gap with US. This happened because in these countries, they manufactured goods which they were importing from US.

21st Century

US experienced recession in 2001 with an unusually slow job recovery overlapped with the building of housing bubble and wider debt bubble, as the ratio of household debt to GDP rose from a record level of 70% in 2001 to 90% in Quarter 1 of 2018.This was done because housing prices were rising. But when housing prices began falling in 2006, the value of the securities booked by mortgages fell dramatically, causing equivalent of bank run in the essentially unregulated non-depository banking system, which had outgrown the traditional, regulated depository banking system. Many mortgage companies and other non-depository banks face a worsening crisis in 2007-08, with the banking crisis peaking in September 2008. This resulted in bankruptcy of Lehman Brothers and bailouts of several other financial institutions.

Bush Government and Obama Government applied banking bailout programmes by maintaining high deficits while Federal Reserve Bank maintained near-zero interest rates. These measures helped the economy recover, as households paid down debts in 2009-2012. There was significant economic recovery and growth of GDP.

In 1980, GDP was $2.8625 trillion which raised to $ 3.2trillion, in 1984 to $ 4.040 trillion, 1989 to $ 5.657 trillion, 2004 to $12.274 trillion and n 2017 to $19.390 trillion.

Employment

US labour force is 160.4 million in 2017. It is the fourth largest labour force after China, India and European Union. Government (Federal, States and Locals) employed 22 million in 2010.Small businesses are the nation's largest employer representing 53% of American workers. The second largest share of employment belongs to large businesses employing 38% of the US workforce.

The nation's private sector employs 91% of the working Americans, Government accounts for 8% of all workers. Over 99% of all employing organisations in the US are small businesses. 30 million small businesses in the US account for 64% of newly created jobs. Jobs in small businesses accounted for 70% of those created in the last decade.

The proportionate of the Americans employed by small business versus big business has remained relatively the same year by year as some small businesses become large businesses and just over half of small businesses survive for more than 5 years. Among the large businesses, several of the largest companies and employers in the world are American companies. Among them are Walmart, Which is the largest company and largest private sector employer in the world. It employs 2.1 million worldwide and 1.4 million in the US alone.

There are nearly 30 million businesses in the US. Minorities such as Hispanios, African Americans and Native Americans (35% of country's population) own 4.1 million of the nation's businesses. Minority-owned businesses generate almost $700 billion in revenue, and they employ 5 million workers in the US. Americans have the highest average employee income among OECD nations. The median household income in the US as of 2008 was $ 52029. About 284000 working people have full time jobs and 7.6 million have part time jobs in addition to their full time employments. Out of all working individuals in the US, 12% belong to the labour union and most union members work for the government. The decline of Union membership in the US over last several decades paralyze that of the labour's share of the Union. The World Bank ranks US first in the ease of hiring and firing workers. The US is only the advanced economy that does not legally guarantee its workers paid vacation or paid sick days, and is one of just few countries in the world without paid family leave as a legal right, with the others being Papua New Guinea, Surname and Liberia. In 2014, the International Trade Union Confederation (ITUC) graded the US a 4 out of 5+, its third lowest score, on the subject of powers and rights granted to labour unions.

Unemployment

As of 31st December 2017, the unemployment rate in the USA was 4.1 % or 6.6 million people. The government's boarder U-6 unemployment rate which includes the part- time under employed was 8.1% or 8.2 million people. These figures were calculated with a civilian labour force of approximately 327 million (4.67% of world population 7 billion people) natural resources like oil, coal 30% of the world resources.

Between the Great Recession in 2009 & 2010, the emerging problem of jobless recoveries resulted in record levels of long-term unemployment with over 6 million workers looking for jobs for more than 6 months as of January 2010. A year after recession ended in June 2009, immigrants gained 856000 jobs in the US while US born workers lost more than a million jobs, due to the partly aging country and demographic shifts. In April 2010, the official unemployment was 9.9%, but US boarder U- 6 unemployment rate was 17.1%. Between February 2008 and February 2010, the number of the people working part-time for economic reasons increased by 4 million to 8.8 million an 83% increase in part-time workers.

By 2013, the unemployment rate fell below 8%. However the number of payroll jobs returned to pre-recession (November 2007) level by May 2014 as the economy recovered.

Pattern of employment in1955 was that 55% of Americans worked in services, 30% -35%in industries and 10%-15% in agriculture. By 1980, the pattern was 65% in Services, 25%-30% in Industries and less than 5% in Agriculture. Male employment was significantly higher than female (at 9.6% vs 75%) being much lower than those for African-American (at 8.5% vs 15.8% in 2009.

The youth unemployment rate was 18.5% in July 2009, highest rate in that month since 1948.In2012, Employment by Sector was: 79.7% in Services, 19.2% in industries and 1.1% in Agriculture.

Income & Wealth

Income Measures

Real (i.e. inflation adjusted) median household income a good measure of middle class income, was $59039 in 2016, a record level. It was, however,just above the provision record set in 1998, indicating the purchasing power of middle class family income has been stagnant for last 20 years. Employer compensation was $8.969 trillion in 2013, while gross private investment totals $2.781 trillion.

Income Inequality

US Income inequality ranked 41st among 156 countries in 2017(i.e. 74% of countries have more equal income distribution) as per CIA World Facebook. The top 1% of income households earned about 9% share of the pre-tax income in 1979 versus 19% in 2017and 17% in 2014.For after-tax income, these figures were7, 17% and 13% respectively. This indicates that share of income earned by top earners more than doubled between 1979 and 2007. Following Recession and higher tax rates and redistribution policies were applied by President Barack Obama in 2013. This resulted in bottom 99% of families average income raising by $7100- Income inequalities in the US has grown from 2005 to 2017 in more than 2 out of three metropolitan areas.

Of the top 1% income earners accounted for 52% of the income gains from 2009 to 2015. Income is defined as market income excluding government transfers. Their share of total income has more than doubled from 9% in 1976 to 20% in 2011.As per OEDC 2014 Report, 80% of the total pre-tax market income growth went to the top 10% from 1935 to 2007.

Household net worth and wealth inequality

As of Q 4 2017, total household net worth in the US was a record of $99 trillion and increase of $ 5.2 trillion from 2016. This increase reflects both

Stock Market and Housing price gains. The measure has been setting records since Q 4 2012. If divided equally, the $ 99 trillion represents an average $782000- per household for about 126.2 million households or $302000-per person. However, median household net worth was $97300-in 2016. The bottom of 25% had a median net worth of zero, while the 25% to 50% had a median net worth of $40000-Wealth inequality is more unequal than income inequality. Top 1% household owns 42% of the net worth in 2012.

Top 10% wealthiest possess 80% of all financial assets. Wealth inequality is greater than in the most developed countries other than Switzerland and Denmak.Inherited wealth may explain why many Americans who have become rich may have had a "substantial Head Start". In September 2012, over 60% of the Forbes richest 400 Americans grew up in substantial privilege'. Median household wealth fell 35% in the US from $106591 to 68839- between 2005 and 2011 due to the Great Recession, but has since recovered as indicated above. About 30% of the entire World's millionaire population resides in US. There are 16.6% millionaires population resides in US. There are 16, 600,000-millionaires in the US Furthermore 34% of the World's billionaires are Americans. US home ownership rate in Q1 2018 was 64.2% well below all-time peak of 69.2 % in Q4, 2014 during the housing bubble.

The average house in the US has more than 700sq.ft.per person which is 50% -100% more than the average in other high income countries.

As of 2018, the number of US citizens are residing in vehicles because they cannot find affordable housing. This is happening because of steep in the cost of living particularly in Los Angles, Portland and San Francisco.

Poverty

From 1980s relative poverty rates have consistently exceeded those of other wealthy nations through analysis using a common data set for comparison tends to find that US has lower absolute poverty rate by market income than most other wealthy nations. Extreme poverty in the US means households Child poverty reached living on less than $2 per day before government benefits, doubled from 1996 levels to 1.5 million households in 2011 including 2.8 million children in 2013. Child poverty reached record high levels, with 16.7 million children living in food insecure households, about 35% more than 2007 levels. As of 2015, 44% children in the US live with low income families.

In 2016, 12.7% of the US population lived in poverty, down from 13.5% in 2007 before the Great Recession to a peak of 15.1% in 2010, before falling back to just above the 2007 level. In 1959-62 period, poverty rate was more than 20% but declined to all time low of 11.1% in 1973 following the war on poverty began during the time of Lyndon Johnson Presidency. In 2016, IMF warned the US that its high poverty rate needs to be tachled urgently.

There were about 643000 sheltered and unsheltered homeless persons in the US on a single night in January 2009. Almost two-third stayed in an emergency shelter or transitional housing programme and other one-third living on the street, in an abandoned building or another place of human habitation. About 1.56 million people or about 0.5% of the US population used an emergency shelter or a transitional housing program during 01-10-2008 to 30-09-2009.

The US has one of the least extensive social safety nets in the developed world, reducing both relative poverty and absolute poverty by considerably less than the mean for wealthy nations. Those in poverty live in conditions rivaling the developing world. Five million people live in "Third World" conditions. Over the last decades the poor in America have been incarcerated at a much higher rate than their counterparts in other developed nations with a penal confinement being "common place for poor men of working age". The shift to neoliberal social and economic policies starting in late 1970s has expanded the penal state, retrenched the social welfare state, deregulated the economy and criminalized poverty, ultimately "transforming what it means to be poor in America."

Health Care: Coverage

The American system is a mix of public and private insurance. The government provides insurance coverage for approximately 53 million elderly via Medicare, 62 million lower income persons via Medio aid and 15 million military via the Veteran's Administrations. About 178 million employed by companies receive subsidized health insurance through their employer while 52 million other persons directly purchase insurance either via the subsidized market place exchanges developed as part of the Affordable Care Act or directly from insurers. The private sector delivers health care services with the exception of the veteran's Administration, where doctors are employed by the government.

The US lags in overall health care performance but is a global leader in medical innovation. America solely developed or contributed significantly to 9 of the top 10 most important medical innovations since 1975 as marked by a 2001 poll of physicians, while the EU and Switzerland together contributed to 5. Since 1966, Americans have received more Noble Prizes in Medicine than the rest of the world combined. From 1989 to 2002, four time more money was invested in private biotechnology companies in America than in Europe.

Five year Cancer survival was significantly higher in US than all 21 European countries.

US healthcare costs are considerably higher than other countries as a share of GDP, among other measures. According to OECD, US healthcare costs in 2015 were 16.9% of GDP, over 5% gap higher than the next most expensive OEDC country. A gap of 5% of GDP represents $1trillion, above

$3000 per person or one-third higher relative to the next most expensive country.

Composition of Economic Sectors

The United States is the world's largest manufacturer with 2013 industrial output of $2.4 trillion which is more than that of Germany, France, India and Brazil combined. The main industries include petroleum, steel, automobiles, construction, Machinery, aerospace, agricultural machinery, telecommunications, chemicals, electronics, food processing, consumer goods, lumber and mining.

Manufacturing

The US leads the world in airplane manufacturing, which represents a large portion of US industrial output. American Companies such as Boeing, Cessna, Lockheed Martin and General Dynamics produce majority of the world's civilian and military aircraft in factories across the US.

Manufacturing Sector of the US economy has experienced substantial job losses over the past several years. In January 2004, number of such jobs stood at 14.3 million, down by 3million or 17.5% since 2000and about 5.2 million since historical peak in 1979.

The US produces 18% of the world's manufacturing output, the share that has declined as other countries developed competitive manufacturing industries. Job loss in manufacturing is due to increased productivity, trade and secular economic trends, growth in communications, pharmaceuticals, aircraft, heavy machinery and other industries. Although agriculture comprises 2% of the economy, The US is net exporter of food with vast tracts of temperate arable land, technological advanced agriculture and agricultural subsidies. US controls almost half of the world's grain exports. Foodgrains production in US is highest in the world with 347 million metric tons. With India 277 million metric tons and China 307 million metric tons.

Transportation

Road

The US economy is heavily dependent on road transport for moving people and goods. Personal transportation is dominated by automobiles, which operate on a network of 4 million miles (6.4 million kilometres). Of public roads, including one of the world's longest highway system 5700miles (91300 km). The world's second-largest aumobile market, the US has the highest rate of per capita vehicle ownership in the world, with 765 vehicles per 1000 Americans. About 40% of the personal vehicles are vans, SUVs, or light trucks.

Rail

Mass transit accounts for 9% of total US trips. Transport of goods by rail is extensive, though relatively low numbers of passengers (approximately 31 million annually) use intercity trains to travel; particularly due to low population density throughout the nation. However, ridership on Amtra, the national intercity passagerail system, grew by almost 37% between 2000and 2010. Also, light rail development has increased in recent years. The state of California is currently constructing the nation's first high-speed rail system.

Airport

The Civil airline is entirely private-owned and has been largely deregulated since 1978. While most major airports are publicly owned prior to 1978. Three Largest US based American Airlines in number one after its 2013 acquisition by US Airways of the world's 30 busiest passenger airports, 12 of them are in US including the busiest Hartfield Johnson Alania International Airport.

Energy

The US is the second largest energy consumer in total use. The US ranks 7th in energy consumption per capita after Canada and a number of other countries. The majority of this energy is derived from fossil fuels in 2005. It was estimated that 40% of the nation's energy came from petroleum, 23% from coal and 23% from natural gas, nuclear power applied 8.4% and renewable energy supplied 6.8% which was mainly from hydroelectric dams although other renewables are included. American dependence on oil imports grew from 24% in 1970 to 65% by the end of 2005. Transportation was the highest consumption rates, according for approximately 69% of the oil used in the US in 2006.

In 2013, the US imported 2808 million barrels crude oil, compared to 3377 million barrels in 2010. US is the largest importer of fuel. The Wall Street Journal reported in 2011 the country was about to become a net exporter for the first time in 62 years. This will continue upto 2020.

Telecommunication

Internet was developed in the US and the country hosts many of the world's largest hubs.

International Trade

The US is the World's second largest trading country. There is a large amount of US dollars in circulation all around the planet, about 60% of funds used in international trade are US dollars. The dollar is also used as the standard unit of currency in the international markets for commodities such as gold and petroleum. The North American Free Trade Agreement or NAFTAcreated one of largest blocs in the world in 1994.

Since 1976, the US has sustained merchandise trade deficits with other nations, and since 1962, the current account deficits are raising. The nation's long –standing surplus in its trade in services was maintained, however, and reached a record of $231 billion in 2013.

The US trade deficit increased from $502 billion in 2016 to $552 billion in 2017, an increase of $50 billion or 10%. During 2017, total imports were $2.9 trillion while exports were $2.35 trillion. The net deficit in goods was $ 807 billion while the net surplus for services was $255 billion. America's 10 largest partners are China, Canada, Mexico, Japan, Germany, South Korea, UK, France, India and Taiwan. The goods trade deficit with China rose from $ 347 billion in 2016 to $ 376 billion in 2017, an increase of $30 billion or 8%.

US had a goods trade deficit with Mexico $7.1 billion and $ 17 billion with Canada. Trade Deficit countrywise in 2017 was as follows:

Country	China	EU	Japan	Mexico	Pacific	Canada	Middle East	Latin America
Trade Deficit $ billion	346.1	106.1	68.6	33.00	29.00	18.7	18.1	
Trade Surplus $ billion								32.3

Thus total trade deficit in 2017 of US was $655.80 billion and trade surplus was $ 32.3 billion. Net trade deficit of USA in 2017 was $623.5 billion.

Due to the continuous trade deficit, present President Trump has imposed heavy customs duty on steel and aluminum imports in the international trade with China and European Union because of unnecessary adverse trade terms against USA. It also cancelled the NAFTA with Canada. Trump has imposed 20%-25% import duties on steel and Alunimium and banned car imports from EU. He insists that the trade terms with USAshould be on equitable principles and there should not be any unjustified deficit for USA in trading unnecessarily with any country specified above. Since then NAFTA was amended in favour of US for trade with Canada, China has been suffering from trade war with USA but still not coming to the terms for trade with USA in future though China's growth rate is seriously affected.

Financial Position

US household and non-profit net worth exceeded $100 billion in the first time in Q 4 2012. National debt is $21.1 trillion in May 2018. US public debt was 77% of GDP in 2017 i.e $ 16.25 trillion. Debt held by the public rose considerably as a result of the Global Recession and its aftermath. It is expected to continue rising as the country ages towards 100% GDP by 2028. In fact from $990 billion in 1980, the debt raised to 130% of GDP i.e. $26.08 trillion as per recent financial indicators. External debt was $19.306 trillion i.e.96% of GDP.

US GDP Nominal as per recent financial indicators, is $20.06 trillion as per Q3 2018. Population below poverty line 12.3% and unemployment 3.7%. Foreign reserves are $121.587 billion and FDI stock was $4.084 trillion. Budget deficit was $ 800 billion which is 39.88% of GDP. This is very high.

Currency & Central Bank

The US dollar is the unit of currency of the USA. Federal Government attempts to use both monetary policy (control of money supply through mechanism such as changes in interest rates) and fiscal policy (taxes and spending) to maintain low inflation, high economic growth, and low unemployment. A private Central Bank, known as Federal Reserve, was formed in 1913 to provided a stable currency and monetary policy. The US dollar has been regarded as the most stable currency. It is an international currency and widely accepted internationally.

Recently US has imposed monetary sanctions on Iran, China, and Russia. These countries find it difficult to do their financial transactions in US dollar. These countries therefore are trying to find the replacement of US dollar with Russian rubble, Yian. These countries have increased stock of gold to support their currency and make it the international currency. Iran has accepted Crep currency. But these countries are not successful in their efforts to make their currencies as the international currency in replacement of US dollar currency. Faith in US dollar currency has not been affected and it is still the international currency and will remain so in future.

Law & Government

US ranked fourth in the ease of doing business.

Some efforts seek, either directly or indirectly to control prices. Traditionally, the government has sought to create state regulated monopolies such as electric utilities. While allowing prices in the level that would ensure them normal profits. At time, government has extended economic control to other kinds of industries as well as in the years following Great Depression. It devised a complex system to stabilize prices to agricultural goods, which tend to fluctuate widely in response to rapidly changing supply and demand.

Another form of economic regulation, antitrust law, seeks to strengthen market forces so that direct application is unnecessary. The government, and sometimes private parties have used antitrust laws to prohibit practices or merger that would unduly limit competition.

American attitudes about regulations substantially changed during the final three decades of 20thcentury.

Policy Makers convinced increasingly that economic regulations protected companies at the expenses of consumers in industries such as airlines and trucking. But technological changes brought new competitors in some industries. Such changes brought new competitors in some industries such as telecommunications that once were considered natural monopolies. Both developments led to a succession of laws easing regulations.

While leaders of America's two most influential political parties generally favoured economic deregulations during 1970s, 1980s and 1990s, there was less agreement concerning regulations designed to achieve social goals. Social regulations had assumed growing importance in the years following the Depression and World War II, and again in the 1960s and 1970s. During 1980s, the government relaxed labour, consumer and environmental rules based on the idea such as regulations interfered with frcc cntcrprise, increase the cost of doing business and thus contributed to inflation. The response to such changes is mixed. Many Americans continued to voice concern about specific events or trends, prompting the government to issue new regulations in some areas, including environment protection.

Taxation

Taxation in the US is a complex system which may involve payment to at least four different levels of government - and many methods of taxation. Taxes are levied by Federal government, by State government and often by local governments, which may include counties, municipalities, township, school districts and other special purpose districts, which include fire, utility and transit districts.

Forms of taxation include taxes on income, sales, imports, payroll, estates and gifts as well as various fees. When taxation by all government levels taken into consideration, total taxation was about 25% of GDP in 2011.Share of black money in US economy is very low compared with other countries.

Although a federal wealth tax is prohibited by the Constitution of US, unless the receipts are distributed to the states by the populations, state and local government property tax amount to a wealth tax on real estates, and because the capital gains are taxed on nominal instead of inflation adjusted profits, the capital gains tax amounts to a wealth tax on the inflation rate.

US taxation is generally progressive, especially at federal level and is among the most progressive in the developed world.

Expenditure

The US public sector spending amounts for 30% of GDP of which federal is spending about 25% and state and local government remaining 5%. Each level of government provides many direct services. The Federal Government, for example, is responsible for national defence, research that often leads to the development of new products, conducts space exploration and runs numerous programmes designed to help workers develop workplace skills and find jobs. Government Spending has a significant effect on local and regional economies – and on the overall pace of economic activities.

State governments are responsible for the construction and maintenance of most highways. State, County or City governments play a leading role in financing and operating public schools. Local governments are particularly responsible for public and fire protection.

Welfare system in the US began in 1930s during the Great Depression, with the passage of the New Deal. The welfare system was then expanded in the 1960s through Great Society legislation, which included Medicare, Medi aid, the Older Americans Act and federal education funding.

Overall, federal, state and local governments spending accounted for almost 28% of GDP in 1998.

Federal Budget & Debt

During F.Y. 2017, the federal government spent $3.98 trillion on a budget or cash basis up $128 billion or 3.3% vs F.Y. 2016 spending of $3.85 trillion. Major categories of F.Y. 2017 spending included Health Care such as Medicare, Medic aid ($1077 billion or 27% of Spending). Social security ($993 billion or 24% of Spending), non – defence discretionary spending used to run federal departments and Agencies ($619 billion or 15% of Spending), Defence department ($590 billion or 15% of Spending) and interest ($269 billion or 7%).

During F.Y. 2017,the Federal government collected approximately $3.32 trillion in the revenue, up $48 billions;1.5% versus F. Y. 2016. Primary receipt categories included individual income taxes $1587 billion or 48% of total receipts. Social security/Social insurance taxes $1162 billion or 35%and corporate taxes $297 Billion or 9%.Other revenue types included excise, estate and gift taxes. F. Y. 2017 revenues were 17.3% of GDP verus 17.7% of GDP in F. Y. 2016.Tax revenues averaged approximately 17.4% GDP over the 1980-2017 period.

The federal budget deficit (i.e. expenditure greater than revenues) was$ 665 billion in F. Y. 2017 versus $585 billion in 2016, an increase of $80 billion or 14%.The budget deficit was 3.5% GDP in 2017 versus 3.2% GDP in 2016. Budget deficit is forecast to rise $804 billion in F. Y. 2018 due to significantly tax cuts and jobs act and other spending bills. An aging country and healthcare inflation are other drivers of deficits and debt over the long-run.

Debt held by the public, a major of national debt, was approximately $14.7 trillion or 77% of GDP in 2017, ranked the 43rd highest of 207 countries. This debt as a percentage of GDP is roughly equivalent to those of many western nations.

Business Culture

A Central feature of the U.S. economy is the economic freedom afforded to the private sector by allowing them to make majority of economic decisions in determining the direction and scale of what the US economy produces. This is enhanced by relatively low levels of regulations and government involvement as well as a court system that generally verifies property rights and enforces contracts. Today, US is home to 296 million small businesses, 30% of the world's millionaires, and 40% of the world's billionaires as well as 139 of the world's 500 largest companies.

Demographic Shift

Beginning in the late 20th century, many Latin Americans immigrated, followed by large number of Asians after removal of nation origin based immigration quotas. The promise of high wages brings many highly skilled workers from around the world to the US as well as millions of illegal immigrants seeking work in the informal economy. Over 13 million people officially entered the US during the 1990s alone.

Labour mobility has also been important to the capacity of the American economy to adapt changing conditions. When immigrants flooded labour markets on the East Coast, many workers moved inland, often to farmland waiting to be tilled. Similarly, economic opportunities in industrial northern cities attracted black Americans from a southern farms in the first half of the 20th century in what was known as the Great Migration.

In the United States, the corporation has emerged as an association of owners, known as stockholders, who form a business enterprise governed by a complex set of rules and customs. Brought on by the process of mass production, corporations, such as General Electric, have been instrumental in shaping the United States. Through the stock market, American banks and investors have grown their economy by investing and withdrawing capital from profitable corporations. Today in the era of Globalization, American investors and corporations have influence all over the world. The American government is also included among the major investors in the American economy. Government investments have been directed towards public works of scale (such as from the Hoover Dam), military-industrial contracts, and the financial industry.

Entrepreneurship

The US has been a leader in technological innovation since the late 19th Century and the scientific research since the middle of 20th century. In 1878 Alexander Graham Bell was awarded the first US patent for the telephone. Thomas Edison laboratory developed phonograph, the first long lasting light bulb and the first viable movie camera. Nikola Texla pioneered the AC induction motor and high frequency power transmission used in radio. In the early 20th century, Hentry Ford popularized the assembly line. Wright brothers, in 1913, made the first sustained controlled heavier-than-air powered flight.

American Society highly emphasizes entrepreneurship and business entrepreneurship is the act of entrepreneur, which can be defined as "one who undertakes innovations, finance and business acumen in an effort to transform innovations into economic goods." This may result in new organisations or may be part of revitalizing mature organisations in response to a perceived opportunities.

Entrepreneurship means the process and engagement of starting businesses. Scope has now been widen and mean "one who undertakes innovations".

"By the time they reach their retirement years, half of all working men in the US probably have a period of self-employment for six or more years participating in a new business creation is a common activity among the US workers over the course of their careers. And in recent years, business creation has been documented by scholars as major drivers of economic growth both in US and Western Europe.

Venture Capital Investment

Venture Capital, as an industry originated in the US which still dominates. According to the National Venture Capital Association, 11% of the private sector jobs come from venture capital backed by the companies and venture capital backed revenue accounts for 21% of US GDP. Today US investment in Venture Capital amounted to $48.3 billion in 2014 from 4356 deals. This represents an increase of 61% in dollars and 4% increase in deals over the prior year. The Organization for Economic Cooperation and Development estimates that venture capital investment in the US has fully recovered by 2014 to pre-recession level since 2008; in biotechnology, $6 billion was invested in 470 deals and, in life sciences overall, $86 billion in 789 deals, Seed stage Co. And late-stage Co. 7%.

Merger & acquisition

Since 1985, there have been three major waves of M. & A. in US. Year 2017 was the most active in terms of the number of deal (12914) whereas 2015 cumulated the biggest overall value of deals ($24 billion)

The biggest merger deal in US history was the acquisition of Time Warner by American online in 2000 where the bid was over $ 164 billion. Since 2000 acquisitions of US companies by Chinese investors increased by 368%. The other way around- US companies acquiring Chinese companies showed a decrease of 25% with a short upholds trend until 2007.

Finance

New York Stock Exchange Market is more than three time larger than any other stock exchange in the world. As of October 2008, the combined capitalization of AAdomestic NYSE listed companies was $10.1 trillion. NASDAQ is another American Stock exchange and the world's third largest exchange after NYSE and Japanese Tokyo Stock Exchange. NASDAQ's trade value is largest than the Japan TSE. NASDAQ is the largest electronic screen based equity securities trading market in US with about 3800 companies and corporations, it has more trading volume per hour than any other stock market.

US finance industry comprised only 10% of the total non-farm business profit in 1947 but it grew to 50% by 2010. Over the same period, Finance Industry income as a proportion of GDP rose from 2.5% to 7.5%.

Mean Salary in New York City's finance industry rose from $80000- in 1981 to $ 360000- in 2011. Average New York City salary rose from $40000- to $70000-. In 1986 there were about 12500 US banks with less than $300 million in deposits, and about 900 with less than $300 million in deposits in the US and over 1800 with more than $300 million in deposits.

Ten top US banks by assets (1) JP Morgan (2) Bank of America (3) CITIGROUP (4) Wells Forgo (5) Goldman Sachs(6) Morgan Stanley (7) US Bank Group (8) Bank of NY (9) HSBC North American Holdings (10) Capital One finance.

IMF Study in 2012 concluded that US financial sector has grown so large that it is slowing economic growth.

US spends $ 300 billion as too much on financial services per year. Sector needs to shrink by 20%.

Present economic Status of USA at Glance

(1) USA has US dollar as its currency which is internationally recognised.

(2) Financial year of USA is October 1st to September 30th

(3) Trade organizations: WTO, DECD and others

(4) GDP Nominal as per 3rd Quarter 2018 was $ 20.06 trillion

(5) GDP Rank: 1st Nominal, 2nd PPP

(6) GDP Growth 3.5% as on Q3, 2018

(7) GDP per Capita $ 62517 (2018)

(8) GDP per Capita 7th Rank GDP Nominal 11th GDP PPP

(9) GDP by Sector: Agriculture 0.9%, Industry 18.9% Services 80.2% 2017 estimates)

(10) Inflation 2.5%

(11) Unemployment 3.7%

(12) Population below poverty line 12.3% (2018)
(13) Labour Force 162. 637 million (50% of Population)
(14) Population 320.87 million
(15) Labour Force by Occupation: Farming, forestry 0.7%, Manicuring, extraction, transportation and crafts 20.3%, Managerial, Professional and technical services 37.3% Sales & Office 24.2%, other services 17.6%
(16) Average Gross Salary $879weekly (Q2, 2018)
(17) Main Industries: Petroleum, Steel, Motor vehicles, aerospace, telecommunications, chemicals, electronics, food processing, consumer goods Lumber mining
(18) Ease of doing Business 8th (2019)

External

(19) Exports $1. 58 trillion
(20) Export Goods: Agricultural products 10.7%, fuels & mining products 9.4%, Manufacturing 74.8% others 5.1%
(21) Main Export Partners: EU 18.7%, Canada 18.3%,Mexico 15.9%, China 8%, Japan 4.4 %, Others 34.8%
(22) Imports: $ 2.35 trillion
(23) Main Imports: Agricultural products 10.5%, fuel & mining 10.7% Manufacturing 78.4% Others 27.9%
(24) Main Import Partners: China 21.4%, EU 18.9%, Mexico 13.2% Canada 12.6%, Japan 6%. Others 27.9%
(25) Trade deficit: 0.77 trillion 3.84% of GDP (2017)
(26) FDI stock $4.084 trillion (2017)
(27) Gross External Debt: $19.306 trillion 96.24% of GDP. debt servicing interest 7% ($269 billion)
(28) Public debt $26.08 trillian 130% of GDP
(29) Revenue $3.3 trillion Expenses $4.1 trillion Fiscal deficit: 0.8 trillion 3.99% of GDP Within limit of 4%.
(30) Economic Aid donors ODA $36.28 billion
(31) Foreign Reserves: $121.587 billion (June1, 2018)
(32) Credit rating: Standard's $ Poor's AA+ (domestic), AA+ (Foreign) Outlook: Stable AAA (T& C Assessment) Outlook: Stable. Moody:AAA. Fitch: AAA outlook Stable. SCOPE: AA

Critical Observations of USA Economy

(1) USA has population of 32.4 crores out of the world population 7 billion (700 crores) which works out to 4.62% of the world population. However, it has ample natural resources /wealth of

about 30% of the world's national resources. Among them are petroleum, mining, fertilized land which give ample production like 347 million metric tons foodgrains production. In fact, USA can maintain 40% of the world population. e.g. population of China and India together. It has thus became the richest country in the world. Nature has created so much inequality that human beings are unable to restrict/control it.

(2) Income distribution in America is not fair and there are wide disparities of income among various classes of income earnings and capitalists. Billionaires and millionairesare the highest in the America while income level of the average American is not increasing substantially 3.7% of labour force 162. 637 million i.e. 6.3 million were unemployed.

(3) USA has started the scheme of unemployment compensation. This has shown an adverse effect. Many workers in America works in factories for minimum days and then make mistake in work purposely so that they are fired and they get unemployment compensation. This leads to laziness and workers are not willing to acquire the skills for the work they do to enhance their productivity. American firms and factories are therefore run by the advanced technical workforce from abroad migrated to USA.

(4) Inflation is 2.4% in America which is well managed.

(5) People below the poverty line is 12.3% of the population of 32.4crores in America which is high compared with 30% natural resources which America owns. Recently measures are taken by President Trump under "American first" policy and stringent restrictions have been introduced for people migrating from other countries.Measures have been taken to eradicate poverty in America.

(6) USA Defence Secretary Dr. Kissinger is known as the best diplomat in USA. But sometimes such brilliant diplomats also make mistake. Dr. Kissinger made error in giving China the status of the most favorite nation. China is dominating country which took advantage of this position and surpassed America in all fields. China's excess in Trade surplus was USD 350 billion in 2016 which ultimately resulted in implementing Trade restrictions/ trriff on China's exports goods.

(7) Trade war with China and European countries as well as the Sanctions on Russia, Iran and North Korea have slowed down financial activities, Industrial production, lower consumer demand and slackness in construction work which will ultimately result in Depression of the economy leading the raising highly unemployment level.

(8) U.S. Defence Secretary Dr. Kissinger's intention that by giving China the most as favourable nation status was partially successful as China did not help USSR from avoiding desolution which occurred in 1991. China and Soviet Russia are now best friends and bitter rivals of USA. Since India had Russia as its best friend, Dr.Kissinger made friendship with Pakistan and sent Seventh fleet in Indian Ocean for war against India as India was supporting Bangladesh. He gave military assistance to Pakistan to wage war with India. Ultimately USA realized this mistake and since Bush II regime, USA has become strategic and military partner of India. Kissinger diplomatic policy proved here also a failure.

(9) Recently President Trump has insisted that Wall at Mexico border should be erected with huge expense USD5.7 billion to protect American Borders from migration, illegal traffic of illicit liquor and girls brought from Mexico for prostitution. House of Commons have rejected Trump claim on the ground that this is not true. House of Commons also rejected Trump proposal to spend USD 5.7 billion for construction of wall on the broader of Mexico. Trump made this as prestigious issue and declared financial shutdown for 35 days. In the "State of Union" speech on 05-02-2019, he said that wall erection was essential and inevitable He declared Emergency. He said he made financial improvement during his rule but not happy and wants to make further improvement in the standard of livings of people in America.

(10) President Trump's whimsical decisions of recently withdrawing troops from Syria and Afghanistan, withdrawal from Automation Agreement with Iran met with wide criticism from Democrats and his own Republican Party and Defence Minister resigned but the president is firm on his decision which will result in World War III.

(11) American President is, however, taking some good decisions in recent years. Prior to Trump, American Presidents showed lenient attitude against Pakistan. This resulted in Pakistan misusing anti-territorism fund $1.3 billion every year from America and encourged heavily territory's Activities. Trump took stern action and stopped these funds to Pakistan and warned the country to discourage territory activities. Since India was neutral country but friend of Russia, American Presidents gave India the Discriminative treatment. Under the principle of the balanced military strength in the Indian Sub-continent, America helped Pakistan with military aid including giving F16 War Aircrafts many years. Under the threat of Russia, China, North Korea, now it has changed its military policy and is giving favorable treatment to India. India is

now USA's Strategic and Military partner. America's relation with India has been improving from regime of President Bush II.

(12) While imposing stringent restrictions on immigration, President Trump is forgetting that his country is country of immigration. Recently high skilled workforce migrated from India and China has made America prosperous. Many Indian and China workforce is trained in American Research Institutions enhancing productivity in industrial production in America. Migrated Indian skilled workforce in UAE, Saudi Arabia, Iran, Iraq, and USA has remitted USD 80 billion to India in 2018.

(13) If President Trump will continue his present immigration ban policy, the country will suffer and American companies will have to outsource these products outside America. Sanctions have been imposed by America and European Countries on Iran, Iran's economy will collapse as its export product is crude oil is banned by US and US have also threatened other countries to penalize them financially if these countries will purchase crude oil from Iran which is Iron's main export and means of live hood..

(14) America is favouring excessively Israel without looking to the right side of Palestine. This creates serious criticism against America. Sanctions imposed on Russia, Iran also resulted in looking for other methods to make payment to these countries which results in settling their claims in their local currencies or gold. This deteriorates recognition of American dollar which is worldwide currency for international payment. This will reduce American dominance on other countries. America should seriously look into this issue urgently.

(15) America should take active steps to reduce inequality in income distribution. Largest capitalists should be pursued to distribute their wealth to poor people. This process will be like "Bhudan" Movement started by Vinoba Bhave in India.

(16) American external debt is USD 19.306 trillion against its GDP USD20.05 trillion which works out to 96.29% which is very high. USA should target to bring down its external debt to USD 5 trillion. Unreasonable ratio of external debt to GDP results in heavy debt servicing and thereby swallows the growth of the country. This also leads to weaken many other financial indicators like unemployment and inflation, industrial production, construction work and will lead the country to serious depression.

(17) American R & D institutions are financed by Federal, States and Local Governments and private companies which result in qualitative manufacturing output demanded by all countries. This expenditure is worth for country's development.

(18) Recently, there was "shut down" for 35 days in US as the Parliament did not approve the Trump proposal to spend $ 5.7 billion on construction of wall on Mexico. Dispute is still going on and President has threaten to declare emergency if the proposal is not approved by House of Commons. This is for the protection of the country and the President is not prepared to make any compromise on this issue.

(19) American extravagant expenditure/spending led to cross limit of expenses specified by the American Constitution resulting in "Shut Down" situations many times. Sometimes such "shut down" lasted for more than15 days.

(20) America has made tremendous progress in space research and is presently doing "Deep Space" research to transfer its residents to other space places.

(21) In the field of Artificial Intelligence, country has made good progress and kept Killer Robot ready for any attack from any country.

(22) On account of Brexit and Recession Atmosphere in the world market, "DO Johns" crashed by 460 points on Friday 22-03-2019.

(23) USA President Trump has made an explosive statement on Friday 22-03-2019 that time has come to declare Gaza Region as part of Israel. This has created lot of controversy among many countries and will result in waging World War III. In fact, Gaza territory was captured by Israel in war with Syria and not returned after the War. Gaza territory is entirely part of Syria and should be returned to Syria unconditionally by Israel. Trump's recent policy to declare Gaza as a part of Israel has been opposed by many countries in Security Council Meeting including EU, China, Russia and other countries but on account of undue support for Israel, Trump does not want to change his decision to resolve the dispute of Israel with Countries like Palestine, Jordon and Syria.

(24) President Trump has stopped the foreign aid $1.3 billion given to Pakistan every year to eradicate the terrorist activities. It is found that Pakistan is in fact applying these funds to support and encourage terrorist activities for terrorist attacks on India and Afghanistan. Trump initiated steps to put Pakistan in Grey List by the Financial Action Task force (FATF) which resulted in banning Pakistan from getting any financial assistance from any international Institutes like IMF and World Bank.

(25) US has made preparations in making large changes in its nuclear policy. In War with any country, America has kept reserve its right to make nuclear attack. America has changed its previous policy of "No First Use" of nuclear weapons. This recent policy change

has resulted in fear in the minds of the Friendly nations of America about their protection from the enemy of countries. America has spent $ 649 billion on manufacturing of defence equipment out of the world defence expenditure of $1.82 trillion which works out to 36% expenditure by USA on defence in 2018.

(26) War fighter planes on publication of "Nuclear Posher Review": From Agreement., America has withdrawn from the"INF" Agreement with Russia. Analysists are of opinion that both countries have withdrawn from this Agreement. This will create havoc because new nuclear weapons competition will start which will create disaster in the world by newly created deadly war weapons by both countries and China.

(27) In order to prevent immigrants entering from Mexico, America has made Agreements with three nations in Mid America namely Hondalus, L Salwador and Gvautemal. It has kept 10000 troops on Mexico border to prevent any immigrates to enter America and Trump will built up defence Border Wall on the Border of Mexico with the expenditure of $7 billion.

(28) On British Naval defence ship "MMS Queen Elizabeth" which has reached "South China Sea" for military clashes, has been equipped with US "F 35" which are the most advanced war fighters.

(29) US has been providing its most advanced war fighter planes "F 35" to Poland, Romania, Greece, Spain and Singapore wef April 2019.

(30) China and America are on "Trade War'. US also suspects that media companies like Huawei are exploited by China as spy companies with result that information on very delicate matter on defence equipments and others are used by China against the interest of US and other countries. Under "G 5" technology, Huawei was doing so. Its Executive Director Vaugzai Meng was arrested in Canada and chart sheet has been filed in the court for further action against her. Australia and other Countries have taken the same action but Britain's Prime Minister Mrs. May has supported and approached the Huawei Company to get G 5 technology knowledge from the company inspite of the danger of China spying and misusing the secret information of Britain by Cyber-attack.

(31) China has threatened US to stop export rare earth metal which is used for computers programme, software, electricity instruments etc., USA has got support from Australia to produce rare earth metals to retaliate trade of rare earth metal with China. Last year USA reduced the import of this metal from China by about 20 percent improving 320 tons of such metal.

Chapter - 16

Economy of China

Introduction

Socialist, market economy of People's Rubric of China is the world's second largest economy by Nominal GDP and the world's largest economy by GDP PPP.

Until 2015, China was the world's fastest growing major economy, with growth rate of 10% over 30 years. Due to the historical and political facts of China's developing economy, China's public sector accounts for bigger share of the national economy than the private sector. According to IMF, on a per capita income basis, China Marked 71st by GDP (Nominal) and 78th by GDP (PPP) per capital in 2016. China has natural resources worth $2.3 trillion, 90% of which are coal and rare earth metals. China's Banking sector is largest with assets of $ 39.9 trillion assets and $ 26.54 trillion in total deposits.

China is the world's largest manufacturing economy and exporter of goods. It is the fastest growing consumer market and second largest importer of goods. China is a net importer of services products. It is the largest trading nation in the world and has increasing engaged in trade organizations and treaties in recent years. China became a member of World Trade Organization (WTO) in 2001. It has also free trade agreements with several nations, including Switzerland, ASEAN, Australia, New Zealand, Pakistan and South Korea. The provinces in the coastal regions of China tend to be industrialized with the regions in the hinterland less developed.

To avoid the long-term socio economic costs of environment pollution in China, it has been suggested that economy of China be shifted to more advanced industrial development with low curbondioxide emissions and better allocation of national resources to innovation and R & D for sustainable economic growth in order to reduce the impact of China's heavy industry.

In recent years, government claimed numbers have come under increased scrutiny since both native and foreign financial and economic observers as well as Chinese government officials claiming that the government has been overstating in economic output. Official figures for GDP growth are inflated by at least 50%.

Regional Economies

China's unequal transportation system combined with important differences in the availibity of natural and human resources and industrial infrastructure has produced a significant variations in the regional economies of China.

Economic development are generally been rapid in coastal provinces than in the interior and there are large disparities in per capita income between regions. Three wealthiest regions are along the Southeast coast, centered on the Pearl Relive Delta, along the east coast, centered on the lower Yangtze River, and near the Boar Gulf, in the Beijing- Tianjin regional economy as a whole and Chinese government policy is designed to remove the obstacles to accelerated growth in these wealthier regions.

History of Chinese Economy

China was not a developed country. Some big territories have been annexed ruthlessly, arbitrarily. Part of India after Mau Se Tung took over as the father of the nation who introduced social liberal economic measures to open the economy in 1950s.Tibet was not a part of China but China started creating dispute on Tibet by ousting Tibetans' highly estimated priest Dalai Lama to whom India extended asylum. China being the dominating country did not approve it. Chinese leaders were aware that India has not made any military preparations and can easily be conquered by military backtracking it. In 1960, China created a dispute on Tibet sovereignty and waged war with India as Tibet was in favour of India. War lasted for about 10 days in which India lost its soldiers heavily. Russia who was India's friend that time did not interfere as China was a communist country and was a brother of Soviet Russia. Prime Minister Mr. Jawaharlal Nehru was shocked with terrible military attack of China and tremendous manpower lost and died on 27-05-1964. India should strongly attack militarily China and snatched Tibet from China to show our overall military, air and naval strength. India's Military should be alert all times to ensure that China will not snatch Nepal and Bhutan which are independent countries to date under Indian control. China eyes on both those countries and looking at the opportunity to conquer these territories. South China Sea has been already captured by China and ownership claims of Philippines, Taiwan and other countries have been ruthlessly ignored by China. It has made this area militarily and navally very strong by establishing ports and Strongest Naval Bases in that area. Philippines has got judgement on in its favour this area by the International Court but China is so adamant that it refused to obey International Court's decision.

In accordance with the one country, two systems policy, the economies of the formal British colony of Hongkong and Portuguese colony of Macau are separate from the rest the rest of China and each other. Both Hongkong and Macau are free to conduct and engage in economic negotiation with foreign countries, as well as participating as full members in various international economic organisations the World Trade Organizationand the Asian Pacific Corporation forum, often under the names "Hongkong China" and "Macau China." China's dominations is refused by Hong Kong population and there are agitation against Government of China is the ...agitation in 1959.

Development

The economic reforms implemented in 1979 helped to propel China into the ranks of the world's major economic powers. China shows a great development potential from its remarkable economic growth in these years.

To guide economic development, Chinese Central Government adopts "five years plans" that detail its economic priorities and essential policies. The Thirteen Five Year Plan (2016-2020) is currently being implemented.

Like Japan and South Korea before it, China has grown steadily, raising the income levels and living standards of its citizens while producing goods that are consumed globally. Between 1978 and 2005, China's per capita GDP grew from $ 153- to $1284-. Its current account surplus increased more than twelvefold between 1982 and 2004 from $5.7 billion to $71 billion. During this time, China also became an industrial powerhouse moving beyond initial success in the low-wage sectors like clothing and footwear to the increasingly sophisticated production of computers, pharmaceuticals and automobiles.

However, it remains unclear how long the China will sustain this growth. No country in the world continues to have growth rate constantly steady. China will place the same situation as USA has engaged in trade war with China by imposing Customs duties on Steel & Alunimium to 25% and also imposed high levels of taxes on about $ 200 billion worth of goods which US imports from China and threatened to impose heavy taxes on imports of goods worth $500 billion. This ban is on account of restricted trade policies of China. China's economy growth is diminishing from 2017 from 8% to 7% and is expected to further diminish to 6.5% and 6.3% in 2018 and 2019 respectively.

China made significant growth in agriculture production and also its industrial production was grown on account of foreign investors entering China. But China's economy is still restrictive and does allow the entry of foreign investors in field like banking sector. This would not be easy as of 2004, China's state owned enterprises were still only partially reorganized and its banks were dealing with burden of $ 205 billion in non-performing loans, monies that had little chance of ever being repaid. The country has the floating exchange rate, and its strict controls on both the current and capital accounts.

In mid-2014 China announced it was taking steps to boost the economy, which at that time was 4% annually but it was slowing. The measures include plans to build multiplied transport network comprising railways, roads and airports to create a new economic belt along the Yangiza river China's " one belt one road" policy was also not accepted by USA, Japan and India as China is trying to trap the countries in debts by this policy. It is dominating country and is not reliable as it is based on the principle that "Mine is mine and yours is also mine".

Issues with over claiming

Chinese provinces and cities long suspected of cooking up numbers, with the focus on local government officials whose performance are often assessed based on how well their respective economies have performed in recent years. China's claimed growth numbers have come under increased scrutiny, with both non-Chinese financial and economic observers as well as Chinese government officials claiming the government has been inflating economic output. Issues of over claiming officially came to light when:

(1) Binhai New Area in the Northern Chinese city of Tiajia's trillion yuan GDP claim for 2016 was in fact a third lower at 665 billion yuan ($103 billion)

(2) Inner Mangolia 's government also stated that about 40% of the region's reported industrial output for 2010 as wells 26% of reported fiscal revenues did not exist.

(3) The provincial government in Liaoning publicly admitted that the government has been asking the books when publishing its economic data from 2011 to 2014. Liaoning frequently called China's rust bell, admitted in 2017 that true local GDP number from 2011 to 2014 had been inflated by about 20%.

Regarding the credibility, a team of Bloombers economists wrote:"we do not have total confidence in the numbers and we are surprised by the acceleration in service output given the collapse in the equity market'.GDP estimates are inflated by China by 2% to 3% and even China's own premier has previously said that "he is far from confident in the country's GDP estimates,calling them "man made" and unreliable.GDP number should be used for reference only". China's official figures are off by 50%. Annual growth rate may be 3.5% rather than 7%.

In January 1985, the State Council of China approved accounting model for new system of national economic system in 1986.

GDP officially declared by IMF was in 1952 $30.55 billion which rose to $1.211 trillion and in 2017 to $ 12.250 trillion.

Other figures are as follows:

Year	*Total Investment*	*Inflation*	*Unemployment*	*Budget Balance.*	*Govt. Debt*	*C/A*
1980	35.50%	-	4.9%			
1996	38.2%	8.3%	3%	-0.7%	21.3%	
2008	43.2%	5.9%	4%		27%	9.1%
2012	47.2%	2.6%	4.1%	-0.3%	34.3%	2.5%
2017	44.4%	1.6%	3.9%	-3.9%	47.8%	1.4%

Systematic Issues and Environment

Over the years, large subsidies were built into the price structure of certain commodities and these subsidies grew substantially in the late 1970s and 1980s.

By 2010, rapidly rising wages and general increase in the standard of living put the increased energy use on a collision course with the need to reduce certain emission in order to control global warning.

National Debt

The IMF, Federal Reserve Bank of St. Louis and other sources, such as the Article IV Consultation Report state that at the end of 2014, "General government gross debt to GDP ratio for China was 41.44% with China's GDP $10.356 trillion, this makes the government debt of China approximately $4.3 trillion. A 2015 IMF report concluded that China's public debt is relatively low and on a stable path in all standard stress tests except for the scenario with the contingent liability shocks" such as "a large scale bank capitalization or financial system bailout to deal with a potential rise in NPLs from deleveraging.

"Shadow Banking" has risen in China posing risks to the fundamental system.

Debt piling facing China is an internal problem given the majority of the borrowings was issued in local currency.

Regulatory Environment & Tax System

Though China's economy has expanded rapidly, its regulatory environment has not kept pace. Since Deng Xiaoping's open market reforms, the growth of new businesses has outpaced the government ability to regulate them. This has created a situation where businesses faced with the mounting competition and poor oversight take drastic measures to increase profit margins, often at the expenses of customer's safety. The issue became more prominent in 2007, when number of restrictions being placed as problematic Chinese exports to USA.

From the 1950s to the 1980s, the Central government revenues derived from the profits of state enterprises, which were remitted to the state. Some government revenues also came from taxes.

The trend, however, has been to remitted profits of the state enterprises to be replaced with taxes on these profits.

Inflation

During the winter of 2007-08 inflation was about 7% which rose to 8.7% in 2008.

Shortage of gasoline and diesel fuel developed in the fall of 2007 due to the reluctance of refiners to produce fuel at low prices set by the state. These prices increased slightly in refineries in 2007 with fuel selling at $2.65 per gallon still significantly below the world prices. Price controls were in effect on numerous basic products and services but ineffective with food prices which were rising at an annual rate of 18.2% in the November 2007. The problem of inflation has caused concern at the highest level of the Chinese government.

In November 2010, the inflation rate rose to 5.1% driven by 11.7% increase in food prices year on year basis. Industrial production went by 13.3%. Prices to fuel and other commodities have risen.

Investment Cycles

Chinese investment has always been highly cyclical.Ever since the 1958 Great Leap Forward, growth in fixed capital formation has typically peaked about every five years. Recent breaks occurred in 1978,1984, 1988, 1993, 2003 and 2009. The corresponding through were in 1981, 1989, 1897 and 2005.

In China, the majority of investment is carried out by entities that are at least partially state owned. Most of these are under the control of local governments. The booms are primarily the result of perverse incentives of local government level. Unlike enterpreneurs in a free-enterprise economy, Chinese local officials are motivated primarily by political considerations. As their performance evaluation are based, to a large extent, on GDP growth within their jurisdiction, they have a strong incentives to promote large-scale investment projects. They also do not face any bankruptcy risk. When localities get into trouble, they are invariably bailed out by state owned banks. Under these circumstances, over-investment is inevitable.

Typical cycle begins with a relaxation of Central government credit and industrial policy. This allows state governments to push investment aggressively, both through state-sector entities they control directly and by offering investment promotion incentives to private investors and enterprises outside their jurisdiction.

The resulting booms put upward pressures on prices and may result in shortage of key input such as coal and electricity. Once inflation has risen to level at which it begins to threaten social stability, Central government will interfere by tightening enforcement of industrial and credit policy. Projects that went ahead without required approvals will be halted. Bank lending to particular type of investors will be restricted. Credit then becomes tight and investment growth begins to decline. This results in bringing inflation to the acceptable levels.

Financial & Banking system

Most of the China's financial institutions are state owned and governed. The chief instruments of financial and fixed control are the people's Bank of China and the ministry of finance, with under the authority of the State Council. The People's Bank of China replaced the Central Bank of China in 1950 and gradually took over private banks. It fulfils many of the functions of Central and commercial banks. It issues the currency, control circulation. And plays an important role in disbursing budgetary expenditures. Additionally it administers the accounts, payments, and receipts of government organisations and other bodies, which enables it to exert through supervision over their financial and general performances in consideration to the government economic plans. PBC is also responsible to international trade and other overseas transactions. Remittances by overseas Chinese are managed by the Bank of China, which has number of branch offices in several countries.

Other financial institutions that are crucial include the China Development Bank which finds economic development and directs foreign investment. The Agriculture Bank of China which provides for the agricultural sector, and China's Construction Bank which is responsible for capitalizing a portion of overall investment and for providing capital funds to certain industrial and construction enterprises, and the Industrial and Commercial Bank of China which conducts ordinary commercial transactions and acts as a Savings Bank for the public.

China's economic reforms generally increased the economic role of the banking system, in theory. Any enterprises or individuals can go to the banks to obtain loans outside the state's plan, in practice 75% of state bank loans go to State Owned enterprises. Even though nearly all investment capital was previously provided on a grant basis according to the state plan, policy has since been the start of reform shifting to a loan basis through the various state owned institutions. In 2014, 14 trillion yuans in loans were outstanding to local governments. Much of that total is believed by outside observers to be non-performing, increasing amounts of funds that are made available through the banks for economic and commercial purposes.

With two Stock Exchanges (Shanghai Stock Market and Shezhen Stock Exchange) mainland China's Stock Market had a market value of $ 4.48 trillion as of November 2014 which makes it the second largest market in the world.

Stock Market

As of 2014 and the first quarter of 2015, the financial industry had been providing 1.5% of China's 7% annual growth. Despite slowing of the economy, as of June 2015, Chinese Stock Index, CSI 300 index, which is based on 300 stocks traded in the Shanghai and Suenhhen stock Market has risen 150% over the last twelve months. In an effort to forestall damages from collapse of a possible economic bubble fueled by the margin trading, the Central government raised requirements for margin trading. Economic damages from a crash of2007-08 was limited due to the margin trading being highly restricted. Chinese stocks fell about 10% during the last week of July 2015with record breaking losses on Monday.

Currency system

The renminbi (people's currency) is the currency of China denominated as the yuan subdivided into 10 Jiao or 100 fen. The renminbi is issued by the People's Bank of China, the monetary authority of China. The ISO 4217 abbreviation is CNY, although also commonly abbreviated as "RMB". As of 2005, the yuan was generally considered by outside observers to be undervalued by about 30%-40%. However IMF stated that the yuan is now correctly valued.

Renminbi is held in a floating exchange rate system managed primarily against the U.S. Dollar. On 21July 2005, China revalued its currency by 2.1% against US dollar and since then has moved to an exchange rate system that references a basket of currencies and has allowed the renminbi to fluctuate at a daily rate up to half a percent.

The rate of exchange (Chinese Yuan per $1) as on 31-03-2008 was RMD 6.8450, in mid-2007 was 7.45 while in early 2006 was RMB 8.07, 8.2793 (January 2000),8.2783 (1999),8.2790 (1998), 8.2898(1997) 8.3142 (1996) per US dollar 1.

China's Central Bank has decisive ability to control its value with relationship with other currencies though RMB is floating.

During the week of 10August 2015, against the background of slow growth of Chinese economy and appreciation of U.S. dollar, the People's Bank of China devalued the renminbi by about 5%. The devaluation was accomplished by pegging the official rate against U.S. dollar.

Recently, like its ambition to dominate the world, China wants its Yuan currency to be internationally recognised and all its international transactions should be done through yuan and not US dollar. It has therefore sold US dollars investments in large quantities like Russia who is also planning to make its rouble as international currency and bought tons of gold as a buffer for their currencies. But chances of their currencies to be internationally recognised are very bleak. These countries can do their international trading business with their currencies with some countries.

We now look the economy of China sector wise.

Agriculture

China is the world's largest producer and consumer of agricultural products –and some 300 million Chinese farm workers are in the industry, mostly laboring on pieces of land. The size of land is almost equal to that of America.

Virtually, all arable land is used for food crops. China is the world's largest producer of rice and is among the principal source of wheat, corn (maize), tobacco, soybean, potatoes, peanuts, barley, oilseed, pork and fish. Major non-food crops, including cotton, other fibres and oilseeds furnish China with a small proportionate of its foreign trade revenues. Agriculture exports such as vegetables and fruits, fish and selfish, grain and meat products are exported to Hongkong. Yields are high because of intensive cultivation, for example, China's crop land area is only 75% of the US total, but China still produces 3)5 more crops and livestock than the US. China hopes to further increase agricultural production through improved plant stocks, fertilizers and technology. China fed 20% of the world population with only 7% of the world's arable land. China stands first worldwide in farm output, and as a result of topographic and climatic factors, only about 10%-15% of the total land area is suitable for cultivation of this, slightly more than half is unirrigated, and the remaining is divided roughly equally between paddy fields and irrigated areas. Nevertheless, about 60% of the population lives in village areas, and until the 1980s a high percentage of them made their living directly from farming. Since then, many have been encouraged to leave the fields and pursue other activities such as light manufacturing, commerce and transportation. By mid 1980s, the farming accounted for less than half of the value of rural output. Today, agriculture contributes only 13% of China GDP.Animal husbandry constitutes the second most important component of agriculture production. China is the world's leading producer of pigs, chicken and egg, and it also has sizable herds of sheep and cattle. Since mid 1970s, greater emphasis has been placed on increasing livestock output. China has a long tradition ofocean and freshwater fishing and agriculture. Pond rising has always been important and has been increasing in size to supplement coastal and inland fisheries threatened by overfishing and to provide such valuable export commodities such as prawns.

Environment factors such as flood, drought and erosion pose serious threat to farms in many parts of the country. The wholesale destruction of forests gave way to an energetic reforestation program that proved inadequate; and forest resources are still failing meagre. In the past decade, the government has been encouraging the agricultural mechanism and land consolidation to raise yields and compensate for the loss of rural workers who have migrated to the cities. The annual growth rate of agricultural mechanization is 6.38%. By 2014, the integrated mechanism rate had risen to nearly 60& with a rate for wheat surpassing 90% and maize appropriately 80%. In addition to standard agricultural equipments like tractors, China's agriculture co-operatives have begun using high technic equipment, including unmanned aerial vechicles which are used to spray crops between pesticides. Good progress has been made in increasing water conservation.Foodgrains Production in China is 302 million metric tons which is second to America which has 347 million metric tons foodgrains productions in 2018.

Housing & Construction

The real estate industry is about 20% of the China economy.

Energy & Mineral Resources

Since 1980, China's energy production has grown dramatically, as has the proportion allocated to domestic consumption production 6.5 trillion hwh (2018). Consumption 2.8248 trillion KWh, Exports 18.7billion KWh and imports 6.2 billion KSh.

Some 80% of all power is generated from fossil fuel as thermal plants with about 17% at hydroelectric installations; only 2% from nuclear energy. Though China has rich overall energy potentials, most have yet to be developed. In addition, the geographical distribution of energy puts most of these resources relatively far from their major industrial users. Basically the northeast is rich in coal and oil, the central part of North China has abundant coal, and has immense hydroelectric potential. But industrialized regions around the Shanghai have too little energy while there is relatively little heavy industry located near major energy sources areas other in the southern part of northeast. Since 1973, China has been a net importer of oil, a large portion of which come from the Middle East. Imported oil accounts for 20% of the processed crude in China. Net imports are expected to rise 3.5 million barrels per day by 2010. China is interested in diversifying the sources of its oil imports and has interested in oil fields around the world. China is developing oil imports from Central Asia. Beijing also plans to increase China's natural gas production, which currently accounts to only 3% of China's total energy consumption and incorporated a natural gas strategy in its 10th Five Year Plan (2000-05) with the goal of expanding gas use from 9.2% share of total energy production to 4% by 2005. (Gas accounts for 25% of US production). Analysists expects China's consumption of natural gas to more than double by 2010.

China has abundant hydroelectric resources. Electricity generated by nuclear power is also projected to grow from 1% in 2000to 5% in 2030. It also plans for 10% of its energy to come from renewable energy sources by 2000. Thermal 70.4%, hydro 17.8%, renewable 7.3%, nuclear 3.8% other 0.7% (2017)

Oil – Production 3631000 barrel/day

577300 per day -2005

Consumption 6534000 barrel per day 91038800 m/d) 2005 and expected 9300000 bb/d (11480000 n/d in 20Outdated mining and ore- processing technologies are being replaced with modern technology'

Net import 2740000bb/d, 436000m/d 2005

Proved reserves 16.3 gbbl

Natural Gas

Production 47.88 km 2005

Consumption 44.73 km 2005

Exports 2.944 km 2005

Imports Nil

Proved Reserves 1448 km (January 2006).

Mining

Outdated mining and ore-processing technologies are being replaced with modern techniques, but China's rapid industrialization requires imports of minerals from abroad, in particular iron ore imports from Australia and the US have soared in the early 2000a as steel production rapidly outstripped domestic iron ore production. Also China has become increasingly active in several African countries to mine the resources it requires for economic growth.

The major areas of production in 2004 were coal (nearly 2 billion tons), iron ore (310 million tons), crude production (175 million tons), natural gas 41 million cubic metres, antimony ore 110000 tons, tin concentrates 110000 tons, nickel ore 64000 tons. In order of magnitude, produced minerals were bauxite sypsum, barite magnetic, talc and related minerals manganese are, fluorspar and zinc. In addition, China produced 2450 tons of silver and 215 tons of gold in 2014. Mining sector accounted for less than 0.9% of total employment in 2002 but produced about 5.3% of the total industrial production.

China has an abundant potential for hydroelectric power production due to its considerable river network and mountainous terrain. Most capacity is situated in southwest of the country, where coal supplies are poor but demand for energy is rising swiftly. The potential in northwest is fairly small but it was there that first hydroelectric stations were built by Japanese during its occupation of Manchuria. Flows of river inflate during winter forcing many power stations to operate at less than normal capacity while in summer floods often interfere with generation.

Thirteen years in construction at a cost of $24 billion the immerse Googes Dam across the Vangize River was essentially completed in 2006 and will revolutionize electrification and flood control of China.

China is well endowed with minerals resources. Most import is coal. China's mineral resources include supplies of nearly all other industrial minerals. Although coal deposits are widely scattered, most of the total is located in northern part of the country. The province of Shanxi is thought to contain half of the total. Other important coal bearing provinces include Liaoning, Hebal andHellonging.

In order to ensure more even distribution of coal supplies, many pits were established after 1960s which produce coal more than half of country's requirements.

Coal makes up the bulk of China's consumption (70% in 2005) and China is the largest producer and consumer of the world. With economy growing, China will require more coal in future.

Oil and gas deposits have been found in the Pearl River of South China production of which is more than the production of coal. In 2013, the pace of China's economy growth exceeded, the domestic oil capacity and flood damaged the nation's oil fields in the middle of the year. Consequently, China imported oil to compensate for the supply reduction and surpassed the US in September 2013 to become the world's largest importer of oil.

Industry & Manufacturing

Industry and Construction account for 46.8% of China's GDP. Between the years 2011and 2013, China used more cement than the US consumed during the entire 20th century. In 2009 around 8% of the total manufacturing output in the world came from China itself and China ranked third worldwide in industrial output that year. (EU was first and USA 2nd). Global insight states that in 2010, China contributed 19.8% of world's manufacturing output and became the largest manufacturer in the world after US had held that position for about 110 years.

In November 2012, the State Council of the People's Republic of China, mandated a "social risk assessment" for all major industrial projects. This requirement followed mass protests in some locations for planned project or expansion.

Since the founding of People's Republic, industrial development has been given considerable attention, as of 2011. 46% of China's national output continued to be devoted to investment, a percentage higher than any other nation. Among the various industrial branches, the machine-building and metallurgic industries have received highest priority. These two areas now alone account for 20%-30% of the total gross value of the industrial output. In these, as most other areas of industry, however, innovation has generally suffered at the hand of the system that has rewarded increase in gross output rather than improvements in variety, sophistication and quality. China still imports significant quantities of specialized steals. Overall industrial output has given at an average rate of more than 10% per year having surpassed all other sectors in the economic growth and degree of mineralization. Some heavy industries and products deemed to be of national strategic importance remain state-owned, but an increasing population of lighter and consumer oriented manufacturing firms are privately held or are private-state joint ventures.

The predominant focus of development in the chemical industry is to expand the output of chemical fertilizers, plastics and synthetic fibres. The growth of this industry has placed China among the world's leading producers of nitrogenous fertilizers. In the consumer goods sector the main emphasis is on textiles and clothing which also form an important part of China's exports. Synthetics, part of textile industry, account for about 10% of the gross industrial output and continues to be important, but less so than before.

In 2011, China was the largest producer of steel in the world producing 45% of the world steel, 683 million tons, increase of 9% from 2010. 6 to 10 of largest steel producers in the world are in China. Profits are low in spite continued high demand due to high debt and overproduction of high end products produced with the equipment financed by the high debt. China is the exporter of steel but its steel exports are restricted due to US imposed import duties on Steel to the extent of 25%.

Automotive Industry

By 2006, China had become the world's third largest automobiles vehicle manufacturer (after US and Japan) and the second largest consumer (only after US).

Year	*Output Aumobile*
1975	139800
1985	443377
1992	1100000
2002	3250000
2007	8880000
2008	9350000
2009	13830000

Automotive Manufacturing

China became the number one automaker in 2009.Domestic sales have pace with production. After respectable annual increase in the mid and late 1990s, passenger car sales soared in the early 2000s. In 2006, a total of 7.22 million automobiles were sold, including 5.18 million units of passenger cars and 2.4 million units of commercial and vehicles.

Other Industries

Substantial investments were made in the manufacture of solar panels and wind generators by number of companies, supported by liberal loans by banks and local government. However by 2012 manufacturing capacity had outstripped domestic and global demands for both products, particularly solar panels, which are subjected to anti-dumping penalties by both US and Europe. The global oversupply has resulted in bankruptcies and production cutbacks both inside and outside China. China has budgeted $50 billion to subsidise production of solar power over the two decades following 2015 but even at the sharply reduced price resulting from oversupply, as of 2012 the cost of solar power remained three times that of power produced by conventional coal-fired power plants.

China is the world's biggest sex toy producer and account for 70% of the worldwide sex toys production. In the country, 1000 manufacturers are active in the industry which generates about 2 billion dollars a year.

As of 2011, China was the world's biggest market for personal computers.

Services

The output of China's services in 2015 ranks 2nd after US. High power and telecom destiny has ensured that the country has remained on a high-growth trajectory over the long term.In 2015, the services sector produced 52.9% of China's annual GDP, second only to manufacturing. However, its proportion of GDP is still low compared to the ratio in more developed countries, and agricultural sector still employs a larger workforce.

Prior to the onset of economic reforms in 1978, China in services sector characterised by state-operated scope, rationing and regulated prices – with reform came private markets, individual enterpreneurs and a commercial sector. The wholesale and retail trade has expanded quickly, with numerous shopping malls, retail shops, restaurant chains and hotel constructed in urban areas. Public administration remains a main component of the service sector, while tourism has become a significant factor in employment and source of foreign exchange.

Telecommunication

China possesses a diversified communication system that links all ports of the country by internet, telephone, telegram, radio and television. China's number of internet users topped 137 million by the end of 2006, an increase of 23.4% from a year before and 162 million by June 2007making China the second largest user after US. China's mobile phones used by 429 billion text messages. For 2007, the number of fixed-linked grew by 79% mainly in rural area.

Tourism

China's tourism industry is one of the fastest growing industries in the national economy. Travel tourism directly contributed $216 billion to the China's economy (about 26% of GDP). In 2011 total international tourism receipts were $ 48 billion.

Domestic tourism market makes up more than 90% of country's tourism traffic and contributes more than 70% of the total tourism revenue in 2002, domestic tourists reached 878 million and tourism revenue was $ 469 billion.

A large middle class with strong consumption power is emerging in China, especially in major cities. China's outbound tourism reached 20.22 million in 2003, overtaking Japan for the first time. China takes 8.6% of world market share to become the world's top tourism industry by 2020.Total business travel spending is expected to reach 195 billion in 2012.

China will overtake France as the leading travel destination by 2030.

Luxury Goods

Luxury spending in China has sky rocked. China bottled water industry is forecast to more than double its size in 2008, becoming $10.5 billion industry. Those who once had no resource but low-quality tap water take advantage of its availability in supermarkets. Tap water production and supply is expected to grow by 29.3% in 2008 expand by 29.5% to newly $200 billion. Also, the consumption of chocolate and other coffeeis to increase by 24.3% as the industry expands to $4.6 billion. Fast food industry has been growing at a 20.8% annual rate as major players such as MacDonnell's enter in the market.

Cybercrime

As of 2016, computer crime is a lucrative illicit proactive in China. Academic study released in 2012 claimed China's cyber black market involved 90000 participants cost of which is $536 billion (English pounds 536 million) negatively impacted upon 110 million internet users (22%) and affected 1.1 million websites (20%). China introduced measure to combatcy bercrime that included increased auditing, security reporting and monitoring, and to reduce the number of internet connection prints.

Labour & Welfare

China promises employment to all able and willing to work and job security with virtually life long tenure. This Socialist- Communist policy is known as the iron rice bowl.

In 1979-80, the state reformed factories by giving wage increase to workers which was immediately offset by sharp rise in inflation rates of 6.7%. The reforms also dismantled the iron rice bowl, which meant reforms also witnessed a rise in unemployment in the economy. In 1979-80, there were 20 million unemployed people.

China estimated employed labour force in 2005 totaled 791.4 million persons or about 60% of the total population. During 2003, 49% of the labour force worked in agriculture, forestry and fishing, 22% in mining, manufacturing, energy and construction industries and 29% in service sector and other categories. In 2004, 25 million persons were employed by 743000 private enterprises. Urban wages rose rapidly from 2004 to 2007, at a rate of 13% to 19% per year with average wage nearly $200 per month in 2007. By 2016, the average monthly wage for workers engaged in manufacturing goods for export was $424. This wage, combined with the other costs of doing business in China had more or less, equalized any Chinese cost advantage with respect to developed countries.

The All-China Federation of Trade Unions (ACFTU) was established in 1925 to represent the interest of trade union councils. ACFTU reported membership of 130 million. out of 248 million urban members at the end of 2002. Chinese trade Unions are organized on broad industrial basis. Membership is open to those who rely on wages for the whole or a large part of their income, a qualification that exclude most agricultural workers.

In 2010, the issues of manufacturing wages caused a strike at a Honda part plant. This resulted in wage increases both at stock plant and other industrial parts.

2010 Census found that China was now half urban and rapidly aging due to one child policy. This is expected to lead to increased demand for labour to take care of an elderly population and reduced supply of migrant labour from the country side.

Due to the worsening pollutions, the corruption and political uncertainties of one-party state and the limited economic freedom in an economy dominated by large state owned enterprises many skilled professionals are either leaving the country or preparing safety nets for themselves abroad. In a decade about 2014, 10 million Chinese migrated to other countries, taking assets and their technical skills. Perceived corruption continued to grow worse in China as it dropped from 75% to 80% in Transparency International's index of state corruption.

External Trade

International trade makes up a sizeable portion of China's overall economy. A meaningful segment of China's trade with the Third World countries was financed through grants, Credit and other forms of assistance. The principal efforts were made in Asia especially, to Indonesia, Burma, Pakistan and Ceylon, but large loans were also granted in Africa (Ghana, Algeria, and Tanzania) and Middle East. However after Mao ending's death in 1976, these efforts were scaled down. Trade with developing countries were negligible; though that time, Hongkong and Taiwan both began to emerge as major trading partners. China's reforms resulted in decentralized its foreign system into the International trading system.

China global trade exceeded $4.16 trillion by end 2013.

Vast majority of China's imports consists of industrial supplies and majority of which come from developed countries, primarily Japan and US regionally, half of China's imports come from East and Southeast Asia., and about one fourth of Chinese exports to the same destinations. Almost 80% of China's exports consist of manufacturing goods, most of which are textiles and electronic equipment with agricultural products and chemicals consisting the remainder out of the five business ports in the world, three are China. US trade deficit with China was $232.5 billion in 2006, as import grew 18%.China's share of total US imports has grown from 75 to 15% since 1996.

Trade volume between China and Russia reached $29.1billion in 2005, an increase of 37.1% compared with 2004. Trade volume between China and Russia is estimated to raise to $ 40 billion in 2007.Chinese imports from Russia are mainly energy sources (crude oil mostly transported by rail) and electricity exports from neighbouring Siberian and Far East in the near future. Russia is building Eastern Siberia Encouraged industries catalog - Pacific Ocean pipeline and hydropower stations. Export of both these commodities are set into increase on completion of these construction.

Export growth has continued to be a major component supporting China's rapid economic growth. To increase exports, China pursued policies such as fostering the rapid development of foreign-invested factories, which assembled imported components into consumer goods for exports and liberalizing trading sights. In the 11th Five Year Plan programme, China placed greater emphasis on developing consumer demand driven economy to sustain economic grants and address imbalances.

Foreign Investment

In early 1980, China restricted foreign investments to export - oriented operations and required foreign investors to form a joint venture partnership with Chinese firms.Encouraged industry catalog sets out the degree of foreign investment allowed in various industry sectors. From the beginning of reforms legalizing foreign investments, capital inflows expanded every year. Till 1999, foreign invested enterprises amount to 59.60% of China's imports and exports.

Since 1990, China has allowed foreign investors to manufacture and sell a wide range of goods on the domestic market, eliminating time restrictions on the establishment of joint ventures and authorised wholly foreign owned enterprises and contractual ventures for foreign companies which invested in energy, communication and transportation.

China authorised some foreign banks to open branches in Shanghai and allowed foreign investors to purchase "B" shares of stock in selected companies. These "B" shares sold to foreigners carried no ownership rights in a company. In 1997, China approved 21046 foreign investment projects and received over $45 billion in Foreign Direct Investment. Foreign investors have been allowed to own upto 51% on domestic financial service companies. Formally it was limited to 49% stake in these firms.

Foreign investment was a strong element in the China's rapid expansion of workers trade. China received $39 billion in 1999 and $41 billion in 2000. China is now one of the leading FDI recipients in the world receiving almost $180 billion in 2005 according to the World Bank statistics. China received $69.47 billion in 2006. China received $260 billion in 2005.

China's FDI declined in 2015 by 5.8%. Foreign exchange reserves were:

Year	*Amount in $ billion*
1999	155
2000	165
2005	819
2006	1066
2008 (January)	1900

US Treasury bills. China surpassed Japan in treasury bills in 2008.

China	Japan
$585 billion	$573 billion (2008)

China has largest foreign exchange reserves.

Chinese Investment Abroad

Local Chinese firms seek to make investments in both developed and developing countries. In 2013, Chinese companies invested $90 billion globally in non-financial sector, 16% more than 2012.

Between 2009 and 2013, China contributed a total of $160.07 billion in outward FDI.

Many Chinese acquire foreign companies and then bring their products/ services to China. China government provides long term low interest capital for companies to expand abroad.

Between January 2009 and December 2013, China contributed a total of $161.03 billion in outward FDI creating about 300000 jobs. Western Europe was the largest regional recipient of Chinese outward FDI, with Germany receiving the highest number of FDI projects for any globally.

There are two ways of Chinese companies choose to enter a foreign market. Organic growth and Merger &Acquisition for the following reasons:

(1) Fast M& A is the fastest way to accompany to expand into another country by acquiring brand, distribution, talents and technology. Chinese CEOs have been used to growing at 50% + speed and do not want to spend capital.

(2) China has become the world's largest economy. Many Chinese acquire foreign companies and bring their products/services to China, anything from premium cars to fashion clothing, to meat to Hollywood movies.

(3) Cheap Capital Access: Huge Chinese Domestic Market help many Chinese companies accumulated financial capital to do M & A.

Chinese government also provides long term low - interest capital to companies to expand abroad.

(4) M & A helped Chinese companies avoid risk of failure of organic growth as they got as estimated company with everything in place.

(5) Some companies may move part of manufacturing in high labour cost countries to China to reduce the cost and make product more attractive in price.

(6) Chinese companies in many sectors face quota limitation and high tax, which prevent them being competitive in foreign markets,

(7) During 2008-10, global economic crisis created liquidity problems for a lot of western countries and reduced their market value. Chinese companies took this opportunity to buy these depressed assets at discount. China's direct foreign investment in non-financial sector growth was from $25 billion in 2007 to $90 billion in 2013, more than 3 times

China is growing in investment and influencing power over Europe, and the EU has begun to take notice. China acquired on 03-02-2016 Switzerland deal for $41.84 billion, UK's deal on 01-02-2008 at $ 14..84 billion and another deal with UK on 02-06-2017at $ 13.740 billion.

China acquired chemical co. and oil & gas co. from Switzerland with value $ 48997.51. In other 15 outbound deals it has spent $ 177 billion since 2005.

However, the fast growth and M & A deals did not change consumer's low quality and low price perception of Chinese goods and brands.

Many M & A deals have failed because companies underestimated the challenges and failed to restructure the Company.

Financial inequity in Chinais highlighted by the fact that China has 66 billionaires at present.

Labour Force

In 2012, for the first time the size of the labour force, people aged 15 to 59, in China shrank slightly to 932.27 million people, a decrees of 3.45million from 2011. This trend, resulting from China's One Child policy of population control, is anticipated to continue to at least 2030.

Ob 29-10-2015, China changed the existing law to a two child policy effective from 01-06-2016.

Transportation and Infrastructure

Development of the country's transportation infrastructure is given high priority because it is so strategically tied to the national economy and national defence. Transportation infrastructure is not fully developed in many aspects and areas, and it constitutes a major hindrance on economic growth and the efficient logistical movement of goods and people. China's transportation policy, influenced by political, military and economic concerns have undergone major changes since 1949.

Immediately after the People Republic was founded, the primary goal was to repair existing transportation infrastructure in order to meet military transport and logistic needs as well as to strengthen territorial integrity. During the most 1950s new roads and rail links were built, while at the same time old ones were improved. During the 1960s, much of the improvement of regional transportation became the responsibility of local governments, and many small railways were constructed. Emphasis was also placed on developing transportation in remote rural, mountainous and forested areas, in order to integrate poorer regions of the country and to help promote economic sale in the agricultural sector.

Before the reform era began in the late 1970s, China's transportation links were mostly concentrated in the coastal areas and access to the inner region were generally poor. This situation has been improved considerably since then, as railways and highways have been built up in the remote and frontier regions of the northeast and southwest. At the same time, the international transportation development was also pursued, and the scope of ocean. Shipping was broadened considerably.

Rail sector is monopolized by China Railway which is controlled by the Ministry of Railways and there is wide variations in services provided. In late 2007, China became one of the few countries in the world to launch its own indigenously developed high speed train. As rail capacity is struggling to meet demand for the transport of goods and raw materials such as coal air routes, roads and waterways are rapidly being developed to provide an increasing proportion of China's overall transportation needs.

Some economic experts have argued that the development gap between China and other emerging economies such as Brazil, Argentina and India can be attributed to a large extent to China's early focus on ambitious infrastructure projects; while China invested roughly 9% of its GDP on infrastructure in 1990s and 2000, most emerging economies invested 2% to 5% of their GDP. This considerable pending gap allowed the Chinese economy to grow at near optimal conditions while many South American economies suffered from various development bottlenecks such as transportation network, aging power-grids and mediocre schools.

Science & Technology

Science and technology in China has in recent decades developed rapidly. The Chinese government has placed emphasis through funding, reform, and social status on Science and technology as a fundamental part of the socio-economic development of the country as well as for national prestige. China has made rapid advances in areas such as education, infrastructure, high tech. manufacturing, academic publishing, patents and commercial application and is now in some areas and by some measures a world leader. China is now increasingly targeting indigenous innovation and aims to reform remaining weakness. These initiatives are dependent on attracting highly educated overseas Chinese back to China to work in the innovation economy and to teach the next generation of Chinese students.

Present Status of Chinese Economy at A Glance

(1) Chinese currency is Yian (CNY) One yian is USD 0.15 i.e. Yian6.666= USD1. Rs. 10.20 =yian1.

(2) Fiscal year of Chana is January- December

(3) Trade Organizations are WTO, G 20 and others, APRC.

(4) GDP $15.175 trillian (Nominal, 2019) 2nd Rank

(5) GDP $30.450 trillion (PPP, 2019) 1st Rank

(6) GDP Growth 6.6%

(7) GDP per Capita $10099 (Nominal, 2019

(8) GDP $19559 (PPP, 2019) GDP per capita rank 71st (Nominal), 78th (PPP)

(9) Population 150 crores

(10) Labour Force 932 million 62.13% of population

(11) GDP by Sector Agriculture 8.6%, industry 39.8%, Services 51.6% (2016)

(12) Inflation 2.1 (March 2011)

(13) Human Development 0.752 (2017) high

(14) Labour Force by Occupation: Agriculture 29.7%, Industry 28.8% Services 43.5% (2016)

(15) Unemployment 3.97%

(16) Main Industries: Mining, Ore processing, iron, steel, armaments, textiles, apparel, petroleum, cement, chemicals, fertilizers, food processing, transportation, equipment, ships, aircrafts, automobiles, satellite, consumer products

(17) Export: 2.49 trillion Imports: $ 2.14 trillionTrade Surplus: 0.35 trillion

(18) Export Goods: Agricultural products 3.2%, Fuel & Mining 2.4%, Manufacturers 94.3%, Others 0.1%

(19) Main export partners: US 18.31%, EU 16%, Hongkong 13.8%, japan 6.1%, South Korea 4.5% and Others 41.2%

(20) Import Goods: Agriculture 9.5%, Fuel & Mining 21.3%, Manufacturing 64.9% Others 48%

(21) Main import partners: EU 13.1%, South Korea 10%, Japan 9.2%, Taiwan 8.8%, US 8.5%, Others 50.4%.

(22) FDI Stock $1.354 trillion (2016)

(23) Gross External debt $1.42 trillion (31-03-2017)

(24) Foreign Reserves $3.15 trillion

(25) Public debt 16.1% of GDP

(26) Revenue $2.94 trillion, Expenses $3.41 trillion, Fiscal Deficit $0.47 billion 3% of GDP within the norms of 4%.

(27) Credit Rating : S & P: A+ (domestic), A+ (foreign) .T &C A+ Outlook Stable, Fitch A+ Outlook: Stable, Scope A+, Outlook: Negative.

(28) Growth rate was 6%. China's commercial profit was $39 billion in January 2019. It was $4 billion in February 2019. Perhaps that compelled Credit Agent SCOPE to rate Outlook as negative.

(29) China's size of economy is lower by 18% than what was declared officially by China. Reported figures were inflated.

(30) On account of trade war, China economy has been seriously affected. Exports reduced by 20.7% and import reduced by 5%.

Critical Observations on China's Economy

(1) In his famous book, "Das Capital" Karl Marx has mentioned the socialist pattern of government. China, Russia, formal Czecosalvika and other communist countries adopted the theory of Das Capita. In his theory, Karl Marx has stated that labour and farmers will prosper by way of this political arrangement and state will 'wither away". But this dream of Karl Marks never came true as farmers and labour improved their income but neither the state withered away nor ruled by peasants and workers... In fact, State and ruling political Party of the state become more powerful and head of the ruling Party became most powerful man in the state. This happened in China, Soviet Russia and other communist country. Marshall Tito of Czecosalvika became the richest man in the world. This is tragedy of the Das Capital theory.

(2) In China, Mao-Se Tung was very powerful man and he planned the county's economy as per his theory. Labour and farmers got some concession but their freedom of speech and opinions were drastically curtailed. Those who opposed him were put in jail and killed and whole country was ruled ruthlessly/oppressively. Any opposition/agitation was ruthlessly crashed and thousands of agitators were ruthlessly killed. Tibet was near to India and the country's priest Mr. Dalai Lama sought protection from India. Tibet was snatched by China as part of China. China also waged war with India on this issue in 1961.India was not prepared for

such war and was defeated.China also annexed to its country many such provinces as China's territory forcibly. Like "one belt one road' present policy, China will make slogan "one world with one China'. This unreasonable lust to rule the world will ruin China in war with USA, European Countries, India and others.

(3) Present President in China Mr. Xi Jinping also has become most powerful leader and assumes all political, military powers. He may wage war with Taiwan at any time as Taiwan has refused to be part of China. Present issue of military and naval base installed by China in South China Ocean will wage war of China with many countries and China will lose most of military defence in the war. Present policy will therefore make China a weak country.

(4) China has the highest population in the world which is 1.52 billion out of world population of 7 billion. This works out to 21% of the world population. Its workforce is 932 million at present. It has 7% of world's arable land and 60 per cent of population lives in rural areas. It has made tremendous progress in agriculture with annual production of about 300 million metric tons foodgrains.

(5) China has natural resources such as iron ore, mining etc. which it has utilized optimal.

(6) China has built up public roads, transportation in remote part of the country. It also built up infrastructure in the broader areas which are disputable with China which facilitates transportation of military equipment and military personnel. It threatens country like India on Boarder issue developing infrastructure on its border areas with India and prepared to attack India at any time.

(7) Dr. Kissinger, US Defence Secretary granted the status as "most favourable country" to China during his regime 1971-1991. Being aggressive country and low developing country, China took advantage of such facility and advanced trade will USA with trade deficit for USA reaching at $350- billion in 2017. President Trump rightfully waged trade ban and trade war with China. This has damaged China's economy drastically and its annual growth has come down from 8% to 6.5% in 2018. This will further declined to 6.3% resulting in tremendous fall in industrial production, domestic consumer demands and construction activities. If the situation continues, China will face badly recession which will further decline its annual economic growth.

(8) China has brought this situation on adopting its own practice of limited opening doors of liberalization to other countries while taking of liberalization policy of USA entered their market by Chinese companies and took active part in merger and acquisition. China slowed down gradually American trade in manufacturing, service industries etc. and acquired 1st position in this field.

(9) China gives financial assistance to many countries on the pretext of making economic growth in that country with high interest rates. When Country is unable to make loan servicing payment, it grasps the part of that country to reimburse itself for such default. Many countries have the fear of this ruthless attitude of China and have cancelled their loan programme with China. China's 'one belt one road" programme has therefore been collapsed. China wanted to invest $1 trillion on this programme but there are very few customers. Its corridor at Pakistan is recently in great dispute.

(10) China's economy has been built up mainly on international trade. Since trade war with USA has dangerously affected the China's growth, President Xi Jing Ping is worried about his existence.

(11) For its own selfishness and greediness, China has captured Sparkly islands and South China ocean region and has established military, naval and nuclear base therein. It prohibited to enter in these areas all countries including Australia, Japan. South Korea, Malaysia, Philippines and other countries who claimed their stake in these areas. It wants to abstract the natural resources in this area like natural gas, iron ore and crude oil etc. in large quantities.All countries including USA, Europe are opposing strongly China for this attitude. International Court decision on this issue also was against China but China has refused to accept International Court decision.USA has brought its naval fleet along with Australia, Japan in this area. Any time this explosive situation may result in third war resulting in heavy losses to China and perhaps Xi Jing Ping may be thrown out of his present position as the President of China.

(12) China has ruthlessly treating Tibet, Hong Kong. Singapore, Taiwan and many other countries which are situated in the remote places. Citizens in these countries are not satisfied with the Chinese rule and they may revolt at any time for their freedom. China will be in trouble that time and its economic growth will be significantly damaged.

(13) Venezuela's economy has been completely financially collapsed but China, Russia, Iran and Cuba are unable to assist it financially as they are troubled by the decline in their economy on account of trade ban and sanctions from USA though they threatened America and Latin American countries for their military interference and also sent their troops to Venezuela for fighting war with USA..

(14) China has technologically strong workforce which is migrated to various countries. Their earnings have been remitted to China in large amounts. This workforce is of high quality skilled workers. China is trying to attract its immigrated workforce to its country by giving them attractive incentives.

(15) External debt and public debt is 8.92% of GDP and is manageable. Public debt works out 16.1% of GDP are well managed.

(16) Growth rate is expected to rise by 6% in 2019. China's Commercial profit has been drastically reduced from $39 billion in January 2019 to $ 4 billion in February 2019. Shanghai Composite Index declined 4% on 08-03-2019 which shows that China's economy has been slowing gradually and may lead to depression in future.

(17) China has surrounded Pag Aasa Port of Philippines with its hundred war ships to capture that port from Philippines and annex it to its empire. President of Philippines Mr. Rodrigo Duarte has instructed China not to do so. If China does so, he warned China that his solidiers will attack China. Suicide attack on Chinese war ships will be made. He appealed China to withdraw these warships surrounding his country. Legal dispute between China and Philippines is old and Philippines has won the case in its favour in the international Court. But China is treated herself as supreme over the International Court and refused to obey the judgement of International Court. Being a small country, Philippines have maintained friendship with China but China is becoming more aggressive. Philippines have made military and strategic partnership with USA to fight and resist China's military attack with military assistance of USA.

(18) UK's present Prime Minister Mrs. Theresa May has permitted Chinese "5G network" in England. In March 2018, executive director of "Huvei" was arrested in Canada. China is collecting the information of US and other countries through medium of Huvei Company as its spy activities which is dangerous for Canada and America. They have therefore put ban on operations of Huvei. By permitting Huvei to UK for 5 G network, UK is taking a great risk. US is advising UK not to take such risk. U.K. has therefore backed out from taking Huawei's help for developing 5G network. But China has threatened UK for sudden back-out.

CHAPTER - 17

ECONOMY OF RUSSIAN SOVIET

(1) Economy of the Union of Soviet Russia - introduction

The economy of the Union of Soviet Socialist Republic was based on a system of state ownership of the means of production, collective farming industrial manufacturing and centralized administrative planning. The economy was characterised by state control of investment, public ownership of industrial assets macroeconomic stability, reliable unemployment and high job security.

Beginning in 1928, the course of the Soviet Union's economy was guided by a series of five years plans. By the 1950s, during the preceding few decades the Soviet Union had rapidly evolved from a mainly agrarian society into a major industrial power. Its transformative capacity – what the White House National Security Council of the United States described as a "proven ability" to carry backward countries speedily through the crisis of modernization and industrialization meant communism consistently appealed to the intellectuals of developing countries in Asia. Impressive growth rates during the three five year plans (1924-1940) are particularly notable given that this period is nearly congruent with the Great Depression. During this period, the Soviet Union encountered a rapid industrial growth while other regions were suffering from crisis. Nevertheless, the impoverished base upon which the five year plans sought to build meant that at the commitment of operations Barbarossa, the country was still poor.

A major strength of the Soviet economy was in enormous supply of oil and gas, which came much more valuable as exports of the world price of oil skyrocketed in the 1970s. The Soviet economy in its final decades was "heavily dependent on vast natural resources – oil and gas in particular." World oil prices collapsed in 1986 putting heavy pressure on the economy. After Mikhail Gorbachev came to power in 1985, he began a process of economic liberalization by dismantling the command economy and moving towards the mixed economy. At the dissolution at the end of 1991, The Soviet Union begat a Russian Federation with a growing pile of $ 66 billion in external debt with barely a few billion in net gold and foreign exchange reserves.

Complex demands of the modern economy somewhat constrained the central planners. Corruption and data fiddling became the common practice among the bureaucracy by reporting fulfilled targets and quotas, thus entrenching the crisis. From the Stalin era to the early Brezhner era, the Soviet economy grew much slower than Japan and slightly faster than the US. GDP in 1950 $510 billion in the Soviet Union, $161billion in Japan and $1456 billion in USA. By 1965, the corresponding values were $1011 billion, $587 billion and $ 2017 billion. The Soviet Union maintained itself as the second largest economy in both Nominal and PPP, values for much of cold war until 1988, when Japan economy exceeded $3 trillion in Nominal value.

The Soviet Union's relatively small consumer market accounted for just under 60% of the country's GDP while the industrial and agriculture sectors contributed 22% and 20% respectively in 1991. Agriculture was predominant occupation in the Soviet Union before massive industrialization underJoseph Stalin. The Services was of the low importance in the Soviet Union, with majority of the labour force employed in the industrial sector. The labour force totaled 152.3 million people. Major industrial products included petroleum, steal, motor vehicles, aerospace, telecommunications, chemical, electronics, food processing, lumber, and mining and defence industry. Though its GDP crossed $1 trillion in the 1970s, and $2 trillion in 1980s, the effects of Central Planning distorted due to the rapid growth of second economy in the Soviet Union.

Planning

Based on the system of state ownerships, the Soviet economy was managed through Gosplan (State Planning Commission), Gosbank (the State Bank) and Gosnab (State Commission for Materials and Equipment Supply). Beginning in 1928, the economy was directed by a series of five year plans with a brief attempt at Seven year plan. For every enterprise, planning ministries (known as the "fund holders") defined the mix of economic inputs (labour and raw materials), a schedule for completion, all wholesale prices and almost all retail prices. The planning process was based around material balances – balancing economic inputs with plan output targets for the planning period. From 1930 until the 1950s the range of mathematics used to assist economic decision – making was, ideological reasons, extremely restricted.

The industry was long concentrated after 1928 on the production of capital goods, though metallurgy, machine manufacture, and chemical industry. In Soviet technology, goods were known as capital. This emphasis was based on the perceived necessity for very fast industrializations and modernalisation of the Soviet Union. After the death of Joseph Stalin in 1953, Consumer goods received with somewhat more emphasis – due to the efforts of Malenkov. However, when Nikita Khrushev consolidated his power backing Georgy Malenkov, one of the accusations against Malenkov was that he permitted "theoretically incorrect and political harmful opposition to the rate of development of heavy industries in favour of the rate of development of light and food industry." Since 1955, the priorities were again given to capital goods. The decision was taken in 20th Congress of the Communist Party of Soviet Union in 1956.

Most information in the Soviet economy flowed from the top down. There were several mechanisms in place for producers and customers to provide input and information that would help in the drafting of economic plans., but the political climate was such that few people ever provided negative inputs or criticism of the plan and thus Soviet planners had very little reliable feedback that they would use to determine the success of their plans. This means that economic planning was often designed based on faulty or outdated information, particularly in sectors with large number of customers. As a result. Some goods tended to be underproduced and led a shortage while other goods tended to be overproduced and accumulated in storage. Low level management often did not report such problems to their superiors, relying instead on each other for support. Some foreign developed a system of barter and either exchanged or shared raw materials and parts without the knowledge of the authorities and outside the parameters of the economic plan.

Heavy industry was always the focus of Soviet economy even in its later years. The fact that it received a special attentions from the planners, combined with the fact that industrial production was relatively easy to plan even without minute feedback, led to a significant growth in that sector. The Soviet Union became one of the leading industrial nations of the world. Industrial production was disproportionately high in the Soviet Union compared to Western economies. However, the production of consumer goods was disproportionally low. Economic planners made little efforts to determine the wishes of household customers, resulting in severe shortage of many consumer goods. Whenever these customer goods would become available on the market, it was routine that customers have to stand in long queues to buy them. The black market grew for such goods as cigarettes that were particularly sought after, but it constantly unproduced.

By the 60s, the Soviet Union was functioning at levels similar in US in terms of food based consumer goods, according to CIA reports claiming caloric consumption in the USSR was higher and that they had similar levels of nutrition. However, critics of Soviet Union point out that there was limited variety, and many people wasted in long queues for food.

Five Yrear Plan

From Joseph Stalin's complex system of planning arrangements had developed and the introduction of the first five year plan 1928.was initiated. Until the late 1980s and early 1990s, when economic reforms backed by Soviet leader Mikhail Gorbachev introduced significant changes in the traditional system.The allocation of resourceswas directed by the planning apparatus rather than through interplay of market forces.

From the Stalin era through the late 1980s, the five year plan integrated short-range planning into a longer time frame. It defined the chief trust of the country's economic development and specified the way the economy could meet the desired goals of the Communist Party of the Soviet Union. Although the five year plan was enacted into law, it contained a series of guidelines rather than a set of direct orders.

Periods covered by the five year plans coincided with those covered by the gathering of the CPSU party Congress. At each CPSU congress, the party leadership presented the targets for the next five year plan, therefore each plan had the approval of the most authoritative body of the country's leading political institution.

Guidelines for the plan

The Central Committee of the CPSU and more significantly its Politburo set basic guidelines for planning. The Politburo set basic guidelines for planning. The Politburo determined the general direction of the economy via control figure. (Preliminary plan targets), major investment projects guidelines were submitted as a report of the Central Committee to the Congress of CPSU to be approved there.

After the approval at the Congress, the list of priorities for the five year plan was processed by the Council of Ministers, which constituted the government of Soviet Union. The Council of Ministers was composed of industrial Ministers. Chairmen of various State Committees and Chairmen of Agencies with ministerial status. The Committee stood at the apex of the vast economic administration, including the state planning apparatus, the industrial ministers, the trusts and finally the state enterprises. The council of Ministers elaborated on Politburo plan targets and sent them to Gosplan, which gathered data on planfulfilment.

Gosplan

Combining the broad goals laid out by the Council of Ministers with data supplied by lower administrative levels regarding the current state of economy, Gosplan worked out through trial and error method a set of preliminary plan target. Among more than twenty state committees, Gosplan needed the government's planning apparatus and was by far the most important agency in the economic administration. The task of planners was to balance resources and requirements to ensure that the necessary inputs were provided for the planned output. Planning apparatus alone was a vast organizational officials, specialists and so no change with executing and monitoring economic policy.

The State Planning agency was subdivided into its own industrial departments, such as coal, iron and machine building; It also had summary departments such as finance, dealing with issues that crossed functional boundaries, with the exception of a brief experiment with regional planning during the Khrushchev era in the 1950s, Soviet planning was done on requirements, a process involving bargaining between ministries and their superiors.

Planning Ministries

Economic ministers performed key roles in the Soviet Organizational structure. When the planning goals had been established by Gosplan, economic ministries drafted plans within their jurisdictions and disseminated planning data to the subordinate enterprises. The planning data were sent downward through the planning hierarchy for progressively more detailed elaboration. The ministry received its control targets which were disaggregated by the branches within the ministry, then by lower writs, eventually until each enterprise received its even control figures (production targets).

Enterprises

Enterprises were called upon to develop in the final period of state planning in the late 1980s and early 1990s. The enterprises' draft plans were then sent back up through the planning ministries for review. This process entailed intensive bargaining with all parties seeking the target levels and input figures that best suited their interest.

Approval of the Plan

The review, revision and approval of the five year plan was followed by another downward flow of information, this time with the amended and final plans containing the specific targets for each sector of the economy. Implementation began at this point and was largely responsibility of enterprise managers.

State Budget

The national state budget was prepared by the Ministry of Finance of the Soviet Union by negotiating with its all - union local organisations. If the State budget was accepted by the Soviet Union, it was then adopted.

Agriculture

Agriculture was organized into a system of collective farming and state farms organized on a large scale and highly mechanized, the Soviet Union was one of the world's leading producer of cereals, almost bad harvest (1972 and 1975) necessitated imports and slowed the economy. The 1976-1980 five-year plan shifted resources to agriculture and 1978 saw a record harvest followed by another drop in overall production in 1979 and 1980 backed to levels attained in 1975. Cotton, sugar beets, potatoes and flax were also major crops. However, despite immense land resources, extensive machinery and chemical industries and large rural workforce, Soviet agriculture was relatively unproductive (75 million metric tons foodgrains), hampered in many areas by the climate (only 10% of Soviet land was arable) and poor work productivity since the collectivization in the 1930. Lack of transport infrastructure also caused most waste.

Foreign Trade & Currency

Largely self -sufficient, the Soviet Union traded little in comparisons to its economic strength. However, trade with non-communist countries increased in 1970 as the government sought to compensate Japan in domestic production with imports.

In general, fuels, metals and timber were exported. Machinery, consumer goods and sometimes grain were imported. In the 1980s, trade with the Council for Mutual Economic Assistance (COMECON) member states accounted for half the country's volume of trade. The Soviet currency (rouble) was non-convertible after 1932 to freely buy or sell foreign currency even though the "exchange rate" was set and published regularly. Buying or selling foreign currency on a black market was a serious crime until the late 1980s. Individual who were paid from abroad normally had to spend their currency in a foreign currency- only chain of state own Birch free stores. Once a force conversion of currency was allowed, the exchange rate plummeted from its official values by almost a factor of 10.

Overall banking system was highly controlled and fully controlled by a single state owned Gosbank, responsive to the fulfilment of government economic plans. Soviet banks furnished short-term credit to state-owned enterprises.

Forms of Property

There were two forms of property in the SU, individual property and collective property. These differed generally in legal status. According to Communist theory, capital (means of production) should not be individually owned, with certain negalible exceptions. In particular, after the end of short period of the New Economic Policy and with collectivization completed, all property and virtually all lands were collective. Land in rural area was allotted for housing and some substantial farming, and persons had certain rights to it, but it was neither their property in full. In particular there was a practice to rotate individual farming lots with collective lots. This resulted in situations where people would immortalize till and cultivate their lots carefully, adapting them to small-scale farming and in 5-7 years those lots would be swapped for kwlkhaz ones, typically with exhausted soil due to intensive, large scale agriculture. There was an extremely small number of remaining individual farmsteads located in isolated rural areas in the Baltic status, Ukraine, Suberia and Cossack lands.

Individual Property

To distinguish between "capitalist" and "socialist", types of the property ownership further, the different forms of individual property were recognised, private property and personal property. The former encompassed capital while the latter described as everything else in a person's possession. This distinction has been a source of confusion when interpreting phrases such as "Socialism" abolished "private property" and might conclude that all individual property was abolished when this was in fact not the case.

Collective Property

There is State and Co-operative property in ownership forms. The most common of co-operative property were housing co-operative in urban areas, Consumers Co-operatives and rural consumer Societies.

History

Early Development

Both the Russian Soviet Federative Socialist and later the Soviet Union were countries in the process of industrialization. For both, this development occurred slowly and allow initial starting point. Because of World War (1914-1918), the Russian Revolution of 1970 and the ensuing Russian Civil War (1917-22) the industrial production had only managed to barely recover its 1913 level by 1926. By this period, about 18% of the population lived in non-rural areas, although only about 7.5% were employed in non-agricultural sector. The remainder remained struck in productivity agricultural.

Soviet Union was typical developing country, characterised by the low capital investment and with most of its population reside in the countryside. Part of the reason for low investment rates lay in the inability to acquire capital from abroad. This in turn, resulted in the repudiation of the debts of the Russian Empire by the Bolsheviks in 1918 as well as from the worldwide financial troubles. Consequently, any kind of economic growth had to be financed by the domestic savings.

The economic problems in agriculture were further exacerbated by natural conditions, such as long cold winters across the country, droughts in the south and acidic soil in the north. However, the Soviet economy did not have "extremely good" potential in the area of raw materials and mineral extraction, for example in the oil fields in Transcaucasia, and this along with a small but growing manufacturing base, helped the Soviet Union avoid any kind of payment problems.

New Economic Policy (1921-29)

By early 1921, it became apparent to the Bolsheviks that forced requisitioning of grains had resulted in low agricultural products and widespread opposition. As a result, the decision was made by Vladimir Lenin and the Politburo to try an alternative approach. So called New Economic Policy (NEP) was approved at the 10th Congress of the Russian communist Party (Bolsheviks).

Everything except "the commanding heights" as Lenin put it, of the economy would be privatized. Commanding heights include foreign trade, heavy industry, communication and transport among the others. In practice, this limited the private sector to artisan and agricultural production/trade. The NEP encountered strong resistance within the Bolshevik party. Lenin had to pursue Communist sceptics that "state capitalism" was a necessary step in achieving communism, while he himself harboured that policy could be abused by private businessmen.

Improvements were immediate. Rationing Cards and quotas had become hallmarks of War Communism had disappeared. However, due to the prolong war, low harvest, and several natural disasters, the Soviet Economy was still in the trouble, particularly its agriculture sector. In 1921, widespread famine broke out in Volges-Ural region. The Soviet government changed its previous course and allowed international relief to come in from abroad, and established a Special Committee chaired by prominent communists and non- communists alike. Despite this, estimated five million people died in famine.

Stalinism

Starting in 1928, the five year plans began building a heavy industrial base at once in an underdeveloped economy without waiting years for capital to accumulate through the expansion of light industry, and without reliance on external financing. NEP was rapidly abandoned and replaced by Stalinism. The country now became industrial at hitherto unprecedented pace, surpassing rising German's place of industrialization in the 19th Century and Japan's earlier in the 20th century.

After the reconstruction of the economy in the wake of destruction caused by the Russian Civil war was completed after the initial plans for further industralisation were fulfilled, the explosive growth showed down until the period of Brezhnev, stagnation in 1970s and 1980s.

Led by the creation go NAMI and by the GAZ Lobby of the Ford model of the 1929, industralisation came with the extension of medical services, which improved labour productivity. Compaigns were carried out against the cholera and malaria, the number of physicians increased as rapidly as facilities and training would permit and death and infant mortality rates steadily decreased.

In respect of evolution of GIVP in comparison with European Power in millions of dollars of 1960:

Country	1900	1913	1925	1938
Russia/SU	32000	52420	32600	75964
Germany	35800	49760	45002	77178
France	23500	27405	36262	39284

As weighted growth rates, economic planning performed very well during the early and mid-1930s. World War II era mobilization, and for the first two decades of postwar era. The Soviet Union became the World's leading producer of oil, coal, iron-ore and cement, manganese, gold, natural gas and other minerals were also of major importance.However, information about Soviet Union in 1932-33 was suppressed by the Soviet authorities until perestroika.

To some estimations, in 1933 workers' real earnings sank more than 11.$5 from 1926 level, though unemployment and perks at work (as, inexpensive meals).Common and political prisoners in labour camps were frequently "mobilized" for various construction projects. The German invasion of World War II inflicted pushing blows to the economy of Soviet Union with Soviet GDP falling 34% between 1940 and 1942. Industrial output did not recover to its 1940 level for almost a decade.

In 1961, a few dominated Soviet ruble was issued. It maintained exchange parity with the sterling until the dissolution of USSR in 1991. After a new leadership, headed by Leonid Brezhnev had come to power, attempts were made to revitalize the economy through economic reforms. Starting in 1965, enterprises and organizations were made to rely on economic methods of profitable production, rather than follow orders from state administration. By 1970, the Soviet economy had reached its zenith and was estimated at about 60% of the size of US in terms of estimated commodities (like steel & coal). In 1989, the official GDP of Soviet Union was $2500 billion. While the GDP of US was $4862 billion with per capita income figures at $8700 and $19800 respectively.

1970-80

The value of all consumer goods manufactured in 1972 in retail price was about $118 billion rubles ($530 billion). The era of stagnation in the mid- 1970s was triggered by the Nixon Stock and aggravated by a War in Afghanistan in 1979 and 1985. Soviet military buildings at the expenses of domestic development kept the Soviet Union's GDP on the same level during the first half of the 1980s. Soviet planned economy was not structured to respond adequately to the demands of complex modern economy, it hoped to forge. The massive quantities of goods produced often did not meet the needs or tastes of consumers.

The volume of decisions facing planners in Moscow became overwhelming. The cumbersome procedures for bureaucratic administration foreclosed the first communications, and flexible response required at the enterprises level for dealing with worker alienation, innovation, customers and supplies. During 1975-85, corruption and data feeding became common practice among bureaucracy to report satisfied targets and quotas thus entrenching the crisis. Effects of the central planning were progressively distorted due to the rapid growth of the second economy in the Soviet Union.

While modern economics were moving rapidly to computerization after 1865, Soviet Union was using IBM360 which proved decisive mistake for it locked scientists into an antiquated system they were unable to improve. They had enormous difficulties in manufacturing the necessary chips reliably and in quantity, in programming workable and efficient programs, in coordinating entirely separate operations, in providing support to computer users.

Soviet Russia's great strength was in vast supplies of oil and natural gas prices of which quadrupled in 1973-74 and again in 1979-80 which made the energy sector the chief driver of Soviet economy. During this period, the Soviet Union had the lowest per capita income among the other socialist countries. Consumer goods scarcity was acute like bread and eating foods. The hard currency from oil export stopped the growing food supply crisis, increased the import of equipment and consumer goods, ensured a financial base for the arms race and the achievement of nuclear parity with US and permitted the realization of such risky foreign policy action as war in Afghanistan.

Awareness of the growing crisis arose initially in KGB which with its extensive network of informants in every region and institution had its finger on the pulse of nation. KGB's special department was devoted to economic analysis and in 1982 it sounded the alarm forcefully to the Soviet leadership. However, Andropov's (Director of KGB) remedy of increased discipline proved ineffective. It was only when Andropov's protégé Gorbochev assumed power that a determined, but ultimately unsuccessful,assault on the economic crisis was undertaken.

Comparison between the US economies (1989)

Description of Heads	*Soviet Union*	*USA*
GDP (GNP) Million $ 1989	2659500	5233300
GDP per capita July 1990	9211	21082
Population July 1990	290938469	250418060
Labour Force	152300000	125557000

The value of all consumer goods manufactured in 1990 in retail prices was about 459 billion ruble (2. 1 trillion). According to CIA estimates by 1989 the size of SU economy was roughly half that in US. According to the

European comparison, Program administered by the UN, the size of Soviet economy was 36% of that of US in 1990.

USSR Workforce

Workforce	1940	1955	1970	1979	1989
Primary (Agriculture & others)	54%	31%	25%	21%	20%
Secondary including Construction, Transports & Communication	28%	44%	46%	48%	41%
Tertiary (Including Trade Finance)	18%	25%	29%	31%	33%
Total	100%	100%	100%	100%	100%

Status of Soviet Union Economy By and 1991 (Before Dissolution) At Glance

(1) Currency: Soviet ruble
(2) Financial Year: Calendar year
(3) Trade Organisations: COMECON, ESCAP &others
(4) GDP: $2.2 trillion in 1985 Nominal 3rd Rank
(5) GDP: $2.6595 trillion 1989 PPP 2nd Rank
(6) GDP per capita: $5800 in 1982 Nominal 32nd Rank
(7) GDP per capita $9211in 1991 GNP, 28th Rank
(8) Population: 29 crores
(9) Labour Force 152.3 million (52.40% of the population).
(10) Inflation 14% (43th Rank, 1991) High
(11) Unemployment 1-2% employment
(12) Labour Force By Occupation: 80% in Industry & others, 20% in agriculture.
(13) Main Industries: Petroleum, steel, motor vehicles, aerospace, telecommunications, chemicals, heavy industries, electronics, food processing, lumber and the defence

External

(14) Exports: $110.7 billion (9th 1989)
(15) Imports: $114.7 billion (10th 1989) Trade Deficit:$4.00 billion)
(16) Export Goods: Petroleum and petroleum products, natural gas, metals, coal, agricultural products and wide variety of manufacturing goods
(17) Main Export Partners: Eastern Bloc 49%, EU 14%, Cuba 5%, US and Afghaistan

(18) Imported goods: Grain and other agricultural products, machinery & equipment, steel products,(including large diameter pipes) consumer manufactures

(19) Import Partners: Eastern Block 54%, EU 11%, Cuba, China, US

(20) External debt: $55 billion (2.5% of GDP)

(21) Economic Aid: $ 147.6 billion

(22) Public Finance: Revenue: $422 billion & Expenses: $510 billion. Fiscal deficit $ 88 billion 4% of GDP.

Chapter - 18

Economy of Russia

Russia has an upper-middle income mixed and transition economy with state ownership in strategic areas of the economy. Market reforms in the 1990s privatized much of Russian industry and agriculture with notable exception to this privatization occurring in the energy and defence-related sectors.

Russia's vast geography is an important determinant of its economic activity, with some sources estimating that Russia contains over 30% of the world's natural resources. The World Bank estimated the total value of the Russia's natural resources of $75 trilllion. Russia relies on energy revenues to drive most of its growth. Russia has an abundance of oil, natural gas and precious metals, which make a major share of Russia's exports. Russia is considered an "energy superpower". It has the world's largest proven natural gas reserves and is the largest exporter of natural gas. It is also the second-largest exporter of petroleum.

Russia has a large and sophisticated arms industry capable of designing and manufacturing high-tech. military equipment, including a fifth-generation fighter jet, nuclear powered submarines, firearms and short/long range ballistic missiles. The value of Russia's arms exports totalled $ 15.7 billion in 2013 second only to the US. Top military exports from Russia include combat aircraft, air defence systems. Ships and submarines.

The economic development of the country has been uneven geographically with the Moscow region contributing a very high share of the country's GDP. There has been a substantial rise .in wealth inequality in Russia since 1990 (far more than China and other Eastern European Countries). Credit Suisse has described Russian wealth inequality as so extreme compared to other countries that it "deserves to be placed in separate category. One study estimates that "the wealth held offshore by Russians is about three times larger than official net foreign reserves and is comparable in magnitude to total household financial assets held in Russia.

Economic History of Soviet Economy

Beginning in 1928, the course of the Soviet Union's economy was guided by five year plans. By the 1950s, during the preceding few decades the Soviet Union had rapidly evolved from a mainly agrarian society into a major industrial power. By the 1970s the Soviet Union entered the era of stagnation. The complex demands of the modern economy and inflexible administration overwhelmed and constrained the central planners. The volume of decisions facing planners in Moscow became overwhelming. The cumbersome procedures for bureaucratic administration foreclosed the free communication and flexible response required at the enterprise level for dealing with worker alienation, customers and suppliers. From 1975 to 1985, corruption and data fiddling became common practice among bureaucracy to report satisfied targets and quotas thus entrenching the crisis. Since 1986, Mikhail Gorbachev attempted address economic problems by moving towards a market oriented socialist economy. Gorbachev's policies had failed to rejuvenate the Soviet economy, though instead, Perestoroika set off a proactive of political and economic disintegration culminating in the breakup of Soviet Union in 1991.

Transition to Market Economy (1991-98)

Following the collapse of the Soviet Union, Russia had undergone a radical transformation, moving from centrally planned economy to a globally integrated market economy. Corrupt and haphazard privatization processes turned over major state-owned firms to politically connected 'Oligarchs" which has full equity ownership highly concentrated.

Yelsin's progress of radical market- oriented reforms came to be known as a "shock therapy". It was based on the policies associated with the Washington Consensus, recommendation of Iman a group of top American economists including Larry Summers. The result was disastrous, with real GDP falling by more than 40% by 1999. Hyperinflation which wiped out personal savings, crime and destitution spreading rapidly. This was accompanied by a drop in standard of living, including surging economic inequality and poverty, alongwith increased excess mortality and decline in life expectancy.

The majority of state enterprises were privatized amid great controversy and subsequently came to be owned by insiders for less than they were worth. For example, the director of a factory during the Soviet regime often become the owner of the same enterprise. Under the government's cover, outrageous financial manipulations were performed that enriched a narrow group of individuals at the key positions of business and government. Many of them promptly invested their new found wealth abroad producing an enormous capital flight.

Difficulties in collecting government revenues amid the collapsing economy and a dependence on short term borrowing to finance the deficits led to 1998 Russian Financial Crisis.

In the 1990s, Russia was "the largest borrower" from IMF with loans totaling $20 billion. The IMF was a subject of criticism for lending so much as Russia introduced little of reforms permitted for the money and large part of these funds could have been diverted from their intended purpose and included in the flow of capital left in the country illegally.

Recovery of Growth (1999-2008)

Russia bounced back from August 1998 financial crisis with surprising speed. Much of the reason for the recovery was the dilution of the rouble, which made domestic producers more competitive nationally and internationally.

Between 2000 and 2008, Russian economy got a major boost from rising commodity prices. GDP grew on average 7% per annual. Disposable income more than doubled and in dollar-denominated terms increased eightfold. The volume of consumer credit between 2000 and 2006 increased 45 times, fueling a boom in private consumption. The number of people living below poverty line declined from 30% to 14% in 2008.

Inflation remained a problem, however, as the central bank aggressively expanded money supply to combat appreciations of the ruble. Nevertheless, in 2007 the World Bank declared that the Russian economy achieved "unprecedented macroeconomic stability". Until October 2007, Russia maintained impressive fiscal disciplion with the budget surpluses every year from 2000.

2009-2014

Russian Banks were hit by the global credit crunch in 2008. Though no long term damage was done thanks to proactive and timely response by the government and Central Bank which shielded the banking system from effect of the global financial crisis. A sharp, but brief recession in Russia was followed by a strong recovery beginning in late 2009.

After 16 years of negotiations Russia's membership to the WTO was accepted in 2011. In 2013, Russia was labeled a high-income economy by the World Bank.

Russian leaders repeatedly spoke of need of diversification of its economy from dependence on oil and gas which constitute 70% of the exports. This economic model has its own limitation and economy is based on prices of oil in the international market as well as recession in international market or export partners country. In 2013, Russian economy expanded by 1.3% on account of decline in oil prices in the international market and recession in EU which is the largest export partner of Russia. Turmoil in nebouring Ukrane also added to the uncertainty and suppressed investment.

According to survey provided by Financial Time in 2012, Russia was second by economic performance among G 20, followed by Saudi Arabia. Economic performance is measured on seven points. GDP growth, budget deficit and government debt for 2012, economic recovery- output compared pre-crisis peak, change in debt since 2009, change in unemployment from 2009 to 2013, and finally the deviation of the current account from balance. The country has made substantial improvement recently in areas like innovations and trade freedom. Since 2008, Moscow has been repeatedly named as the "billionaire capital of the world" by Forbes,

2014 –Present

Following the annexation of Crimea in March 2014 and Russia's involvement in the outgoing conflict in Ukraine, US, the EU, Canada and Japan imposed sanctions on Russia's financial, energy, and defence sectors. Some EU member countries were split on further sanctions but have nominated to go down the sanction route. This led to the decline of the Russian rubble and sparked fears of a Russian financial crisis. Russia responded with sanctions against a number of countries, including one-year total ban on food imports from EU and US. As of 2018 it is estimated that Western sanctions may have reduced Russian economy by as much as 6%.

GDP growth declined to 0.6% in 2014. As of the 2nd and 3rd quarter of 2015, inflation was 8%, the economy has contracted by 4.6% economy entered recession. To balance the state budget in 2015, oil price would need to be around \$74 as opposed to \$104 for 2014. Russia has \$500 billion in foreign reserves, but holds \$360 billion in 2015. Russian economy is not a crisis but a new reality" to which it should adopt primarily due to the low oil prices. GDP has fallen 3.7%, income – by 4.3% Salaries- by 9.3% and inflation 12.9%. Number of people living poverty line were having monthly income \$140 increased by more than 2.3 million people. Russia is rated as the most unequal of the world's major countries.

During 2014-15, a quarter of banks in Russia left the market, the enterprises of Russian Bank Guarantee fund reached 1 trillion rouble.

At the end of 2016, the US imposed further sanctions on the Russian Federation in response to the 2016 the US government election where Russia suspected to interfere in the election. In 2016, the Russian economy was the sixth largest economy in the world by PPP and twelfth largest at market exchange rates. Income is unequally distributed and 110 billirains in Russia hold 35% of all financial assets. Russia has second largest volume of illicit money outflows, having lost over \$880 billion between 2002 and 2011.

Russian economy risked going into recession from early 2014 mainly due to falling oil prices, sanctions and subsequent capital flights. While in

2014, GDP growth remained positive at 0.6% in 2015, Russian economy shrunk by 3.7% and was expected to shrink further in 2016.

A poll completed in 2018 among 1400 managers of non-hydrocarbons Russian businesses demonstrated huge level of pessimism, with majority describing the economic situation in the country as catastrophic. 73% of respondents in large business and 77% in medium and small are dealing with a "crisis.", while only 4% described it as "good". 50% suffered from increased real tax rates, 60% were hit by increasing public utility tariffs.

Year	*GDP (in Billion $) Nominal*	*GDP $ billion PPP*	*Growth %*	*Inflation rate%*	*Unemployment %*	*Govt. debt %*
1992	1730	11482	-	-	5.2	-
1993	1591.9	10724	8.7	874.6	5.9	
1997	1406.3	9557	1.4	14.8	11.8	
2000	1635.3	11170	10	20.8	10.6	55.7
2008	3298.9	23054	5.2	14.1	6.2	7.4
2014	3892	27072	0.7	7.8	5.2	15.6
2017	4007.8	27834	1.5	3.7	5.2	17.4

Currency & Central Bank

Russia rouble is the unit of currency of Russian Federation. It is accepted as legal tender in the partially recongnised states of Abkhazia and South Ossetia and the unrecognized Donets Republic and Logan.

The Russian monetary system is managed by the Bank of Russia. Founded on 13 July 1990 as the State Bank of the RSFSR, Bank of Russia assumed responsibilities of the Central Bank following the breakup of the Soviet Union in 1991.

According to the Constitution, Bank of Russia is an independent entity, with the primary responsibility of protecting the stability of the national currency, the rouble. It is also chief regulator and a lender of last resort for the banking industry in Russia. Bank of Russia is governed by a board of directors, headed by a governor who is appointed by the President of Russia.

Large current account surpluses caused rapid real appreciation of the rouble between 2000 and 2008. Bank of Russia attempted to combat this trend aggressively accumulating foreign currency resources. This was a major contributing to relatively high inflation rates during this period. Central Bank policy evolved following the global financial crisis. Instead of targeting a fixed exchange ratesvs dollar and euro, Bank of Russia shifted in focus to inflation targeting. In April 2012, Russian inflation reached record level low of 3.6%.

The Russian Central Bank has been planning to free float the Russian rouble and has been widening the currency trading band and expects the rouble to be fully free floating in 2015. However, the rouble has fallen significantly since 2013 when the Central bank announced the plans. On 3rd October 2014 the US-rouble exchange rate was 40 Russian roubles to USD 1, up from 32.19 roubles for the same period last year. This represents a decline of 24.26%. The Russian Central Bank has stated that Russian banks are also able to withstand a devaluation of upto 25% - 30% in January 2014 when the rouble has just began to decline. The Russian Central Bank spent $88billion in order to stem the fall of rouble in 2014. Due to the Central Bank intervention and stronger oil prices, the rouble rebounded sharply at the beginning of 2015. In April 2015, Ksenia Kidaeva, Central Bank's Deputy Governor stated that hebelieved the currency has stabilized at the present rate of around 50 roubles to USD1.

Along with a rapid devaluation of the ruble, inflation in Russia has greatly raised. In October 2014, the rate of inflation was reported to be 8% although this was well below the 2013.30% inflation rate experienced in 1992. In November 2007, inflation was at its lowest ever point since the fall of Soviet Union @2, 5%.

Public Policy

Fiscal Policy

Russia was expected to have a Government budget deficit of $21 billion in 2016. The budget deficit was narrowed to 0.6% in 2017 from 2.28% in 2016 of GDP.

National Wealth Fund

On 01-01-2004, the Government of Russia established Stabilization fund of Russian Federation as a part of the federal budget to balance it if oil prices fails. On 01-02-2008 the Stabilization fund was divided into two parts. The first part is a reserve fund equal to 10% of GDP (10% of GDP equals to $200 billion) and was to be invested in a similar way as the Stabilization fund. The Second Fund is to be invested into more risky investments, including the shares of foreign companies.

Public debt

Russia has very low debt to GDP ratio, it is among the lowest ratio in the world. Most of its external debt is private. In 2016, its debt to GDP ratio was 12%.

As a Chief Successor state to the Soviet Union, Russia took up the responsibility for paying USSR's external debt which was $166 billion.

Protectionism

Russia is one of the leading nations to protectionist policies. Russia put significant protectionist policies in place. Russia's strategic trade block consisting of Russia, Belarus and Karcukstan is responsible for a significant portion of worldwide protectionism during 2013. Of the protectionist policies, 43% were targeted bailouts and subsidies for local companies while 15% were tariff measures. Since 2008, Russia has implemented many protectionist measures, about the same scale as did India,however, the most protectionist state was the US.

Corruption

Starting from Russia's second term, very few corruption cases have been the subject of outrange. Putin system is remarkable for its uniquitous and open merging of the civil service and business, as well as its use of relatives, friends and acquaintances to benefit from budgetary expenditures and take over the state property. Corporate property and land raiding is common place. Corruption in Russia is perceived a significant problem impacting all aspects of life, including administration, law enforcement, healthcare and education. The phenomenon of corruption is strongly established in the historical model of public governance in Russia and attributed to general weakness of rule of law in Russia. According to 2016 results of corruption Perception Index a Transparency International, Russia ranked 13th place out of 176 countries.

There are many different estimates of actual costs of corruption. According to official government statistics Rosstat, "shadow economy" occupied only 15% of Russia's GDP in 2011 amounted to only 3.5% to 7% of GDP. In comparison, some independent experts maintain the corruption consumes as much as 25% of Russia's GDP. A World Bank report puts the figure of 48%. There is also the interesting shift in main forces of bribery: whereas previously officials took bribe to shut their eyes to legal infractions, they now take them simply to perform their duties. Many experts admit that in recent years, corruption in Russia become a business. In 1990s, businessmen had to pay different criminal groups to provide protection. Nowadays this "protective" function is performed by officials. Corrupt hierarchies characterize different sectors of economy including education.

In the end, the Russian population pays for this corruption. Some experts believe that rapid increases in monthly bills significantly outplacing the rate of inflation are a direct result of high volume of corruption at the highest level.

Sectors

In Russia, services are the biggest sector of economy and account for 58% of GDP within the services, the most significant segments are wholesale and retail trade, repair of motor vechicles, motorcycles and personal and household goods (17% of total GDP), public administration, health and education (12%) real estate (9%) and transport storage and communication (7%). Industry contributes 40% to total output mining 11%, manicure 13%

and construction 4% are most important industries segment. Agriculture accounts for the remaining 2%.

Primary

Energy

The mineral – packed Ural Mountains are the vast fossil fuel (oil, gas, cold) and timber reserves of Siberia and the Russian Far East make Russia rich in natural resources, which dominate Russian exports. Oil and Gas exports, specifically, continue to be the main source of hard currency.

The petroleum Industry in Russia is one of the largest in the world. Russia has the largest reserves, and is the largest exporter of natural gas. It has the second highest coal reserves, the eighth highest oil reserves and the largest export of oil in the world in absolute number. Per Capita oil production in Russia, though, is not that high. As of 2007, Russia was producing 69603 bb/day per 1000 people., much less than Canada (102575bb/day), South Arabia (371363bb/day) or Norway 554244 bb/day) or UK(27,807 bb/day.

Mining

Russia is also a leading producer and exporter of minerals and gold. Russia is largest diamond producing nation in the World, estimated to produce over 33 million carats in 2013, or 25% of global output valued over $3.4 billion with state owned ALROSA accounting for approximately 95% of all Russian production.

Expecting the area to become more accessible as climate change melts Arctic ice, and believing the area contains large reserves of untapped oil and natural gas, Russia explores on 2 August 2007 in submersibles planted the Russian flag on Arctic seabed, staking a claim of energy source right up to the North Pole. Reaction to the event was mixed. President Vladimir Putin congratulated to explorers for the" outstanding scientific project" while Canadian officials stated the expedition was just a public show.

Under the Federal law on continental shelf developed upon proposal from the federal agency managing the state funds of mineral resources, or its territorial office, the Russian government approves the list of some section of mined resources that are passed for development without any contests or auctions. Some sections of mineral resources of federal importance that are situated in Russia and stretch out of item continent shelf, some gas deposits of Federal importance that are handed over to prospecting and developing mineral resources under a joint licence. The Russian government is also empowered to decide on the handover of previously mentioned sections of mineral resources for development without any contest or auction.

Forestry

Russia has more than a fifth of world's forestry which makes it the largest forest country in the world. However, according to 2012 study by the Food & Agriculture Organization of the UN and the Government of Russian Federation, the considerable potential of Russian forests is underutilized and Russians share the global trade in forest production is less than 4%.

Agriculture

Russia comprise roughly three quarters of the territory of the former Soviet Union, Following the break- up of the Soviet Union in 1991 nearly 10 years of decade, Russian Agriculture began to show signs of improvement due to organizational and technology modernization. Northern areas concentrate mainly of livestock and the southern parts and western Siberia produce grains. The restructuring formal state farms has been an extremely slow process. The new land code passed by Duma in 2002 should speed restructuring and attract new domestic investment to Russian agriculture. Private farms and garden pilots of individuals account for over one-half of all agricultural production. In 2016, agriculture has surpassed the arms industry as Russia's second largest export sector after oil and gas.

Study of economy of Soviet Russia is divided between the economy of Soviet Union known as USSR which was dissolved in 1991 and Russian Empire was formed.

USSR economy was based on system of state ownership of the means of production, collective farming, industrial manufacturing and central administrative planning. Economy east state controlled investment, public ownership of industrial assets, macroeconomic stability, reliable unemployment and high job security.

From 1928, Soviet Union's economy was guided by five years plan. By 1950, Soviet Union had rapidly evolved from an agrarian society into a major industrial power. Its transformative capacity attracted developing countries who adopted Soviet planning system as their economic development model consistently appealed to the intellectuals of developing countries in Asia. Impressive growth rate during the first five year plans (1928 onwards) are particularly notable given that this period is nearly congruent with Great Depression during the period, the Soviet Union encountered a rapid industrial growth while other regions were suffering from crisis. Netherthless, impoverished base upon which five year sought to build meant that at the commencement of operation Barbarossa's the country was still poor.

Soviet Union had oil and gas ample. After oil prices collapsed in 1986. Mikhail Gorbachev came to power in 1985, he began the process of liberalization by dissenting the command economy and moving towards a mixed economy. At its desolution at the end of 1991, the Soviet Union begat a Russian Federation with the growing pile of $66 billion in external loan and with barely few billion dollars in net gold and foreign exchange reserves.

Transportation

Russian Railways accounts for 2.5% of Russia's GDP. The percentage of freight and passenger traffic that goes by rail is unknown, since no statistics are available for private transportation such as private automobiles or company-owned trucks. In 2007, about 1.3 billion passengers, 1.3 billion tons of freight went via Russian Railways. In 2007 the company owned 19,700 goods and passenger locomotives, 24,200 passenger cars (carriages) (2007) and 526,900 freight cars (goods wagons) (2007). A further 270,000 freight cars in Russia are privately owned. In 2009 Russia had 128,000 kilometres of common-carrier railroad line, of which about half was electrified and carried most of the traffic; over 40% was double track or better.

Construction

In 2009 the Russian construction industry survived its most difficult year in more than a decade. The 0.8% reduction recorded by the industry for the first three quarters of 2010 looked remarkably healthy in comparison with the 18.4% slump recorded the previous year, and construction firms became much more optimistic about the future than in previous months. The most successful construction firms concluded contracts worth billions of dollars and planned to take on employees and purchase new building machinery. The downturn served to emphasize the importance of the government to the construction market compulsory.

Insurance

According to the Central Bank of Russia 422 insurance companies operate on the Russian insurance market by the end of 2013. The concentration of insurance business is significant across all major segments except compulsory motor third party liability market, as the Top 10 companies in 2013 charged 58.1% premiums in total without compulsory health insurance (CHI). Russian insurance market in 2013 demonstrated quite significant rate of growth in operations. Total amount of premiums charged (without CHI) in 2013 is RUB 904.9 bln (increase on 11.8% compared to 2012), total amount of claims paid is RUB 420.8 bln (increase on 13.9% compared to 2012). Premiums to GDP ratio (total without CHI) in 2013 increased to 1.36% compared to 1.31% a year before. The share of premiums in household spending increased to 1.39%. Level of claims paid on the market total without CHI is 46.5%, insufficient increase compared to 2012. The number of policies in 2013 increased on 0.1% compared to 2012, to 139.6 mlllion policies.

Although relative indicators of the Russian insurance market returned to pre-crisis levels, the progress is achieved mainly by the increase of life insurance and accident insurance, the input of these two market segments in premium growth in 2013 largely exceeds their share on the market. As before, life insurance and accident insurance are often used by banks as an appendix to a credit contract protecting creditors from the risk of credit default in case of borrower's death or disability. The rise of these lines is connected, evidently, with the increase in consumer loans, as the total sum of credit obligations of population in 2013 increased on 28% to RUB 9.9 trillion. At the same time premium to GDP ratio net of life and accident insurance remained at the same level of 1.1% as in 2012. Thus, if "banking" lines of business are excluded, Russian insurance market is in stagnation stage for the last four years, as premiums to GDP ratio net of life and accident insurance remains at the same level of 1.1% since 2010.

Information technology

The IT market is one of the most dynamic sectors of the Russian economy. Russian software exports have risen from just $120 million in 2000 to $3.3 billion in 2010.Since the year 2000 the IT market has started growth rates of 30–40% a year, growing by 54% in 2006 alone. The biggest sector in terms of revenue is system and network integration, which accounts for 28.3% of the total market revenues.Meanwhile, the fastest growing segment of the IT market is offshore programming.

Currently Russia controls 3% of the offshore software development market and is the third leading country (after India and China) among software exporters]. Such growth of software outsourcing in Russia is caused by a number of factors. One of them is the supporting role of the Russian Government. The government has launched a program promoting construction of IT-oriented technology parks (Techno parks)—special zones that have an established infrastructure and enjoy a favorable tax and customs regime, in seven different places around the country: Moscow, Novosibirsk, Nizhny Novgorod, Kaluga, Tumen, Republic of Tatarstan and St. Petersburg Regions. Another factor stimulating the IT sector growth in Russia is the presence of global technology corporations such as Intel, Google, Motorola and others which have intensified their Software development activities and opened their R & D centers in Russia.

Tourism

Tourism in Russia has seen rapid growth since the late Soviet period, first domestic tourism and then international tourism. Rich cultural heritage and great natural variety place, Russia is among the most popular tourist destinations in the world.

In 2013, Russia was visited by 28.4 million tourists being the ninth most visited country in the world. The most visited destinations in Russia are Moscow and Saint Petersburg, recognized as world cities.

Mergers and Acquisitions

Between 1985 and 2018 almost 28,500 mergers or acquisitions have been announced in Russia. This cumulates to an overall value of around 984 bil. USD which translates to 5.456 bilion RUB. In terms of value, 2007 has been the most active year with 158 bil. USD, whereas the number of deals peaked in 2010 with 3,684 (964 compared to the value record year 2007). Since 2010 value and numbers have decreased constantly and another wave of M&A is expected.

The majority of deals in, into or out of Russia have taken place in the financial sector (29%), followed by banks (8.6%), oil and gas (7.8%) and Metals and Mining (7.2%).

Present Status of Russian Federation Economy At Glance

(1) Currency: Russian rouble rouble= 0.15 USD

(2) Fiscal year: Calder year

(3) Trade Organizations: WTO, GECT, CIC, APEC, EACO, G-20 and others

(4) GDP: $1.579 trillion (Nominal 2017, 11th Rank)
$4.007 trillion (PPP 2017, 6th Rank)

(5) GDP Growth: 0.1% in 2016, 1.5% in 2017, 1.6% 2018 and 1.5% in 2019 (estimated)

(6) GDP per capita: $100608 (Nominal, 62nd Rank $ 27899 (PPP, 48th Rank)

(7) Population: 159 million

(8) Labour Force: 76.8 million 48.92% of population

(9) GDP by Sector: Agriculture 4.7%, Industry 32.4% & Services 62.3 – 2017

(10) Inflation 2.5%

(11) Unemployment 4.5% employment assured lifetime.

(12) Labour by Occupation: Agriculture 9.4%, Insurance 27.6%, Services 63%

(13) Average net monthly salary: 37758 roubles/$503 per month - 2018

(14) Main Industries: Petroleum, natural gas, mining, coal, chemicals, metals, rolling mills, machine building, aircraft, space vehicles, defence equipment, medical instruments, scientific instruments, consumer durables, textiles, foodstuffs, handicrafts, transportation equipments, communication equipments, agricultural machinery

(15) Ease of doing business: 35th rank.

(16) Exports: $528.9 billion Imports $182.3 billion Trade Surplus $346.6 billion.

(17) Export Goods: Petroleum and petroleum products, natural gas, metals, wood & wood products, chemicals, wide variety of civilian and military manufactures

(18) Main Export Partner: EU 45.8%, China9.8%, Belarus 4.9% Turkey 4.8%, South Korea 3.5%, others 31.2%

(19) Import Goods: Machinery, Vechicles, pharamaceuticals products, plastic, semi-finished metals, proke meat, fruits, medical insruments, iron,steel

(20) Import Main Partners: EU38.2%, China 20.9%, US 6.1%, Belarus 5.2%, Japan 3.7% Others 26%

(21) FDI Stock: $361billin

(22) Foreign Reserves: $475 billion (Feb.2019)

(23) Gross Extenal debt $529.6 billion - 2017 33.54% of GDP (Nominal)

(24) Public debt: 10.6 % of GDP i.e. $157. 9 Billion - 2017

(25) Fiscal: Revenues $221.886 - 2016 Expenses: $258.42 billion – 2017 Fiscal Deficit $36.534 billion 2.31% of GDP. Well managed

(26) Credit Rating S & P AB+ (Domestic), BBB+ Foreign)
T & C BB+ Outlook Positive
Moody Ba1, Outlook Stable, FITCH BBB-, Outlook- Positive.

Critical Observations on Economy of Soviet Union (USSR, upto 1991 prior to dissolution) and Russia (after 1991).

(1) Study of the Economy of Soviet Union and Russia is divided into 2 parts; (a) Economy of USSR prior to its dissolution in 1991 and (b) Economy of present Russia after 1991

(2) USSR economy was based on system of state ownership of the means of production, collective farming, industrial manufacturing and central administrative planning. Economy was state controlled investment, public ownership of industrial assets, macroeconomic stability, negligible unemployment and high job security.

(3) From 1928, Soviet Union's economy was guided by five years plan. By 1950, Soviet Union had rapidly evolved from a mainly agrarian society into a major industrial power. Its transformative capacity i.e. "proven ability to carry backward countries speedily through the crisis of modernization and industrialization meant communism consistently appealed to the intellectuals of developing countries in Asia. Impressive growth rate during the first five years plans (1928-1940) are particularly notable given that this period is nearly congruent with Great Depression. During the period, Soviet Union encountered a rapid economic growth while other regions were suffering from crisis. Nevertheless impoverished base upon which five year plans sought to build meant that at the commencement of operation Barbarossa the country was still poor.

(4) Oil and gas stocks were ample. But prices of oil and gas came down drastically in 1986 which resulted in crisis and slow down of Soviet Union economy.

(5) President Mikhail Gorbachev came to power in 1985. He began the process of economic liberalization by dismantling the commercial economy and moving towards a mixed economy. At the dissolution at the end of 1991, the Russian Federation with a growing pile had $66 billion in external loan and with barely a few billion dollars in gold and foreign exchange reserves. This loan was waived by World Bank under Moratorium.

(6) Though the Soviet Union economy was primarily based on planning, complex demands of the modern economy somewhat constrained the central planners. Corruption and data fiddling became common practice among the bureaucrats by reporting fulfilled targets and quotas. From the Stalin era to the early Brezhnev era, Soviet Union grew much slower than Japan and slightly faster than US. GDP levels in 1950 were $510 billion in Soviet Union, $161 billion in Japan and $ 1456 billion in USA. In 1965, corresponding values were $1011billion, $587 billion and $2607 billion respectively. Soviet Union maintained itself as a sound largest economy in both Nominal and Purchasing Power Parity value for much of Cold War till 1988, when Japan's economy exceeded $3 trillion in Nominal value.

(7) Soviet Union small consumer sector under 60% of GDP in 1990 while industrial and agriculture sectors continued to 22% and 20% respectively. Agriculture was Predominant occupation in Soviet Union in 1980 before massive industrialization under Joseph Stalin. Service sector was of low importance.

(8) Though GDP crossed $1trillion in 1970 and $2 trillion in 1980, the effects of central planning was progressively distorted due the rapid growth in Soviet Union.

(9) We shall observe that though the planning was the main base of economy, planning process was not consistent and it depended on priority given by the Head of the State. Head of State used to give sometimes priority to capital goods resulting in ample production of capital goods which were not bought by the people and large stock used to remain unutilized. Consumer goods were in scarcity that time and needed to be imported. Then priority was given to consumer goods and reverse situation used to occur. Corruption and data fiddling added fuel to the fire and target reported as achieved were not in practice achieved. Economy figures were unreliable.

(10) Control over communist nation in Soviet Union was weaken which resulted in dissolution of Soviet Union in 1991. Perhaps Gorbachev's economic liberalization policy was the immediate cause for dissolution.

(11) Soviet Union helped India in developing economy by drawing Five Year Plans. Soviet Union was a strategic partner of India and Pokhran automic energy plant was set up by USSR in India. It helped India in becoming self-sufficient in defence. Also Bombay IIT was a great contribution of Russian Federation for higher technological education for Indian students.

Russian Federation

Critical Observations of Economy of Russia after dissolution in 1991

(1) Russia has an upper middle income mixed and transmission economy with state ownership in strategic areas of the economy. Market reforms in the 1990s privatized much of the Russian industry and agriculture, with notable exception to this privatization occurring in the energy and defence-related sectors.

(2) Russia has 30% of natural resources of the world resources in the form of petrol, natural gas and gold mining with the population of 27 crores. Value of Russia's 30% natural resources have been estimated $ 75 trillion. USA also has natural resources of 30% of the world resources with32 crores population. That means 2 countries with 64 crores population have 60% of the world's natural resources. Rest of the world has population of 636 crores with 40% of world natural resourceswhich works out to 0.0628% world's naturalre sources per 1 crore population. In case of Russia and USA together, this ratio works out to approximately 0.9375% world's natural resources per 1 crore population i.e. 15 times more than the population in rest of the world.

(3) Thus nature has divided the world into very rich people and poor people. This wide disparity has resulted in poor becoming poorer and rich becoming richer. There is no perfect system/machinery to resolve this disparity.

(4) There was financial crisis on dissolution of Soviet Russia in 1991. As a main Successor, Russia took the responsibility for the financial liability of USSR of external debt $166 billion.

(5) Following the collapse of the Soviet Union, in 1991, Russia had undergone a radical transformation, moving from centrally planned economy to a globally integrated market economy. Corrupt and half hazard privatization processes turned over major state-owned firms to politically connected "oligarchs" which has felt equity ownership highly concentrated.

(6) Yelsin's program of radical market oriented reforms came to be known as a "Shock Therapy". It was based on the politics associated with the Washington Consensus, recommendation of IMF and a group of top American economists, including Larry Summers. The result was disastrous, with real GDP falling by 40% by 1999. Hyperinflation which wiped out personal savings, crime and destitution spreading rapidly. This was accompanied by a drop in the standard of living, including surging economic inequality and poverty, alongwith increased excess mortality and a decline in life expectancy. But subsequently, the economy recovered.

(7) The majority of state enterprises were privatized amid great controversy and subsequently came to be owned by insiders for less than what there were worth. The director of a factory during the Soviet regime often become owner of the same enterprise. Under the government's cover, outrigger financial manipulation were performed that enriched a narrow group of individuals at key positions of business and government. Many of them promptly invested their new wealth abroad producing an enormous capital flight.

(8) Difficulties in collecting government revenues amid collapsing economy and a dependence on short term borrowing to finance the deficits led to the 1998 Russian financial crisis.

(9) In the 1990s Russia was "a large borrower" from the IMF with loans totaling $20 billion. The IMF was the subject of criticism for lending so much as Russia introduced little of reforms promised for the money and a large part of these funds could have been diverted from their intended purpose and included in the flow of capital left in the country illegally.

(10) Russia bounced back from August 1998 financial crash by devaluation of Rubble which made domestic producers more competitive nationally and internationally.

(11) Russia became a member of WTO in 1999. Russian exports were 70% in oil and gas. It wanted to diversify to foster a high technology sector.

(12) Russia's financial growth was merely 1.3 %in 2013 due to recession in European Union and fall in oil prices, lack of spare industrial capacity.

(13) Political turmoil in Ukraine by separating Crimea from Ukraine, Russia under military force resulted in imposing financial sanctions by USA, EU and other countries in 2014 slowed down the Russian economy by growth rate of about 1% in 2014. But it bounced back and achieved recovery by growth rate 5% in the next year because

of export of oil, natural gas and artillery. Russian economy is however hit by 6%.

(14) Russian economy has strong military base and presently it is exporting defence machinery consisting of most advanced defence aircraft AS400. India has imported AS400 from Russia. In fact, India's main defence machinery is imported in India from Russia such as military aircrafts as Mig etc. Russia is also exporting AS400 to many countries like Turkey, japan. After nuclear test by India, there was large opposition from all countries including US who banned to make any cooperation with India in weapons and other matters, Russia is the only country who backed India and supported its automic tests. Russia gave India nuclear reactors for developing additional nuclear capacity of India. Russia was a strategic partner of India that time and even today.

(15) Russia has also made tremendous progress in space research and America and Russia are planning to send people in orbit in Mars and other satellites.

(16) Due to Sanctions on account of Ukraine and Russia interference in the American election in 2016, Russia is suffering from sanctions from US. This creates exchange problem for Russia, China, and Iran. These countries are therefore settling their monetary payments in their local currency. China and Russia are planning to make their currency as world currency backed by gold. Infact, China is in the basket of currencies. It has invested its huge surpluses into US dollar denominated Treasury bonds. Recently China has sold huge amount of US treasury bonds and the huge dollar fund has been converted in purchasing and accumulating huge gold stock to support its currency as international recognised currency. Russia has also invested and accumulated in gold stock to support its currency as internationally recognised currency. But their currencies will be unlikely to be accepted as world currency as nations in the world are not treating these communist countries as reliable. US dollar's status may be reduced but it will be worldwide accepted currency for exchange. Whether these currencies will be recognised as international currencies in lieu of US dollar currency is an open question and may be resolved in future.

(17) Putin is the head of Russia for many years. He has developed relation with many countries and is in a dominating position competing US and China. In Seria's issue, IS territorism was destroyed by Russia alongwith US and other countries. It has good relation with Iran who is also subject to Sanctions from USA on the issue of creating automic weapons by Iran.

(18) Russia has external debt \$529 billion with GDP 1.579 billion. Ratio of external debt works out to 33.50% which is high and

should be curtailed to 15 -20% to enable Russia to avoid debt servicing trap.

(19) In Country like Russia where jobs are secured, 4.5% unemployment looks high and needs to be reduced. Further, assurance of job will instigate workers to work slow thereby affecting productivity. This should be avoided in any case. Productivity of labour should be increased and government should concentrate on this issue.

(20) Though main export of Russia is petroleum, petroleum products and natural gas, Russia has also developed the manufacturing of civilian and military equipments and Russia is mainly exporting these equipments to many countries. This gives good income resource to Russia.

(21) Russia is preparing for "deep Space" research to assess the possibility to send people from Russia other planet for permanent residence. This also includes research in the planets for remote places.

(22) Based on Artificial Intelligence, Russian Killer Robot Army is ready to do work in defence area.

(23) Russia has withdrawn from "INF" Agreement with US resulting in competition of creating new nuclear war dangerous weapons which is disastrous to the world and mankind.

(24) In Merger &Actuation, Russia has made good progress.

CHAPTER - 19

ECONOMY OF UNITED KINGDOM (U.K.)

Background

In the 18th century the UK was the first country to industrialize and in the 19th century it had a dominant role in the global economy, accounting for 9.1% of the World's GDP in 1870. The Second Industrial Revolution was also taking place in the US and German Empire; this presented an increasing economic challenge for the UK. The costs of fighting World War I and World War II further weakened the UK's relative position. In the 21st century, however, it remains a global power and has an influential role in the world economy.

Her Majesty's Treasury headed by the Chancellor of the Exchequer exercised government's involvement. Since 1979, broadly laissez-faire approach was taken by the British government. From 1997, its Monetary Policy Committee has been setting interest rates, qualitative easing and forward guidance.

The currency of the UK is pound sterling, which is the world's fourth largest reserve currency after US dollar, Euro and Japanese yens and 10th most valued currencies in the world.

The UK is a member of the Commonwealth, European Union (upto 30-03-2019), the G7, the G20, and the World Bank, the OFSACIE, the WTO, and AIIBUN

Current economic status of UK

The economy of the United Kingdom is highly developed and market oriented. It is the fifth national economy of the world measured by Nominal Gross GDP and ninth largest by GDP PPP. Britain's GDP is 3.6% of World GDP.

In International trade, UK was the ninth largest goods exporter and sixth largest goods importer in 2016.It had also third largest inward foreign exchange direct investment and third largest outward foreign exchange direct investment.

Britain consists of England, Scotland, Wales and North Ireland. It is of the most globalized economies. Service sector contributes 80% of the GDP and London is the largest financial market in the world. British aerospace industry is second largest national economy and its pharmaceutical industry is the tenth largest national economy. 26 out of 500 largest companies have headquarters in Britain. Though UK is the net importer of oil since 2005, its economy is boosted by North oil and natural gas production with 2.8 billion barrels in 2016. There is regional disparity in prosperity with South East England and North East Scotland areas being richest in per capita income Size of London economy makes it the largest city by in Europe.

History

British Empire ruling in India from 1797 -1947

Till recently (till 1947/1980), British government ruled many countries as their colonies like India, Australia and Hongkong.

As far as India's experience is concerned, British were not the good rulers. During the Mughal Empire, Indian economy was prosperous with agriculture as its leading industry. Foodgains were produced largely and exported to countries like Japan and Indonesia. Cotton textile of India was leading and exporting large quantities to UK and other Far East countries. India and China had 75% -80% world trade. Fashion of various countries depend on the design of cotton manufacturing in India. Tell 1795, India was financially very prosperous country.

After British came to India, the picture changed completely. British Rulers ignored the agriculture production, cultivation completely. This resulted in droughts and famines in many parts of India resulting in thousands of casualties Epidemics were also ruthlessly and mercilessly handled by Britishers killing thousands of people in Famines.

Britishers had eye on the cotton textile industry of India which was prosperous. Due to the hatred of Indians and their financial prosperity, Britishers concentrated on cotton production in India but shifted all cotton output to Manchester to manufacture cotton into cloth in the name of Industrial Revolution which was brought back to India to sell in the Indian large market to make huge profits. Indian loom owners who were manufacturing cloth in India were ruthlessly prohibited to do this business by imposing very heavy taxes on their products with the result that Indians were completely ruined in cotton business.

British rulers improved road and rail transport facilities but that too for face-lifting transport of cotton from India to UK through ports Of course, these roads and railway facilities were also used by the Indian public.

Sati ban act was passed to stop the Sati custom in India. Standard education system was also established by Britishers. They encouraged Indian students to learn English language. Those who took advantage of the same and completed their education got government jobs in the Government offices. Of course these government servants never actively participated in the Independent movement.

Inequality in India on casteism was also tried to reduce by Britishers. Britishers also introduced Indiam Civil Service examination to select capable administrators. This examination was tuff and free from interference from political leaders. Mr. C. D. Deshmukh, Mr. Netaji Subhash Chandra Bose and many other Indian sappeared and passed this examination (ICS) with top ranks and proved to be good administrators, After Independence, Government of India adopted this system to select capable administrators under IAS examination process free from the political interference.

Independent states in India used to adopt sons/daughters as their heir for future kings of the Independent States if they have no children. This practice was abolished by the British rulers by passing law prohibiting adopted sons/ daughters to give right for future kings of the independent states. There was lot of agitation by the independent states on this issue. This was one of the reason for coup in 1857.

British laws were in favour of British citizens in India and Indians hardly got any justice from these laws especially the freedom Fighters. In fact, freedom Fighters like Vir Sawarkar were mercilessly treated in Andaman-Nikobar jail.

Second World War Prime Minister Mr. Winston Churchill made remarks about India that Indian have no capacity to rule and therefore they should not be given independence. His statement was completely false and full of hatred as persons like C.D. Deshmukh and Subhash Chandra Bose passed the ICS examination with top ranks. Whimsical Churchill was removed as Prime Minister of Great Britain after end of the World War II.

Jalianawala Baug massacre was the glaring example of hatred and mercilessness of Britishers. General Dyer who gave orders to his military soldiers in Jalianawala Baug episode to close all doors of the Baug and shoot the people participated in the Meeting on 13-04-1919 without complying with normal rules of shooting. This resulted in killing thousands of people participated in the Meeting on the spot. There was large agitation in protest all over the country spontaneously. British Rulers enquired with General Dyer about this incidence. He was transferred but not given any capital punishment for this deed. Ultimately, he died of serious desease. British government has yet not expressed any apology for this painful incidence.

Britain broke completely in World War II financially and militarily by losing thousands of Soldiers and by costs of World War I and World War II. British rulers realised that they cannot rule India any more. They granted Indepenance to India on 15th August 1947 but intentionally divided the undivided India into India and Pakistan ensuring that there will be boarder issue between both the countries constantly. USA showed many times the pictures of ruthless treatment given to the mob of Independence fighters in their newspapers and pressurized Britishers to give independent to India forthwith. Efforts of American government also helped to get Indian independence on 15 August 1947.

However, the relationship between India and UK were cordial after Indian Independence. UK was a strategic partner of India in anti-terrorism moment, peace and defence. India purchased from UK a naval warship "Vishal" which was in services of Indian Navy for about 30 years. Another War ship nuclear sub-marine will be built up in India with technical knowhow and skills from UK in the Indian Dockyard. New War Ship will be as strong and mighty as War Ship"Elizabeth" in UK. After inclusion and in service of the new warship, India's Navy strength will tremendously increase to compete with China and Pakistan who are both main enemies of India.

1945-1979

After the Second World War, new Labour Government nationalized the Bank of England, civil aviation, telephone networks, railways, gas, electricity, and coal, iron and steel industries, affecting 2.3 million workers.After World War II, UK enjoyed a long period without a major recession and made a rapid growth in prosperity in which its unemployment rate was very low in 1950-60 not exceeding 3.5% until 1970.Annual rate of growth from 1960 to 1973 was averaged 2.9%, though this rate was far behind than other European countries such as France, Germany and Italy.

Disindustralisation meant closure of operations in mining, heavy industry, and manufacturing, resulting in the loss of highly paid working –class jobs. The UK's share of manufacturing output had risen from 9.5% in 1830 during the Industrial Revolution to 22.9% in the 1870s. It fell to 13.6% by 1913, 10.7% by 1938, and 4.9% by 1973. Overseas competition, lack of innovation, trade unionism, the welfare state, loss of British Empire and cultural attitudes have all been put forward as explanations. It reached crisis point in the 1970s against the backdrop of world-wide energy crisis, high inflation, and a dramatic influx of low-cost manufactured goods from Asia, workforce distribution in Great Britain from 1841-1911, and in England and Wales from 1921-2011.

During the 1973 oil crisis, the 1973-74 Stock Market crash, and the secondary banking crisis of 1973-75, the British economy fell into the 1973-75 recession and the government of Edward Health was ousted by the Labour Party under Harold Wilson, which had previously governed from 1964 to 1970. Wilson formed a minority government in March 1974 after the general election on 28 February ended in a hung parliament. Wilson secured a three-seat overall majority in a second election in October that year.

UK recorded weaker growth than many other European nations in the 1970s;

Even after the recession, the economy was blighted by using unemployment and double-digit inflation which exceeded 20% more than once and was rarely below 10% after 1973.

In 1976, the UK was forced to applying for a loan of Sterling pounds 2.3 billion from the International Monetary Fund. Denis Healey, then Chancellor of the Exchequer, was required to implement public spending cuts and other economic reforms in order to secure the loan, and for a while the British improved, with a growth of 4.3%in early 1979.However, UK was hit by numerous public strike and this unrest resulted in replacing Cunningham in the General Election in May 1979 by Conservative Party Prime Minister Mrs. Margaret Thatcher as a new government.

1979-1997

A new period of neo-liberal economics began with Mrs. Margaret Thatcher as Prime Minister of UK. During the 1980s, many state-owned industries and utilities were privatized, taxes cut, trade union reforms passed and market deregulated. GDP fell by 5.9% initially, but growth subsequently returned and rose to an annual rate of 5% at its peak in 1988which was the highest in Europe.

Unemployment rates in the United Kingdom from 1881 until 2017 reached levels not seen in the UK since the Great Depression of the 1930s.

Thatcher's modernization of the economy was far from trouble-free; her battle with inflation, which in 1980 had risen to 21.9%, resulted in a substantial increase in unemployment from 5.3% in 1979 to over 10.4% by the start of 1982, peaking at nearly 11.9% in 1984 – a level not seen in Britain since the Great Recession. The rise in unemployment coincided with the recession after which UK GDP did not reach its pre-recession rate until 1983. In spite of this, Thatcher was re-elected in June 1983 with a landslide majority. Inflation had fallen to 3.7%, while interest rates were relatively high at 9.56%.

The increase in unemployment was largely due to the government's economic policy which resulted in the closure of outdated factories and coal pits. Manufacturing in England and Wales declined from around 38% of jobs in 1961 to around 22% in 1981. This trend continued for most of the 1980s, with newer industries and the service sector enjoying significant growth. Many jobs were also lost as manufacturing became more efficient and fewer people were required to work in the sector. Unemployment had fallen below 3 million by the time of Thatcher's third successive election victory in June 1987; and by the end of 1989 it was down to 1.6 million.

Britain's economy slid into another global recession in late 1990; it shrank by a total of 6% from peak to through, and unemployment increased from around 6.9% in spring 1990 to nearly 10.7% by the end of 1993. However, inflation dropped from 10.9% in 1990 to 1.3% three years later. The subsequent economic recovery was extremely strong, and unlike after the early 1980s recession, the recovery saw a rapid and substantial fall in unemployment, which was down to 7.2% by 1997, although the popularity of the Conservative government had failed to improve with the economic upturn. The government won a fourth successive election in 1992 under John Major who had succeeded Thatcher in November 1990, but soon afterwards came Black Wednesday, which damaged the Conservative government's reputation for economic competence, and from that stage onwards, the Labour Party was ascendant in the opinion polls, particularly in the immediate aftermath of Tony Blairs election as party leader in July 1994 after the sudden death of his predecessor John Smith.

Despite two recessions, wages grew consistently by around 2% per year in real terms from 1980 until 1997, and continued to grow until 2008.

1997 to 2008.

In May 1997, Labour, led by Tony Blair, won the general election by a landslide after 18 years of Conservative government, and inherited a strong economy with low inflation,falling unemployment, and current account surplus. Four days after the election, Gorden Brown, the new Chancellor of Exchequer, gave the Bank of England the freedom to control monetary policy, which until then had been directed by the government. During Blair's 10 years in office there were 40 successive quarters of economic growth, lasting until the second quarter of 2008. GDP growth, which had briefly reached 4% per year in the early 1990s, gently declining thereafter, was relatively anemic compared to prior decades, such as the 6.5% per year peak in the early 1970s, although growth was smoother and more consistent, annual growth rates averaged 2.68% between 1992 and 2007, with the finance sector accounting for a greater part than previously. The period saw one of the highest GDP growth rates of any developed economy and the strongest of any European nation. At the same time, household debt rose from £420 billion in 1994 to £1 trillion in 2004 and Sterling pounds 1.46 trillion in 2008 – more than the entire GDP of the UK.

GDP year-on-year growth rates (seasonally adjusted) in the UK from 1949 to 2017, showing the four major recessions that have taken place.

UK entered a recession in Q2 of 2008 due to global financial crisis. UK's financial sector was closely connected with any major economy. UK was therefore vulnerable to the crisis.

Beginning with the collapse of Northern Rock, which was taken into public ownership in February 2008, other banks had to be partly nationalized. The Royal Bank of Scotland group, at its peak the fifth-largest bank in the world by market capitalization, was effectively nationalized in October 2008. By mid-2009, HM Treasury had a 70.33% controlling shareholding in RBS, and a 43% shareholding, through UK Financial Investments Limited, in Lloyds Banking Group. The Great Recession, as it came to be known, saw unemployment rise from just over 1.6 million in January 2008 to nearly 2.5 million by October 2009.

The UK had been one of the strongest economies in terms of inflation interest rates and unemployment, all of which remained lower until the 2008–09 recession. In August 2008 the IMF warned that the country's outlook had worsened due to a twin shock: financial turmoil and rising commodity prices. Both developments harmed the UK more than most developed countries, as it obtained revenue from exporting financial services while running deficits in goods and commodities, including food. In 2007, the UK had the world's third largest deficit, due mainly to a large deficit in manufactured goods. In May 2008, the IMF advised the UK government to broaden the scope of fiscal policy to promote external balance. The UK's output per hour worked was on a par with the average for the "old"EU-15 countries.

2009 to present

It took 30 quarters for GDP per capita to recover from the recession.

In March 2009, the Bank of England (BoE) cut interest rates to a historic low of 0.5% and began quantitative easing (QE) to boost lending and shore up the economy. The UK exited the Great Recession in Q4 of 2009 having experienced six consecutive quarters of negative growth, shrinking by 6.03% from peak to trough, making it the longest recession since records began and the deepest since World War II. Support for Labour slumped during the recession, and the general election of 2010 resulted in a coalition government of the Conservatives and the Liberal Democrats, which made deep spending cuts to ease the budget deficit.

In 2011, household, financial, and business debts stood at 420% of GDP in the UK, compared to 279% in Japan, 253% in France, 209% in the United States, 206% in Canada, and 198% in Germany. As the world's most indebted country, spending and investment in the UK were held back after the recession, creating economic malice. However, it was recognised that government borrowing, which rose from 52% to 76% of GDP, helped to avoid a 1930's like Recession. Within three years of the general election, government cuts had led to public sector job losses well into six figures, but the private sector enjoyed strong jobs growth.

Productivity, 1971 to 2016

The 10 years following the Great Recession were characterised by extremes. In 2015, employment was at its highest since records began, and GDP growth had become the fastest in the Group of Seven (G7) and Europe, but workforce productivity was the worst since the 1820s, with any growth attributed to a fall in working hours. Output per hour worked was 18% below the average for the rest of the G7. Real wage growth was the worst since the 1860s, and the Governor of Bank of England described it as a lost decade. Wages fell by 10% in real terms in the eight years to 2016, whilst they grew across the OECD by an average of 6.7%. For 2015 as a whole, the current account deficit rose to a record high of 5.2% of GDP (£96.2bn), the highest in the developed world. In Q4 2015, it exceeded 7%, a level not witnessed during peacetime since records began in 1772. The UK relied on foreign investors to plug the shortfall in its balance of payments. Homes had become less affordable, a problem exacerbated by QE, which kept house prices 22% higher than they would otherwise have been, and equities 25% higher, according to the BoE's own analysis.

A rise in unsecured household debt added to questions over the sustainability of the economic recovery in 2016. The BoE insisted there was no cause for alarm, despite having said two years earlier that the recovery was "neither balanced nor sustainable". It was still very unbalanced, with consumption accounting for 100% of growth in that year. Households ran an unprecedented deficit of 3% of GDP. Unemployment continued to fall, resulting in a 42-year low of 4.4% in June 2017, but real earnings also fell. Following the UK's decision to leave the European Union, the BoE cut interest rates to a new historic low of 0.25% for just over a year to bolster confidence in the economy. It also bought government and corporate bonds, taking the amount of QE since the start of the Great Recession to £435bn.

Government spending and economic management

UK interest rate from 1800 to 2017

Government involvement in the economy is primarily exercised by HM Treasury, headed by the Chancellor of Exchequer. In recent years, the UK economy has been managed in accordance with principles of market liberalization and low taxation and regulation. Since 1997, the Bank of England Monetary Policy Committee headed by the Governor of Bank, has been responsible for setting interest rates at the level necessary to achieve the overall inflation target for the economy that is set by the Chancellor each year. The Scottish Government, subject to the approval of the Scottish Parliament, has the power to vary the basic rate of income tax payable in Scotland by plus or minus 3 pence in the pound, though this power has not yet been exercised.

In the 20-year period from 1986/87 to 2006/07 government spending in the UK averaged around 40% of GDP. In July 2007, the UK had government debt at 35.5% of GDP. As a result of the 2007-10 financial crisis and the late-2010 great recession, government spending increased to a historically high level of 48% of GDP in 2009–10, partly as a result of the cost of a series of bank bailout In terms of net government percentage of GDP, at the end of June 2014 public sector net debt excluding financial sector interventions was

£1304.6 billion, equivalent to 77.3% of GDP. For the financial year of 2013–2014 public sector net borrowing was £93.7 billion. This was £13.0 billion higher than in the financial year of 2012–2013.

Taxation

Taxation in the United Kingdom may involve payments to at least two different levels of government: local government and central government. Local government is financed by grants from central government funds, business rates, council tax, and, increasingly, fees and charges such as those from on-street parking. Central government revenues are mainly from income tax, national insurance contributions, value added tax, corporation tax and fuel duty.

Sectors

Agriculture

Agriculture & Forestry in United Kingdom

Agriculture in the UK is intensive, highly mechanized and efficient by European standards, producing about 50% of food needs in 2008 (down from about 65% in 1993), with less than 1.6% of the labour force (535,000 workers. It contributes around 0.6% of British national value added. Around two-thirds of the production is devoted to livestock, one-third to arable crops. Agriculture is subsidized by the European Union's Common Agricultural Policy.

The UK retains a significant, though reduced, fishing industry. Its fleets, based in towns such as Kingston upon Hull, Grimsy, Fleetwood, Newlyn, Great Yarmath, Peterhead, francerburg, and Lowesstoff bring home fish ranging from sole to herring.

The Blue Book 2013 reports that "Agriculture" added gross value of £9,438 million to the UK economy in 2011.

Construction

Construction Industry in UK

The construction industry of the United Kingdom contributed gross value of £86 billion to the UK economy in 2011. The industry employed around 2.2 million people in the fourth quarter of 2009.There were around 194,000 construction firms in the United Kingdom in 2009, of which around 75,400 employed just one person and 62 employed over 1,200 people. In 2009 the construction industry in the UK received total orders of around £18.7 billion from the private sector and £15.1 billion from the public sector.

The largest construction project in the UK is Cross rail. Due to open in 2018, it will be a new railway line running east to west through London and into the surrounding countryside with a branch to Heathrow Airport. The main feature of the project is construction of 42 km (26 mi) of new tunnels connecting stations in central London. It is also Europe's biggest construction project with a £15 billion projected cost.

Prospective construction projects include High Speed 2 line between London and the West Midlands and Crossroad 2.

Production industries

Electricity, gas and water supply

Energy in United Kingdom

The Blue Book 2013 reports that this sector added gross value of £33,289 million to the UK economy in 2011. The United Kingdom is expected to launch the building of new nuclear reactors to replace existing generators and to boost UK's energy reserves.

Manufacturing

Manufacturing in UK

A Roll-Royle Trent 900 aircraft jet engine is setup on an Airbus A380.

In the 1970s, manufacturing accounted for 25 percent of the economy. Total employment in manufacturing fell from 7.1 million in 1979 to 4.5 million in 1992 and only 2.7 million in 2016, when it accounted for 10% of the economy.

A 2009 report from Pricewaterhouse Coopers, citing data from the UK Office for National Statistics, stated that manufacturing output (gross value added at 2007 prices) has increased in 35 of the 50 years between 1958 and 2007, and output in 2007 was at record levels, approximately double that in 1958.

In 2011 the UK manufacturing sector generated approximately £140,539 million in gross value added and employed around 2.6 million people.Of the approximately £16 billion invested in R&D by UK businesses in 2008, approximately £12 billion was by manufacturing businesses. In 2008, the UK was the sixth-largest manufacturer in the world measured by value of output.

In 2008 around 180,000 people in the UK were directly employed in the UK automotive manufacturing sector.In that year the sector had a turnover of £52.5 billion, generated £26.6 billion of exports and produced around 1.45 million passenger vehicles and 203,000 commercial vehicles The UK is a major centre for engine manufacturing, and in 2008 around 3.16 million engines were produced in the country.

The aerospace industry of UK is the second- or third-largest aerospace industry in the world, depending upon the method of measurement. The industry employs around 113,000 people directly and around 276,000 indirectly and has an annual turnover of around £20 billion. British companies with a major presence in the industry include BAE Systems (the world's second-largest defence contractors) and Rolls-Royle the world's second-largest aircraft engine maker). Foreign aerospace companies active in the UK include EADS and its Airbus subsidiary, which employs over 13,000 people in the UK.

The pharmaceutical industry employs around 67,000 people in the UK and in 2007 contributed £8.4 billion to the UK's GDP and invested a total of £3.9 billion in Research & Development sector in 2007 exports of pharmaceutical products from the UK totalled £14.6 billion, creating a trade surplus in pharmaceutical products of £4.3 billion. The UK is home to Glaxo Smith Kine and Astrazeneca respectively the world's third- and seventh-largest pharmaceutical companies.

Mining, quarrying and hydrocarbons

Mining in UK

UK trade balance in crude oil and petroleum from 1890 until 2015:

After 25 years of net exports, the UK became a net importer of oil in 2005.

The Blue Book 2013 reports that this sector added gross value of £31,380 million to the UK economy in 2011 In 2007 the UK had a total energy output of 9.5 quadrillion Btus (10 exajoules), of which the composition was oil (38%), natural gas (36%), coal (13%), nuclear (11%) and other renewables (2%). In 2009, the UK produced 1.5 million barrels per day (bbl/d) of oil and consumed 1.7 million bbl/d.Production is now in decline and the UK has been a net importer of oil since 2005. As of 2010 the UK has around 3.1 billion barrels of proven crude oil reserves, the largest of any EU member state.

In 2009 the UK was the 13th largest producer of natural gas in the world and the largest producer in the EU. Production is now in decline and the UK has been a net importer of natural gas since 2004. In 2009 the UK produced 19.7 million tons of coal and consumed 60.2 million tons. In 2005 it had proven recoverable coal reserves of 171 million tons. It has been estimated that identified onshore areas have the potential to produce between 7 billion tonnes and 16 billion tonnes of coal through Underground Coal gasification (UCG).Based on current UK coal consumption, these volumes represent reserves that could last the UK between 200 and 400 years.

The UK is home to a number of large energy companies, including two of the six oil and gas "super-majors – BP and Royal Dutch ".

The UK is also rich in a number of natural resources including coal, tin, limestone, iron ore, salt, clay, chalk, gypsum, lead and silica.

Service industries

The service sector is the dominant sector of the UK economy, and contributes around 80.2% of GDP as of 2016.

Creative industries

The creative industry accounted for 7% of gross value added (GVA) in 2005 and grew at an average of 6% per annum between 1997 and 2005. Key areas include London and the North West of London, which are the two largest creative industry clusters in Europe. According to the British Fashion Council, the fashion industry's contribution to the UK economy in 2014 is 26 billion, up from 21 billion pounds in 2009.The UK is home to the world's largest advertising company, WPP.

Education, health and social work

Education & Health Care in UK

The Qeen Elizabeth Health Hospital in Birghimton, a major NHS hospital According to The Blue Book 2013 the education sector added gross value of £84,556 million in 2011 whilst human health and social work activities added £104,026 million in 2011.

In the UK the majority of the healthcare sector consists of the state funded and operated National Health Service (NHS), which accounts for over 80% of all healthcare spending in the UK and has a workforce of around 1.7 million, making it the largest employer in Europe, and putting it amongst the largest employers in the world. The NHS operates independently in each of the four constituent countries of the UK. The NHS in England is by far the largest of the four parts and had a turnover of £92.5 billion in 2008.

In 2007/08 higher education institutions in the UK had a total income of £23 billion and employed a total of 169,995 staff.In 2007/08 there were 2,306,000 higher education students in the UK (1,922,180 in England, 210,180 in Scotland, 125,540 in Wales and 48,200 in Northern Ireland).

Financial and business services

Financial Services Industry in UK

The UK Financial Services Industry added gross value of £116,363 million to the UK economy in 2011. The UK's exports of financial and business services make a significant positive contribution towards the country's balance of payments.

Paternoster Exchange, home of the London Stock Exchange

London is a major centre for international business and commerce and is one of the three "command centres" of the global economy (alongside New

York City and Tokyo). There are over 500 banks with offices in London, and it is the leading international centre for banking, insurance, Eurobonds, foreign exchange trading and energy future. London's financial services industry is primarily based in the City of London and Canary Wharf. The City houses the London Stock Market, the London International Financial Future & Option Market, the London Metal Exchange, Lloyds of London, and the Bank of London. Canary Wharf began development in the 1980s and is now home to major financial institutions such as Barclays Bank, Citigroup and HSBC, as well as the UK Financial Services Industry.London is also a major centre for other business and professional services, and four of the six largest law firms in the world are headquartered there.

Several other major UK cities have large financial sectors and related services. Edinburgh has one of the largest financial centres in Europe and is home to the headquarters of the Royal Bank of Scotland Group and Standard Life. Leeds is the UK's largest centre for business and financial services outside London, and the largest centre for legal services in the UK after London.

According to a series of research papers and reports published in the mid-2010s, Britain's financial firms provide sophisticated methods to launder billions of pounds annually, including money from the proceeds of corruption around the world as well as the world's drug trade, thus making the City a global hub for illicit finance. According to a Deutsche Bank study published in March 2015, Britain was attracting circa one billion pounds of capital inflows a month not recorded by official statistics, up to 40 percent probably originating from Russia, which implies misreporting by financial institutions, sophisticated tax avoidance, and the UK's "safe-haven" reputation.

Hotels and restaurants

The Blue Book 2013 reports that this industry added gross value of £36,554 million to the UK economy in 2011. Intercontinental Hotels Group (IHG), headquartered in Denham, Buckinghamshire, is currently the world's largest hotelier, owning and operating hotel brands such as Intercontinental, Holiday Inn and Crowne Plaza. The international arm of Hilton Hotels, the world's fifth largest hotelier, used to be owned by Ladbrokes Plc, and was headquartered in Watford, Hertfordshire from 1987 to 2005. It was sold to Hilton Hotels Group of the US in December 2005.

Informal

A study in 2014 found that prostitution and associated services added over £5 billion to the economy each year.

Public administration and defence

The Blue Book 2013 reports that this sector added gross value of £70,400 million to the UK economy in 2011.

Real estate and renting activities

Real Estate in UK

Transport shopping complex in Manchestar was sold for £1.6 billion in 2011 in the largest property sale in British history.

The real estate and renting activities sector includes the letting of dwellings and other related business support activities. The Blue Book 2013 reports that real estate industry added gross value of £143,641 million in 2011. Notable real estate companies in the United Kingdom include British Land, Land Securities, and The Peel Group.

The UK property market boomed for the seven years up to 2008, and in some areas property trebled in value over that period. The increase in property prices had a number of causes: low interest rates, credit growth, economic growth, and rapid growth in buy-to-let property investment, foreign property investment in London and planning restrictions on the supply of new housing. In England and Wales between 1997 and 2016, average house prices increased by 259%, while earnings increased by 68%. An average home cost 3.6 times annual earnings in 1997 compared to 7.6 in 2016.

Rent has nearly doubled as a share of GDP since 1985, and is now larger than the manufacturing sector. In 2014, rent and inputed rent– an estimate of how much home-owners would pay if they rented their home – accounted for 12.3% of GDP.

Tourism

Tourism in UK

Tourism is very important to the British economy. With over 32.6 million tourists arriving in 2014, the United Kingdom is ranked as the eighth major tourist destination in the world. London is the second most visited city in the world with 17.4 million visitors in 2014, behind first-placed Hong Kong (27.8 million visitors)

Transport, storage and communication

Transport & Communication in UK

From 1994 to 2016, showing the initial rise in car use, which peaked in 1994 and declined gently as rail use increased.[176]

The transport and storage industry added a gross value of £59,179 million to the UK economy in 2011 and the telecommunication industry added a gross value of £25,098 million in the same year.

The UK has a total road network of 246,700 miles (397,025 km) with 31,400 miles (50,533 km) of major roads, including 2,300 miles (3,701 km) of motorway. The railway infrastructure, in Great Britain, is owned by Network rail which has 19,291 miles (31,046 km) of railway lines, of which 9,866 miles (15,878 km) is open for traffic. There are a further 206.5 miles (332.3 km) of track in Northern Ireland, owned and operated by Northern Ireland. Since the privatization of British Rail, passenger trains in Britain are run by Train Operating Companies. As of 2019, there are 32 TOCs. The government is to spend £56 billion on a new high-speed railway line, HS2, with the first phase from London to Birmingham costing £27 billion. Crosrail, due to open in London during autumn2019, is Europe's largest infrastructure project with a £15 billion projected cost.

The Highways Agency is the executive agency responsible for trunk roads and motorways in England apart from the privately owned and operated M6TollDepartment for Transport states that traffic congestion is one of the most serious transport problems and that it could cost England an extra £22 billion in wasted time by 2025 if left unchecked. According to the government-sponsored Eddington Report of 2006, congestion is in danger of harming the economy, unless tackled by road pricing and expansion of the transport network.

In the year from February 2017 to January 2018, UK airports handled a total of 284.8 million passengers.In that period the three largest airports were London Healthrow Airport (78.0 million passengers), Garwick Airport (45.6 million passengers) and Manchestar Airport (27.8 million passengers). London Heathrow Airport, located 14 $^{1}D_{2}$ miles (23.3 km) west of the capital,has the most international passenger traffic of any airport in the world. It is the hub for the UK flag carrier British Airways, as well as BMI and Virgin Aratic. London's six commercial airports form the world's largest city airports measured by the passengers with 171 million passengers in 2017.

Wholesale and retail trade

This sector includes the motor trade, auto repairs, and personal and household goods industries. The Blue Book 2013 reports that this sector added gross value of £151,785 million to the UK economy in 2011.

As of 2016, high-street retail spending accounted for about 33% of consumer spending and 20% of GDP. Because 75% of goods bought in the United Kingdom are made overseas, the sector only accounts for 5.7% of gross value added to the British economy.

The UK grocery market is dominated by four companies: Asda (owned by Walmart Store), Morrisons, Sainsbury and Tesco.

London is a major retail centre and in 2010 had the highest non-food retail sales of any city in the world, with a total spend of around £64.2 billion. The UK-based Tesco is the third-largest retailer in the world measured by revenues (after Wal-Mart Stores and Carrefour) and as of 2011 was the leader in the UK market with around a 30% share.

Currency

Pound Sterling

Bank of England is the Central bank of the United Kingdom

London is the world capital for foreign exchange trading, with a global market share of nearly 41% in 2013 of the daily $5.3 trillion global turnover. The highest daily volume, counted in trillions of dollars US, is reached when New York enters the trade.

The currency of the UK is the pound sterling, represented by the symbol "£'. The Bank of England is the central bank, responsible for issuing currency. Banks in Scotland and Northern Ireland retain the right to issue their own notes, subject to retaining enough Bank of England notes in reserve to cover the issue. The pound sterling is also used as a reserve currency by other governments and institutions, and is the third-largest after the US dollar and the euro.

The UK chose not to join the euro at the currency's launch. The government of former Prime Minister Tony Blair had pledged to hold a public referendum to decide on membership should "five economic tests" be met. Until relatively recently there was debate over whether or not the UK should abolish its currency and adopt the euro. In 2007 the Prime Minister, Growden Brown, pledged to hold a public referendum based on certain tests he set as Chancellor of Exchequer. When assessing the tests, Gordon Brown concluded that while the decision was close, the United Kingdom should not yet join the euro. He ruled out membership for the foreseeable future, saying that the decision not to join had been right for the UK and for Europe. In particular, he cited fluctuations in house prices as a barrier to immediate entry. Public opinion poll have shown that a majority of Britons have been opposed to joining the single currency for some considerable time, and this position has hardened further in the last few years. In 2005, more than half (55%) of the UK were against adopting the currency, while 30% were in favour. The possibility of joining the euro has become a non-issue since the referendum decision to withdraw from the European U7795= 1.nion.

Exchange rates GBP

Average for each year, in USD (US dollar) and EUR (euro) per GBP; and in GBP 0.7795=$1: GBP per USD and EUR. (Synthetic Euro). These averages conceal wide intra-year spreads. The coefficient of variation gives an indication of this. It also shows the extent to which the pound tracks the euro or the dollar. Note the effect of Black Wednesday in late 1992 by comparing the averages for 1992 and for 1993.

In 1990, exchange rate of Sterling pound was GBP 0.5633 = $1.775 and GDP 0.7161=Euro1.397. In 1992, it was GBP 0.5699=$1.7550 and GBP

0.7365= Euro 1.3580. There was fall of GBP in 1993. GBP0.6663= $1.501 and GBP 0.7795= Euro 1.2830

Economy by region

List of ceremonial countries in England by GVA (Gross Value Added)

Per capita in 2007 (in euros) showing the distribution of economic activity.

The strength of the UK economy varies from country to country and from region to region. Excluding the effects of North Sea oil and gas (which is classified in official statistics as extra-region), England has the highest gross value added (GVA) and Wales the lowest of the UK's constituent countries.

Rank	*Country*	*GDP per capita, 2015*
1	England	£26,160/ $40,000
2	Scotland	£23,685/ $36,200
3	Northern Ireland	£18,584/ $28,400
4	Wales	£18,002/ $27,500

Within England, GVA per capita is highest in London. The following table shows the GVA per capita of the nine statistical regions of England.

Rank	*Region*	*GVA per capita, 2013*[202]
1	Greater London	£40,215
2	South East England	£25,843
3	East of England	£21,897
4	South West England	£21,163
5	North West England	£19,937
6	West Midlands	£19,428
7	East Midlands	£19,317
8	Yorkshire and the Humber	£19,053
9	North East England	£17,381

Two of the riches 10 areas in the European Union are in the United Kingdom. Inner London is number 1 with a GDP per capita of €65 138, and the Thames Valley (Berkshire, Buckinghamshire and Oxford shire)) is number 7 with a GDP per capita of €37 379. Edinburgh is also one of the largest financial centres in Europe.

At the other end of the scale, Cornwall has the lowest GVA per head of any county or unitary authority in England, and it has received EU Convergence funding (formerly Objective One funding) since 2000.

Trade

UK exports at constant prices, 1995–2016

The total trade deficit (goods and services) narrowed £0.2 billion to £7.9 billion in the three months to November 2018 as both goods and services exports each increased £0.1 billion more than their respective imports.

Excluding erratic commodities (mainly aircraft) the total trade deficit widened £1.2 billion to £9.5 billion in the three months to November 2018.

Large increases in export prices of oil and aircraft drove the narrowing of the total trade deficit; removing the effect of inflation, the total trade deficit widened £0.3 billion to £6.5 billion in the three months to November 2018.

The trade in goods deficit widened £0.8 billion with EU countries and narrowed £0.9 billion with non-EU countries in the three months to November 2018, due mainly to increases in imports from EU countries and exports to non-EU countries.

The total trade deficit widened £4.1 billion in the 12 months to November 2018 due mainly to a £4.4 billion narrowing in the trade in services surplus.

Investment

In 2013 the UK was the leading country in Europe for inward foreign direct investment (FDI) with $26.51bn. This gave it a 19.31% market share in Europe. In contrast, the UK was second in Europe for outward FDI, with $42.59bn, giving a 17.24% share of the European market.

In October 2017, the ONS revised the UK's balance of payments, changing the net international investment position from a surplus of £469 bn to a deficit of £22bn. Deeper analysis of outward investment revealed that much of what was thought to be foreign debt securities owned by British companies were actually loans to British citizens. Inward investment also dropped, from a surplus of £120bn in the first half of 2016 to a deficit of £25bn in the same period of 2017. The UK had been relying on a surplus of inward investment to make up for its long-term current account deficit.

Mergers and Acquisitions (M&A)

Since 1985, 103,430 deals with UK participation have been announced.

There have been three major waves of increased M&A activity (2000, 2007 and 2017; see graph "M&A in the UK"). 1999 however, was the year with the highest cumulated value of deals (490.bil GBP, which is about 50% more than the current peak of 2017). The Finance industry and Energy & Power made up most of the value from 2000 until 2018 (both about 15%).

In most cases both the acquiring and target companies have/had shareholders spread throughout the world, not only in the stated countries.

European Union membership

The proportion of the country's exports going to the EU has fallen from 54 percent to 47 percent over the past decade. The total value of exports however, has increased in the same period from £130 billion (€160 billion) to £240 billion (€275 billion).

In June 2016 the UK voted to leave the EU in a national referendum on its own membership of the EU. After the activation of Article 50 of the Lisbon Treaty, the UK is set to leave the EU on Friday 29 March 2019. The future relationship between the UK and EU is under negotiation, although there are still attempts to prevent the UK's departure from the European Economic Area

Poverty

The United Kingdom is developed country with social welfare infrastructure, thus discussions surrounding poverty tend to use a relatively high minimum income compared to developing countries. According to the OECD, the UK is in the lower half of developed country rankings for poverty rates, doing better than Italy and US but less well than France, Austria, Hungary, Slovakia and the Nordic countries. Eurostat figures show that the numbers of Britons at risk of poverty has fallen to 15.9% in 2014, down from 17.1% in 2010 and 19% in 2005 (after social transfers were taken into account). Poverty is countered in United Kingdom with the welfare state. There have been protests over the recent welfare changes of introducing Universal Credit. The aim of the government was to simplify the welfare state. People have protested sanctioning of people on Universal Credit, as well as disabled people protesting changes.

The poverty line in the UK is commonly defined as being 60% of the median household income. In 2007–2008, this was calculated to be £115 per week for single adults with no dependent children; £199 per week for couples with no dependent children; £195 per week for single adults with two dependent children under 14; and £279 per week for couples with two dependent children under 14. In 2007–2008, 13.5 million people, or 22% of the population, lived below this line. This is a higher level of relative poverty than all but four other EU members. In the same year, 4.0

million children, 31% of the total, lived in households below the poverty line, after housing costs were taken into account. This is a decrease of 400,000 children since 1998–1999.

Present Position of The Economy of UK At A Glance

(1) Currency of UK is the Sterling Pound. GBP 1= $.7795or !GBP= $1.3575

(2) Fiscal year 6th April previous year to 5th April present year

(3) Trade Organisations: EU, OECD, AIIB & World Trade.

(4) GDP: $2.88 trillion (GDP Nominal,5thRank)

(5) GDP: $3.034 trillion (GDP PPP, 9th rank)

(6) GDP growth: 0.6% Q 3, 2018, 1.5% in 2016

(7) GDP per capita: $44177 (Nominal, 22nd rank)

(8) GDP per capita: $45043 (PPP, 26th rank)

(9) GDP by sector: 0.6% in Agriculture, 19.2% in Industry & 80.2% in Services – 2016

(10) Inflation 1.8% - January 2019, RPI 2.7% - December 2018

(11) Base borrowing rate: 0.75%

(12) Population: 65 million

(13) Labour Force: 32.71 million in January 2019 50.32% of population

(14) Employment rate 76.1%

(15) Unemployment 3.9%

(16) Population below poverty line 22% i.e. 143 million. Quite high.

(17) Labour by occupation: Agriculture 1.5% Industry 18.8% & Services 79.7%

(18) Average Gross salary GBP 530 weekly

(19) Poverty line measurement in 2007-08: GBP 115 per adult with no dependent, GBP 199 for couple with no children. GBP 195 for single adult with two children under 14 and GBP 297 wit couple and two children under 14. These are weekly requisition.

(20) Ease of doing business: 9th rank.

(21) External Trade: Exports: $ 412 billion (10th, 2018) & Imports $ 581.6 billion (5th, 2016) Trade Deficit $169.6 billion. 5.88% of GDP

(22) Export Goods: Manufactured goods, fuels, chemicals, food, beverages, tobacco

(23) Main Export partners: US 14.6%, Germany 10.1%, Switzerland 7%, China 6%, France 5.9% Netherland 5.8%, Ireland 5.5%

(24) Import Goods: Manufactured goods, machinery, fuel

(25) Main Import Partners: Germany 14.8%, China 9.8%, US 9.2%, Netherland 7.5%, France 5.5%, Belgium 5%

(26) FDI Inwards$1.996 trillion, FDI outwards $1.443 trillion Net Surplus $ 555 billion

(27) Gross External debt: 7.499 trillion 260.38% High in Fluctuating economy.

(28) Public debt 88.8% of GDP i.e. 2.55 trillion

(29) Fiscal: Revenues: GBP 1.4 trillion, Expenses: GBP 842 billion Fiscal surplus: GBP 98 billion (in 2019, estimated) but in 2018 deficit was GBP 127 billion which was 6% of GDP. As per standard norms, it should be maximum 4% of GDP.

(30) Economic Aid ODA GDP 146 billion in 2017

(31) Foreign Reserves: $ 164.2 billion as at 31-03-2018

(32) Credit Rating: S & P – AA (Domestic), AA (Foreign), AAA & Outlook: Negative (T & C), Moody Aa2 & Outlook Stable, Fitch AA AA & Outlook Negative, Scope AA & Outlook: Negative.

Three Credit agencies have granted outlook negative on account of financial turmoil and rising of commodity prices. UK should perform well financially to achieve "Stable" Outlook by all credit rating agencies. Also concentrates on Brexit created recession and industry index is jumping.

Critical Observations of Economy of United Kindgom

(1) Unlike USA which is made a big nation with 50 states, Europe is divided into small independent states like U.K., France, and Germany etc. For their own protection, these countries have formed the European Union and their financial transactions are settled by Euro as their common currency U.K. is a member of EU but has an independent currency as GBP. All financial transactions of UK are settled through GBP. How financial transactions of UK will be settled with countries in EU is not yet agreed upon between UK and EU after Brexit in 2016.

(2) U.K.is composed of England, Wales, Scotland and Northern Ireland.

(3) The economy of the U.K. is highly developed and market oriented. It is the fifth largest nation economy in the world measured by GDP and ninth largest by PPP, 22nd largest by GDP per capitacomprising world's 3.3% GDP.

(4) In 2016, the U.K. was the ninth largest goods exporter in the world and sixth largest goods importer. It is the third largest inward foreign direct investment and third largest outward foreign direct investment. It is the most globalized economy.

(5) Service sector dominates, contributing 80% of GDP. The financial service industry is particularly important and London is the world's largest financial centre.

(6) Britain's airspace industry is the second largest national aerospace industry with BAE & Ross-Royce Trent manufacturing Jet engines and Airbus 380. In defence also, it manufactures missiles and defence aircrafts such as Euro Fighters which are in great demand from many countries.

(7) British pharmaceutical industry is the largest in the world.

(8) South East England and North East Scotland are richest areas per capita. The size of London economy makes it the largest city by GDP in Europe.

(9) U.K. ruled India and other countries as its colonies for more than 200 years. India was financially very sound when U.K. captured it. But under the British Rule, India was ruined and U.K. became prosperous at the cost of India under the name of Industrial revolution. U.K. ruthlessly ruined Indian trade and was the main cause for serious famine in India. Epidemics were ruthlessly handled causing millions of people. Though the transport communication was improved and railways were set up, these were for easing transportation of raw cotton from India and bringing manufactured cloth to India thus making huge profit by taking advantage of India with oppressive methods. British claims that they had the rule of law. But that is also not true because the most of the laws were in their favour and were giving nothing but injustice to the Indian citizens. During the British Raj, Indians were treated as worse than slaves and they showed cruelty. However, Britishers also made some good improvement in Indian Social life by passing Sati prohibition Legislature, introduction of standard education system, to select capable administrators, ICS examination process and reducing inequility in the society by casteim.

(10) Costs of fighting World WarI & II resulted in weakening British economy and U.K. was compelled to give independence to colonial countries forcibly and unwillingly.

(11) U.K. set up Monetary Policy Committee under Central Bank i. e. Bank of England which was regulating interest, quantitative easing and future guidance.

(12) U.K. took opinion poll on Brexit to withdraw from EU in 2016. Voters favoured Brexit by marginal majority. This was not financially good step. Negotiations were held continuously with European Union as to how trade and financial transactions with EU will be carried out in future but Agreement on Brexit was not satisfactory which has been twice resulted by British Parliament

and British citizens are demanding resignation from the Prime Minister Mrs. May. On Brexit, another poll is demanded and British people are in the mood to cancel Brexit. Financial condition in U.K. is very bad and Recession is adding fuel to the fire. Prime Minister Mrs. May is compelled to resign in June 2019.

(13) During the 20 years period from 1986-1987 to 2006-07, the government is spending in UK average of 40% of GDP. In July 2007, UK government debt was @ 35.5% of GDP. As a result of financial crisis between 207-10 and late 2000s, global recession, government spending increased to the historical high of 48% of GDP in 2009-10, partly as a result of series of bank bailout. In terms of net government debt excluding financial sectors interventions was pound 1304.6 billion equaling to 79.3% of GDP. This was very high and must be controlled urgently.

(14) Taxation involves payment to local and central governments.

(15) According to a series of research papers and reports published in mid-2010, Britain's financial firms provided sophisticated methods to launder billions of pounds annually, including money from proceeds of corruption around the world and drug trade. This makes City a global hub for illicit finance. Prostitution and associated services added over pounds billion to the economy each year.

(16) Inflation was @21.9% in 1980and unemployment was 5.3%, 18.4% in 1982, 11.9% in 1984 and 7.2% in 1997. Inflation came down subsequently to 3.7% but interest rate was still high @ 9.56% p.a. This shows that economy is not steady stable.

(17) UK's external debt works out to 260% of GDP and Domestic Loan as 85.8% of GDP which are at very dangerous levels which will definitely create the debt servicing problem and the restructuring of loan by IMF will impose the stringent conditions like substantial reduction in Social welfare measures, public expenditure and taxation which will further deteriorate the economy. There should be realistic planning to reduce these high levels of debts which will become unproductive. Credit Rating Agencies have already given the financial outlook of UK as "Negative" to caution the country.IMF highlighted financial turmoil and rising commodities prices while granting bail-out package of GBP 2.3 billion applied by UK in 1976. IMF also advised reduction in public spending.

CHAPTER - 20

ECONOMY OF FRANCE

France has the world's 6th largest economy by GDP 2018 nominal figures and the 10th largest economy by PPP figures. It has the 3rd largest economy in the European Union after Germany and United Kingdom.

France has a diversified economy. The chemical industry is a key sector for France, helping to develop other manufacturing activities and contributing to economic growth. France's Tourism Industry is a major component of the economy, as France is the most visited destination in the world. Sophia is the major technology hub for the economy of France. Paris is ranked as the most elegant city in the world, which propels the agglomeration of the fashion industry. According to the IMF, in 2013, France was the 20th country by GDP per capita with $44,600 per inhabitant. In 2013, France was listed on the United Nation's Human Development Index with 0.884 (very high human development) and 25th on the Corruption Perception Index. The OECD is headquartered in Paris, the nation's financial capital.

France's economy entered the recession of the late 2000s later and appeared to leave it earlier than most affected economies, only enduring four-quarters of contraction. However, France experienced stagnant growth between 2012 and 2014, with the economy expanding by 0% in 2012, 0.8% in 2013 and 0.2% in 2014, though growth picked up in 2015 with a growth of 0.8% and a growth of 1.1% for 2016, to a growth of 2.2% for 2017 and to later reach 2.1% for 2018.

Corporations

With 28 of the 500 biggest companies of the world in 2018, France ranks 5th in the Fortune Global 500, behind the USA, China, Japan and Germany

Several French corporations rank amongst the largest in their industries such as AXA in insurance and Air France in air transportation. Luxury and consumer good are particularly relevant, with L'Oréal being the world's largest cosmetic company while LVMH and PPR are the world's two largest luxury product companies. In energy and utilities, GDF-Suez and EDF are amongst the largest energy companies in the world, and Areva is a large nuclear-energy company.

Rise and decline of dirigisme

France embarked on an ambitious and very successful programme of modernization under state coordination. This programme of dirigisme, mostly implemented by governments between 1944 and 1983, involved the state control of certain industries such as transportation, energy and telecommunications as well as various incentives for private corporations to merge or engage in certain projects.

The 1981 election of President Francois Mitterland saw a short-lived increase in governmental control of the economy, nationalizing many industries and private banks. This form of increased dirigisme, was criticized as early as 1982. By 1983, the government decided to renounce dirigisme and start an era of rigour corporatization. As a result, the government largely retreated from economic intervention; dirigisme has now essentially receded, though some of its traits remain. The French economy grew and changed under government direction and planning much more than in other European countries.

Despite being a widely liberalized economy, the government continues to play a significant role in the economy: government spending, at 56% of GDP in 2014, is the second highest in the European Union. Labour conditions and wages are highly regulated. The government continues to own shares in corporations in several sectors, including energy production and distribution, automobiles, transportation, and telecommunications. However these shareholdings are being rapidly sold, the state keeping mostly symbolic stakes in those companies (aside rail transportation and energy).

Government finance

Budget & Taxation in France

In April and May 2012, France held a presidential election in which the winner Francois Hollande had opposed austerity measures, promising to eliminate France's budget deficit by 2017. The new government stated that it aimed to cancel recently enacted tax cuts and exemptions for the wealthy, raising the top tax bracket rate to 75% on incomes over a million euros, restoring the retirement age to 60 with a full pension for those who have worked 42 years, restoring 60,000 jobs recently cut from public education, regulating rent increases; and building additional public housing for the poor.

In June 2012, Hollande's Socialist Party won an overall majority in the legislative elections, giving it the capability to amend the French Constitution and allowing immediate enactment of the promised reforms. French government bond interest rates fell 30% to record lows,less than 50 basis points above German government bond rates.

National debt

The Government of France has run a budget deficit each year since the early 1970s. In mid-2012, French government debt levels reached €1,833 billion. This debt level was the equivalent of 91% of French GDP.

Under European Union rules, member states are supposed to limit their debt to 60% of output or be reducing the ratio structurally towards this ceiling, and run public deficits of no more than 3.0% of GDP.

In late 2012, credit-rating agencies warned that growing French government debt levels risked France's AAA credit rating, raising the possibility of a future credit downgrade and subsequent higher borrowing costs for the French government. In 2012 France was downgraded by ratings agencies Moody's, Standard & Poor's, and Fitch to the AA+ credit rating.

In December 2014 France's credit rating was further downgraded by Fitch (and S&P) to the AA credit rating.

Data of Economic Indicators

In 1980-81, inflation was 13.1% and 13.3% and emolument was 6.2% and 7.4%.

In 1987-88, inflation was 3.3& and 2.7% and unemployment was 9.2% and 8.8%

In 2000-2001, inflation was 1.8% and 1.8% and unemployment was 9.2% and 8.5%

In 2016-2017, inflation was 1.1% and 1.8% and unemployment was 10% and 9.4%

Budget deficit was ranging from 0.4% to 2.6% of GDP. While GDP was Euro 453.2 billion in 1987, it was euro @.2.288 trillion in 2017 showing the growth of 1.8% in 1980 to 1.8%, same level, in 2017. It was highest in 1988 @4.7% and Lowest @ -2.9% in 2009 during the period 1980-2016.

Economic sectors

Industry

2006 electricity production of France

Nuclear power (78.1%)

Hydroelectric power (11.1%)

Fossil fuel power (9.5%)

Other (1.3%)

The leading industrial sectors in France are telecommunications (including communication satellites), aerospace and defense, ship building (naval and specialist ships), pharmaceuticals, construction and civil engineering, chemicals, textiles, and automobile production.

Research and development spending is also high in France at 2.26% of GDP, the fourth-highest in the OECD.

Energy

France is the world-leading country in nuclear energy, home of global energy giants Areva, FDF and GDF Suez: nuclear power now accounts for about 78% of the country's electricity production, up from only 8% in 1973, 24% in 1980, and 75% in 1990. Nuclear waste is stored on site as reprocessing facilities. Due to its heavy investment in nuclear power, France is the smallest emitter of carbon dioxide among the seven most industrialized countries in the world.

In 2006 electricity generated in France amounted to 548.8 Twh.

In November 2004, EDF (which stands for Electricity de France), the world's largest utility company and France's largest electricity provider, was floated with huge success on the French stock market. Notwithstanding, the French state still retains 70% of the capital.

Other electricity providers include Cimpagnie nationale du Roune (CNR) and Endesa (through SNET).

Agriculture

A wheat field in lie-de-France region.

France is the world's sixth largest agricultural producer and EU's leading agricultural power, accounting for about one-third of all agricultural land within the EU.

Northern France is characterized by large wheat farms. Dairy products, pork, poultry, and apple production are concentrated in the western region. Beef production is located in central France, while the production of fruits, vegetables, and wine ranges from central to southern France. France is a large producer of many agricultural products and is currently expanding its forestry and fishery industries. The implementation of the Common Agricultural Policy (CAP) and the Uraguay of the General Agreement of Tariff and Trade (GATT) have resulted in reforms in the agricultural sector of the economy.

As the world's second-largest agricultural exporter, France ranks just after the United States. The destination of 49% of its exports is other EU members' states. France also provide agricultural exports to many poor African countries (including its former colonies) which face serious food shortages. Wheat, beef, pork, poultry, and dairy products are the principal exports.

Exports from the United States face stiff competition from domestic production, other EU member states, and third-world countries in France. US agricultural exports to France, totaling some $600 million annually, consist primarily of soybeans and soybean products, feeds and fodders, seafood, and consumer products, especially snack foods and nuts. French exports to the United States are much more high-value products such as its cheese, processed products and its wine.

The French agricultural sector receives almost €11 billion in EU subsidies. France's competitive advantage is mostly linked to the high quality and global renown of its produce, such as cheese and wine.

Tourism

The Palace of Versailles is one of the most popular tourist destinations in France.

France is the most popular tourist destination with more than 83.7 million foreign tourists in 2014, ahead of Spain (58.5 million in 2006) and the United States (51.1 million in 2006). This figure excludes people staying less than 24 hours in France, such as northern Europeans crossing France on their way to Spain or Italy during the summer.

France is home to cities of much cultural interest (Paris being the foremost), beaches and seaside resorts, ski resorts, and rural regions that many enjoy for their beauty and tranquility. France also attracts many religious pilgrims to Lourdes, a town in the Hautes-Pyrénées department, which hosts several million visitors a year.

Arms industry

Assault Rafael

The French arms industry's main customer, for whom they mainly build warships, guns, nuclear weapons and equipment, is the French government.

Record high defence expenditure (currently[1] at €35 billion), which was considerably increased under the government of Prime Minister Jean-Pierre Refrain, goes largely to the French arms industries.

During the 2000–2015 period, France was the fourth largest weapons exporter in the world.

French manufacturers export great quantities of weaponry to Saudi Arabia, the United Arab Emirates, Brazil, Greece, India, Pakistan, Taiwan, Singapore and many others.

It was reported that in 2015, French arms sales internationally amounted to 17.4 billion U.S. dollars, more than double the figure of 2014. Vice News explained that "While the United Kingdom has lapsed somewhat in this regard, France has maintained a high-level of production of military equipment for land, air, and sea defense – an expensive approach that relies on the export of arms and technology." India has purchased 35 Rafael aircrafts from France to strengthen its military and air power

Transport

Transport in France

Transportation in France relies on one of the densest networks in the world with 146 km of road and 6.2 km of rail lines per 100 km. It is built as a web with Paris at its center. The highly subsidized rail transport network makes up a relatively small portion of travel, most of which is done by car. However the high-speed TGV trains make up a large proportion of long-distance travel, partially because intercity buses were prevented from operating until 2015.

France also boasts a number of seaports and harbors, including Bayonne, Bordeaux, Boulogne-suMer, Brest, Calais etc. There are approximately 470 airports in France and by a 2005 estimate, there are three heliports. 288 of the airports have paved runways, with the remaining 199 being unpaved. The national carrier of France is Air France, a full service global airline which flies to 20 domestic destinations and 150 international destinations in 83 countries (including Overseas France) across all 6 major continents.

Labour market

According to a 2011 report by the American Bureau of Labour Statistics (BLS), France's GDP per capita at our purchasing power parity is similar to that of the UK, with just over US$35,000 per head. To explain why French per capita GDP is lower than that of the United States, the economist Paul Krugman stated that "French workers have roughly as productive as US workers", but that the French have allegedly a lower Work force Partition rate and "when they work, they work fewer hours". According to Krugman, the difference is due to the French making "different choices about retirement and leisure".

The labour productivity level in France is one of highest in Europe. OECD in 2015.

Keynesian economist sought different solutions to the unemployment issue in France, and their theories led to the introduction of the 35-hour workweek law in 1999. Between 2004 and 2008, the government attempted to combat unemployment with supply-side reforms, but was met with fierce resistance; the central nouvelle embauche and the central premiere embauche (which allowed more flexible contracts) were of particular concern, and both were eventually repealed. The Sarkozy government used the revenue de solodarite active (in-work benefits) to redress the allegedly negative effect of the revenue minimum d'insertion (unemployment benefits which do not depend on previous contributions, unlike normal unemployment benefits in France) on the incentive to accept even jobs which are insufficient to earn a living.

French employment rates for 15–64 years is one of the lowest of the OECD countries: in 2012, only 71% of the French population aged 15–64 years were in employment, compared to 74% in Japan, 77% in the UK, 73% in the US and 77% in Germany. This gap is due to the low employment rate for 15–24 years old: 38% in 2012, compared to 47% in the OECD. Neoliberal economists attribute the low employment rate, particularly evident among young people, to allegedly high minimum wages that would prevent low productivity workers from easily entering the labour market.

A December 2012 New York Times article reported on an allegedly "floating generation" in France that formed part of the 14 million unemployed young Europeans documented by the Euro found research agency. In the same article, Anne Sonnet, a senior economist studying unemployment at the OECD claimed that nearly two million young people in France had given up looking for employment at that time, while French labour minister Michel Sapin said that 82 percent of people hired were only on temporary contracts. Sapin further explained that, in his opinion, the challenge at that time was to create a more flexible system, in which greater trust existed between unions and companies, and "partial unemployment" was accommodated during difficult periods. The so-called floating generation was attributed to an allegedly dysfunctional system: "an elitist educational tradition that does not integrate graduates into the work force, a rigid labour market that is hard to enter for newcomers, and a tax system that makes it expensive for companies to hire full-time employees and both difficult and expensive to lay them off". In July 2013, the unemployment rate for France was 11%.

In early April 2014, employers' federations and unions negotiated an agreement with technology and consultancy employers, as employees had been experiencing an extension of their work time through smartphone communication outside of official working hours. Under a new, legally binding labour agreement, around 250,000 employees will avoid handling work-related matters during their leisure time and their employers will, in turn, refrain from engaging with staff during this time.

Every day, about 80,000 French citizens are commuting to work in neighbouring Luxembourg, making it the biggest cross-border workforce group in the whole of the European Union. They are attracted by much higher wages for the different job groups than in their own country and the lack of skilled labour in the booming.

External trade

List of Exports in France

Luxembourgish economy

France is the second-largest trading nation in Europe (after Germany). Its foreign trade balance for goods had been in surplus from 1992 until 2001, reaching $25.4 billion (25.4 G$) in 1998; however, the French balance of trade was hit by the economic downturn, and went into the red in 2000, reaching a US$15bn deficit in 2003. Total trade for 1998 amounted to $730 billion, or 50% of GDP—imports plus exports of goods and services. Trade with European Union countries accounts for 60% of French trade.

In 1998, US–France trade stood at about $47 billion – goods only. According to French trade data, US exports accounted for 8.7% – about $25 billion – of France's total imports. US industrial chemicals, aircraft and engines, electronic components, telecommunications, computer software, computers and peripherals, analytical and scientific instrumentation, medical instruments and supplies, broadcasting equipment, and programming and franchising are particularly attractive to French importers.

The principal French exports to the US are aircraft and engines, beverages, electrical equipment, chemicals, cosmetics, luxury products and perfume. France is the ninth-largest trading partner of the US.

Total Trade in Billion US-Dollar		
Rank	Country	Total Trade (2016)
1.	Germany	169.9
2.	Italy	79.0
3.	United States	78.3
4.	Belgium Luxembourg	78.3
5.	Spain	71.7
6.	China	66.5
7.	United Kingdom	57.7
8.	Netherlands	43.2
9.	Switzerland	32.0
10.	Japan	19.0

Region's' economy

List of French and overseas collectivities by GDP

Nominal GDP per capita, 2015 Eurostat

The economic disparity between French regions is not as high as that in other European countries such as the UK, Italy or Germany, and higher than in countries like Sweden or Denmark, or even Spain. However, Europe's wealthiest and second largest regional economy, Ile-de-France (the region surrounding Paris), has long profited from the capital city's economic hegemony.

The rural areas are mainly in Auvergne, Limousin, and Centre-val de Loire, and wine production accounts for a significant proportion of the economy in Aquitaine(Bordeaux (orclaret), and produced in .

Paris is France's largest urban economy (and the world's third)

In terms of income, important inequalities can be observed among the French departments.

According to the 2008 statistics of the INSEE, the Yvelines is the highest income department of the country with an average income of €4,750 per month. Hauts-de-Seine comes second, Essonne third, Paris fourth, Seine-et Marne fifth lle-de-France is the wealthiest region in the country with an average income of €4,228 per month (and is also the wealthiest region in Europe) compared to €3,081 at the national level. Alsce comes second, Rhone-Aples third, Picady fourth, and Upper Normandy fifth.

The poorest parts of France are the French overseas departments, French Guiana being the poorest department with an average household income of €1,826. In Metropolitan France it is Creuse in the Limosin region which comes bottom of the list with an average household income of €1,849 per month.

Urban income inequalities

Huge inequalities can also be found among cities. In the Paris metropolitan area, significant differences exist between the higher standard of living of *Paris Ouest* and lower standard of living in areas in the northern banlieues of Paris such as Seine-Saint-Denis.

For cities of over 50,000 inhabitants, Neuilly-sur-Seine, a western suburb of Paris, is the wealthiest city in France with an average household income of €5,939, and 35% earning more than €8,000 per month. But within Paris, four around dissidents' surpass wealthy Neuilly-sur-Seine in household income: the 6th, the 7th, the 8th and the 16th; the 8th "arrondissement" being the wealthiest district in France (the other three following it closely as 2nd, 3rd and 4th wealthiest ones.

Wealth

Overview

In 2010, the French had an estimated wealth of US$14.0 trillion for a population of 63 million.

- In terms of aggregate wealth, the French are the wealthiest Europeans, accounting for more than a quarter of wealthiest European households. Globally, the French nation ranks fourth-wealthiest.

- In 2010, wealth per French adult was a little higher than $290,000, down from a pre-crisis high of $300,000 in 2007. According to this ratio, French are the wealthiest in Europe. The tax on wealth is paid by 1.1M of people in France, the payment of this tax starts when a €1.3M of assets is reached (there is a discount on the principal residence value).
- Almost every French household has at least $1,000 in assets. Proportionally, there are twice as many French with assets of over $10,000 and four times as many French with assets of over $100,000 than the world average.
- The French are also among the least indebted populations in the developed world with personal debt accounting for "little more than 10% of household assets".

Millionaires

France has the third highest number of millionaires in Europe as of 2017. There were 1.617 million millionaire households (measured in terms of US dollars) living in France in 2017, behind the UK (2.225M) and Germany (1.637).

The wealthiest man in France is the LVMH CEO and owner Bernard Arnault.

Present Position of Economy of France At A Glance

(1) La De fense is the financial hub of France
(2) Currency: Euro 1 Euro= $1.14
(3) Fiscal year: Calendar year
(4) Trade organisations: EU, WTO, OECD
(5) GDP Nominal $2.794 trillion ($6^{th}$ rank, 2018)
(6) GDP PPP $2.968 trillion ($10^{th}$ rank, 2018)
(7) GDP growth: 1.6% - 2018
(8) GDP per capita $43600 (Nominal, 21st rank)
(9) GDP per capita $$45474 (PPP, 29th rank)
(10) GDP by sector: Agriculture 1.6%, industry 19.4%, Services 78.9% - 2017 (est)
(11) Inflation 2% (May 2018)
(12) Population 64.08 million
(13) Population below poverty line 14.2% 9.10 million - 2015
(14) Labour Force: 35.5 million (2017) 55% of population
(15) Labour force by occupation: agriculture 3.8%, industry 24.3% & services 71.8%.
(16) Unemployment 8.8%

(17) Average Gross Salary: Euro 35584 /$42300 annually 2017

(18) Average Net Salary: Euro26700/$30840 – 2017

(19) Main Industries: Machinery, chemicals, automobiles, metallurgy, aircraft, electronics, textiles, food processing, tourism

(20) EXTERNAL : Exports: $522.8 billion

(21) Imports: $611.7 billion
Trade Deficit: $88.9 billion. 3% of GDP

(22) Export Goods: machinery and equipment, aircraft, plastics, chemicals, pharmaceutical products, iron & steel, beverage

(23) Main Export Partners: Germany 16%, Spain 7.6%, US 7.3%, Italy 7.2%, UK7%, Belgium 6.8% - 2016

(24) Import goods: machinery & equipment, vehicles, crude oil, aircraft, plastic, chemicals

(25) Main Import Partners: Germany 19.5%, Belgium 10.6%, Netherland 7.9%, Italy 7.8%, Spain 7%, US 5.8%, UK 4.2% - 2016

(26) FDI Stock: $842.50 billion - 31-03-2017
Foreign Reserves: $153.8 billion – March 2016

Economic Aid: Donor ODA $9.50 billion

(27) Gross External debt: $5.250 trillion. 187.90% of GDP. Very high

(28) Public debt: 96.8% of GDP i.e. $2.7045 trillion Very high

(29) FISCAL: Revenues: $1.3 trillion, Expenses: $1.5 trillion

(30) Fiscal Deficit: $200 billion 7% of GDP as per existing norms, this should not exceed 4% of GDP.

(31) Credit Rating: S & P: AA, Outlook: Stable, Scope AA Outlook: Stable, Moody's Aa2 Outlook: Stable, Fitch AA Outlook: Stable

Critical Observations of Economy of France

(1) France is a member of EU and her financial transactions are settled by EU's common currency Euro. Euro value is Euro 1 = $1.14

(2) France is the world 6th largest economy by 2018 nominal figure and 10th largest economy by PPP.

(3) France has diversified economy. The chemical industry is the key sector for France, helping to develop other manufacturing activities and contributing to economic growth. France's tourism is a major component of the economy, as France is the most visited destination in the world. Sophia Antipolis is the major technology hub for the economy of France.

(4) France economy entered the recession of the late 2000s but appeared to leave it earlier than most affected economies. France

experienced stagnant growth between 2012 and 2014 with economy expanding by 0.0% in 2012, 0.8% in 2013, 0.02% in 2014, and then picked up in 2015 with a growth of 0.8% and 1.1% in 2016, 2.2% in 2017 and 2.1% in 2018.

(5) Though the France is liberized economy, it spends 56% of GDP by playing significant role in the economy. It purchases shares of 7.16 various corporates in sectors like telecommunication, transportation, automobiles, energy production.

(6) Mr.Franeois Hollande won the legislative elections in 2017 by overall majority. National debt was 91% of GDP which was far excess of EU rule of maximum 60% of GDP and needs to be reduced drastically. Under EU rule, fiscal deficit should not be more than 3% per year. In 2018, Revenue was Euro 1.3 trillion and expenses 1.5 trillion showing 0.2 trillion deficit which works out to 7.16% of GDP which is ought to be reduced to 4%.

(7) France expenses on R&D for various sectors is 2.28% of GDP.

(8) Desalt Rafael has been manufactured by France which are war aeroplane. France spends Euro 35 billion on defence and exports the Defence weapon to various countries like Saudi Arabia, UAE, India, Pakistan, and Brazil with export earning $17.4 billion. India has recently made Agreement to purchase 36 Desalt Rafael planes from France.

(9) France has highest labour productivity. However its labour force of age 15-64 years is lowest @ 71% of the population compared with 74% Japan,77% UK, 73% US, 77% Germany.

(10) Domestic war in France to expel present President Mr. Emanuel Macron under "Yellow West" agitation is in dangerous situation under the opposition Party Leadership of Christoph Shaulencon. Referendum agreed to by the President has not satisfied the agitators. Macron is the main leader with German President Angel to encourage to take migrated population to France from other countries. This has made country unsafe from migrated people attack and completely collapsing the economy of these countries. Citizens in these countries are not in favour of accepting migrated people and there is a strong resistance.

(11) International trade deficit is $ 88.9 billion on imports $ 611.7 billion and exports $522.8 billion.

(12) International debt is $ 5.250 trillion and GDP is 2.794 trillion which works out to external debt 187.90% of GDP. Should be curtailed to avoid the problem of debt servicing and Debt restructuring resulting in imposing stringent conditions and restrictions by IMF. As per Euro rule, Domestic loan should not exceed 60% of GDP but France's domestic loan is 96.8% of GDP

i.e.2.70 trillion and should be reduced to $1.6764 trillion. Unemployment figure at 8.8% is also high which will result in recession. Keynesian economists sought different solutions to the unemployment in France such as 35 working hours per week.

CHAPTER - 21

ECONOMY OF GERMANY

Introduction of German Economy

The economy of Germany is a highly developed social market economy. It has the largest national economy in Europe, the fourth largest by Nominal GDP in the world, and fifth by GDP (PPP). In 2017, the country accounted for 28% of the euro area economy according to the IMF. Germany is a founding member of the European Union (EU) and the Eurozone.

In 2016, Germany recorded the highest trade surplus in the world worth $310 billion, making it the biggest capital exporter globally. Germany is the third largest exporter in the world with 1.21 trillion euros ($1.28 trillion) in goods and services exported in 2016. The Service Sector contributes around 70% of the total GDP, industry 29.1%, and agriculture 0.9%. Exports account for 41% of national output. The top 10 exports of Germany are vehicles, machinery, chemical goods, electronic products, electrical equipment, pharmaceuticals, transport equipment, basic metals, food products, and rubber and plastics. The economy of Germany is the largest manufacturing economy in Europe and it is less likely to be affected by the financial downturn and conduct applied research with practical industrial value and sees itself as a bridge between the latest university insights and industry-specific product and process improvements, and by generating a great deal of knowledge in its own laboratories as well. In July 2017, the IMF gave the country's economy "yet another bill of good health" and some advice on steps it might take to maintain this level in the long run.

Germany is rich in timber, lignite, potash, and salt. Some minor sources of natural gas are being exploited in the state of Lower Saxony. Until reunification, the German Democratic Republic mined for uranium in the Ore mountains (see also: SAG/SDAG Wismut). Energy in Germany is sourced predominantly by fossil fuels (50%), followed by nuclear power second, then gas, wind, biomass (wood and biofuels), hydro and solar. Germany is the first major industrialized nation to commit to the renewable energy transition called

Energiewende. Germany is the leading producer of wind turbines in the world. Renewables now produce over 27% of electricity consumed in Germany.

99 percent of all German companies belong to the German "Mitterland", small and medium-sized enterprises, which are mostly family-owned. Of the world's 2000 largest publicly listed companies measured by revenue, the Fortune Global 2000, 53 have headquartered in Germany, with the Top 10 being Aiilinz, Volkawagen, Siemens, BNW, DeuscheTelecom Bayer, BASF, Munich, Re and SAP.

Germany is the world's top location for trade fairs. Around two thirds of the world's leading trade fairs take place in Germany. The largest annual international trade fairs and congresses are held in several German cities such as Hanover, Frankfurt, Cologne, Leipzig, and Dusseldort.

Economic History of Germany

Age of Industrialization

The Industrial Revolution in Germany got underway approximately a century later than in England, France, and Belgium, partly because Germany only became a unified country in 1871.

The establishment of the Deutscher zollverein (German Customs Union) in 1834 and the expansion of railway systems were the main drivers of Germany's industrial development and political union. From 1834, tariff barriers between increasing numbers of the Kleindeutchland German states were eliminated. In 1835 the first German railway linked the Franconian cities of Nuremberg and Furth - it proved so successful that the decade of the 1840s saw "railway mania" in all the German states. Between 1845 and 1870, 5,000 more miles of rail had been built and in 1850 Germany was building its own locomotives. Over time, other German states joined the customs union and started linking their railroads, which began to connect the corners of Germany together. The growth of free trade and of a rail system across Germany intensified economic development which opened up new markets for local products, created a pool of middle managers,increased the demand for engineers, architects and skilled machinists, and stimulated investments in coal and iron.

Another factor which propelled German industry forward was the unification of the monetary system, made possible in part by political unification. The Deutsche Mark, a new monetary coinage system backed by gold, was introduced in 1871. However, this system did not fully come into use as silver coins retained their value until 1907.

The victory of Prussia and her allies over Napoleon III of France in the Franco- Prussian War of 1870-1871 marked the end of French hegemony in Europe and resulted in the proclamation of the German Empire in 1871. The establishment of the empire inherently presented Europe with the reality of a new populous and industrializing polity possessing a considerable, and undeniably increasing, economic and diplomatic presence. The influence of French economic principles produced important institutional reforms in Germany, including the abolition of feudal restrictions on the sale of large landed estates, the reduction of the power of the guilds in the cities, and the introduction of a new, more efficient commercial law. Nonetheless, political decisions about the economy of the empire were still largely controlled by a coalition of "rye and iron", that is the Prussian Junker landowners of the east and the Ruhr heavy industry of the west.

Regarding politics and society, between 1881 and 1889 Chancellor Otto von Bismarck promoted laws that provided social insurance and improved working conditions. He instituted the world's first welfare state. Germany was the first to introduce social insurance programs including universal healthcare, compulsory education, sickness insurance, accident insurance, disability insurance, and a retirement pension. Moreover, the government's universal education policy bore fruit with Germany achieving the highest literacy rate in the world – 99% – education levels that provided the nation with more people good at handling numbers, more engineers, chemists, opticians, skilled workers for its factories, skilled managers, knowledgeable farmers and skilled military personnel.

By 1900 Germany surpassed Britain and the United States in steel production. The German economic miracle was also intensified by an unprecedented population growth from 35 million in 1850 to 67 million in 1913. From 1895 to 1907, the number of workers engaged in machine building doubled from half a million to well over a million. Only 40 percent of Germans lived in rural areas by 1910, a drop from 67% at the birth of the Empire. Industry accounted for 60 percent of the gross national product in 1913. The German chemical industry became the most advanced in the world, and by 1914 the country was producing half the world's electrical equipment.

The rapid advance to industrial maturity led to a drastic shift in Germany's economic situation - from a rural economy into a major exporter of finished goods. The ratio of finished product to total exports jumped from 38% in 1872 to 63% in 1912. By 1913 Germany had come to dominate all the European markets. By 1914 Germany had become one of the biggest exporters in the world.

Weimar Republic and Third Reich

Gross national product and GNP deflator, year on year change in %, 1926 to 1939, in Germany. Via google top Pf-file of the German Publication.

The Nazis rose to power while unemployment was very high, but achieved full unemployment later thanks to massive public works programs such as the Reichsbahn, Reichspost and the Reichsautobahn projects. In 1935 rearmament in contravention of the Treaty of Versailles added to the economy.

Weimar and Nazi Germany by Stephen J. Lee

The post 1931 financial crisis economic policies of expansionary fiscal policies (as Germany was off the gold standard) was advised by their non-Nazi Minister of Economics, Hijalmar Scratch, who in 1933 became the president of the central bank. Hijalmar Schacht later abdicated from the post in 1938 and was replaced by Hemann Goring.

The trading policies of the Third Reich aimed at self-sufficiency but with a lack of raw materials Germany would have to maintain trade links but on bilateral preferences, foreign exchange controls, import quotas and export subsidies under what was called the "New Plan"(Nuclear Plan) of 19 September 1934. The "New Plan" was based on trade with less developed countries who would trade raw materials for German industrial goods saving currency. Southern Europe was preferable to Western Europe and North America as there could be no trade blockades. This policy became known as the Grosswirtschaftsraum ("greater economic area") policy.

Eventually, the Nazi party developed strong relationships with big business and abolished trade unions in 1933 in order to form the National Labour Service (RAD), German Labour Front (DAF) to set working hours, Beauty of Labour (SDA) which set working conditions and Strength through Joy (KDF) to ensure sports clubs for workers.

West Germany

The Volkswagen Beetle was an icon of West German reconstruction.

Beginning with the replacement of the Reinchsmark with the Deusche Mark as legal tender, a lasting period of low inflation and rapid industrial growth was overseen by the government led by German Chancellor Kornad Adenauer and his minister of economics, raising We Europe. Germany from total wartime devastation to one of the most developed nations in modern Europe.

In 1953 it was decided that Germany was to repay $1.1 billion of the aid it had received. The last repayment was made in June 1971.

A part from these factors, hard work and long hours at full capacity among the population in the 1950s, 1960s and early 1970s and extra labor supplied by thousands of "guest workers" provided a vital base for the economic upturn.

East Germany

Economy of the German Democratic Republic

By the early 1950s the Soviet Union had seized reparations in the form of agricultural and industrial products and demanded further heavy reparation payments. Silesia with the Upper Silesian Coal Basin, and Stettin, a prominent natural port, were lost to Poland.

Exports from West Germany exceeded $323 billion in 1988. In the same year, East Germany exported $30.7 billion worth of goods; 65% to other communist states. East Germany had zero unemployment.

In 1976 the average annual GDP growth was roughly 5.9%.

Federal Republic

As of 2013, Germany is the third largest exporter and third largest importer in the world, producing the largest trade surplus as a national economy.

The German economy practically stagnated in the beginning of the 2000s. The worst growth figures were achieved in 2002 (+1.4%), in 2003 (+1.0%) and in 2005 (+1.4%). Unemployment was also chronically high. Due to these problems, together with Germany's aging problem, the welfare system came under considerable strain. This led the government to push through a wide-ranging program of belt-tightening reforms, Agenda 2010, including the labour market reforms known as Hartz I -IV.

In the later part of the first decade of 2000 the world economy experienced high growth, from which Germany as a leading exporter also profited. Some credit the Hartz reforms with achieving high growth and declining unemployment but others contend that they resulted in a massive decrease in standards of living, and that its effects are limited and temporary.

The nominal GDP of Germany contracted in the second and third quarters of 2008, putting the country in a technical recession following a global and European recession cycle. German industrial output dropped to 3.6% in September vis-à-vis August. In January 2009 the German government under Angela Marke approved a €50 billion ($70 billion) economic stimulus plan to protect several sectors from a downturn and a subsequent rise in unemployment rates. Germany exited the recession in the second and third quarters of 2009, mostly due to rebounding manufacturing orders and exports - primarily from outside the Euro Zone - and relatively steady consumer demand.

Germany is a founding member of the EU, the G8 and the G20, and was the world's largest exporter from 2003 to 2008. In 2011 it remained the third largest exporter and third largest importer. Most of the country's exports are in engineering, especially machinery, automobiles, chemical goods and metals. Germany is a leading producer of wind turbines and solar-power technology. Annual trade fairs and congresses are held in cities throughout Germany. 2011 was a record-breaking year for the German economy. German companies exported goods worth over €1 trillion ($1.3 trillion), the highest figure in history. The number of people in work has risen to 41.6 million, the highest recorded figure.

Through 2012, Germany's economy continued to be stronger relative to local neighboring nations.

Components of Gross National Income

As of January 2015, the unemployment rate was 4.8 percent.

As of December 2014, the CPI rate was 0.6 percent.

The main economic indicators in 1980–2017 show that the inflation was below 2%.

Companies

Of the world's 500 largest stock-market-listed companies measured by revenue in 2010, the Fortune Global 500, 37 are headquartered in Germany. 30 Germany-based companies are included in the DAX the German stock market index. Well-known global brands are Mercedes –Benz, BMW, SAP Siemen, Volkswagen, Addis, Allianz, Porsche, Bayer, BASF, Bosch, and Nivea.

Germany is recognised for its specialized small and medium enterprises, known as the Mittelstand model. Around 1,000 of these companies are global market leaders in their segment and are labelled hidden champions.

From 1991 to 2010, 40,301 merger and acquisitions with an involvement of German firms with a total known value of 2,422 bil. EUR have been announced. The largest transactions since 1991 are: the acquisition of Mannesmann by Vodafone for 204.8 bil. EUR in 1999, the merger of Dailmier-Benz with Chrysler to form DaimierChrysler in 1998 valued at 36.3 bil. EUR.

Economy of Berlin developed an international Startup ecosystem and became a leading location for venture capital funded firms in the European Union.

Mergers and Acquisitions

Since the German reunification there have been 52,258 mergers or acquisitions deals inbound or outbound Germany. The most active year in terms of value was 1999 with a cumulated value of 48.billion EUR, twice as much as the runner up which was 2006 with 24.billion. EUR.

Economic region

Eurozone

Germany is part of a monetary union, the Eurozone, and of the EU single market.

Germany as a federation is a polycentric country and does not have a single economic center. The stock exchange is located in Frankfurt am Main, the largest Media company is headquartered in Gutesion; the largest car manufacturers are in (Wolfsburg) Wolfsburg, Stuttgart and Munich.

Germany is an advocate of closer European economic and political integration. Its commercial policies are increasingly determined by agreements among European Union (EU) members and EU single market legislation.

Germany introduced the common European currency, the euro on 1 January 1999. Its monetary policy is set by the European Central Bank in Frankfurt.

The southern states ("Bundesländer"), especially Bayern, Baden-Württemberg and Hessen, are economically stronger than the northern states. One of Germany's traditionally strongest (and at the same time oldest) economic regions is the Ruhr areain the west, between Duisburg and Dortmund. 27 of the country's 100 largest companies are located there. In recent years, however, the area, whose economy is based on natural resources and heavy industry, has seen a substantial rise in unemployment (2010: 8.7%).

The economy of Bayern and Baden-Wuttermberg, the states with the lowest number of unemployed people (2018: 2.7%, 3.1%), on the other hand, is based on high-value products. Important sectors are automobiles, electronics, aerospace and biomedicine, among others. Baden-Württemberg is an industrial center especially for automobile and machine building industry and the home of brands like Mercedes-Benz (Daimler), Porsche and Bosch.

With the reunification on 3 October 1990, Germany began the major task of reconciling the economic systems of the two former republics. Interventionist economic planning ensured gradual development in eastern Germany up to the level of former West Germany, but the standard of living and annual income remains significantly higher in western German states. The modernization and integration of the eastern German economy continues to be a long-term process scheduled to last until the year 2019, with annual transfers from west to east amounting to roughly $80 billion. The overall unemployment rate has consistently fallen since 2005 and reached a 20-year low in 2012. The country in July 2014 began legislating to introduce a federally mandated minimum wage which would come into effect on 1 January 2015.

German States

List of selected German states by GRP in 2017 (in billions)

Nominal GRP was Euro 3.263.35 trillion in 2017 with State Rhine West phalia having euro 691.52billion, Bavaria euro 594.45 billion and Lower saxony euro 433.27 billion as GRP in 2017 which works out as 21.2%, 18.2% and 13.3%.

Wealth

The following top 10 list of German billionaires is based on an annual assessment of wealth and assets compiled and published by Forbes magazine on 1 March 2016.

1. $27.9 billion Beate Heister (b. Albrecht) & Karl Albrecht Jr.
2. $20.3 billion Theo Albrecht Jr.
3. $18.5 billion Susanne Klatten

4. $18.1 billion Georg Schaeffler
5. $16.4 billion Dieter Schwarz
6. $15.6 billion Stefan Quandt
7. $15.4 billion Michael Otto
8. $11.7 billion Heinz Hermann Thiele
9. $10 billion Klaus-Michael Kühne
10. $9.5 billion Hasso Plattner

Wolfsburg is the city in Germany with the country's highest per capital GDP at $128,000.

Sectors

German exports in 2006

Germany has a social market economy characterised by a highly qualified labour force, a developed infrastructure, a large capital stock, a low level of corruption, and a high level of innovation. It has the largest national economy in Europe, the fourth largest by nominal GDP in the world, and ranked fifth by GDP (PPP) in 2015.

The service sector contributes around 70% of the total GDP, industry 29.1%, and agriculture 0.9%.

Primary

In 2010 agriculture, forestry, and mining accounted for only 0.9% of Germany's gross domestic product (GDP) and employed only 2.4% of the population, down from 4% in 1991. Agriculture is extremely productive, and Germany is able to cover 90% of its nutritional needs with domestic production. Germany is the third largest agricultural producer in the European Union after France and Italy. Germany's principal agricultural products are potatoes, wheat, barley, sugar beets, fruit, and cabbages.

Despite the country's high level of industrialization, almost one-third of its territory is covered by forest. The forestry industry provides for about two-thirds of domestic consumption of wood and wood products, so Germany is a net importer of these items.

Lignite at Tagebau Garzweiler near Grevenbroich, Germany

The German soil is relatively poor in raw materials. Only lignite (brown coal) and potas salt (Kalisalz) are available in significant quantities. However, the former GDR's Wismut mining company produced a total of 230,400 tonnes of uranium between 1947 and 1990 and made East Germany the fourth largest producer of uranium ore worldwide (largest in USSR's sphere of control) at the time. Oil, natural gas and other resources are, for the most part, imported from other countries.

Potash salt is mined in the center of the country. The most important producer is K+ S AG.

Germany's bituminous coal deposits were created more than 300 million years ago from swamps which extended from the present-day South England, over the Ruhr area to Poland Lignite deposits developed in a similar way, but during a later period, about 66 million years ago. Because the wood is not yet completely transformed into coal, brown coal contains less energy than bituminous coal.

Lignite is extracted in the extreme western and eastern parts of the country, mainly in Nordrhein-Westfalen, Sachsen and Brandenburg. Considerable amounts arc burned in coal plants near to the mining areas, to produce electricity. Transporting lignite over far distances is not economically feasible, therefore the plants are located practically next to the extraction sites. Bituminous coal is mined in Nordrhein-Westfalen and Saarland. Most power plants burning bituminous coal operate on imported material, therefore the plants are located not only near to the mining sites, but throughout the country.

Industry

Industry and construction accounted for 30.1% of gross domestic product in 2017, and employed 24.2% of the workforce. Germany excels in the production of automobiles, machinery, electrical equipment and chemicals. With the manufacture of 5.2 million vehicles in 2009, Germany was the world's fourth largest producer and largest exporter of automobiles. German automotive companies enjoy an extremely strong position in the so-called premium segment, with a combined world market share of about 90%.

Small- to medium-sized manufacturing firms (Mitterlstand companies) which specialize in technologically advanced niche products and are often family-owned form a major part of the German economy. It is estimated that about 1500 German companies occupy a top three position in their respective market segment worldwide. In about two thirds of all industry sectors German companies belong to the top three competitors.

Germany is the only country among the top five arms exporters that is not a permanent member of the United Nations Security Council.

Services

Tourism in Germany

Bavaria (l.) is a tourism destination and Berlin (r.) a centre of creative industries.

In 2008 services constituted 69% of gross domestic product (GDP), and the sector employed 67.5% of the workforce. The subcomponents of services are financial, renting, and business activities (30.5%); trade, hotels and restaurants, and transport (18%); and other service activities (21.7%).

Germany is the seventh most visited country in the world,with a total of 407 million overnights during 2012. This number includes 68.83 million nights by foreign visitors. In 2012, over 30.4 million international tourists arrived in Germany. Berlin has become the third most visited city destination in Europe. Additionally, more than 30% of Germans spend their holiday in their own country, with the biggest share going to Mecklenburg -Vorpommern. Domestic and international travel and tourism combined directly contribute over EUR43.2 billion to German GDP. Including indirect and induced impacts, the industry contributes 4.5% of German GDP and supports 2 million jobs (4.8% of total employment). The largest annual international trade fairs and congresses are held in several German cities such as Hannover, Frankfurt, and Berlin.

Government finances

Taxation & Federal Budget in Germany

The debt-to-GDP ratio of Germany had its peak in 2010 when it stood at 80.3% and decreased since then. According to Eurostat, the government gross debt of Germany amounts to €2,152.0 billion or 71.9% of its GDP in 2015. The federal government achieved a budget surplus of €12.1 billion ($13.1 billion) in 2015. Germany's credit rating by credit rating agencies stands at the highest possible rating *AAA* with a stable outlook in 2016.

Germany's "debt clock" (*Schuldenuhr*) reversed for the first time in 20 years in January 2018. It is now running backwards at €78 per second.

Infrastructure

Energy

Energy in Germany

Germany is the world's fifth largest consumer of energy, and two-thirds of its primary energy was imported in 2002. In the same year, Germany was Europe's largest consumer of electricity, totaling 512.9 terawatt-hours. Government policy promotes energy conservation and the development of renewable energy sources, such as solar, wind, biomass, hydroelectric, and geothermal energy. As a result of energy-saving measures, energy efficiencies has been improving since the beginning of the 1970s. The government has set the goal of meeting half the country's energy demands from renewable sources by 2050.

The largest solar power and third largest wind power capacity in the world is installed in Germany.

In 2000, the red-green coalition under Chancellor Schroder and the German nuclear power industry agreed to phase out all nuclear power plants by 2021. The conservative coalition under Chancellor Merkel reversed this decision in January 2010, electing to keep plants open. The nuclear disaster of the Japanese nuclear plant Fusushima in March 2011 however, changed the political climate fundamentally: Older nuclear plants have been shut down. And a general phase out until 2020 or 2022 is now probable. Renewable energy yet still plays a more modest role in energy consumption, though German solar and wind power industries play a leading role worldwide.

In 2009, Germany's total energy consumption (not just electricity) came from the following sources: Oil 34.6%, Natural gas 21.7%, Lignite 11.4%, Bituminous coal 11.1%, Nuclear power 11.0%, Hydro and wind power 1.5%, others 9.0%.

There are 3 major entry points for oil pipelines: in the northeast (the Druzhba pipeline, coming from Gdansk), west (coming from Rotterdam) and southeast (coming from Nelahozeves). The oil pipelines of Germany do not constitute a proper network, and sometimes only connect two different locations. Major oil refineries are located in or near the 11 cities.

Germany's network of natural gas pipelines, on the other hand, is dense and well-connected. Imported pipeline gas comes mostly from Russia, the Netherland and the UK. Although gas imports from Russia have been historically reliable, even during the cold war, recent price disputes between Gazprom and the former Soviet states, such as Ukraine, have also affected Germany. As a result, high political importance is placed on thc construction of the Nord Stream pipeline, running in Russia along the Baltic Sea to Greifswald in Germany. This direct connection avoids third-party transit countries. Germany imports 50% to 75% of its natural gas from Russia.

Transport

With its central position in Europe, Germany is an important transportation hub. This is reflected in its dense and modern transportation networks. The extensive motorway (Autobahn) network that ranks worldwide third largest in its total length and features a lack of blanket speed limits on the majority of routes.

Germany has established a polycentric network of high-speed trains. The InterCity Express or *ICE* is the most advanced service category of the Deutsche Bahn and serves major German cities as well as destinations in neighbouring countries. The train maximum speed varies between 200 km/h and 320 km/h (125-200 mph). Connections are offered at either 30-minute, hourly, or two-hourly intervals. German railways are heavily subsidized, receiving €17.0 billion in 2014.

The largest German airports are the Frankfurt & Munich International Airports, both are global hubs of Lufthansa. Other major airport is Berlin.

Technology

Science and Technology in German

Germany is a pioneer research center for nanotechnology and materials engineering.

Germany's achievements in sciences have been significant, and research and development efforts form an integral part of the economy.

Germany is also one of the leading countries in developing and using green technologies. Companies specializing in green technology have an estimated turnover of €200 billion. German expertise in engineering, science and research is eminently respectable.

The lead markets of Germany's green technology industry are power generation, sustainable mobility, material efficiency, energy efficiency, waste management and recycling, sustainable water management.

With regard to triadic patents Germany is in third place after the US and Japan. With more than 26,500 registrations for patents submitted to the European Patent Office, Germany is the leading European nation. Siemens, Bosch and BASF, with almost 5,000 registrations for patents between them in 2008, are among the Top 5 of more than 35,000 companies registering patents. Together with the US and Japan, with regard to patents for Nano, bio and new technologies Germany is one of the world's most active nations. With around one third of triadic patents Germany leads the way worldwide in the field of vehicle emission reduction.

According to Winfried Kreschmann, who is premier of the region where Daimler is based, "China dominates the production of solar cells. Tesla is ahead in electric cars and Germany has lost the first round of digitalization to Google, Apple and the like. Whether Germany has a future as an industrial economy will depend on whether we can manage the ecological and digital transformation of our economy".

Present Position of Economy of Germany At Glance

(1) Frankfurt is the financial capital of Germany.

(2) Currency: Euro Euro1= $1.14

(3) Financial year: Calendar year

(4) Trade Organisations: EU, WTO, OECD

(5) GDP: $4.029 trillion (Nominal, 2017 4th rank) GDP PPP $4.379 trillion (2017, 5th rank)

(6) GDP Growth: 0.2% (Q.3, 2018), 1.5% (2018, YTD)

(7) GDP per Capita: $48669 (Nominal, 17th rank), $52896 (PPP, 18 rank).

(8) GDP by Sector: Agriculture 0.6%, Industry 30.1%, Services 69.3%

(9) GDP by components: Household Consumption 53.7%, Government 19.9%, Investment 0.1%Imports of Goods & Services -40%

(10) Population: 82.78 million

(11) Labour Force: 45.9 million 55.44% of population

(12) Unemployment 3.4% (July 2018)

(13) Inflation 2%

(14) Labour Force by Occupation: Agriculture 1.4%, Industry 24.2% Services 74.3%

(15) Average Gross Salary: Euro 3771/$4638 per month, Average Net Salary: Euro 2269/$2791 Monthly 15th rank for Gross, 14th rank for Net. – 2017 & 2016

(16) Main Industries: Iron, steel, coal, cement, chemicals, machinery, vehicles, machine tools, electronics, automobiles, food & beverages, ship building, textiles

External:

(17) Exports: $1.401 trillion, Imports: $1.104 trillion trade surplus: $297 billion.

(18) Export Goods: Motor cycles, machinery, chemicals, computer & electronic products, electric equipments, pharmaceuticals, metal, textile, rubber.

(19) Main Export Partners: EU 58%, US 8.8%, China6.4%, Switzerland 4.1%, Turkey 1.9%, Others20.8%

(20) Import Goods: Machinery, data processing equipments, vehicles, chemicals, oil & gas, metals, electric equipments, pharmaceuticals, foodstuffs, agricultural products

(21) Main Import Partners: EU 57.6%, China 9.9%, US 6.2%, Switzerland 4.7%, Russia 2.8%, Others 18.8%

(22) FDI Stock: 41.455 trillion, Foreign Reserves: $360 billion, Economic Aid: ODA $24.67 billion

(23) Gross External debt: $ 5.084 trillion (31-07-2017) 126.18% of GDP

Fiscal

(24) Public Debt: 64.13% of GDP i.e. 2.58 trillion

(25) Revenues: $1.598 trillion, Expenses: $1.573 trillion Fiscal Surplus: $25 billion i.e. 0.62% of GDP

(26) Credit Rating: S & P: AAA Outlook: Stable, Moody's: Aaa Outlook: Stable, Fitch: AAA Outlook: Stable, Scope: AAA Outlook: Stable.

(27) Population below poverty line is not registered.

Critical Observations of Economy of Germany

(1) The economy of Germany is a high developed social market economy. It is the largest national economy in Europe with 8.28 crores population at present. It is fourth largest economy by GDP (Nominal) and fifth largest by GDP (PPP).

(2) It is the founding member of EU and Eurozone. Leader in directing the countries in EU in their economic activities.

(3) German recorded trade surplus Euro 310 billion in 2016. It is the largest manufacturing economy in EU.It has ample stocks of natural gas, potest stand timber.

(4) Industrial revolution started in Germany a century later than England, France and Belgium. Invention of automobiles by Karl Benz with his wife Betha Benz with Victoria model in 1884 was well known and was in demand.

(5) Germany is first in introducing Social Insurance scheme there by improving labour conditions. It expands railways and other transportation infrastructure facilities. In 1937, Nazi rose to power when unemployment was high. But soon it was improved and came down to 4.8%. New foreign exchange control, import quotas were also introduced.

(6) Population in Germany is 8.28 crores and labour force 4.59 which works out to 55.35% of population. Euro is the main and exclusive currency for exchange in Germany and EU. Value of Euro is $1.14.There is no fiscal deficit but fiscal surplus of 0.25 trillion. Domestic/Public loan is 64.13% of GDP compared with EU rule that maximum Public Loan of any EU Country should not exceed 60% of GDP. External loan is 5.084 trillion i.e. 126.185% of GDP $ 4.029 trillon which is on high side and may compel the government to restructure loan servicing with accepting austerity measures like cut in public spending from IMF.

(7) Adlodt Hitler came into power as Nazi's head in 1937 and he waged World War II in 1939 and defeated Poland, France and England miserably. Russia succeeded in defeating his attack on Russia. Japan who was military partner of Hitler suffered from terrible bombing on Nagasaki and Hiroshima where millions of people died and/or permanently became handicapped. Immediately Japan showed White flag and withdrew from World War II in 1945. Azad Hind Sena of Subhash Chandra Bose was very active in Japan in waging war against British which resulted in tremendous military and financial loss to England. Unfortunately Subhash Chandra Bose died in Plane accident in 1945. Adolf Hitler committed suicide and World War II ended abruptly. War finance was provided to Russia mainly by US which was never repaid by

Russia. War damages were recovered from Germany by USA, UK and Russia. Hilter's goal to conquer the world was not achieved.

(8) World War II made Germany's position very pathetic and German was divided into East Germany and West Germany.

(9) West Germany became part of USA and East Germany became a part oF Russia. Germany was oppressed by these country heavily as retaliation. Germany's Economy completely collapsed like Venezuela at present but it came back to normal after few years.

(10) After precarious war like and political conditions in Seria, Africa and other countries, citizens from those country started migrating in European Countries. German President Mrs. Angel Markel and France President Mr. Emyual Macron are strong supporters of migrating people from other countries in their countries. Under the initiative of France and Germany, EU specified minimum quotas for each member country of EU for immigration which was strongly opposed by Italy, Poland, Denmark, Hungary and other countries and these countries are taking drastic actions against immigration officially and sending them back to their countries. Strong opposition is faced by both Presidents Germany and France and agitatorsin Germany and France want these both leaders to resign. At present no President has resigned but Markel has announced that she will not contest next election. Macron is still hoping to satisfy agitators on "Yellow West "movement but has not yet been successful.

(11) Main issue of migration is that terrorists also have migrated with these folks and created terrorist acts in migrated countries. Perhaps, in next EU election, there will be drastic changes or EU may be dissolved.

(12) In the past, German has faced complete crash of its economy worse than Venezuela at present but it successfully came out of that situation and is now performing very well. Its Credit rating as given by the Credit Rating Agencies is also satisfactory.

CHAPTER - 22

ECONOMY OF JAPAN

Introduction

The economy of Japan is a highly developed and market oriented economy. It is the third largest in the world by GDP Nominal and 4th largest in the world by GDP PPP. It is the 2nd largest developed economy after USA. Japan is the member of G7. Japanese yen is the currency of the country which is volatile and widely fluctuating currency. With this fluctuation, Japan's GDP (PPP) works out to \$ 38937- per capita income (2016). It is the fastest growing economy. It is the world's third largest automobile manufacturing country and has largest econotronic goods industry. Manufacturing in Japan is highly technical and of precision goods. It is highly innovative country with energetic productive workforce who is very laborious and proud of nation's image.

The size and industrial structure of cities in Japan have maintained tight regularities despite substantial churning of population and industries across cities. Japan is the world's largest creditor nation. Japan generally runs an annual trade surplus and has a considerable net international investment surplus. As of 2010, Japan possesses 13.7% of the world's private financial assets) at an estimated \$13.5 trillion. As of 2015, 54 of the Fortune Global 500 companies are based in Japan, down from 62 in 2013.

Japan has the highest ratio of public debt GDP of any developed nation. However, the national debt is predominantly owned by Japanese nationals. The Japanese economy faces considerable challenges posed by a declining population. Statistics showed an official decline for the first time in 2015, while projections suggest that it will continue to fall from 127 million down to below 100 million by the middle of the 21st century.

Overview of economy

In the three decades of economic development following 1960, rapid economic growth referred to as the Japanese post-war economic miracle occurred. After the Bomb dropping on Hiroshima and Nagasaki, the Japanese economy was completely collapsed but with young workforce and their enthusiasm to build up their country prosperous as before has resulted in such miracle. Japan could achieve an average growth rates of 10% in the 1960s, 5% in the 1970s and 4% in the 1980s. Japan was able to establish and maintain itself as the world's second largest economy from 1978 until 2010, when it was surpassed by China. By 1990, income per capita in Japan equaled or surpassed that in most countries in the West.

During the second half of the 1980s, rising stock and real estate prices created an economic bubble which came to an abrupt end as the Tokyo Stock Market crashed in 1990–92 and real estate prices peaked in 1991. Growth in Japan throughout the 1990s at 1.5% was slower than global growth, giving rise to the term Lost Decade. After another decade of low growth rate, the term became the Lost 20 Years. Nonetheless, GDP per capita growth from 2001 to 2010 has still managed to outpace Europe and the United States.

With this low growth rate, the national debt of Japan has expanded due to its considerable social welfare spending in an aging society with a shrinking tax-base. The scenario of "Abandoned homes" continues to spread from rural areas to urban areas in Japan.

A mountainous, volcanic island country, Japan has inadequate natural resources to support its growing economy and large population, and therefore exports goods in which it has a comparative advantage such as engineering-oriented research and development-led industrial products in exchange for the import of raw materials and petroleum. Japan is among the top-three importers for agricultural products in the world next to the European Union and United States in total volume for covering of its own domestic agricultural consumption. Japan is the world's largest single national importer of fish and fishery products.

Though many kinds of minerals were extracted throughout the country, most mineral resources had to be imported in the postwar era. Local deposits of metal-bearing ores were difficult to process because they were low grade. The nation's large and varied forest resources, which covered 70 percent of the nation's entry in the late 1980s, were not utilized extensively. Because of political decisions on local, prefectural, and national levels, Japan decided not to exploit its forest resources for economic gain. Domestic sources only supplied between 25 and 30 percent of the nation's timber needs. Agriculture and fishing were the best developed resources, but only through years of painstaking investment and toil. The nation therefore built up the manufacturing and processing industries to convert raw materials imported from abroad. This strategy of economic development necessitated the establishment of a strong economic infrastructure to provide the needed energy, transportation, communications, and technological know-how.

Deposits of Gold, Magnesium and silver meet current industrial demands, but Japan is dependent on foreign sources for many of the minerals essential to modern industry. Iron ore, copper, bauxite and alumina must be imported, as well as many forest products.

Economic history of Japan

The economic history of Japan Edo is one of the most studied economies for its spectacular growth in three different periods. First was the foundation of Edo (in 1603) to whole inland economic developments, second was the Meiji Restoration (in 1868) to be the first non-European power, third was after the defeat of World War II (in 1945) when the island nation rose to become the world's second largest economy.

First contacts with Europe (16th century)

Japan was considered as a country rich in precious metals, mainly owing to Marco Polo's accounts of gilded temples and palaces, but also due to the relative abundance of surface ores characteristic of a massive huge volcanic country, before large-scale deep-mining became possible in Industrial times. Japan was to become a major exporter of silver, copper, and gold during the period until exports for those minerals were banned.

Renounce Japan was also perceived as a sophisticated feudal society with a high culture and a strong pre-industrial technology. It was densely populated and urbanized. Prominent European observers of the time seemed to agree that the Japanese *"excel not only all the other Oriental peoples, they surpass the Europeans as well."*

Early European visitors were amazed by the quality of Japanese craftsmanship and metalsmithing. This stems from the fact that Japan itself is rather rich in natural resources found commonly in Europe, especially iron.

The cargo of the first Portuguese ships (usually about 4 smaller-sized ships every year) arriving in Japan almost entirely consisted of Chinese goods (silk, porcelain). The Japanese were very much looking forward to acquiring such goods, but had been prohibited from any contacts with the European Emperor of China, as a punishment for Wako pirate raids. The Portuguese (who were called Namban, lit. Southern Barbarians) therefore found the opportunity to act as intermediaries in Asian trade.

Edo period (1603–1868)

Japanese export porcelain in the European shape of a barber's basin, with copulating cock, around 1700.

The beginning of the Edo period coincides with the last decades of the Nanban trade period during which intense interaction with European powers, on the economic and religious plane, took place. It is at the beginning of the Edo period that Japan built her first ocean-going Western-style warships, such as the San Juan Bautista, a 500-ton galleon-type ship that transported a

Japanese embassy headed by Hasekura Tsunenaga to the Americas, which then continued to Europe. Also during that period, the bakufu commissioned around 350 Red Seal Ships three-master and armed trade ships, for intra-Asian commerce. Japanese adventurers, such as Yamada Nagasasa, were active throughout Asia.

In order to eradicate the influence of Christianization, Japan entered in a period of isolation called sakoku, during which its economy enjoyed stability and mild progress. But not long after, in the 1650s, the production of Japanese export porcelain increased greatly when civil war put the main Chinese center of porcelain production, out of action for several decades. For the rest of the 17th century most Japanese production was for export, mostly in Kyushu. The trade dwindled under renewed Chinese competition by the 1740s, before resuming after the opening of Japan in the mid-19th century.

Economic development during the Edo period included urbanization, increased shipping of commodities, a significant expansion of domestic and, initially, foreign commerce, and a diffusion of trade and handicraft industries. The construction, trades flourished, along with banking facilities and merchant associations. Increasingly, authorities oversaw the rising agricultural production and the spread of rural handicrafts.

By the mid-eighteenth century, Edo had a population of more than 1 million and Osaka and Kyoto each had more than 400,000 inhabitants. Many other castle towns grew as well. Osaka and Kyoto became busy trading and handicraft production centers, while Edo was the center for the supply of food and essential urban consumer goods.

Rice was the base of the economy, as the daimyô collected the taxes from the peasants in the form of rice. Taxes were high, about 40% of the harvest. The rice was sold at the fudasashi market in Edo. To raise money, the daimyô used forward contracts to sell rice that was not even harvested yet. These contracts were similar to modern future trading.

During the period, Japan progressively studied Western sciences and techniques through the information and books received through the Dutch traders in Dejima. The main areas that were studied included geography, medicine, natural sciences, astronomy, art, languages, physical sciences such as the study of electrical phenomena, and mechanical sciences as exemplified by the development of Japanese clock watches, inspired from Western techniques.

Pre-war period (1868–1945)

Since the mid-19th century, after the Meiji Restoration, the country was opened up to Western commerce and influence and Japan has gone through two periods of economic development. The first began in earnest in 1868 and extended through to World War II; the second began in 1945 and continued into the mid-1980s.

Economic developments of the prewar period began with the "Rich State and Strong Army Policy" by the Meiji Government. During the Meiji period (1868–1912), leaders inaugurated a new Western-based education system for all young people, sent thousands of students to the United States and Europe, and hired more than 3,000 Westerners to teach modern science, mathematics, technology, and foreign languages in Japan. The government also built railroads, improved road, and inaugurated a land reform program to prepare the country for further development.

To promote industrialization, the government decided that while it should help private business to allocate resources and to plan, the public sector was best equipped to stimulate economic growth. The greatest role of government was to help provide good economic conditions for business. In short, government was to be the business guide of the producer. In the early Meiji period, the government built factories and shipyards that were sold to entrepreneurs at a fraction of their value. Many of these businesses grew rapidly into the larger conglomerates. Government emerged as chief promoter of private enterprise, enacting a series of pro-business policies.

In the mid-1930s, the Japanese nominal wage rates were "10 times less" than the one of the U.S (based on mid-1930s exchange rates), while the price level is estimated to have been about 44% the one of the U.S.

Postwar period (1945–present)

Japanese Trade in 2005

From the 1960s to the 1980s, overall real economic growth was extremely large: 10% average in the 1960s, 5% average in the 1970s and 4% average in the 1980s as mentioned above.By the end of said period, Japan had moved into being a high-wage economy.

Growth slowed markedly in the late 1990s also termed the Lost Decade, after the collapse of the Japanese assets price bubble. As a consequence Japan ran massive budget deficits (added trillions in Yen to Japanese financial system) to finance large public works programs.

By 1998, Japan's public works projects still could not stimulate demand enough to end the economy's stagnation. In desperation, the Japanese government undertook "structural reform" policies intended to wring speculative excesses from the stock and real estate markets. Unfortunately, these policies led Japan into deflation on numerous occasions between 1999 and 2004. Japan had a new option. Krugman's plan called for a rise in inflation expectations to, in effect, cut long-term interest rates and promote spending.

Japan used another technique, somewhat based on Krugman's, called Quantitative easing. As opposed to flooding the money market with newly printed money, the Bank of Japan expanded the money supply internally to raise expectations of inflation. Initially, the policy failed to induce any growth, but it eventually began to affect inflationary expectations. By late 2005, the economy finally began what seems to be a sustained recovery. GDP growth for that year was 2.8%, with an annualized fourth quarter expansion of 5.5%, surpassing the growth rates of the US and European Union during the same period. Unlike previous recovery trends, domestic consumption has been the dominant factor of growth.

Despite having interest rates down near zero for a long period of time, the Quantitative easing strategy did not succeed in stopping price deflation. This led some economists, such as Paul Krugman, and some Japanese politicians, to advocate the generation of higher inflation expectations. In July 2006, the zero-rate policy was ended. In 2008, the Japanese Central Bank still had the lowest interest rates in the developed world, but deflation had still not been eliminated and the Nikkei 225 has fallen over approximately 50% (between June 2007 and December 2008). However, on 5 April 2013, the Bank of Japan announced that it would be purchasing 60–70 trillion yen in bonds and securities in an attempt to eliminate deflation by doubling the money supply in Japan over the course of two years. Markets around the world have responded positively to the government's current proactive policies, with the Nikkei 225 adding more than 42% since November 2012. The Economist has suggested that improvements to bankruptcy law, land transfer law, and tax laws will aid Japan's economy. In recent years, Japan has been the top export market for almost 15 trading nations worldwide.

Infrastructure

Energy and transportation in Japan

In 2005, one half of Japan's energy was produced from petroleum, a fifth from coal, and 14% from natural gas. Nuclear power in Japan made a quarter of electricity production but due to the Fukushima Daiichi nuclear disaster there has been a large desire to end Japan's nuclear power program. In September 2013, Japan closed its last 50 nuclear power plants nationwide, causing the nation to be nuclear free.

Japan's spending on roads has been considered large. The 1.2 million kilometers of paved road are one of the major means of transportation. Japan has left-hand traffic. A single network of speed, divided, limited-access toll roads connects major cities and are operated by toll-collecting enterprises. New and used cars are inexpensive, and the Japanese government has encouraged people to buy hybrid vehicles. Car ownership fees and fuel levies are used to promote energy-efficiency.

Rail Transport is a major means of transport in Japan. Dozens of Japanese railway companies compete in regional and local passenger transportation markets; for instance, 6 passenger JR enterprises, Kintetsu Railway, Seibu

Railway, Seibu Railway and Keio Corporation. Often, strategies of these enterprises contain real estate or department stores next to stations, and many major stations have major department stores near them. All trains are known for punctuality, and a delay of 90 seconds can be considered late for some train services.

There are 98 passenger and 175 total airports in Japan, and flying is a popular way to travel. The largest domestic airport, Tokyo International Airport, is Asia's second busiest airport. The largest international gateways are Narita International Airport (Tokyo area), Kansai International Airport (Osaka/Kobe/Kyoto area), and Chubu Cenrair International Airport (Nagoya area).

About 84% of Japan's energy is imported from other countries. Japan is the world's largest liquefied natural gas importer, second largest coal importer, and third largest net oil importer. Given its heavy dependence on imported energy, Japan has aimed to diversify its sources. Since the oil shocks of the 1970s, Japan has reduced dependence on petroleum as a source of energy from 77.4% in 1973 to about 43.7% in 2010 and increased dependence on natural gas and nuclear power. Other important energy source includes coal, and hydroelectricity, Japan's biggest renewable energy source. Japan's solar market is also currently booming. Kerosene is also used extensively for home heating in portable heaters, especially farther north. Many taxi companies run their fleets on liquefied natural gas. A recent success towards greater fuel economy was the introduction of mass-produced Hybrid vehicles. Prime Minister Shinzo Abe, who was working on Japan's economic revival, signed a treaty with Saudi Arabia and UAE about the rising prices of oil, ensuring Japan's stable deliveries from that region.

Macro-economic trend

Real GDP growth rate from 1956 to 2008

Quarterly change in the real GDP (blue) and the unemployment rate (red) of Japan from 2000 to 2010 shows that in 2010, Japanese GDP was $ 477 billion and Nominal per-capita GDP was 89.8% as % of US.

GDP composition

In 2012, Japan's GDP Nominal was $5,268 trillion. Main Industry-wise classification to the nation's Nominal GDP were as follows:

Development of main indicators

The main economic indicators in 1980–2017shows that Inflation under 2 %

In 1980, GDP was $1.046 billion PPP with unemployment 2% and inflation rate was7.8% while in 2017 GDP PP was $5.421 billion with unemployment @2.9% and inflation over 0.5%.

Industry	*GDP in 2012 in $ billion*	*Percentage Nation GDP in 2012 $ 5268 billion*
Oher services activities	1238	23.5%
Manufacturing	947	18%
Real Estate	697	13.2%
Wholesale & Retail trade	660	12.5%
Transport & Communication	358	6.8%
Public administration Construction	329 & 327 respectively	6.2% each

Sectors of the economy

Agriculture, Forestry and fishing in Japan

The Japanese agricultural sector accounts for about 1.4% of the total country's GDP.Only 12% of Japan's land is suitable for cultivation. Due to this lack of arable land, a system of terraces is used to farm in small areas. This results in one of the world's highest levels of crop yields per unit area, with an overall agricultural self-sufficiency rate of about 50% on fewer than 56,000 km (14 million acres) cultivated.

Japan's small agricultural sector, however, is also highly subsidized and protected, with government regulations that favor small-scale cultivation instead of large-scale agriculture as practiced in North America. There has been a growing concern about farming as the current farmers are aging with a difficult time finding successors.

Rice accounts for almost all of Japan's cereal production. Japan is the second-largest agricultural product importer in the world. Rice, the most protected crop, is subject to tariffs of 777.7%.

Although Japan is usually self-sufficient in rice (except for its use in making rice crackers and processed foods) and wheat, the country must import about 50% of its requirements of other grain and fodder crops and relies on imports for half of its supply of meat. Japan imports large quantities of wheat and soybeans. Japan is the 5th largest market for EU agricultural exports. Over 90% of mandarin oranges in Japan are grown in Japan. Apples are also grown due to restrictions on apple imports.

Fishery

Fishing Industry in Japan

Japan ranked fourth in the world in 1996 in tonnage of fish caught. Japan captured 4,074,580 metric tons of fish in 2005, down from 4,987,703 tons in 2000, 9,558,615 tons in 1990, 9,864,422 tons in 1980, 8,520,397 tons in 1970, 5,583,796 tons in 1960 and 2,881,855 tons in 1950. In 2003, the total aquaculture production was predicted at 1,301,437 tonnes. In 2010, Japan's total fisheries production was 4,762,469 fish. Offshore fisheries accounted for an average of 50% of the nation's total fish catches in the late 1980s although they experienced repeated ups and downs during that period.

Coastal fishing by small boats, set nets, or breeding techniques accounts for about one third of the industry's total production, while offshore fishing by medium-sized boats makes up for more than half the total production. Deep-sea fishing from larger vessels makes up the rest. Freshwater fishing, including salmon, trout and eel hatcheries and fish farms, takes up about 30% of Japan's fishing industry. Among the nearly 300 fish species in the rivers of Japan are native varieties of catfish, chub, herring and goby, as well as such freshwater crustaceans as crabs and crayfish. Marine and freshwater aquaculture is conducted in all 47 prefectures in Japan.

Industry

Manufacturing in Japan

Japanese manufacturing and industry is extremely diversified, with a variety of advanced industries that are highly successful. Industry accounts for 24% of the nation's GDP.

Industry is concentrated in several regions, with the Kango region surrounding Tokyo, as well as the Kansai region surrounding Osaka and the Tokai region surrounding Nagoya. Other industrial centers include the southwestern part of Honshu and northern Shikoku around the Seto Inland Sea; and the northern part of Kyushu. In addition, a long narrow belt of industrial centers called the Taiheiyo belt is found between Tokyo and Fukuoka, established by particular industries that have developed as mill towns.

Japan enjoys high technological development in many fields, including consumer electronics, automobile manufacturing, semiconductor manufacturing, fibers, optical fibers, optoelectronics, optical media, facsimile and copy machines, and fermentation processes in food and biochemistry. However, many Japanese companies are facing emerging rivals from the United States, South Korea, and China.

Automobiles

Manufacturing in Japan

The rapid growth and success of Toyato's Lexus and other Japanese automakers reflects Japan's strength and global dominance in the automobile industry.

Japan is the third biggest producer of automobiles in the world. Toyato is currently the world largest car maker, and the Japanese car makers Nissan, Honda, Suzuki, and Mazda also count for some of the largest car makers in the world.

Mining and petroleum exploration

Mining in Japan

Japan's mining production has been minimal, and Japan has very little mining deposits. However, massive deposits of rare earths have been found off the coast of Japan. In the 2011 fiscal year, the domestic yield of crude oil was 820 thousand kiloliters, which was 0.4% of Japan's total crude processing volume.

Services

Trade and services in Japan

Japan Airlines, though faced with massive debts as of 2010, is considered one of the largest airlines in the world.

Japan's service sector accounts for about three-quarters of its total economic output. Banking, insurance, real estate, retailing, transportation, and telecommunications are all major industries such as Mitsubishi UFJ, Mizuho, NTT, TEPCO, Nomula, Mitsubishi Estate EON, Miysui Sumitomo, Softbank, JR East, Seven & I.KDDI and Japan Airlines counting as one of the largest companies in the world. Four of the five most circulated newspapers in the world are Japanese newspapers. The Koizumi Japan Post., one of the country's largest providers of savings and insurance services for privatization by 2015. The six major keiretsus are the Mitsubhishi, Sumitomo, Fuyo, Mitsui, Dai-Ichi Kangyoand SanwaGroups Japan is home to 251 companies from the Forbes Global 2000 or 12.55% (as of 2013).

Tourism

Tourism in Japan

Himeji Castle, in Himeji, Hyogo Prefecture, is one of the most visited sights in Japan.

In 2012, Japan was the fifth most visited country in Asia and the Pacific, with over 8.3 million tourists. In 2013, due to the weaker yen and easier visa requirements for southwest Asian countries, Japan received a record 11.25 million visitors which was higher than the government's projected goal of 10 million visitors. The government hopes to attract 40 million visitors a year by the 2020 Summer Olympics in Tokyo. Some of the most popular visited places include the cities of Osaka, Kobe and Kyoto, as well as Himeji Castle.

Finance

The Tokyo Stock Exchange is the third largest stock exchange by market capitalization, as well as the 2nd largest stock market in Asia, with 2,292 listed companies. The Nikkei 225 and the TOPIX are the two important stock market indexes of the Tokyo Stock Exchange. The Tokyo Stock Exchange and the Osaka Stock Exchange, another major stock exchange in Japan, merged on 1 January 2013, creating one of the world's largest stock exchanges. Other stock exchanges in Japan include the Nagoya Stock Exchange, Fukuoka Stock Exchange and Sapporo Securities Exchange.

Labor force

Labour Market of Japan

Unemployment rate of Japan

The unemployment rate in December 2013 was 3.7%, down 1.5 percentage points from the claimed unemployment rate of 5.2% in June 2009 due to the strong economic recovery.

In 2008 Japan's labour force consisted of some 66 million workers—40% of whom were women—and was rapidly shrinking. One major long-term concern for the Japanese labor force is its low birthrate. In the first half of 2005, the number of deaths in Japan exceeded the number of births, indicating that the decline in population, initially predicted to start in 2007, had already started. While one countermeasure for a declining birthrate would be to remove barriers to immigration despite taking new steps towards it, the Japanese government has been reluctant to do so, since foreign immigration to Japan has been unpopular among citizens.

In 1989, the predominantly public sector union confederation, SOHYO (General Council of Trade Unions of Japan), merged with RENGO (Japanese Private Sector Trade Union Confederation) to form the Japanese Trade Union Confederation. Labor union membership is about 12 million.

Law and Government

Japan ranks 27th of 185 countries in the ease of doing business index 2013.Japan has one of the smallest tax rates in the developed world.After deductions, the majority of workers are free from personal income taxes. Consumption tax is only 8%, while corporate tax rates are high, second highest corporate tax rate in the world, at 36.8%. However, the House of Representatives has passed a bill which will increase the consumption tax to 10% in October 2015.The government has also decided to reduce corporate tax and to phase out automobile tax.

In 2016, the IMF encouraged Japan to adopt an income policy that pushes firms to raise employee wages in combination with reforms to tackle the labor market dual retired employment system to drive higher wages, on top of monetary and fiscal stimulus. Shinzo Abe has encouraged firms to raise wages by at least three percent annually (the inflation target plus average productivity growth).

Shareholder is rare despite the fact that the corporate law gives shareholders strong powers over managers. Under Prime Minister Shinzo Abe, corporate governance reform has been a key initiative to encourage economic growth. In 2012 around 40% of leading Japanese companies had no any independent directors while in 2016 most all have begun to appoint independent directors.

The government's liabilities include the second largest public debt of any nation with debt of over one quadrillion yen, or $8,535,340,000,000 in USD. Former Prime Minister Naoto Kan has called the situation 'urgent'.

Japan's central bank has the second largest foreign exchange reserves after the People's Republic of China, with over one trillion US Dollars in foreign reserves.

Culture

Our expansion could be much bigger and quicker, but we are held back. Nowhere in the world do the [regulatory approvals] take so long. (The process is) old fashioned. — Tony Fernandes, *AirAsia chief.*

Overview

"Consensus building", in Japanese culture is an informal process of quietly laying the foundation for some proposed change or project, by talking to the people concerned, gathering support and feedback, and so forth. It is considered an important element in any major change, before any formal steps are taken, and successful *nemawashi* enables changes to be carried out with the consent of all sides.

Japanese companies are known for management methods such as "The Toyata Way. Kaizen, Japanese for "improvement" is a Japanese philosophy that focuses on continuous improvement throughout all aspects of life. When applied to the workplace, Kaizen activities continually improve all functions of a business, from manufacturing to management and from the CEO to the assembly line workers.By improving standardized activities and processes, Kaizen aims to eliminate waste). Kaizen was first implemented in several Japanese businesses during the country's recovery after World War II, including Toyota, and has since spread to businesses throughout the world. Within certain value systems, it is ironic that Japanese workers labor amongst the most hours per day, even though kaizen is supposed to improve all aspects of life.

Some companies have powerful enterprise unions and shunto. The Nenko System or Nenko Joretsu, as it is called in Japan, is the Japanese system of promoting an employee based on his or her proximity to retirement. The advantage of the system is that it allows older employees to achieve a higher salary level before retirement and it usually brings more experience to the executive ranks. The disadvantage of the system is that it does not allow new talent to be combined with experience and those with specialized skills cannot be promoted to the already crowded executive ranks. It also does not guarantee or even attempt to bring the "right person for the right job".

Relationships between government bureaucrats and companies are often close. Amakudari *amakudari*, "descent from heaven" is the institutionalized practice where Japanese senior bureaucrats retire to high-profile positions in the private and public sectors. The practice is increasingly viewed as corrupt and a limitation on efforts to reduce ties between the private sector and the state that prevent economic and political reforms. Lifetime employment and seniority-based career advancement have been common in the Japanese work environment. Japan has begun to gradually move away from some of these norms.

Salaryman refers to someone whose income is salary based; particularly those working for corporations. Its frequent use by Japanese corporations, and its prevalence in Japanese manga and anime has gradually led to its acceptance in English-speaking countries as a noun for a Japanese white-collarbusinessman. The word can be found in many books and articles pertaining to Japanese culture. Immediately following World War II, becoming a salaryman was viewed as a gateway to a stable, middle-class lifestyle. In modern use, the term carries associations of long working hours, low prestige in the corporate hierarchy, the term salaryman refers almost exclusively to males.

An office lady, often abbreviated OL, is a female office worker in Japan who performs generally pink collar tasks such as serving tea and secretarial or clerical work. Like many unmarried Japanese, OLs often live with their parents well into early adulthood. Office ladies are usually full-time permanent staff, although the jobs they do usually have little opportunity for promotion, and there is usually the tacit expectation that they leave their jobs once they get married.

Freeter is a Japanese expression for people between the age of 15 and 34 who lack full-time employment or are unemployed, excluding homemakers and students. They may also be described as underemployed or freelance workers. These people do not start a career after high school or university but instead usually live as parasite singles with their parents and earn some money with low skilled and low paid jobs. The low income makes it difficult for freeters to start a family, and the lack of qualifications makes it difficult to start a career at a later point in life.

Karoshi which can be translated quite literally from Japanese as "death from overwork", is occupational sudden death. The major medical causes of karôshi deaths are heart attack and stroke due to stress.

Sokaiya (sometimes also translated as *corporate bouncers*, *meeting-men*, or *corporate blackmailers*) are a form of specialized racketeer unique to Japan, and often associated with the yakuza that extort money from or blackmail companies by threatening to publicly humiliate companies and their management, usually in their annual meeting (*sôkai*). Sakarin is a Japanese term for moneylender, or loan shark. It is a contraction of the Japanese words for salaryman and cash. Around 14 million people, or 10% of the Japanese population, have borrowed from a *sarakin*. In total, there are about 10,000 firms (down from 30,000 a decade ago); however, the top seven firms make up 70% of the market. The value of outstanding loans totals $100 billion. The biggest *sarakin* are publicly traded and often allied with big banks.

The first "Western-style" department of store in Japan was Mitsukoshi, founded in 1904, which has its root as a kimono store called Echigoya from 1673. When the roots are considered, however, Matsuzakaya has an even longer history, dated from 1611. The kimono store changed to a department store in 1910. In 1924, Matsuzakaya store in Ginza allowed street shoes to be worn indoors, something innovative at the time.These former kimono shop department stores dominated the market in its earlier history. They sold, or rather displayed, luxurious products, which contributed for their sophisticated atmospheres. Another origin of Japanese department store is that from railway company. There have been many private railway operators in the nation, and from the 1920s, they started to build department stores directly linked to their lines' tenimi Seibu and Hankyu are the typical examples of this type. From the 1980s onwards, Japanese department teministores face fierce competition from supermarkets and convenience stores, gradually losing their presences. Still, *depâto* are bastions of several aspects of cultural conservatism in the country. Gift certificates for prestigious department stores are frequently given as formal presents in Japan. Department stores in Japan generally offer a wide range of services and can include foreign exchange, travel reservations, ticket sales for local concerts and other events.

Keiretsu

Keiretsu ("system" or "series") is a set of companies with interlocking business relationships and shareholdings. It is a type of business group. The prototypical *keiretsu*appeared in Japan during the "economic miracle" following World War II. Before Japan's surrender, Japanese industry was controlled by large family-controlled vertical monopolies called zaibatsu. The Allies dismantled the *zaibatsu* in the late 1940s, but the companies formed from the dismantling of the *zaibatsu* were reintegrated. The dispersed corporations were re-interlinked through share purchases to form horizontally integrated alliances across many industries. Where possible, *keiretsu* companies would also supply one another, making the alliances vertically integrated as well. In this period, official government policy promoted the creation of robust trade corporations that could withstand pressures from intensified world trade competition.

The major *keiretsu* were each centered on one bank, which lent money to the *keiretsu's* member companies and held equity positions in the companies. Each central bank had great control over the companies in the *keiretsu* and acted as a monitoring entity and as an emergency bail-out entity. One effect of this structure was to minimize the presence of hostile takeovers in Japan, because no entities could challenge the power of the banks.

There are two types of *keiretsu*: vertical and horizontal. Vertical keiretsu illustrates the organization and relationships within a company (for example all factors of production of a certain product are connected), while a horizontal *keiretsu* shows relationships between entities and industries, normally centered on a bank and trading company. Both are complexly woven together and sustain each other.

The Japanese recession in the 1990s had profound effects on the keiretsu. Many of the largest banks were hit hard by bad loan portfolios and forced to merge or go out of business. This had the effect of blurring the lines between the keiretsu: Sumitomo Bank of Mitsui Bank, for instance, became Sumitomo Mitsui banking Corporation in 2001, while Sanwa Bank (the banker for the Hankyu-Toho Group) became part of Bank of Tokyo-Mitsubishi UFJ. Additionally, many companies from outside the keiretsu system, such as Sony, began outperforming their counterparts within the system.

Generally, these causes gave rise to a strong notion in the business community that the old Keiretsu system was not an effective business model, and led to an overall loosening of keiretsu alliances. While the keiretsu still exist, they are not as centralized or integrated as they were before the 1990s. This, in turn, has led to a growing corporate acquisition industry in Japan, as companies are no longer able to be easily "bailed out" by their banks, as well as rising derivative litigation by more independent shareholders.

Mergers and Acquisitions corporation acquisition

Japanese companies have been involved in 50,759 deals between 1985 and 2018. This cumulates to a total value of 2,636 bil. USD which translates to 281,469.9 bil. YEN. In the year 1999 there was an all-time high in terms of value of deals with almost 220 bil. USD. The most active year so far was 2017 with over 3,150 deals, but only a total value of 114 bil. USD.

Among the top 50 deals by value, 92% of the time the acquiring nation is Japan. Foreign direct investment is playing a much smaller role than national M&A in Japan.

Exchange:

Japanese Yen per US$1 – 88.67 (2010), 93.57 (2009), 103.58 (2008), 117.99 (2007), 116.18 (2006), 109.69 (2005), 115.93 (2003), 125.39 (2002), 121.53 (2001), 105.16 (January 2000), 113.91 (1999), 130.91 (1998), 120.99 (1997), 108.78 (1996), 94.06 (1995).

Present Position of Japanese Economy At Glance

(1) Currency: Japanese yen 110 yens =$1

(2) Fiscal year: 1st April-31st March

(3) Trade Organisations: APEC, WTO, OECD, G 20, G 8 & Others

(4) GDP: $5.221 trillion (Nominal, 3rd Rank, $5.809 Trillion (PPP, 4th Rank)

(5) GDP growth: 1.4% (2015), 1% (2018)

(6) GDP per capita: $41418(Nominal, 23rd Rank), $46069 (PPP, 28th Rank)

(7) Population: 126 million

(8) Labour Force: 65 million 51.58% of Population

(9) Labour Force by Occupation: agriculture 2.9%, Industry 26.2%, Services 70.9%

(10) Unemployment 2.8%

(11) Inflation 0.5%

(12) Main Industries: Motor Vehicles, electronic equipments, machine tools, steel, nonferrous metals, ships, chemicals, textiles, processed food

(13) Ease of doing business: 39thRank

(14) External

(15) Exports: $697.2 billion, Imports: $670.97 billion Trade Surplus:$26.23 billion

(16) Export Goods: Motor Vehicles 14.9%, Iron & Steel products 5.4%, semiconductors 55, automobiles 4.8%, power generating machines 3.5%, Plastic materials 3.3%

(17) Main export Partners: US 20.2%, China 17.6%, EU 11.4%, South Korea 7.2%, Taiwan 6.1%, Others 37.4%

(18) Import Goods: Petroleum 16.1%, liquid natural gas 9.1%, Clothing 3.8%, Semiconductors 3.3%, coal 2.4%, audio & visual apparatus 1.4

(19) Import Partners: China 25.8%, EU 12.45, US 11.4%, Australia 5%, South Korea 4.1%, Others 41.35

(20) FDI stock: $252.9 billion

(21) Foreign Reserves: 1.249 trillion

(22) Gross External debt: $3.408 trillion 65% of GDP

(23) Public Debt: $12.41 trillion 237.6% of GDP Very high

(24) Fiscal:

(25) Revenue: $ 1.714 trillion Expenses: 1.885 trillion Fiscal Deficit: $0.171 trillion $171 billion 3.27% of GDP Within limit of 4% of GDP.

(26) Credit Rating: S & P A+ Domestic & Foreign), T & C AA+ Outlook: Stable, Moody A1 Outlook: Stable, SCOPE A+, Outlook: Stable

Critical Observations of Economy of Japan

(1) The economy of Japan is a highly developed and market oriented economy. It is third largest in the World by Nominal GDP and 4th by PPPGDP.This is the World's second largest developed economy member in G7.

(2) Due to a volatile currency exchange rate, Japan's GDP as measured in USD fluctuates widely. According to these fluctuations through use of Atlas method, Japan is estimated to have a GDP per capita annual $38490. The Japanese economy is forecast by the quarterly Tankan Survey of business sentiment conducted by Bank of Japan. Nikki 225 presents Monthly Report of top blue chip equities on Japan Exchange Group.

(3) Japan is the third largest automobiles manufacturing country, largest electronic goods industry. It is an innovative country of global patent filing.

(4) Faced with competition from China and South Korea, manufacturing in Japan now focusses primarily on high tech and precision goodslike hybrid vechicles and robotics.

(5) Japan Possesses 13.7% of World's private financial assets as of 2010 as at estimated $13.5 trilion.

(6) As of 2015, 54 of the Fortune Global 500 companies based in Japan.

(7) Japan has the highest ratio of 237.6 % of GDP of Public debt which stands at $12.41 trillion against GDP 5.221 trillion. But most of this public loan is owned by Japanese nationals. National debt expanded due to considerable social welfare activities and shrinking tax base

(8) Japanese population is 12.60 crores with labour force 6.5 crores which works out to 51.58% of the population. It is forecasted that Japanese population will fall to 10 crores by mid-21st century because of birth rate lesser than death rate. Workforce is also reducing from 66 million in 2013 to 65 million at present. One way is to encourage immigration but Japanese's citizens are strongly opposing immigration.

(9) In World War II, Japan suffered the highest when atom bombs were dropped on its two cities i.e.Nagasaki and Hiroshima. Millions died and millions became permanently disabled to do any business. US then took responsibility of defence of Japan. Japan young labour force was highly productive and with nationalist

spirit and zeal to make their country as financially stronger and efficient on before. It made economic miracle and presently a country which was in ashes has become the highly developed country competing US.

(10) Industrial growth is Japan was 10% in 1960, 5% in 1970 and 4% in 1980.

(11) Japan is the largest importer of agriculture products in the world after EU. Only 12% of total land is used for agriculture. Agriculture is highly subsidized and protected. 84% of Japan's energy is also imported.

(12) In Tourism, Japan is 5th most visited country in Asia and Pacific. 83 million tourists visiting the country annually.

(13) Japan has 98 passenger and 175 international airports. It has 250 high speed trains. It has also offered to establish bullet train from Mumbai to Ahmedabad in Gujarat at no interest on loan for such train.

(14) Tokyo is the largest wholesale market for primary products. There is a high quality of Japanesecraft ship and metal smithing.

(15) Japan was not spending anything on defence and the defence of Japan is undertaken by US. However, recently Prime Minister of Japan Shinzo Abe has planned to focus on military preparation and is spending large amount of purchasing and manufacturing defence equipment to counter aggressive behavior of China on South China Ocean region. Abe also encouraged firms to raise workers' wages. There was a deflation in Japan during 1999-2014. On 5 April 2013, Bank of Japan purchased 60-70 trillion yen bonds to avoid deflation which showed positive results.

(16) In 2013, there was nuclear disaster in Fukushima Daichi Nuclear power plant which resulted in heavy damages. Japan has thereafter closed 50 nuclear power plants.

(17) Extenal debt \$3.408 trillion compared with GDP \$5.221 works out to 65.27% and needs to be reduced to avoid any debt servicing problems in future.

(18) Japan has created good economic atmosphere to boost business.

(19) Japan has the smallest tax rate. Personal tax 8% and Corporate Tax 36.8%. It raised the Personal tax to 10% and took measures to raise workers' wages during Prime Minister Shinzo Abe.

(20) China's aggressively occupying South China East Sea portion has created conflict with China by many countries including Japan. Japan is therefore preparing for war against China on this issue for its legitimate rights in Senkaku in Eastern China sea by spending large amount of money on defence and making war preparation jointly with US as its strategic partner and installing anti missiles

on its boarder. In East China Sea, America and Japan tests their capacity by mock war preparations.

(21) Yen was always widely fluctuating and Japan has many times currency crisis but every time it recovered and yen is now very strong. In terms of Indian Rupee, yen was 1Yen = Indian Re 0.04 upto 1972. It has now be valued at Yen1 =Indian Re 0.70 which means yen has been revalued by 17.5 times.

(22) In 2017, Japan registered 3150 Meager & Acquisition deals with value $114 billion.

(23) Japan is not at trap with China on "one belt one road" policy.

Chapter - 23

Economy of Australia

Introduction

With a GDP of A$1.69 trillion, Australian economy as a mixed-market economy stood in 2017 as the 14th largest economy in the world as GDP Nominal and 20th in GDP PPP. It surpassed Switzerland in 2018 and became the country with the largest median wealth per adult with total Australian wealth as A$ 8.9 trillion in June 2016. Australia was the 25th largest goods exporter and 20th largest goods importer. Generally the economic growth of any country does not remain constant and is always fluctuating and sometimes volatile. But Australia has the record of uninterrupted GDP growth in the developed world with March 2017 financial quarter for 103rd quarter which marked 26 years since the country had a technical recession.

The Australian economy is dominated by its service sector, comprising 61.1% of the GDP and employing 79.2% of the labour force in 2016. East Asia (including ASEAN and Northeast Asia) is a top export destination, accounting for about 64% of exports in 2016. Australia has the eighth-highest total estimated value of natural resources, valued at US$19.9 trillion in 2016. At the height of the mining boom in 2009–10, the total value-added of the mining industry was 8.4% of GDP.Despite the recent decline in the mining sector, the Australian economy has remained resilient and stable and has not experienced a recession since July 1991.

The Australian Securities Exchange in Sydney is the 16th-largest stock exchange in the world in terms of domestic market capitalization and has the largest interest rate derivatives market in Asia. The currency of Australia and its territories is the Australian dollar which it shares with several Pacific nation states.

Australia is a member of the APEC, G20, OECD and WTO. The country has also entered into free trade agreements with ASEAN, Canada, Chile, China, South Korea, Malaysia, New Zealand, Peru, Japan, Singapore, Thailand and the United States. The ANZCERTA agreement with New Zealand has greatly increased integration with the economy of New Zealand and in 2011 there was a plan to form an Australasian Single Economic Market by 2015.

History

Economic History of Australia

20th century

Australian Settlement

Australia's average GDP growth rate for the period 1901–2000 was 3.4% annually. As opposed to many neighbouring Southeast Asian countries, the process towards independence was relatively peaceful and thus did not have significant negative impact on the economy and standard of living. Growth peaked during the 1920s, followed by the 1950s and the 1980s. By contrast, the late 1910s/early 1920s, the 1930s, the 1970s and early 1990s were marked by financial crises.

Economic liberalization

From the early 1980s onwards, the Australian economy has undergone intermittent economic liberalization. In 1983, under prime minister Bob Hawke, but mainly driven by Treasurer Paul Keating, the Australian dollar was floated and financial deregulation was undertaken.

Early 1990s recession

The early 1990s recession came swiftly after the Black Monday of October 1987, as a result of a stock collapse of unprecedented size which caused the Dow Jones Industrial Average to fall by 22.6%. This collapse, larger than the stock market crash of 1929, was handled effectively by the global economy and the stock market. Stock market crash of 1929 began to quickly recover. But in North America, the lumbering savings and loans industry was facing decline, which eventually led to a savings and loan crisis which compromised the well-being of millions of US people. The following recession thus impacted the many countries closely linked to the US, including Australia. Paul Keating, who was prime minister at the time, famously referred to it as "the recession that Australia had to have." During the recession, GDP fell by 1.7%, employment by 3.4% and the unemployment rate rose to 10.8%. However, the recession did assist in reducing long-term inflation rate expectations and Australia has maintained a low inflation environment since the 1990s to the present day.

Mining

Mining in Australia

Mining has contributed to Australia's high level of economic growth, from the gold rush in the 1840s to the present day. The opportunities for large profits in pastoralism and mining attracted considerable amounts of British capital, while expansion was supported by enormous government outlays for transport, communication, and urban infrastructures, which also depended heavily on British finance. As the economy expanded, large-scale immigration satisfied the growing demand for workers, especially after the end of convict transportation to the eastern mainland in 1840. Australia's mining operations secured continued economic growth and Western Australia itself benefited strongly from mining iron ore and gold from the 1960s and 1970s which fueled the rise of suburbanization and consumerism in Perth, the capital and most populous city of Western Australia, as well as other regional centres.

2007-2012 Global financial crisis

Rudd Government (2007-2010)

The Australian government stimulus package ($11.8 billion) helped to prevent a recession.

The World Bank expected Australia's GDP growth rate to be 3.2% in 2011 and 3.8% in 2012. The economy expanded by 0.4% in the fourth quarter of 2011, and expanded by 1.3% in the first quarter of 2012. The growth rate was reported to be 4.3% year-on-year.

The International Monetary Fund in April 2012 predicted that Australia would be the best-performing major advanced economy in the world over the next two years; the Australian Government Department of the Treasury anticipated "forecast growth of 3.0% in 2012 and 3.5% in 2013", the National Australian Bank in April 2012 cut its growth forecast for Australia to 2.9% from 3.2%., and JP Morgan in May 2012 cut its growth forecast to 2.7% in calendar 2012 from a previous forecast of 3.0%, also its forecast for growth in 2013 to 3.0% from 3.3%. Deutsche Bank in August 2012, and Societe Generale in October 2012, warned that there is risk of recession in Australia in 2013.

While Australia's overall national economy grew, some non-mining states and Australia's non-mining economy experienced a recession.

Data

While in 1980, GDP PPP was $155.1 billion, GDP growth was 2.9% and GDP per capita was $10480 with inflation and Unemployment were 10.1% and 6.1% respectively. Inflation and unemployment ratios came down in 1981 to 9.5% and 5.8% respectively while GDP growth was 4.1%, GDP per capita PPP was $11744 and GDP $176.6 billion. GDP, GDP per capita PPP was constantly rising and Inflation and unemployment rates were continuously reduced and in 2016 and 2017, GDP PPP were $1.197 trillian and $ 1.246 trillion respectively. GDP PPP per capita were $49096 in 2016 and $50334 in 2017 while inflation was fluctuating with 1.3% in 2016 and 2% in 2017,

Unemployment 5.7% in 2016 and 5.6% in 2017 and Government debt reached the red line with 40.6% of GDP in 2016 and 41.6% of GDP in 2017.

Overview

Australia's annual inflation rate per-capita is higher than that of the UK, Canada, Germany and France in terms of PPP. In GDP (PPP), Australia is ranked 18th in the world. The country was ranked 2nd in the United Nations Human Development Index and 6th in the Economist worldwide quality-of-life 2005. Using constant exchange rate, Australian wealth had grown by 4.4% annually in 2014 since 2007 compared with 9.2% rate over 2000-2007. Australia's sovereign credit rating is "AAA" for all three major rating agencies, higher than the United States of America.

The emphasis on exporting commodities rather than manufactures underpinned a significant increase in Australia's terms of trade during the rise in commodity prices since 2000. However, due to a colonial heritage a lot of companies operating in Australia are foreign-owned and as a result, Australia has had persistent current account deficits for over 60 years despite periods of positive net merchandise exports; given the net income outlay between Australia and the rest of the world is always negative. The current account deficit totalled AUD$44.5 billion in 2016 or 2.6% of GDP.

Inflation has typically been between 2–3% and the pre-GFC cash rate typically ranged between 5–7%, however, partly in response to the end of the mining boom the cash rate has recently been steadily falling, dropping from 4.75% in October 2011 to 1.5% in Aug 2016. The service sector of the economy, including tourism, education and financial services, constitutes 69% of GDP.Australian National University in Canberra also provides a probabilistic interest-rate-setting project for the Australian economy, which is compiled by shadow board members from the ANU academic staff.

Rich in natural resources, Australia is a major exporter of agricultural products, particularly wheat and wool, minerals such as iron ore and gold, and energy in the forms of liquefied natural gas and coal. Although agriculture and natural resources constitute only 3% and 5% of GDP, respectively, they contribute substantially to Australia's export composition. Australia's largest export markets are Japan, China, South Korea, India and the US.

At the turn of the current century, Australia experienced a significant mining boom. The mining sector's contribution to overall GDP grew from around 4.5% in 1993–94, to almost 8% in 2006–07. The services sector also grew considerably, with property and business services in particular growing from 10% to 14.5% of GDP over the same period, making it the largest single component of GDP (in sectoral terms). This growth has largely been at the expense of the manufacturing sector, which in 2006–07 accounted for around 12% of GDP. A decade earlier, it was the largest sector in the economy, accounting for just over 15% of GDP.

Regional differences

Between 2010 and 2013, much of the economic growth in Australia was attributed to areas of the country where mining- and resource-based industries and services are mostly located. Western Australia and the Northern Territory are the only states that have economic growth. During 2012 and 2013 Australian Capital Territory, Queensland, Tasmania, South Australia, New South Wales and Victoria experiences recessions at various times. The Australian economy is characterised as a "two-speed economy". From June 2012 to March 2013 Victoria experienced a recession. In 2012 the Government of Victoria cut 10% of all jobs in the public service.The period since has seen these trends reversed with West Australia and the Northern Territory, who are heavily dependent on mining, experience significant downturns in GDP while the eastern states returned to growth, led by strong upturns in NSW and Victoria.

Taxation in Australia

Quarterly taxation revenue ($millions) since 1959.

Taxation in Australia is levied at the federal, state, and local government levels. The federal government raises revenue from personal income taxes and business taxes. Other taxes include the goods and services tax General Service Tax), excise and customs duties. The federal government is the main source of income for state governments. As a result of state dependence on federal taxation revenue to meet decentralized expenditure responsibilities, Australia is said to have a vertical fiscal imbalance.

Besides receipts of funds from the federal government, states and territories have their own taxes, in many cases as slightly different rates. State taxes commonly include payroll tax levied on businesses, a poker-machine tax on businesses that offer gambling services, land tax on people and businesses that own land and most significantly, stamp duty on sales of land (in every state) and other items (chattels in some states, unlisted shares in others, and even sales of contracts in some states).

The states effectively lost the ability to raise income tax during the Second World War. In 1942, Canberra invoked its Constitutional taxation power (s. 51 (ii)) and enacted the *Income Tax Act* and three other statutes to levy a uniform income tax across the country. These acts sought to raise the funds necessary to meet burgeoning wartime expenses and reduce the unequal tax burden between the states by replacing state income taxes with a centralized tax system. The legislation could not expressly prohibit state income taxes (s. 51(ii) does not curtail the power of states to levy taxes) but the federal government's proposal made localized income tax extremely difficult politically. The federal government offered instead compensatory grants authorised by s. 96 of the Constitution for the loss of state income (*State Grants (Income Tax Reimbursement) Act 1942*).

The states rejected Canberra's regime and challenged the legislation's validity in the First Uniform Tax Case (South Australia v Commonwealth) of 1942. The High Court of Australia held that each of the statutes establishing Commonwealth income tax was a valid use of the s. 51(ii) power, in which Latham CJ noted that the system did not undermine essential state functions and imposed only economic and political pressure upon them.

The Second Uniform Tax Case (*Victoria v Commonwealth* (1957)) reaffirmed the court's earlier decision and confirmed the power of the federal government's power to make s. 96 grants conditionally (in this case, a grant made on the condition that the recipient state does not levy income tax).

Since the Second Uniform Tax Case, a number of other political and legal decisions have centralized fiscal power with the Commonwealth. In *Ha vs. New South Wales* (1997), the High Court found that the *Business Franchise Licences (Tobacco) Act 1987* (NSW) was invalid because it levied a customs duty, a power exercisable only by the Commonwealth (s.90). This decision effectively invalidated state taxes on cigarettes, alcohol and petrol. Similarly, the imposition of a Commonwealth goods and services tax (GST) in 2000 transferred another revenue base to the Commonwealth.

Consequently, Australia has one of the most pronounced vertical fiscal imbalances in the world: the states and territories collect just 18% of all governmental revenues but are responsible for almost 50% of the spending areas. Furthermore, the centralization of revenue collection has allowed Canberra to force state policy in areas well beyond the scope of its constitutional powers, by using the grants power (s.96) to mandate the terms on which the states spend money in areas over which it has no power (such as spending on education, health and policing).

Local governments (called *councils* in Australia) have their own taxes (called rates) to enable them to provide services such as local road repairs, local planning and building management, garbage collection, street cleaning, park maintenance services, libraries, and museums. Councils also rely on state and federal funding to provide infrastructure and services such as roads, bridges, sporting facilities and buildings, aged care, maternal and child health, and childcare.

In 2000, GST was introduced, similar to the European-style VAT.

Employment

According to the Australian Bureau of Statistics (ABS) seasonally estimates, the unemployment rate decreased 0.1% to 5.5% in September 2017 while the labour force participation rate remained steady at 65.2%. The trend participation rate for 15- to 24-year-olds increased by 0.3 percentage points to 67.7 per cent while unemployment rate for this group declined by less than 0.1% to 12.7%, decreasing by 0.3% over the year. According to the Australian

Bureau of statistics, in August 2017, the quarterly underemployment rate decreased by 0.2% to 8.6% while the quarterly underutilization rate (the unemployed plus the under-employed)decreased by 0.2% to 14.1 per cent.

According to Roy Morgan Research the unemployment rate in August 2017 was 10.2%, while Australian workers who were considered either unemployed or underemployed was estimated to be 19.7% (2.565 million) in the same month. Around 4.247 million were estimated to be in part-time employment.

In 2007 228,621 Newstart unemployment allowance recipients were registered, a total that increased to 646,414 or 5.3% of the total labour force by March 2013. As of March 2017, the number of Newstart recipients stands at 746,681 or 5.8% of the labour force; a proportional increase of 0.5% in four years.

The accuracy of official unemployment figures has been brought into question in the Australian media due to discrepancies between the methods of different research bodies (Roy Morgan versus the ABS), differing definitions of the term 'unemployed' and the ABS' practice of counting under-employed people as "employed".

As of May 2017, the Australia labour force were employed in the following industries:

Total labour force 121.13 million. Specifical/selected industries have employed workforce as under:

Industry	*No.of employees*	*% of total*
Health care and Social assistance	15..62 million	12.9%
Retail trade	12.28 million	10.1%
Construction	11.08 million	9.1%
Professional, scientific and technical services	10.18 million	8.4%
Education and training	9.71 million	8%
Manufacturing	9.06 million	7.5%
Accommodation and food services	8.72 million	7.2%
Public administration	8.12 million	6.7%

Employment for newly qualified professionals

According to the Australian Graduate Survey done by *Graduate Careers Australia*, full-time employment for newly qualified professionals from various occupations (around four months after the completion of their qualifications) experienced some declines between 2012 and 2015. Some examples are:

Field of Education	*2012*	*2013*	*2014*	*2015*	*Change 2012–2015*
Dentistry	83.6%	83.3%	79.6%	86.7%	+3.1%
Computer Science	74.7%	70.3%	67.2%	67%	-7.7%
Architecture	63.9%	60.0%	57.8%	70.2%	+6.3%
Psychology	63.1%	56.1%	52.1%	55.2%	-7.9%
Business studies	74.5%	71.8%	69.7%	70.8%	-3.7%
Electronic/Computer engineering	79.5%	80.9%	74.9%	78.1%	-1.4%
Mechanical engineering	88.4%	82.4%	71.0%	72.2%	-16.2%
Surveying	93.0%	86.5%	83.9%	90.7%	-2.3%
Health other	73.3%	69.7%	70.4%	69.2%	-4.1%
Nursing (initial)	92.2%	83.1%	80.5%	79%	-13.2%
Nursing (post-initial)	86.1%	71.4%	75.8%	74.9%	-11.2%
Medicine	98.1%	96.9%	97.5%	96.3%	-1.8%
Education (initial)	74.9%	70.8%	70%	71.8%	-3.1%
Education (post-initial)	58.8%	71.4%	69.2%	72.7%	+13.9%

The Graduate Careers Survey 2014 explained, "However, GCA's Beyond Graduation Survey (BGS) indicates that the middle- and longer-term outlook is very positive, with the employment figures for 2010 graduates growing by 14 percentage points three years later." The Beyond Graduation Survey 2013 included 12,384 responses and the Graduate Careers Survey 2014 survey included 113,263 responses ("59.3 per cent of the almost 191,000 Australian resident graduates who were surveyed responded to the AGS." The professional associations of some of these occupations expressed their criticism of the immigration policy in 2014.

States and territories ranked by unemployment rates

Rank	*States*	*Unemployment rate (September 2017)*[87]
1	Victoria	6.0%
2	Queensland	5.9%
3	South Australia	5.8%
4	Tasmania	5.7%
5	Western Australia	5.7%
6	New South Wales	4.6%
7	Australian Capital Territory	4.4%
8	Northern Territory	4.1%

Note: All data in the table above are seasonally adjusted, except for the Northern Territory and the Australian Capital Territory, which are trend data.

In September 2017, South Australia's seasonally adjusted unemployment rate rose from 5.8% to 5.9% but the trend unemployment rate fell below 6% for the first time in four years to 5.8%.

Sectors

Gross operating profits across all industries since 1994 ($millions/ quarter)

List of companies of Australia

Industry

Mining

Coal, Energy and Mining in Australia

In 2014–15 mineral extraction in Australia was valued at 212 billion Australian dollars. Of this, Coal represented 45,869 million, oil and natural gas 40,369 million, Iron ore 69,486 million, Gold ore 13,685 million, and other metals 7,903 million.

Coal is mined primarily in Queensland, New South Wales and Victoria. Fifty-four per cent of the coal mined in Australia is exported, mostly to East Asia. In 2000–01, 258.5 million tonnes of coal was mined, and 193.6 million tonnes exported. Coal provides about 85% of Australia's electricity production. In fiscal year 2008–09, 487 million tonnes of coal was mined, and 261 million tonnes exported. Australia is the world's leading coal exporter.

The Australian mining corporations Rio Tinto Group and BHP are among the largest in the world.

Australia's Argyle mine is the second-largest diamond mine in the world estimated to produce 12.6 million carats in 2014, worth over $500 million. Argyle is known for producing some of the world's most valuable pink and red diamonds.

Manufacturing

Manufacturing in Australia

The manufacturing industry in Australia has declined from 30% of GDP in the 1960s to 12% of GDP in 2007.

In 2008, four companies mass-produced cars in Australia.Mitsubishi ceased production in March 2008, followed by Ford in 2016, and Holden and Toyota in 2017.

Until trade liberalization in the mid-1980s, Australia had a large textile industry. This decline continued through the first decade of the 21st century. Since the 1980s, tariffs have steadily been reduced; in early 2010, the tariffs were reduced from 17.5 per cent to 10 per cent on clothing, and 7.5–10% to 5% for footwear and other textiles. As of 2010, most textile manu-facturing, even by Australian companies, is performed in Asia.

Total employment in Australian textile, clothing and footwear manufacturing (thousands of people) was since 1984.

Agriculture

Agriculture contributes 3% of Australia's GDP at the farm gate and when value-added processing beyond the farm is included this figure rises to 12%. Sixty per cent of farm products are exported. Irrigation is an important and widespread practice for a country where many parts receive low rainfall. Agriculture, Forestry and Fishing was the second-strongest industry from 2013 to 2015, with the number of employees growing from 295,495 in February 2013 to 325,321 in February 2015.

Services

IT related jobs (such as computer system design and engineering) are defined as Professional, Scientific and Technical Services by the Department of Education, Employment and Workplace Relations of Australia. IT job creation occurs mostly in the state capital cities of Australia.

Finance

Australia's "big four banks" (National Australia Bank, Commonwealth Bank, Australia and New Zealand Banking Group and Westpac) are among the 'World's 50 Safest Banks' as of April 2012.

Between 1991 and 2013, 36,720 mergers and acquisitions with a total known value of US$2,040 billion with the involvement of Australian firms have been announced. In the year 2013, 1,515 transactions valued at US$78 billion had been announced which was a decrease in terms of numbers ("18%) and value ("11%) compared to 2012. The largest takeover or merger transaction involving Australian companies was the 2007 takeover of the Coles Group by Westfarmers, totalling A$22 billion.

Tourism

Tourism in Australia

In the financial year 2014/15, tourism represented 3.0% of Australia's GDP contributing A$ 47.5 billion to the national economy. Domestic tourism is a significant part of the tourism industry, representing 73% of the total direct tourism GDP.

In calendar year 2015, there were 7.4 million visitor arrivals. Tourism employed 580,800 people in Australia in 2014–15, 5% of the workforce. About

43.7% of persons employed in tourism were part-time. Tourism also contributed 8.0% of Australia's total export earnings in 2010–11.

Media and Telecommunications in Australia

In 2011–12, Australia was ranked 30th out of 179 countries in accordance to press freedom. Media is a strong industry in Australia, with Fairfax Media and News Corporation representing two of the country's largest media companies.

Education

School attendance is compulsory in Australia, from the age of 5 up until approximately 16 (although it varies between each state and territory). Australia also has an adult literacy rate that was estimated to be 99% in 2003.

In the Programme for International Student Assessment, Australia regularly scores among the top five of thirty major developed countries (member countries of the Organization for Economic Co-operation and Development). In 2018 there were 525,054 international students in Australia, comprising a market of 32.2 billion A$.

Transport in Australia

Infrastructure

Energy

The Australian economy is dependent on imported crude oil and petroleum products, the economy's petroleum import dependency is around 80%- crude oil + petroleum products.

Trade and economic performance

In the second half of the 20th century, Australian trade shifted away from Europe and North America to Japan and other East Asian markets. Regional franchising businesses, now a $128 billion sector, have been operating co-branded sites overseas for years with new investors coming from Western Australia and Queensland.

In the late 19th century, Australia's economic strength relative to the rest of the world was reflected in its GDP. In 1870, Australia had the highest GDP per capita in the world due to economic growth fueled by its natural resources. However, as Australia's population grew rapidly over the 20th century, its GDP per capita dropped relative to countries such as the US and Norway. However, the Australian economy has been performing nominally better than other economies of the OECD and has supported economic growth for over 20 consecutive years. According to the Reserve Bank of Australia, Australian per capita GDP growth is higher than that of New Zealand, US, Canada and Netherlands. The past performance of the Australian economy has been heavily influenced by US, Japanese and Chinese economic growth.

Australian national debt

Australia's net external debt exceeded $1 trillion in April 2017 as a result of Australia's structural current account deficits. Although these deficits have narrowed over the last decade due to an increase in net merchandise trade, this effect has been partly offset by the return of Australian government debt; net federal debt was estimated at $326.0 billion in the 2016–17 federal budget of which 60% is owed to foreigners. The entirety of the debt has been accumulated through ten straight budget deficits as Australia had negative net government debt (i.e. The Australian government had net positive bond holdings) a decade earlier in the 2006–07 fiscal year.

Chinese investment

There is substantial export to China of iron ore, wool and other raw materials, and over 120,000 Chinese students study in Australian schools and universities. China is the largest purchaser of Australian debt. In 2009, offers were made by state-owned Chinese companies to invest $22 billion in Australia's resource extraction industry.

The Signing of the China-Australia Free-Trade Agreement, signed November 2014, has the potential to drastically increase Chinese Investments as agriculture and services become more lenient.

Australia's special investor visa program introduced in 2012 encouraged Chinese investment. The visa program fast-tracks visas and eases the residency requirement for a permanent visa for those ready to invest over five million Australian dollars into state government bonds, specific infrastructure and property investments. Wealthy Chinese interested in retirement houses, top schools and cleaner air, began looking to Australia after Canada started scaling back its investment visa program in 2012 and eliminated its main investor visa program in 2014. In early 2014 it was reported that the Australia's special investor visa was granted to 65 mostly Chinese millionaires who brought over $440 million into the country. By 2017, almost 90% of the more than 1,300 foreigners who used Australia's special investor visa program were from China. Australia also has an investor visa program with a required investment of one million Australian dollars but with more restrictions and a lengthier period of time to get a permanent visa.

In 2017, it was reported that Australia is the third-most popular destination for Chinese to invest wealth offshore, with a 7% increase in Chinese private wealth flowing into Australia while interest in the top two investment destinations, Hong Kong and the United States, fell by 18% and 3%, respectively. In 2017 there were 1.6 million high-net-worth Chinese (with at least 10 million Chinese yuan to invest) and 24 per cent of the 3,000 wealthy Chinese surveyed had private investments in Australia. Migration was one of the top three reasons for Chinese investment offshore.

In 2018, in the Lowy Institute poll there had a sharp rise in the proportion of the Australian population who say the Australian government is "allowing too much investment from China".

This number rose from 56 per cent in 2014 to 72 per cent in 2018.

Australia's balance of payments

Australia's current account (in $M) since 1959

Trade terms, the Australian economy has had persistently large current account deficits (CADs) for more than 50 years. One of the factors that undermines balance of payment is Australia's export base, making it highly vulnerable to the volatility in the prices of commodity goods. In addition, due to a colonial heritage a lot of companies operating in Australia are foreign-owned and, as a result, Australia's net income outlay between it and the rest of the world is always negative; this results in persistent current account deficits even when there is a positive export.

Dependent upon commodities, the Australian government endeavored to redevelop the Australian manufacturing sector. This initiative, also known as microeconomic reform, helped Australian manufacturing to grow from 10.1% in 1983–1984 to 17.8% in 2003–2004.

There are other factors that have contributed to the extremely high current account deficit in Australia such as lack of international competitiveness.

However, as Australia's CAD is almost entirely generated by the private sector, as outlined in Professor John Pitchford's 'Consenting Adults Thesis' in the early 1990s, there is an argument that the CAD is not a significant issue. Historically, Australia has relied on overseas capital to fill the gap between domestic savings and investment, and many of these investment opportunities could not have been pursued if Australia did not have access to foreign savings. This suggests that Australia's apparently low savings level and CAD are not necessarily a significant problem. As long as the investment that is being funded by overseas capital inflow generates sufficient returns to pay for the servicing costs in the future, the increase in foreign liabilities can be viewed as sustainable in the longer term.

Personal wealth

GNI per capita in 2015

According to the 2011 Credit Suisse Global Wealth report, Australia's wealth per adult had quadrupled over the past decade, and its total wealth was US$6.4 trillion. In the report Australia was the second-wealthiest country in the world behind Switzerland based on average wealth per adult, and had the highest median wealth in the world (US$222,000, nearly four times the amount of each US adult) and a proportion of people with wealth above US$100,000 that was eight times the world average. This was attributed to a resilient Australian dollar, property ownership levels and a strong labour market. Compared to the rest of the world, very few Australians had a net worth of less than US$1,000, which was attributed to relatively low credit card and student loan debt. In 2013, Australia was identified by the Credit Suisse as retaining its 2012 position as the nation with the second-highest average wealth per adult (US$403,000); however, the nation's poverty rate was also reported to have increased from 10.2% in 2000–01 to 11.8% at the time of the 2013 report on global wealth.

Despite the economic slowdown, in the 2014 Credit Suisse Global Wealth Report, Australia continued to have the second-highest average wealth per adult (US$430,800) and the highest median wealth (US$225,400), with a total wealth of $7.2 trillion. The average level of real estate (US$319,700) was the second-highest in the world after Norway and 60% of gross household assets. The report explained that this partly reflects a large endowment of land and natural resources relative to population, and also high urban real estate prices. Only 6% of Australians had a net worth below US$10,000, compared to 29% in the USA and 70% for the world as a whole. The average debt was 20% of gross assets. The proportion of people with wealth above US$100,000 was the highest in the world (eight times the world average). Australia had 3.8% (1,783,000 people) of the top 1% of global wealth holders while having 0.4% of the world's adult population. The wealth share by Australia's top decile was 51.1% in 2000, 50.7% in 2007, and 51.1% in 2014. In 2016, Australia continued to be the second-wealthiest nation in terms of wealth per adult.

In 2017, Australia was the world's top destination for millionaires, beating the United States for the second consecutive year. An estimated 11,000 millionaires moved to Australia in 2016, compared with the 10,000 who moved to the United States. Australia was especially attractive to Chinese millionaires due to its relative proximity, cleaner environment, political and economic stability, and investor visa program. Also, the primary reason for millionaires leaving China is top schools abroad that will give their children a better education and career connections.

Mergers and acquisitions

All in all over 43,150 deals have been completed national, inbound or outbound Australia. This cumulates to an overall value of US$2,554 billion. There was a strong upward trend between 1989 and 2007. In this peak year almost 3,100 deals took place, which is almost 60% more than in 2017, the current low. Australian companies are particularly investing in the fields of metals and minerals (15% of all deals from Australia into foreign countries). Runner-up is the oil and gas industry with only 6.4%.

Politics

The Liberal/National Coalition and its forebears (right wing) and the Labor Party (left wing) have formed every Australian Government since Federation, and continue to be the major forces in the predominantly two-party system under which Australia operates.

Poverty

In 2017 ACOSS released a new report revealing that poverty is growing in Australia, with an estimated 2.9 million of people, or 13.3% of all people, living below the internationally accepted poverty line it also estimated that there are 731,000 children in poverty, and 17.5% of children under the age of 15 are in poverty.

Homelessness

There were 105,237 people experiencing homelessness on census night in 2011. This equated to 1 in 200 Australians, and represented an increase of 17% from the 2006 census, with the rate of homelessness increasing from 45 per 10,000 to 49 per 10,000.

The number of homeless people in Australia jumped by more than 14,000- or 14 per cent-in the five years to 2016, according to census data. The Australian Bureau of Statistics (ABS) said 116,000 people were homeless on census night in 2016, representing 50 homeless people per 10,000.

Present Position of Austrlian Economy At Glance

(1) Currency: AUD1 = $ 0.72

(2) Financial year: 1st July- 30th June

(3) Trade organisations: APEC, G20, OECD, WTO

(4) GDP: $1.530 trillion (Nominal, 13th rank), GDP PPP $ 1.315 trillion -19th rank

(5) GDP Growth: 0.6%

(6) GDP per capita: $58941 (Nominal, 10th rank), $52141 (PPP, 19th rank)

(7) GDP by Sector: Services 61.1%, Construction 8.1%, Mining 6.9%, Agriculture 2.2%

(8) Inflation 1.8%

(9) Population: 259.6 million

(10) Workforce: 127 million, 48.92% of population

(11) Unemployment: 5.5%

(12) Population below poverty line; 17.5%

(13) Population which are homeless: 0.5% of population or 116000 people

(14) GINI coeffiency: 0.333

(15) Average Gross salary: AUD Weekly A$ 1605 (fulltime employment), A$ 1170 (All employment)

(16) Main Industries: Financial 7 Insurance services, construction, mining, professional, scientific & technical services, manufacturing

(17) Ease of doing business: 18th

(18) EXTERNAL

(19) Exports: $190.2 billion

(20) Imports: $ 196.1 billion

(21) Trade deficit: 5.9 billion 0.3% of GDP

(22) Export Goods: Iron ore, coal, petroleum gases, gold, synthetic corundum, wheat & mesin, bovine meal, wool, neat of sheep& goats

(23) Main Export Partners: China 31.6%, Japan 13.9%, EU7.5%, South Korea 6.7%, US 4.6% & others 35.6%

(24) Import goods: cars, petroleum, automatic data, processing equipments, medicaments, food preparation, cigars, wine, baked goods, alcohol of less than 80% volume

(25) Main Export Partners: China 23.4%, EU 19.3%, US 11.5%, Japan 7.7%, Thailand 5.7%, Others 32.5%

(26) FDI Stock: Inward $ 576.037billion, Outward $401.506 billion. Net Inward: $175. 529 billion

(27) Gross External debt: $ 1.487 trillion (97.19 of GDP). High

(28) Public debt 42.3% of GDP ($647 billion) Manageable

(29) Fiscal: Revenue: $461 billion, Expenses: $484 billion Deficit: $23 billion (4.99% of GDP) exceeding limit of 4%. Of GDP

(30) Economic Aid Donor ODA $3.02 billion

(31) Foreign Reserves: 451.838 billion

(32) Credit Rating: S&P AAA+ Outlook: Negative, Moody AAA+ Outlook: Stable. Fitch AAA+ Outlook: Stable.

Critical Observations on Economy of Australia

(1) Economy of Australia is a large mixed- market economy with a GDP of A$ 1.69 trillion as at 2017.It out tookSwitzerland and became the country with largest median wealth per adult.

(2) Australia's total wealth was A$ 8.9 trillion as of June 2018. It was the 14th largest economy by Nominal GDP and 20th by PPP GDP. It was the 25th largest goods exporters and 20th largest goods importer.

(3) Australian economy is dominated by service sectors comprising 61.1% of GDP and employing 79.2% of the labour force in 2016. East Asian (including ASEAN and Northeast Asia) is a top export destination, accounting for 64% of exports in 2016.

(4) Australia took the record for the longest run for uninterrupted GDP growth in the developed world with March 2017 financial quarter, 103rd quarter and marked 26 years since the country had a technical recession. (Two consecutive quarters of negative growth).

(5) Australia has the eighth highest total estimated value of natural resources valued at $19.9 trillion in 2016. At the height of mining boom in 2009-10, total value added of the mining industry was 8.4%of GDP. Despite recent decline in mining sector, the Australian economy has remained resilient and stable and has not experienced a recession since 1991.

(6) Australian securities exchange in Sydney is the 16th largest stock exchange in the world in terms of domestic market capitalization and the largest interest rate derivatives market in Asia.

(7) From the early 1980 onwards, the Australian economy has undergone intermittent economic liberalization. In 1983, under the prime minister Bob Hawke but mainly driven by Treasurer Paul Keating, the Australian dollar was floated and the financial deregulation was undertaken.

(8) In 1991, there was a recession which came swiftly after the Black Monday of October 1987 as a result of stock market collapse of unprecedented size which cause the DOW Jones Industrial Average to fall by 22.6%. The collapse larger than stock market crash in 1912 was handled effectively by the global economy and the stock markets began to quickly recover. But in North America, the limbering savings and loan industry was facing decline, which eventually led to a savings & Loan Crisis which compromised the well-being of millions of US people. The following recession imparted many countries closely linked to US including Australia. Paul Keating who was then the prime minister at that time, famously referred to it as "the recession that Australia had to have". During the recession, GDP fell by 1.7%, employed by 3.4% and unemployment rate rose to 10.8%. However, the recession did assist in reducing long-term inflation rate expectations and Australia has maintained a low inflation environment since the 1990 to the present day.

(9) Mining has contributed a high-level economic growth to Australia from the gold rush in the 1840s to the present day. The opportunities for the large profits in pastoralism and mining attracted considerable amounts of British Capital while expansion was supported by

enormous government outlays for transport, communication,and urban intra structures which also depended heavily on British finance. Large immigration satisfied the growing demand for workers, especially after the end of growing demand convict transportation to the eastern mainland in 1840.

(10) The Australian government stimulus package ($11.8 billion) helped to prevent a recession.

(11) GDP growth was 4.3% year-on-year basis from 2011 onwards. IMF predicted Australian growth at 3.2% but it was reduced by the credit agencies. There was also prediction than there will be recession in 2013, but except non-mining states in Australia, no other part of the country experienced any recession in 2013.

(12) Rich in natural resources, Australia is a major exporter of agricultural products particularly wheat and wool, minerals such as iron ore and gold, energy in the form of liquefied natural gas and coal. Property and business services also grew from 10% to 14.5% of GDP between 1993 and 2006-7.

(13) In terms Taxation is levied at federal, state and local government levels. Federal Government raises revenue from personal tax and business taxes. Other taxes include goods and service tax (General Service Tax, excise and customs duties). Federal Government is the main source of income for State Governments. States' dependence on federal taxation revenues is to meet decentralized expenditure. States levy pay-roll taxes on businesses, Machine tax on businesses that offer gambling services, land tax on people and businesses that own land. Stamp duty on sale of land is also levied by the states. In order to raise funds for wartime expenses for World War II, income tax was raised in 1942 by some states to reduce the unequal tax burden between the states and Federal. State territories collect 18% of all government revenue but responsible for almost 50% of the spending areas. Local governments have their own taxes (called rates) to enable them to provide services such as local and road repairs, local planning, building managements, garbage collection street cleaning, park maintenance services.

(14) Unemployment rate was 5.5% in 2017 which is slightly high of total work force of 59% of population.

(15) Also started unemployment allowance in which 228621people were registered in 2013. These figures increased to 646414 in 2015 and 746681 in 2017. During the last four years, only 0.5% increase was seen in this area.

(16) Public debt at 42.3% is manageable but external debt at 1.487 i.e. 97.18% of GDP is very high and should be reduced drastically to

avoid any debt servicing problem in future. Fiscal deficit at 5% is also normal.

(17) Australia has a bad experience of China in media handling and it does not participate in "One Belt One Road "policy of China.

(18) On South China Sea issue, there is tuff dispute between China and other Asian neighbouring countries including Australia which is also affected. In co-operation with USA, Australia is preparing to wage war against China on this issue.However, many millionaires Chinese have invested in Australia as a residential place in Australia after retirement. Lacs of Chinese students are taking education in Australia.

(19) In trade terns, the Australian economy has had persistently large current account deficits (CAD) for more than 50 years. Balance of payment is Australia's base, making it highly vulnerable to the volatility in the price of commodity goods. In addition, due to colonial heritage a lot of companies operating in Australia are foreign - owned companies and, as a result, Australia's net income outlay between it and next of the world is always negative which results in persistent current account deficits even when there is a positive effort.

There are other factors that have contributed to the extremely high current account deficit in Australia such as lack of international competitiveness.

Australia's CAD is almost entirely generated by the private sector. CAD is therefore not a significant issue, according to some Economists. Australia has relied on overseas capital to fill the gap between domestic savings and investment and many of these investment opportunities could not have been pursued if Australia did not have access to foreign savings. This suggests that Australia's apparently low saving level and CAD are not necessarily a significant problem. As long as the investment that is being funded by overseas capital inflow generates sufficient returns to pay for the servicing costs in the future, the increase in foreign liabilities can be viewed as sustainable in the long run.

Chapter - 24

Economy of Argentina

Introduction

The economy of Argentina is a high income economy for fiscal year 2017 according to the World Bank. It is Latin America's third largest economy, and the second largest in South America behind Brazil.

The country benefits from rich natural resources, a highly literate population, an export-oriented agricultural sector, and a diversified industrial base. Argentina's economic performance has historically been very uneven, in which high economic growth alternated with severe recessions, particularly since the late twentieth century, and income maldistribution and poverty increased. Early in the twentieth century Argentina had one of the ten highest per capita GDP levels in the world, at par with Canada and Australia and surpassing both France and Italy. Argentina's currency declined by about 50% in 2018 to more than 38 Argentine pesos per US Dollar and today is under a stand-by program from the International Monetary Fund.Many famous Rating Agencies have downgraded the country's rating so that Argentina finds it very difficult to get additional external debt from International Financial institutions.

Argentina is considered an emerging market by the FTSE Global Equity Index (2018), and is one of the G-20 major economy. Recently, G-20 Conference was arranged in Buenos Aires, Argentina's capital in 2018.

Economic History of Argentina

Historical growth of Argentina from 1961 to 2016

Prior to the 1880s, Argentina was a relatively isolated backwater, dependent on the salted meat, wool,leather, and hide industries for both the greater part of its foreign exchange and the generation of domestic income and profits. The Argentine economy began to experience swift growth after 1880 through the export of livestock and grain commodities, as well as through British and French investment, marking the beginning of a fifty-year era of significant economic expansion and mass European Immigration.

During its most vigorous period, from 1880 to 1905, this expansion resulted in a 7.5-fold growth in GDP, averaging about 8% annually. One important measure of development, GDP per capita, rose from 35% of the United States average to about 80% during that period. Growth then slowed considerably, such that by 1941 Argentina's real per capita GDP was roughly half that of the U.S. Even so, from 1890 to 1950 the country's per capita income was similar to that of Western Europe; although income in Argentina remained considerably less evenly distributed.

The Great Depression caused Argentine GDP to fall by a fourth between 1929 and 1932. Having recovered its lost ground by the late 1930s partly through import substitute, the economy continued to grow modestly during World War II (in contrast to the recession caused by the previous world war). The war led to a reduced availability of imports and higher prices for Argentine exports that combined to create a US$1.6 billion cumulative surplus, a third of which was blocked as inconvertible deposits in the Bank of England by the Roca-Runcian Treaty. Benefiting from innovative self-financing and government loans alike, value added in manufacturing nevertheless surpassed that of agriculture for the first time in 1943, employed over 1 million by 1947, and allowed the need for imported consumer goods to decline from 40% of the total to 10% by 1950.

The populist administration of Juan Peron nationalized the Central Bank, railways, and other strategic industries and services from 1945 to 1955. The subsequent enactment of developmentalism after 1958, though partial, was followed by a promising fifteen years. Inflation first became a chronic problem during this period (it averaged 26% annually from 1944 to 1974);but though it did not become fully "developed," from 1932 to 1974 Argentina's economy grew almost fivefold (or 3.8% in annual terms) while its population only doubled. While unremarkable, this expansion was well-distributed and so resulted in several noteworthy changes in Argentine society - most notably the development of the largest proportional middle class (40% of the population by the 1960s) in Latin America as well as the region's highest-paid, most unionized working class.

The economy, however, declined during the military dictatorship from 1976 to 1983, and for some time afterwards. The dictatorship's chief economist, Jose Alfredo Martinezde Hoz, advanced a corrupt, anti-labour policy of financial liberalization that increased the debt burden and interrupted industrial development and upward social mobility. Over 400,000 companies of all sizes went bankrupt by 1982, and neoliberal economic policies prevailing from 1983 through 2001 failed to reverse the situation.

Record foreign debt interest payments, tax evasion, and capital flight resulted in a balance of payments crisis that plagued Argentina with severe stagflation from 1975 to 1990, including a bout of hyperinflation in 1989 and 1990. Attempting to remedy this situation, economist Domingo Cavallo pegged the peso to the U.S. dollar in 1991 and limited the growth in the money supply. His team then embarked on a path of trade liberation, deregulation, and privatization. Inflation dropped to single digits and GDP grew by one third in four years.

External economic shocks, as well as a dependency on volatile short-term capital and debt to maintain the overvalued fixed exchange rate, diluted benefits, causing erratic economic growth from 1995 and the eventual collapse in 2001. That year and the next, the economy suffered its sharpest decline since 1930; by 2002, Argentina had defaulted on its debt, its GDP had declined by nearly 20% in four years, unemployment reached 25%, and the peso had depreciated 70% after being devalued and floated.

Argentina's socio-economic situation has since been steadily improving. Expansionary policy and commodity exports triggered a rebound in GDP from 2003 onward. This trend has been largely maintained, creating over five million jobs and encouraging domestic consumption and fixed investment. Social programs were strengthened, and a number of important firms privatized during the 1990s were renationalized beginning in 2003. These include the postal service, AySA (the water utility serving Buenos Aires), Pension funds (transferred to ANSES), Aerolineas Argentnas, the energy firm YPF, and the railways.

The economy nearly doubled from 2002 to 2011, growing an average of 7.1% annually and around 9% for five consecutive years between 2003 and 2007. Real wages rose by around 72% from their low point in 2003 to 2013. The global recession did affect the economy in 2009, with growth slowing to nearly zero; but high economic growth then resumed, and GDP expanded by around 9% in both 2010 and 2011.Foreign exchange controls, austerity measures, persistent inflation, and downturns in Brazil, Europe, and other important trade partners, contributed to slower growth beginning in 2012, however. Growth averaged just 1.3% from 2012 to 2014, and rose to 2.4% in 2015.

The Argentine government bond market is based on GDP-linked bonds, and investors, both foreign and domestic, netted record yields amid renewed growth. Argentina's debt restructuring offers in 2005 and 2010 resumed payments on the majority of its almost US$100 billion in defaulted bonds and other debt from 2001.

Holdouts controlling 7% of the bonds, including some small investors, hedge funds, and vulture funds led by Paul Singer's Cayman Islands, rejected the 2005 and 2010 offers to exchange their defaulted bonds. Singer, who demanded US$832 million for Argentine bonds purchased for US$49 million in the secondary market in 2008,attempted to seize Argentine government assets abroad and sued to stop payments from Argentina to the 93% who had accepted the earlier swaps despite the steep discount. Bondholders who instead accepted the 2005 offer of 30 cents on the dollar, had by 2012 received returns of about 90% according to estimates by Morgan Stanley. Argentina settled with virtually all holdouts in February 2016 at a cost of US$9.3 billion; NML received US$2.4 billion, a 392% return on the original value of the bonds.

While the Argentine Government considers debt left over from illegimate unconstitutional odious debt, it has continued servicing this debt despite the annual cost of around US$14 billion and despite being nearly locked out of international credit markets with annual bond issues since 2002 averaging less than US$2 billion (which precludes most debt roll over).

Argentina has nevertheless continued to hold successful bond issues, as the country's stock market, consumer confidence, and overall economy continue to grow. The country's successful, US$16.5 billion bond sale in April 2016 was the largest in emerging market history.

In May 2018, Argentina's government asked the international Monetary Fund for its intervention, with an emergency loan for a $30 billion bailout, as reported by Bloomberg.

In May 2018 the official estimated inflation had peaked up to 25 percent a year, and on 4 May Argentina's central bank raised interest rates on pesos to 40 percent from 27.25 percent, which is the highest in the world, since the national currency had lost 18% of its value since the beginning of the year.

Data

The following table shows the main economic indicators in 1980–2017. Inflation below 5 % is in green.

Year	*GDP (in Bil. US$ PPP)*	*GDP per capita (in US$ PPP)*	*GDP per capita 2011 constant price (in US$ PPP)*	*GDP growth (real)*	*Inflation rate (in Percent)*	*Unemployment (in Percent)*	*Government debt (in % of GDP)*
1980	176.6	6,318	14,709	▲0.1 %	n/a	3.0 %	n/a
1983	▲201.9	▲6,880	▲13,269	▲3.7 %	n/a	▲5.0 %	n/a
1989	▼230.7	▼7,240	▼11,616	▼ −7.0 %	n/a	▲8.0 %	n/a
1998	▲439.7	▲12,212	▲15,999	▲3.9 %	▲0.9 %	▼14.7 %	▲35.2 %
1999	▼431.3	▼11,850	▼15,290	▼ −3.4 %	▼−1.2 %	▲16.1 %	▲40.1 %
2015	▲883.9	▲20,492	▲19,244	▲2.7 %	n/a	n/a	▲55.1 %
2016	▼878.8	▼20,156	▼18,690	▼ −1.8 %	n/a	▲8.5 %	▼53.3 %
2017	▲920.2	▲20,875	▲19,013	▲2.9 %	▲25.7 %	▼8.4 %	▼52.6 %

Sectors

Agriculture in Argentina

Argentina is one of the world's major agricultural producers, ranking among the top producers in most of the following, exporters of beef, circitrus, fruit, grapes, honey, maize, sorghum, soyabean, squash, sunflower seeds, wheat, and verba mate. Agriculture accounted for 9% of GDP in 2010, and around one fifth of all exports (not including processed food and feed, which are another third). Commercial harvests reached 103 million tons in 2010, of which over 54 million were oilseeds (mainly soy and sunflower), and over 46 million were cereals (mainly maize, wheat, and sorghum).

Soy and its byproducts, mainly animal feed and vegetable oil, are major export commodities with one fourth of the total; cereals added another 10%. Cattle-raising is also a major industry, though mostly for domestic consumption; beef, leather and dairy were 5% of total exports.Sheep-raising and wool are important in Patagonia, though these activities have declined by half sincc 1990. Biodiesel, however, has become one of the fastest growing agro-industrial activities, with over US$2 billion in exports in 2011.

Fruits and vegetables made up 4% of exports: apples and pears in the Rio Negro valley; rice, oranges and other cicitus in the northwest and Mesopotamia; grapes and strawberries in Cuyo (the west), and berries in the far south. Cotton and tobacco are major crops in the Gran Chaco, sugarcane and Chile peppers in the northwest, and oilvers and garlic in the west. Yerba mate tea (Misiones), tomatoes (Salta) and peaches (Mendoza) are grown for domestic consumption. Organic farming is growing in Argentina, and the nearly 3 million hectares (7.5 million acres) of organic cultivation is second only toAustralia, Argentina is thc world's fifth-largest wine producer, and fine wine production has taken major leaps in quality. A growing export, total viticulture potential is far from having been met. Mendoza is the largest wine region, followed by San Juan.

Government policy towards the lucrative agrarian sector is a subject of, at times, contentious debate in Argentina. A grain embargo by farmers protesting an increase in export taxes for their products began in March 2008, and, following a series of failed negotiations, strikes and lockouts largely subsided only with the 16 July, defeat of the export tax-hike in the Senate.

Argentine fisheries bring in about a million tons of catch annually, and are centered on Argentina hake, which makes up 50% of the catch; Pollock, squid, and centolla crab are also widely harvested. Forestry has long history in every Argentine region, apart from the pampas, accounting for almost 14 million of round wood harvests. Eucalyptus, pine,and elm (for cellulose) are also grown, mainly for domestic furniture, as well as paper products (1.5 million tons). Fisheries and logging each account for 2% of exports.

The Vaca Muerta tight oil (shale oil) field holds 16.2 billion barrels of oil and 308 cubic feet of natural gas. It is estimated to be the third largest in the world.

Natural resources

Mining in Argentina

Mining and other extractive activities, such as gas and petroleum, are growing industries, increasing from 2% of GDP in 1980 to around 4% today.

The northwest and San Juan Province are the main regions of activity. Coal is mined in Santa Cruz province. Metals and minerals mined include borate, copper, lead, magnesium, sulfur, tungsten, uranium, zinc, silver, titanium, and gold., whose production was boosted after 1997 by the Bajo de Alumbrera mine in Catamarca Province and Barrick Gold investments a decade later in San Juan. Metal ore exports soared from US$200 million in 1996 to US$1.2 billion in 2004, and to over US$3 billion in 2010.

Around 35 million each of petroleum and petroleum fuels are produced, as well as 50 billion of natural gas, making the nation self-sufficient in these staples, and generating around 10% of exports.The most important oil fields lie in Patagonia and Cuyo. A network of pipelines (next to Mexico's, the second-longest in Latin America) send raw product to Bahia Blanca, center of the petrochemical industry, and to the La Plata-Greater Buenos Aires-Rosario industrial belt.

Industry

Manufacturing is the largest single sector in the nation's economy (15% of GDP), and is well-integrated into Argentine agriculture, with half the nation's industrial exports being agricultural in nature. Based on food processing and textiles during its early development in the first half of the 20th century, industrial production has become highly diversified in Argentina. Leading sectors by production value are: Food processing and beverages; motor vechicles and auto parts; refinery products, and biodiesel; chemicals and pharmaceuticals; steel and aluminium; and industrial and farm machinery; electronics and home appliances. These latter include over three million big ticket items, as well as an array of electronics, kitchen appliances and cellular phones, among others.

Argentina's auto industry produced 791,000 motor vehicles in 2013, and exported 433,000 (mainly to Brazil, which in turn exported a somewhat larger number to Argentina); Argentina's domestic new auto market reached a record 964,000 in 2013. Beverages are another significant sector, and Argentina has long been among the top five wine producing countries in the world; beer overtook wine production in 2000, and today leads by nearly two billion liters a year. Other manufactured goods include: glass and cement; plastics and tires; lumber products; textiles; tobacco products recording; and print media; furniture; apparel and leather.

Most manufacturing is organized in the 314 industrial parks operating nationwide as of 2012, a fourfold increase over the past decade. Nearly half the industries are based in the Greater Buenos Aires area, although Cordoba, Rosario, and Ushuaia are also significant industrial centers; the latter city became the nation's leading center of electronics production during the 1980s. The production of computers, laptops, and servers grew by 160% in 2011, to nearly 3.4 million units, and covered two-thirds of local demand. Argentina has also become an important manufacturer of cell phones, providing about 80% of all devices sold in the country. Another important rubric historically dominated by imports – farm machinery - was similarly replaced by domestic production, which covered 60% of demand by 2013. Production of cell phones, computers, and similar products is actually an "assembly" industry, with the majority of the higher technology components being imported, and the designs of products originating from foreign countries. High labour costs for Argentina assembly work tend to limit product sales penetration to Latin America, where regional trade treaties exist.

Construction permits nationwide covered over 15 million m (160 million ft²) in 2013. The construction sector accounts for over 5% of GDP, and two-thirds of construction is for residential buildings.

Argentine electric output totaled over 133 billion Kwh in 2013. This was generated in large part through well-developed natural gas and hydrofluoric resources. Nuclear energy is also of high importance, and the country is one of the largest producers and exporters, alongside Canada and Russia of cobaiting 60, a radioactive isotope widely used in cancer therapy.

Services

The service sector is the largest contributor to total GDP, accounting for over 60%. Argentina enjoys a diversified service sector, which includes well-developed social, corporate, financial, insurances, real estate, transport, communication services, and tourism.

The telecommunications sector has been growing at a fast pace, and the economy benefits from widespread access to communications services. These include: 77% of the population with access to mobile phones, 95% of whom use smartphones Internet (over 32 million users, or 75% of the population) and broadband services (accounting for nearly all 14 million accounts). Regular telephone services, with 9.5 million lines, and mail services are also robust. Total telecom revenues reached more than $17.8 billion in 2013, and while only one in three retail stores in Argentina accepted online purchases in 2013 E-commerce reached US$4.5 billion in sales.

Trade in services remained in deficit, however, with US$15 billion in service exports in 2013 and US$19 billion in imports. Business Process Outsourcing became the leading Argentine service export, and reached US$3 billion. Advertising revenues from contracts abroad were estimated at over US$1.2 billion.

Tourism is an increasingly important sector and provided 4% of direct economic output (over US$17 billion) in 2012; around 70% of tourism sector activity by value is domestic.

Banking

Banking in Argentina

Argentine banking, whose deposits exceeded US$120 billion in December 2012, developed around public sector banks, but is now dominated by the private sector. The private sector banks account for most of the 80 active institutions (over 4,000 branches) and holds nearly 60% of deposits and loans, and as many foreign-owned banks as local ones operate in the country. The largest bank in Argentina by far, however, has long been the public Banco de la Nacion Argentina. Not to be confused with the Central Bank, this institution now accounts for 30% of total deposits and a fifth of its loan portfolio.

During the 1990s, Argentina's financial system was consolidated and strengthened. Deposits grew from less than US$15 billion in 1991 to over US$80 billion in 2000, while outstanding credit (70% of it to the private sector) tripled to nearly US$100 billion.

The banks largely lent US dollars and took deposits in Argentina pesos, and when the peso lost most of its value in early 2002, many borrowers again found themselves hard pressed to keep up. Delinquencies tripled to about 37%. Over a fifth of deposits had been withdrawn by December 2001, when Economy Minister Domingo Cavallo imposed a near freeze on cash withdrawals. The lifting of the restriction a year later was bittersweet, being greeted calmly, if with some umbrage, at not having these funds freed at their full U.S. dollar value. Some fared worse, as owners of the now-defunct Velox Bank defrauded their clients of up to US$800 million.

Credit in Argentina is still relatively tight. Lending has been increasing 40% a year since 2004, and delinquencies are down to less than 2%. Still, credit outstanding to the private sector is, in real terms, slightly below its 1998 peak, and as a percent of GDP (around 18%) quite low by international standards. The prime rate, which had hovered around 10% in the 1990s, hit 67% in 2002. Although it returned to normal levels quickly, inflation, and more recently, global instability, have been affecting it again. The prime rate was over 20% for much of 2009, and around 17% since the first half of 2010.

Partly a function of this and past instability, Argentines have historically held more deposits overseas than domestically. The estimated US$173 billion in overseas accounts and investment exceeded the domestic monetary base (M3) by nearly US$10 billion in 2012.

Tourism

Tourism in Argentina

According to World Economic Forum's 2017 Travel & Tourism Competitiveness Report, tourism generated over US$22 billion, or 3.9% of GDP, and the industry employed more than 671,000 people, or approximately 3.7%

of the total workforce.Tourism from abroad contributed US$5.3 billion, having become the third largest source of foreign exchange in 2004. Around 5.7 million foreign visitors arrived in 2017, reflecting a doubling in visitors since 2002 despite a relative appreciation of the peso.

Argentines, who have long been active travelers within their own country, accounted for over 80%, and international tourism has also seen healthy growth (nearly doubling since 2001). Stagnant for over two decades, domestic travel increased strongly in the last few years, and visitors are flocking to a country seen as affordable, exceptionally diverse, and safe.

Foreign tourism, both to and from Argentina, is increasing as well. INDEC recorded 5.2 million foreign tourist arrivals and 6.7 million departures in 2013; of these, 32% arrived from Brazil, 19% from Europe, 10% from the United States and Canada, 10% from Chile, 24% from the rest of the Western Hemisphere, and 5% from the rest of the world. Around 48% of visitors arrived by commercial flight, 40% by motor travel (mainly from neighboring Brazil), and 12% by sea. Cruise liner arrivals are the fastest growing type of foreign tourism to Argentina; a total of 160 liners carrying 510,000 passengers arrived at the Port of Buenos Aires in 2013, an eightfold increase in a just a decade.

Energy

Energy in Argentina

Electricity generation in Argentina totaled 133.3 billion Kwh in 2013. The electricity sector in Argentina constitutes the third largest power market in Latin America. It mainly still relies on centralized generation by natural gas power generation (51%), hydroelectricity (28%), and oil-fired generation (12%). Reserves of shale gas and tight oil in the Vaca Muerta oil field and elsewhere are estimated to be the world's third-largest.

Despite the country's large untapped wind and solar potential new renewable energy technologies and distributed energy generation are barely exploited. Wind energy is the fastest growing among new renewable sources. Fifteen wind farms have been developed since 1994 in Argentina, the only country in the region to produce wind turbines. The 55 MW of installed capacity in these in 2010 will increase by 895 MW upon the completion of new wind farms begun that year. Solar power is being promoted with the goal of expanding installed solar capacity from 6 MW to 300, and total renewable energy capacity from 625 MW to 3,000 MW.

Argentina is in the process of commissioning large centralized energy generation and transmission projects. An important number of these projects are being financed by the government through trust funds, while independent private initiative is limited as it has not fully recovered yet from the effects of the Argentine economic crisis.

The first of the three nuclear reactors was inaugurated in 1974, and in 2015 nuclear power generated 5% of the country's energy output.

The electricity sector was unbundled in generation, transmission and distribution by the reforms carried out in the early 1990s. Generation occurs in a competitive and mostly liberalized market in which 75% of the generation capacity is owned by private utilities. In contrast, the transmission and distribution sectors are highly regulated and much less competitive than generation.

Infrastructure

Transportation in Argentina

Argentina's transport infrastructure is relatively advanced, and at a higher standard than the rest of Latin America.There are over 230,000 km (144,000 mi) of roads (not including private rural roads) of which 72,000 km (45,000 mi) are paved, and 2,800 kilometres (1,700 mi) are expressways, many of which are privatized tollways. Having tripled in length in the last decade, multilane expressways now connect several major cities with more under construction. Expressways are, however, currently inadequate to deal with local traffic, as over 12 million motor vehicles were registered nationally as of 2012 (the highest, proportionately, in the region).

The railway network has a total length of 37,856 kilometres (23,523 mi), though at the network's peak this figure was 47,000 km (29,204 mi). After decades of declining service and inadequate maintenance, most intercity passenger services shut down in 1992 following the privatization of the country's railways and the breaking up of the state rail company, while thousands of kilometers fell into misuse. Outside Greater Buenos Aires most rail lines still in operation are freight related, carrying around 23 million tons a year. The metropolitan rail lines in and around Buenos Aires remained in great demand owing in part to their easy access to the Buenos Aires Underground, and the community rail network with its 833 kilometres (518 mi) length carries around 1.4 million passengers daily.

In April 2015, by overwhelming majority the Argentina Senate passed a law which re-created Ferro carriers Argentnos as Nuevos Ferrocarriers Argentinos, effectively re-nationalizing the country's railways. In the years leading up to this move, the country's railways had seen significant investment from the state, purchasing new rolling stock, re-opening lines closed under privatization and re-nationalizing companies such as the Belgrano Cargas freight operator. Some of these re-opened services include the General Roca Railway service to Mar de Plata, the Tren a las Nubes tourist train and the General Mitre Railway service from Buenos Aires to Cordoba, while brand new services include the Posadas-Encarnacion International Train.

Inaugurated in 1913, the Buenos Aires Underground was the first underground rail system built in Latin America, the Spanish speaking world and the Southern Hemisphere. No longer the most extensive in South America, its 60 kilometres (37 mi) of track carry a million passengers daily.

Argentina has around 11,000 km (6,835 mi) of navigable waterways, and these carry more cargo than do the country's freight railways.This includes an extensive network of canals, though Argentina is blessed with ample natural waterways as well, the most significant among these being the Rio de la Plata, Parana, Uruguay, Rio Negro, and Paraguay rivers. The Port of Buenos Aires, inaugurated in 1925, is the nation's largest investor handling 11 million tons of freight and transported 1.8 million passengers in 2013.

Aerolineas Argentinas is the country's main airline, providing both extensive domestic and international service. Austral Lineas Aereas is Aerolíneas Argentinas' subsidiary, with a route system that covers almost all of the country. LADE is a military-run commercial airline that flies extensive domestic services. The nation's 33 airports handled air travel totaling 25.8 million passengers in 2013, of which domestic flights carried over 14.5 million; the nation's two busiest airports, Jorge Newbery and Ministro Pistarini International Airports, boarded around 9 million flights each.

Foreign trade

Foreign Trade of Argentina

Argentine exports are fairly well diversified. However, although agricultural raw materials are over 20% of the total exports, agricultural goods still account for over 50% of exports when processed foods are included. Soy products alone (soyabeans, vegetable oil) account for almost one fourth of the total. Cereals, mostly maize and wheat, which were Argentina's leading export during much of the twentieth century, make up less than one tenth now.

Industrial goods today account for over a third of Argentine exports. Motor vehicles and auto parts are the leading industrial export, and over 12% of the total merchandise exports. Chemicals, steel, aluminum, machinery, and plastics account for most of the remaining industrial exports. Trade in manufactures has historically been in deficit for Argentina, however, and despite the nation's overall trade surplus, its manufacturing trade deficit exceeded US$30 billion in 2011. Accordingly, the system of non-automatic import licensing was extended in 2011, and regulations were enacted for the auto sector establishing a model by which a company's future imports would be determined by their exports (though not necessarily in the same rubric).

A net energy importer until 1987, Argentina's fuel exports began increasing rapidly in the early 1990s and today account for about an eighth of the total; refined fuels make up about half of that. Exports of crude petroleum and natural gas have recently been around US$3 billion a year. Rapidly growing domestic energy demand and a gradual decline in oil production, resulted in a

US$3 billion energy trade deficit in 2011 (the first in 17 years)[143] and a US$6 billion energy deficit in 2013.

Argentine imports have historically been dominated by the need for industrial and technological supplies, machinery, and parts, which have averaged US$50 billion since 2011 (two-thirds of total imports). Consumer goods including motor vehicles make up most of the rest. Trade in services has historically in deficit for Argentina, and in 2013 this deficit widened to over US$4 billion with a record US$19 billion in service imports. The nation's chronic current account deficit was reversed during the 2002 crisis, and an average current account surplus of US$7 billion was logged between 2002 and 2009; this surplus later narrowed considerably, and has been slightly negative since 2011.

Foreign investment

Foreign Direct Investment in Argentina is divided nearly evenly between manufacturing (36%), natural resources (34%), and services (30%). The chemical and plastics sector (10%) and the automotive sector (6%) lead foreign investment in local manufacturing; oil and gas (22%) and mining (5%), in natural resources; telecommunications (6%), finance (5%), and retail trade (4%), in services. Spain was the leading source of foreign direct investment in Argentina, accounting for US$22 billion (28%) in 2009; the U.S. was the second leading source, with $13 billion (17%); and China grew to become the third-largest source of FDI by 2011. Investments from the Netherlands, Brazil, Chile, and Canada have also been significant; in 2012, foreign nationals held a total of around US$112 billion in direct investment.

Several bilateral agreements play an important role in promoting U.S. private investment. Argentina has an Overseas Private Investment Corporation (OPIC) agreement and an active program with the U.S. Export-Import Bank. Under the 1994 U.S.–Argentina Bilateral Investment Treaty, U.S. investors enjoy national treatment in all sectors except shipbuilding, fishing, nuclear-power generation, and uranium production. The treaty allows for international arbitration of investment disputes.

Foreign direct investment (FDI) in Argentina, which averaged US$5.7 billion from 1992 to 1998 and reached in US$24 billion in 1999 (reflecting the purchase of 98% of YRF stock by Repsol), fell during the crisis to US$1.6 billion in 2003. FDI then accelerated, reaching US$8 billion in 2008.The global crisis cut this figure to US$4 billion in 2009; but inflows recovered to US$6.2 billion in 2010, and US$8.7 billion in 2011, with FDI in the first half of 2012 up by a further 42%.

FDI volume remained below the regional average as a percent of GDP even as it recovered, however; Kirchner Administration policies and difficulty in enforcing contractual obligations had been blamed for this modest performance. The nature of foreign investment in Argentina nevertheless shifted significantly after 2000, and whereas over half of FDI during the 1990s consisted in privatizations and merger and acquisitions, foreign investment in Argentina became the most technologically oriented in the region – with 51% of FDI in the form of medium and high-tech investment (compared to 36% in Brazil and 3% in Chile).

Issues

The economic performance of Argentina (100 = Latin American average GDP per capita PPP).

The economy recovered strongly from the 2001–02 crisis, and was the 21st largest in purchasing power parity terms in 2011; its per capita income on a purchasing power parity basis was the highest in Latin America. A lobby representing US creditors who refused to accept Argentina's debt-swap programmes has campaigned to have the country expelled from the G20. These holdouts include numerous vulture funds which had rejected the 2005 offer, and had instead resorted to the courts in a bid for higher returns on their defaulted bonds. These disputes had led to a number of liens against central bank accounts in New York and, indirectly, to reduced Argentine access to international credit markets.

The government under President Mauricio Macri announced to be seeking a new loan from the International Monetary Fund in order to avoid another economic crash similar to the one in 2001. The May 2018 announcement comes at a time of high inflation and falling interest rates. The loan would reportedly be worth $30 billion.

Following 25 years of boom and stagnation, Argentina's economy doubled in size from 2002 to 2013, and officially, income poverty declined from 54% in 2002 to 5% by 2013; an alternative measurement conducted by CONICET found that income poverty declined instead to 15.4%. Poverty measured by living conditions improved more slowly, however, decreasing from 17.7% in the 2001 Census to 12.5% in the 2010 Census. Argentina's unemployment rate similarly declined from 25% in 2002 to an average of around 7% since 2011 largely because of both growing global demand for Argentine commodities and strong growth in domestic activity.

Given its ongoing dispute with holdout bondholders, the government has become wary of sending assets to foreign countries (such as the presidential plane, or artworks sent to foreign exhibitions) in case they might be impounded by courts at the behest of holdouts.

The government has been accused of manipulating economic statistics.

Reliability of official CPI estimates

Official CPI inflation figures released monthly by INDEC have been a subject of political controversy since 2007 through 2015. Official inflation data are disregarded by leading union leaders, even in the people sector, when negotiating pay rises.Some private-sector estimates put inflation for 2010 at around 25%, much higher than the official 10.9% rate for 2010. Inflation estimates from Argentina's provinces are also higher than the government's figures. The government backed up the validity of its data, but has called in the International Monetary Fund to help it design a new nationwide index to replace the current one.

The official government CPI is calculated based on 520 products, however the controversy arises from these products not being specified, and thus how many of those products are subject to price caps and subsidies. Economic analysts have been prosecuted for publishing estimates that disagree with official statistics. The government enforces a fine of up to 500,000 pesos for providing what it calls "fraudulent inflation figures". Beginning in 2015, the government again began to call for competitive bids from the private sector to provide a weekly independent inflation index.

Inflation

High inflation has been a weakness of the Argentine economy for decades. Inflation has been unofficially estimated to be running at around 25% annually since 2008, despite official statistics indicating less than half that figure; these would be the highest levels since the 2002 devaluation. A committee was established in 2010 in the Argentina Chamber of Deputies by opposition Deputies Patricia Bullrich, Ricardo Gil Lavedra, and others to publish an alternative index based on private estimates.Food price increases particularly that of beef, began to outstrip wage increases in 2010, leading Argentines to decrease beef consumption per capita from 69 kg (152 lb.) to 57 kg (125 lb.) annually and to increase consumption of other meats.

Consumer inflation expectations of 28 to 30% led the national mint to buy banknotes of its highest denomination (100 pesos) from Brazil at the end of 2010 to keep up with demand. The central bank pumped at least 1 billion pesos into the economy in this way during 2011.

As of June 2015, the government said that inflation was at 15.3%; approximately half that of some independent estimates. Inflation remained at around 18.6% in 2015 according to an International Monetary Fund estimate; but following a sharp devaluation enacted by the Maurico Macri administration on December 17, inflation reignited during the first half of 2016 - reaching 42% according to the Finance Ministry.

Supermarkets in Argentina have adopted electronic price tags, allowing prices to be updated quicker.

Income distribution

In relation to other Latin American countries, has a moderate to low level of income inequality. Its Gini coefficient is of about 0.427 (2014). The social gap is worst in the suburbs of the capital, where beneficiaries of the economic rebound live in gated communities, and many of the poor live in slums known as villas miseries.

In the mid-1970s, the most affluent 10% of Argentina's population had an income 12 times that of the poorest 10%. That figure had grown to 18 times by the mid-1990s, and by 2002, the peak of the crisis, the income of the richest segment of the population was 43 times that of the poorest. These heightened levels of inequality had improved to 26 times by 2006, and to 16 times at the end of 2010. Economic recovery after 2002 was thus accompanied by significant improvement in income distribution: in 2002, the richest 10% absorbed 40% of all income, compared to 1.1% for the poorest 10%; by 2010, the former received 29% of income, and the latter, 1.8%.

Argentina has an inequality-adjusted human development index of 0.707, compared to 0.578 and 0.710 for neighboring Brazil and Chile, respectively. The 2010 Census found that poverty by living conditions still affect 1 in 8 inhabitants, however; and while the official, household survey income poverty rate (based on U$S 100 per person per month, net) was 4.7% in 2013, the National Research Council estimated income poverty in 2010 at 22.6%, with private consulting firms estimating that in 2011 around 21% fell below the income poverty line. The World Bank estimated that, in 2013, 3.6% subsisted on less than US$3.10 per person per day.

Present Position of Agentina Economy At A Glance

(1) Currency Agentine peso (ARS) Exchange rate 38 peso=U.S.$1

(2) Financial year Calendar year

(3) Trade Organisations: WTO, Mercosur, G-20

(4) GDP $475.429 billion (Nominal), $718 billion (PPP)

(5) GDP growth 2.9% 2017, -1.7% 2019

(6) GDP per capita $10067 (Nominal), $20609 (PPP)

(7) GDP by Sector: Agriculture, forestry & fishing 6%, Mining 3.6%, Manufacturing 17.2%, Construction 5.6%, Commerce & industries 16.9%. Transport, communication & utilities 7.9 %, Govt. 9.5%, business, social & other services 33.3%

(8) Inflation 47.8% Oct.2018, 24.8% 2017, 40.9% 2016

(9) GINI coeffeciency: 0.440 2018

(10) Population 47.25 million

(11) Labour Force 18 million 38% of Population

(12) Labour force by occupation: Agriculture 7.3%, Manufacturing 13.1%, Construction 7.6%, Commerce & Tourism 21.40 %, Transport, communication 7.8%, financial, real estate and business services 9.4%, public administration and defence 6.3%s ocial services & others 27.1%

(13) Unemployment 9.6%2018, 8.4% 2017

(14) Average gross salary: ARS 21248 monthly

(15) Main Industries: food processing and beverages, motor vehicles, auto parts, appliances and electronics, machinery & equipment, chemicalspharmaceuticals, glass, steal &aluminum, cement, textiles, tobacoproducts, publishing, furniture, leather

(16) Ease of doing business: 119th

External

(17) Exports: $58.45 billion

(18) Export Goods: Soyabean and derivatives, petroleum & gas, vehicle, corn, wheat

(19) Main Export Partners: Brazil 16%, US 7.9%, China 7.5%, Chile 4.4%

(20) Imports: $63.97 billion Deficit $5.52billion (11.62% of GDP)

(21) Import goods: achinery, motor vehicles, petroleum and natural gas, organic chemicals, plastic

(22) Main Import Partners: Brazil 26.7%, China 18.5%, US 11.3%, Germany 4.9%

(23) FDI Stock: 76.58 billion 2017 Abroad $40.94 billion 2017

(24) Current Account: -31.32 billion 2017

(25) Gross External debt: $214.9 billion 45.20% of GDP. $163.2 billion Public and $92 .5 billion Market

(26) Public debt: 97.7% of GDP $464.50 billion

(27) Budget Balance: -6% of GDP

(28) Revenue: $120.6 billion Expenses: $ 158.6 billion fiscal deficit $ 38 billion. 8% of GDP

(29) Foreign Reserves $55.33 billion

(30) Credit Rating (S & P) B- Domestic SD(Foreign)
B- (T &C)

Critical Observations of Economy of Argentiina

(1) Economy of Argentina is a high income economy for fiscal year 2017 according to the World Bank. It is the third largest economy and the second largest in South America after Brazil. It is the most volatile and fluctuating economy. Government has made default in repaying their bonds borrowings many time. Bail out packages are also taken from IMF.Recently in 2018, it has applied for $30 billion bailout package and the country is under observation of IMF prior to sanctioning if its bailout package.Peso was devalued in USD terms by 50% in 2018. Its cereal production is 46 million metric tons.

(2) The country benefits from rich natural resources, a highly literate population, and export oriented agricultural sector and a diversified industrial base.

(3) Argentina's economic performance has historically been very uneven, in which high economic growth alternated with severe recessions since the late twentieth century and, a diversified industrial base.

(4) Early in twentieth century, Argentina had one of the ten highest per capita GDP levels surpassing both France and Italy.

(5) Argentina's currency 'peso" declined by about 50% in 2018 to more than 38 Argentina peso per dollarand today it is under the stand by program from the IMF. America supported it in giving financial assistance of $57 billion from IMF. In spite of this, Argentina is allowing China to install Military Base in Argentina which is strongly opposed by US President. Argentina has therefore postponed this programme. Argentina was the hosted country for G-20 summit in 1918.

(6) Argentina is considered as emerging market by FTSE.Global Equity Index and is one of G-20 major economies.

(7) Prior to the 1880s, Argentina was relatively isolated backwater dependent on salted meat, wool, leather and hide industries for both the greater part of foreign exchange and generation of domestic income and profit.

(8) Argentina economy began to experience rapid growth after 1880 through the livestock and grain commanding as well as through British and France investment making the beginning of 50 year era of significant expansion and mass European immigrations.

(9) During the most vigorous period from 1880-1905, this expansion resulted in a 7.5 times growth in GDP, averaging about 8% annually. GDP per capita rose from 35% of US average to about 80% during the subsequent period.

(10) In 1941, it was 50% of the GDP of USA. During the period 1890 to 1950, country's per capita income was similar as that of Western Europe.

(11) Income in Argentina remained considerably less evenly distributed.

(12) Great Depression caused to fall GDP by forth between 1929 and 1932, recovered its lost ground by late 1932. Recovered its loss around by late 1932.

(13) War led to a reduced availability of imports and higher prices for Argentina's exports. This created $1.6 billion cumulative surplus for Argentina but this was locked by Roca-Ranchman Treaty.

(14) Populist administration of Juan Perron nationalized National Central Bank, railways and other strategic industries and services

between 1945 and 1955. Argentina economy grew about fivefold from 1944 to 1974, 3.8% in annual term.

(15) Economy declined during military dictatorship from 1976 to 1983 on account of advanced corruption, anti-labour policy, financial liberalization that increased debt burden and affected industrial development.

(16) Economist Cavolloin pegged peso to USD in 1991.

(17) Nuclear plant generated electric energy of 133.3 billion Kwh in 2013.

(18) Overall study of Argentina reveals that the country is not economically sound for the following reasons: (a) Peso currency is fluctuating and its movement are volatile. (b) Economy is temporarily becomes stable under correct steps taken by the Ruler but inside the economy appears to be very weak. (c) Public debt 97.7% of GDP is very high and should be reduced drastically. (d) Credit Rating by Credit Rating Agency also shows that its future prospects are not bright. (e) Unemployment is 9% of labour force which should be reduced to eradicate poverty. (f) Inflation is above 40% which eats the economic growth of Argentina, (g) Fiscal deficit is 8% of GDP which is high. (h) Further external borrowing will not be available unless it improves its current rating. Debt serving at approximately 9% slighilty high. External debt outstanding is 214.9 billion against GDP 475 billion looks reasonable but the country had defaulted on $100 billion bonds issued by it so the creditors may not be confident about repayment of debt by the country on time to avoid default.

(19) The Argentina government bond market is based on GDP-linked bonds, and investors, both foreign and domestic, netted record yields amid renewed growth. Argentina debt restructuring offers in 2005 and 2010 resumed payments on the majority of almost $100 billion in defaulted bonds and other debt from 2001. Holdouts controlling 7% of the bonds, including some small investors, hedge funds, and vulture funds led by Paul Singer's Cayman Islands rejected the 2005 and 2010 offers to exchange their defaulted bonds. Singer demanded $232 billion for Argentina bonds purchased for $49 million in the secondary market in 2008 attempted to seize Argentine government assets abroad and sued to stop payments from Argentina to the 93% who had accepted the earlier swap discount. Bondholders had accepted the earlier swaps despite the steep discount. Bondholders who instead accepted the 2005 offer of 30 cent on the dollar, had by 2012 received returns of about 90% according to the estimates by Morgan Stanley. Argentina settled with virtually all holdouts in

February 2016 at a cost of $9.3 billion; NML received $ 2.4 billion, a 392% return on the original value of the bonds. This shows that delay in settling liability by Argentina government will lose the confidence of investors in its future bond borrowings.

(20) Venezuela country's financial status is very bad and it has been experimenting economic crisis in their country. Nobody is financially assisting Mathura to come out this situation and no country is interested in doing any trading or business with that country. Argentina should take appropriate step to avoid this trap and make sincere efforts to improve its credit rating to come out of this future economic crisis.

Chapter - 25

Economy of Mexico

Introduction

The economy of Mexico is 15th rank in the world in GDP Nominal terms and the 11th largest by GDP PPP as per IMF. Since the 1994 crisis, administrations have improved country's macroeconomic fundamentals. Though low rates were maintained by the country during the South American Crisis in 2002, it was not negatively affected but showed positive results. However, Mexico was one of the Latin American nations most affected by 2008 recession with GDP contracting more than 6% in that year.

The Mexican economy has had an unprecedented macroeconomic stability, which has reduced inflation and interest rates to record lows and has increased per capita income. In spite of this, enormous gaps remain between the urban and the rural population, the northern and southern states, and the rich and the poor. Some of the unresolved issues include the upgrade of infrastructure, the modernization of the tax system and labor laws, and the reduction of income inequality. Tax revenues, all together 19.6 percent of GDP in 2013, are the lowest among the 34 OECD countries.

The economy contains rapidly developing modern industrial and service sectors, with increasing private ownership. Recent administrations have expanded competition in ports, railroads, telecommunications, electricity generation, natural gas distribution and airports, with the aim of upgrading infrastructure. As an export-oriented economy, more than 90% of Mexican trade is under free trade agreements (FTAs) with more than 40 countries, including the European Union, Japan, Israel, and much of Central and South America. The most influential FTA is the North American Free Trade Agreement (NAFTA), which came into effect in 1994, and was signed in 1992 by the governments of the United States, Canada and Mexico but was cancelled by American President Mr. Trump in 2017 and after long negotiation with Mexico and Canada, new Agreement has been signed by US which reduces trade deficit of US with these countries. In 2006, trade with Mexico's two northern partners accounted for almost 90% of its exports and 55% of its imports. Recently, the Countries of the Union approved important tax, pension and judicial reforms, and reform to the oil industry is currently being debated. Mexico had 15 companies in the Forbes Global 2000 list of the world's largest companies in 2016.

Mexico's labor force is 52.8 million as of 2015. The OECD and WHO both rank Mexican workers as the hardest-working in the world in terms of the number of hours worked yearly, although profitability per man-hour remains low.

History

Economic History of Mexico

Porfirio Diaz, (1876–1911) in whose presidency rapid industrialization took place in foreign capital.

Mexican president Porifioro Diaz brought unprecedented economic growth during the last quarter of the nineteenth century. This growth was accompanied by foreign investment and European immigration, the development of an efficient railroad network and the exploitation of the country's natural resources. Annual economic growth between 1876 and 1910 averaged 3.3%.

Political repression and fraud, as well as huge income inequalities exacerbated by the land distribution system based on the system where large lands were owned by a few but worked by millions of underpaid peasants living in precarious conditions, led to the Mexican Revolution (1910–1920), an armed conflict that drastically transformed Mexico's political, social, cultural, and economical structure during the twentieth century under a premise of social democracy. The war itself left a harsh toll on the economy and population, which decreased over the 11-year period between 1910 and 1921. The reconstruction of the country was to take place in the following decades.

The period from 1930 to 1970 was dubbed by economic historians as the Mexican Miracle, a period of economic growth that followed the end of the Mexican Revolution and the resumption of capital accumulation during peacetime. During this period the nation adopted the economic model of import substitution industralisation (ISI) which protected and promoted the development of national industries. Mexico experienced an economic boom through which industries rapidly expanded their production. Important changes in the economic structure included free land distribution to peasants under the concept of ejido, the nationalization of the oil and railroad companies and the introduction of social rights into the constitution, the birth of large and influential labor unions, and the upgrading of infrastructure. While population doubled from 1940 to 1970, GDP increased six fold during the same period.

President Jose Lopez Portillo (1976-1982), during whose administration the economy soared with the discovery of oil and then crashed when the price dropped.

Growth while under the ISI model had reached its peak in the late 1960s. During the 1970s, the presidential administrations of Echeverria (1970–76) and Lopez Portillo (1976–82), tried to include social development in their policies, an effort that entailed more public spending. With the discovery of vast oil fields in a time in which oil prices were surging and international interest rates were low -and even negative- the government decided to borrow from international capital markets to invest in the state-owned oil company, which in turn seemed to provide a long-run income source to promote social welfare. This method produced a remarkable growth in public expenditure, and President Lopez Portillo announced that the time had come to "manage prosperity" as Mexico multiplied its oil production to become the world's fourth largest exporter.

Average annual GDP growth was 3.4% during 1900-1929, 4.2% during 1929-1945, 6.5% during 1945-72, -4.2% and -6.2% during Debt Crisis and Peso Crisis in 1983 and 1995 respectively.

It was contracted in 2009 by -6.5%.

In the period of 1981–1982 the international panorama changed abruptly; oil prices plunged and interest rates rose. In 1982, President López Portillo, (1976–82) just before ending his administration, suspended payments of foreign debt, devalued the peso and nationalized the banking system, along with many other industries that were severely affected by the crisis, among them the steel industry. While import substitution had been in use during an era of industrialization, by the 1980s it was evident that the protracted protection had produced an uncompetitive industrial sector with low productivity gains.

President de la Madrid (1982–88) was the first of a series of presidents that began to implement neoliberal reforms. After the crisis of 1982, lenders were unwilling to return to Mexico and, in order to keep the current account in balance, the government resorted to currency devaluations, which in turn sparked unprecedented inflation, which reached a historic high in 1987 at 139.7%.

The first step toward the liberalization of trade was Mexico's signature of the General Agreement on Tariffs and Trade (GATT) in 1986 under President de la Madrid. During the Sailinas administration (1988–94) many state-owned companies were privatized. The telephone company Telmex, a government monopoly, became a private monopoly, sold to Carlo Slim. Also not opened to private investors were the government oil company Premex or the energy sector. Furthermore, the banking system that had been nationalized in the waning hours of the López Portillo administration in 1982 were privatized, but with the exclusion of foreign banks. Salinas pushed for Mexico's inclusion in the North American Free Trade Agreement, expanding it from a U.S.-Canada agreement. The expanded NAFTA was signed in 1992, after the signature of two additional supplements on environments and labor standards, it came into effect on January 1, 1994.

Salinas also introduced strict price controls and negotiated smaller minimum wage increments with the labor union movement under the aging Fidel Velazquez with the aim of curbing inflation. While his strategy was successful in reducing inflation, growth averaged only 2.8 percent a year. By fixing the exchange rate, the peso became rapidly overvalued while consumer spending increased, causing the current account deficit to reach 7% of GDP in 1994. The deficit was financed through public debt instrument that reassured payment in dollars.

The assassinations of the ruling party's presidential candidate in March 1994, and the Secretary-General of the party and brother of the Assistant-Attorney General in 1994, sent a disquieting message to investors. Public debt holders rapidly sold their *tesobonos*, depleting the Central Bank's reserves, while portfolio investments, which had made up 90% of total investment flows, left the country as fast as they had come in.

This unsustainable situation eventually forced the entrant Zedillo administration to abandon the fixed exchange rate. The peso sharply devalued and the country entered into an economic crisis. The boom in exports, as well as an international rescue package crafted by U.S. president Bill Clinton (1993-2001), helped cushion the crisis. In less than 18 months, the economy was growing again, and annual rate growth averaged 5.1 percent between 1995 and 2000. More critical interpretations argue that the crisis and subsequent public bailout "preserved, renewed, and intensified the structurally unequal social relations of power and class characteristic of finance-led neoliberal capitalism" in forms institutionally specific to Mexican society.

President Zedillo (1994–2000) and President Fox (2000–06), of the National Action Party (Mexico), the first opposition party candidate to win a presidential election since the founding of the precursor of the Institutional Revolutionary Party in 1929, continued with trade liberalization. During Fox's administrations, several FTAs were signed with Latin American and European countries, Japan and Israel, and both strove to maintain macroeconomic stability. Thus, Mexico became one of the most open countries in the world to trade, and the economic base shifted accordingly. Total trade with the United States and Canada tripled, and total exports and imports almost quadrupled between 1991 and 2003. The nature of foreign investment also changed with a greater share of foreign-direct investment (FDI) over portfolio investment.

Macroeconomic, financial and welfare indicators

Main indicators

Mexico's Gross Domestic Product (GDP) in purchasing power parity (PPP) was estimated at US $2,143.499 billion in 2014, and $1,261.642 billion in nominal GDP terms. It is the leader of the MINT group. Its standard of living, as measured in GDP in PPP per capita, was US $16,900. The World Bank reported in 2009 that Mexico's Gross National Income in market exchange rates was the second highest in Latin America, after Brazil at US $1,830.392 billion, which lead to the highest income per capita in the region at $14,400. As such, Mexico is now firmly established as an upper middle-income country. After the slowdown of 2001 the country has recovered and has grown 4.2, 3.0 and 4.8 percent in 2004, 2005 and 2006, even though it is considered to be well below Mexico's potential growtt. Population under poverty is 13.8%, unemployment 5.5% and inflation 2.21% in November 2015.

The Mexican peso is the currency (ISO 4217: MXN; symbol: $). One peso is divided into 100 *centavos* (cents). MXN replaced MXP in 1993 at a rate of 1000 MXP per 1 MXN. The exchanged rate remained stable between1998-2012 was between 10.20 and 11=3.50 MXN per US$, recently the Mexican peso parity took a hit under president Enrique Peña Nieto, lost in single year 19.87% of its value and is currently at MXN 20.37per US$. (2017).Interest rates in 2007 were situated at around 7 percent, having reached a historic low in 2002 below 5 percent. Inflation rates are also at historic lows; the inflation rate in Mexico in 2006 was 4.1 percent, and 3 percent by the end of 2007. Compared against the US Dollar, Mexican Peso was devalued over 7,500% since 1910.

Unemployment rates are the lowest of all OECD member countries at 3.2 percent. However, underemployment is estimated at 25 percent. Mexico's Human development index was reported at 0.829, (comprising a life expectancy index of 0.84, an education index of 0.86 and a GDP index of 0.77), ranking 52 in the world within the group of high-development.

Development

The following table shows the main economic indicators in 1980–2017. Inflation under 5 % is in green.

Year	*GDP (in Bil. US$ PPP)*	*GDP per capita (in US$ PPP)*	*GDP growth (real)*	*Inflation rate (in Percent)*	*Unemployment (in Percent)*	*Government debt (in % of GDP)*
1980	403.6	5,818	▲9.5 %	▲26.5 %	1.2 %	n/a
1981	▲478.8	▲6,745	▲8.5 %	▲27.9 %	▼0.9 %	n/a
1988	▲619.8	▲7,550	▲1.3 %	▲113.5 %	▼3.5 %	n/a
1994	▲939.8	▲10,099	▲4.9 %	▲7.0 %	▲3.7 %	n/a
2001	▲1,288.0	▲12,612	▼−0.4 %	▲6.4 %	▲2.8 %	▼39.4 %
2010	▲1,806.5	▲15,811	▲5.1 %	▲4.2 %	5.3 %	▼42.0 %
2017	▲2,458.4	▲19,902	▲2.0 %	▲6.0 %	▼3.4 %	▼54.2 %

Poverty

Poverty in Mexico

Poverty in Mexico is measured under parameters such as nutrition, clean water, shelter, education, health care, social security, quality and basic services in the household, income and social cohesion as defined by social development laws in the country. It is divided in two categories: Moderate poverty and Extreme poverty.

While less than 2% of Mexico's population lives below the international poverty line set by the World Bank, as of 2013, Mexico's government estimates that 33% of Mexico's population lives in moderate poverty and 9% lives in extreme poverty, which leads to 42% of Mexico's total population living below the national poverty line. The huge gap might be explained by the government's adopting the multi-dimensional poverty method as a way to measure poverty, so a person who has an income higher than the "international poverty line" or "well-being income line" set by the Mexican government might fall in the "moderate poverty" category if he or she has one or more deficiencies related to social rights such as education (did not complete studies), nutrition (malnutrition or obesity), or living standards (including elemental, such as water or electricity, and secondary domestic assets, such as refrigerators). Extreme poverty is defined by the Mexican government as persons who have deficiencies in both social rights and an income lower than the "well-being income line". Additional figures from SEDESOL (Mexico's social development agency) estimates that 6% (7.4 millions of people) live in extreme poverty and suffer from food insecurity.

Recently, extensive changes in government economic policy and attempts at reducing government interference through privatization of several sectors, for better or worse, allowed Mexico to remain the biggest economy in Latin America, until 2005 when it became the second-largest; and a so-called "trillion dollar club" member.Despite these changes, Mexico continues to suffer great social inequality and lack of opportunities. The current administration has made an attempt at reducing poverty in the country, to provide more opportunities to its citizens such as jobs, education, and the installation of universal healthcare.

Income inequality

The GDP per capita of Mexican States in USD, 2012.

A single person in Mexico, Carlos Slim, has a net worth equal to six percent of GDP. Additionally, only ten percent of Mexicans represent 25% of Mexican GDP. A smaller group, 3.5%, represent 12.5% of Mexican GDP.

According to the OECD, Mexico is the country with the second highest degree of economic disparity between the extremely poor and extremely rich, after Chile – although this gap has been diminishing over the last decade. The bottom ten percent on the income rung disposes of 1.36% of the country's resources, whereas the upper 10% dispose of almost 36%. OECD also notes that Mexico's budgeted expenses for poverty alleviation and social development is only about a third of the OECD average – both in absolute and relative numbers. According to the World Bank, in 2004, 17.6% of Mexico's population lived in extreme poverty, while 21% lived in moderated poverty.

Agriculture

Agriculture in Mexico

Agriculture as a percentage of total GDP has been steadily declining, and now resembles that of developed nations in that it plays a smaller role in the economy. In 2006, agriculture accounted for 3.9% of GDP, down from 7% in 1990, and 25% in 1970.Given the historic structure of ejidos, it employs a considerably high percentage of the work force: 18% in 2003, mostly of which grows basic crops for subsistence, compared to 2–5% in developed nations in which production is highly mechanized. Foodgrains production is 20 million metric tons. Besides Foodgains, mangoes, oranges, onions, limes lemons, sunflower seeds are also produced.

After the Mexican Revolution Mexico began an agrarian reform, based on the 27th article of the Mexican Constitution that included transfer of land and/or free land distribution to peasants and small farmers under the concept of the ejido. This program was further extended during President Cardenas' administration during the 1930s and continued into the 1960s at varying rates. The cooperative agrarian reform, which guaranteed small farmers a means of subsistence livelihood, also caused land fragmentation and lack of capital investment, since commonly held land could not be used as collateral. In an effort to raise rural productivity and living standards, this constitutional article was amended in 1992 to allow for the transfer of property rights of the communal lands to farmers cultivating it. With the ability to rent or sell it, a way was open for the creation of larger farms and the advantages of economies of scale. Large mechanized farms are now operating in some northwestern states (mainly in Sinaloa). However, privatization of ejido continues to be very slow in the central and southern states where the great majority of peasants produce only for subsistence.

Up until the 1980s, the government encouraged the production of basic crops (mainly corb and beans) by maintaining support prices and controlling imports through the National Company for Popular Subsistence (CONASUPO). With trade liberalization, however, CONASUPO was to be gradually dismantled and two new mechanisms were implemented: Alianza and Procampo. Alianza provides income payments and incentives for mechanization and advanced irrigation systems. Procampo is an income transfer subsidy to farmers. This support program provides 3.5 million farmers who produce basic commodities (mostly corn), and which represent 64% of all farmers, with a fixed income transfer payment per unit of area of cropland. This subsidy increased substantially during President Fox's administration, mainly to white corn producers in order to reduce the amount of imports from the United States. This program has been successful, and in 2004, roughly only 15% of corn imports are white corn –the one used for human consumption and the type that is mostly grown in Mexico– as opposed to 85% of yellow and crashed corn –the one use for feeding livestock, and which is barely produced in Mexico.

Crops

In spite of being a staple in the Mexican diet, Mexico's comparative advantage in agriculture is not in corn, but in horticulture, tropical fruits, and vegetables. Negotiators of NAFTA expected that through liberalization and mechanization of agriculture two-thirds of Mexican corn producers would naturally shift from corn production to horticultural and other labor-intensive crops such as fruits, nuts, vegetables, coffee and sugar cane. While horticultural trade has drastically increased due to NAFTA, it has not absorbed displaced workers from corn production (estimated at around 600,000). Corn production has remained stable (at 20 million metric tons), arguably, as a result of income support to farmers, or a reluctance to abandon a millenarian tradition in Mexico: not only have peasants grown corn for millennia, corn *originated* in Mexico. Mexico is the seventh largest corn producer in the world.

Potatoes

The area dedicated to potatoes has changed little since 1980 and average yields have almost tripled since 1961. Production reached a record 1.7 million tonnes in 2003. Per capita consumption of potato in Mexico stands at 17 kg a year, very low compared to its maize intake of 400 kg. On average, potato farms in Mexico are larger than those devoted to more basic food crops. Potato production in Mexico is mostly for commercial purposes; the production for household consumption is very small.

Sugar cane

Approximately 160,000 medium-sized farmers grow sugar cane in 15 Mexican states; currently there are 54 sugar mills around the country that produced 4.96 million tons of sugar in the 2010 crop, compared to 5.8 million tons in 2001. Mexico's sugar industry is characterized by high production costs and lack of investment. Mexico produces more sugar than it consumes. Sugar cane is grown on 700,000 farms in Mexico with a yield of 72 metric tons per farm.

Industry

The industrial sector as a whole has benefited from trade liberalization; in 2000. It accounted for almost 50% of all export earnings.

Among the most important industrial manufacturers in Mexico is the automotive industry, whose standards of quality are internationally recognized. The automobile sector in Mexico differs from that in other Latin American countries and developing nations in that it does not function as a mere assembly manufacturer. The industry produces technologically complex components and engages in some research and development activities, an example of that is the new Volkswagen Jetta model with up to 70% of parts designed in Mexico.

The "Big Three" (General Motors, Ford and Chryster) have been operating in Mexico since the 1930s, while Volkswagen and Nissan built their plants in the 1960s. Later, Toyato, Honda, BMW, and Mercedes-Benz joined in. Given the high requirements of North American components in the industry, many European and Asian parts suppliers have also moved to Mexico: in Puebla alone, 70 industrial part-makers cluster around Volkswagen.

The relatively small domestic car industry is represented by DINA Camiones S.A. de C. V., a manufacturer of trucks, busses and military vehicles, which through domestic production and purchases of foreign bus manufacturers has become the largest bus manufacturer in the world; Vehizero that builds hybrid trucks and the new car companies Mastretta design that builds the Mastretta MXT sports car and Autobuses King that plans to build 10000 microbuses by 2015, nevertheless new car companies are emerging among them CIMEX that has developed a sport utility truck, the Conin, and it is to be released in September 2010 in Mexico's national auto show, And the new electric car maker Grupo Electrico Motorizado. Some large industries of Mexico include Cemex, the world's largest construction company and the third largest cement producer the alcohol beverage industries, including world-renowned players like Group Modela; conglomerates like FEMSA, which apart from being the largest single producer of alcoholic beverages and owning multiple commercial interests such OXXO convenience store chain, is also the second-largest Coca-Cola bottler in the world; Gruma, the largest producer of corn flour and tortillas in the world; and Grupo Bimbo, Telmex, Televisa, among many others. In 2005, according to the World Bank, high-tech industrial production represented 19.6% of total exports.

Maquiladoras (manufacturing plants that take in imported raw materials and produce goods for domestic consumption and export on behalf of foreign companies) have become the landmark of trade in Mexico. This sector has benefited from NAFTA, in that real income in the maquiladora sector has increased 15.5% since 1994, though from the non-maquiladora sector has grown much faster. Contrary to popular belief, this should be no surprise since maquiladora's products could enter the US duty-free since the 1960s industry agreement. Other sectors now benefit from the free trade agreement, and the share of exports from non-border states has increased in the last 5 years while the share of exports from maquiladora-border states has decreased.

Currently Mexico is focusing in developing an aerospace industry and the assembly of helicopter and regional jet aircraft fuselages is taking place. Foreign firms such as MD Helicopters, Bell, Cessna, and Bombardier build helicopter, aircraft and regional jets fuselages in Mexico. Although the Mexican aircraft industry is mostly foreign, as is its car industry, Mexican firms have been founded such as Aeromarmi, which builds light propeller airplanes, and Hydra Technologies, which builds Unmanned Aerial Vechicles such as the S4 Ehecati, other important companies are Frisa Aerospace that manufactures jet engine parts for the new Mitsubishi Regional jet and supplies Prat & whittney and rolls Royce jet engine manufacturers of casings for jet engines and Kuo Aerospace that builds parts for aircraft landing gear and Supplies bombardier plant in Querétaro.

As compared with the United States or countries in Western Europe a larger sector of Mexico's industrial economy is food manufacturing which includes several world class companies but the regional industry is undeveloped. There are national brands that have become international and local Mom and Pop producers but little manufacturing in between.

Electronics

The electronics industry of Mexico has grown enormously within the last decade. Mexico has the sixth largest electronics industry in the world after China, United States, Japan, South Africa and Taiwan. Mexico is the second largest exporter of electronics to the United States where it exported $71.4 billion worth of electronics in 2011. The Mexican electronics industry is dominated by the manufacture and OEM design of televisions, displays, computers, mobile phones, circuit boards, semiconductors, electronic appliances, communications equipment and LCD modules. The Mexican electronics industry grew 20% between 2010 and 2011, up from its constant growth rate of 17% between 2003 and 2009. Currently electronics represent 30% of Mexico's exports.

Televisions

The design and manufacture of flat panel plasma, LCD and LED televisions is the single largest sector of the Mexican electronics industry, representing 25% of Mexico's electronics export revenue. In 2009 Mexico surpassed South Korea and China as the largest manufacturer of televisions, with Sony, Toshiba,Samsung, Sharp (through Semex), others manufacturing CRT, LCD, LED and Plasma televisions in Mexico. Due to Mexico's position as the largest manufacturer of television it is known as the television capital of the world in the electronics industry.

Computers

Mexico is the third largest manufacturers of computers in the world with both domestic companies and foreign companies manufacturing various types of computers across the country. Most of the computers manufactured in Mexico are from foreign companies. Mexico is Latin America's largest producer of electronics and appliances made by domestic companies.

OEM and ODM manufacturing

A Lanix LT10.1 high definition LCD assembled under OEM contract by Lanix for use in a Sharp LCD television.

Mexico is also home to a large number of OEM and ODM manufactures both foreign and domestic. Companies assemble finished electronics or design and manufacture electronic components on behalf of larger companies such as Sony or Microsoft using locally sourced components, for example the ODM, Flextronics manufactures Xbox video games systems in, Mexico for Microsoft using components such as power systems and printed circuit boards from a local company, Falco Electronics which acts as the OEM.

Engineering and Design

The Monterrey Institute of Technology and Higher Education is one of Mexico's most prestigious technology and engineering universities and is ranked one of the leading engineering institutions in Latin America.

The success and rapid growth of the Mexican electronics sector is driven primarily by the relatively low cost of manufacturing and design in Mexico; its strategic position as a major consumer electronics market coupled with its proximity to both the large North American and South American markets whom Mexico shares free trade agreements with; government support in the form of low business taxes, simplified access to loans and capital for both foreign multinational and domestic startup tech-based firms; and a very large pool of highly skilled, educated labor across all sectors of the tech industry. For example, German multinational engineering and electronics conglomerate Siemens has a significant Mexican base, which also serves as its business and strategy hub for Central American countries and the Caribbean region.

There are almost half a million (451,000) students enrolled in electronics engineering programs with an additional 114,000 electronics engineers entering the Mexican workforce each year and Mexico had over half a million (580,000) certified electronic engineering professionals employed in 2007. From the late 1990s, the Mexican electronics industry began to shift away from simple line assembly to more advanced work such as research, design, and the manufacture of advanced electronics systems such as LCD panels, semi-conductors, printed circuit boards, microelectronics, microprocessors, chipsets and heavy electronic industrial equipment and in 2006 the number of certified engineers being graduated annually in Mexico surpassed that of the United States. Many Korean, Japanese and American appliances sold in the US are actually of Mexican design and origin but sold under the OEM's client names. In 2008 one out of every four consumer appliances sold in the United States was of Mexican design.

Joint Production

While many foreign companies like Phillips, Vizio and LG simply install wholly owned factories in Mexico, a number of foreign companies have set up semi-independent joint venture companies with Mexican businesses to manufacture and design components in Mexico. These companies are independently operated from their foreign parent companies and are registered in Mexico. These local companies function under Mexican law and retain a sizable portion of the revenue. These companies typically function dually as in-company OEM development and design facilities and manufacturing centers and usually produce most components needed to manufacture the finished products. An example would by Sharp which has formed Semex.

Semex was founded as a joint venture between Sharp and Mexican investors which acts as an autonomous independent company which Sharp only maintains partial control over. The company manufactures whole products such televisions and designs individual components on behalf of Sharp such as LCD modules and in return Semex is granted access to sharp capital, technology, research capacity and branding. Notable foreign companies which have set up joint venture entities in Mexico include Samsung which formed Samex, a local designer and manufacturer of finished televisions, white goods and individual electronic components like printed circuit boards, LCD panels and semiconductors, Toshiba, who formed Toshiba de México, S.A. de C.V., an administratively autonomous subsidiary which produces electronics parts, televisions and heavy industrial equipment.

Some of these subsidiaries have grown to expand into multiple branches effectively becoming autonomous conglomerates within their own parent companies. Sony for example started operations in Mexico in 1976 with a group of Mexican investors, and founded the joint venture, Sony de Mexico which produces LED panels, LCD modules, automotive electronics, appliances and printed circuit boards amongst other products for its Japanese parent company, Sony KG. Sony de Mexico has research facilities in Monterrey and Mexico City, designs many of the Sony products manufactured in Mexico and has now expanded to create its own finance, music and entertainment subsidiaries which are Mexican registered and independent of their Japanese parent corporation.

Domestic Industry

Although much of Mexico's electronics industry is driven by foreign companies, Mexico also has a sizeable domestic electronics industry and a number of electronics companies including Mabe, a major appliance manufacturer and OEM which has been functioning since the nineteen fifties and has expanded into the global market, Meebox, a designer and manufacturer desktop and tablet computers, solar power panels and electronics components, Texa, which manufactures computers laptops and servers, Falco, a major international manufacturer of electronic components such as printed circuit boards, power systems, semiconductors, gate drives and which has production facilities in Mexico, India and China, and Lanix, Mexico's largest electronics company which manufactures products such as computers, laptops, smartphones, LED and LCDs, flash memory, tablets, servers, hard drives, RAM, optical disk drive, and printed circuit boards and employs over 11,000 people in Mexico and Chile and distributes its products throughout Latin America. Another area being currently developed in Mexico is Robotics, Mexico's new Mexone robot has been designed with the idea that in future years develop a commercial application for such advanced robots.

Oil

Petroleum Industry in Mexico

Mineral resources are the "nation's property" (i.e. public property) by constitution. As such, the energy sector is administered by the government with varying degrees of private investment. Mexico is the sixth-largest oil producer in the world, with 3,700,000 barrels per day (590,000 m^3/d). Pemex, the public company in charge of administering research, exploration and sales of oil, is the largest company (oil or otherwise) in Mexico and the second largest in Latin America after Brazil's Petrobras. Pemex is heavily taxed of almost 62 per cent of the company's sales, a significant source of revenue for the government.

Without enough money to continue investing in finding new sources or upgrading infrastructure, and being protected constitutionally from private and foreign investment, some have predicted the company may face institutional collapse. While the oil industry is still relevant for the government's budget, its importance in GDP and exports has steadily fallen since the 1980s. In 1980 oil exports accounted for 61.6% of total exports; by 2000 it was only 7.3%.

Energy

Electricity sector in Mexico

Mexico's installed electricity capacity in 2008 was 58 GW. Of the installed capacity, 75% is thermal, 19% hydro, 2% nuclear and 3% renewable other than hydro. The general trend in thermal generation is a decline in petroleum-based fuels and a growth in natural gas and coal. Since Mexico is a net importer of natural gas, higher levels of natural gas consumption (i.e. for power generation) will likely depend upon higher imports from either the United States or via liquefied natural gas (LNG).

Manufacturing in Mexico

Automobiles

The automotive sector accounts for 17.6% of Mexico's manufacturing sector. Companies like General Motors and others produce 2.8 million vehicles annually at 20 plants across the country, mostly in Puebla. Mexico manufactures more automobiles of any North American nation.The industry produces technologically complex components and engages in research and development.

The "Big Three" (General Motors, Ford and Chrysler) have been operating in Mexico since the 1930s, while Volkswagen and Nissan built their plants in the 1960s. In Puebla 70 industrial part-makers cluster around Volkswagen. In the 2010s expansion of the sector was surging. In 2014 more than $10 billion in investment was committed in the first few months of the year. Kia Motors in August 2014 announced plans for a $1 billion factory in Nuevo Leon.

Retailing

Mexico has a MXN 4.027 trillion retail sector (2013, about 300 billion USD at the 2013 exchange rate) including an estimated $12 billion USD (2015) in e-commerce. The largest retailer is Walmart, while the largest Mexico-based retailers are Soriana super/hypermarkets, FEMSA incl. its OXXO convenience stores.

Services

In 2013 the tertiary sector was estimated to account for 59.8% of Mexico's GDP. In 2011 services employed 61.9% of the working population. This section includes transportation, commerce, warehousing, restaurant and hotels, arts and entertainment, health, education, financial and banking services, telecommunications as well as public administration and defense. Mexico's service sector is strong, and in 2001 replaced Brazil's as the largest service sector in Latin America in dollar terms.

Tourism in Mexico

Tourism is one of the most important industries in Mexico. It is the fourth largest source of foreign exchange for the country. Mexico is the eighth most visited country in the world (with over 20 million tourists a year).

Finance

Banking system

According to the IMF the Mexican banking system is strong, in which private banks are profitable and well-capitalized. The financial and banking sector is increasingly dominated by foreign companies or mergers of foreign and Mexican companies with the notable exception of Banorte. The acquisition of Banamex, one of the oldest surviving financial institutions in Mexico, by Citigroup was the largest US-Mexico corporate merger, at US $12.5 billion. In spite of that, the largest financial institution in Mexico is Bancomer associated to the Spanish BBVA.

The process of institution building in the financial sector in Mexico has evolved hand in hand with the efforts of financial liberalization and of inserting the economy more fully into world markets. Over the recent years, there has been a wave of acquisitions by foreign institutions such as US-based Citigroup, Spain's BBVA and the UK's HSBC. Their presence, along with a better regulatory framework, has allowed Mexico's banking system to recover from the 1994–95 peso devaluation. Lending to the public and private sector is increasing and so is activity in the areas of insurance, leasing and mortgages However, bank credit accounts for only 22% of GDP, which is significantly low compared to 70% in Chile. Credit to the Agricultural sector has fallen 45.5% in six years (2001 to 2007), and now represents about 1% of total bank loans. Other important institutions include savings and loans, credit unions (known as "cajas populares"),government development banks, "non-bank banks "bonded warehouses, bonding companies and foreign-exchange firms.

A wave of acquisitions has left Mexico's financial sector in foreign hands. Their foreign-run affiliates compete with independent financial firms operating as commercial banks, brokerage and securities houses, insurance companies, retirement-fund administrators, mutual funds, and leasing companies.

Securities market

Mexico has a single securities market, the Mexican Stock Exchange (Bolsa Mexicana de Valores, known as the Bolsa). The market has grown steadily, with its main indices increasing by more than 600% in the last decade. It is Latin America's second largest exchange, after Brazil's. The total value of the domestic market capitalization of the BMV was calculated at US$ 409 billion at the end of 2011, and raised to US$ 451 billion by the end of February this year.

The Indice de Precious v Cotizaciones (IPC, the general equities index) is the benchmark stock index on the Bolsa. In 2005 the IPC surged 37.8%, to 17,802.71 from 12,917.88, backed by a stronger Mexican economy and lower interest rates. It continued its steep rise through the beginning of 2006, reaching 19,272.63 points at end-March 2006. The stock market also posted a record low vacancy rate, according to the central bank. Local stock market capitalization totalled US$236bn at end-2005, up from US$170 bn at end-2004. As of March 2006 there were 135 listed companies, down from 153 a year earlier. Only a handful of the listed companies are foreign. Most are from Mexico City or Monterrey; companies from these two cities compose 67% of the total listed companies.

Mexico's stock market is closely linked to developments in the US. Thus, volatility in the New York stock exchanges, as well as interest-rate changes and economic expectations in the US, can steer the performance of Mexican equities. This is both because of Mexico's economic dependence on the US and the high volume of trading in Mexican equities through American Depositary Receipts (ADRs). Currently, the decline in the value of the dollar is making non-US markets, including Mexico's, more attractive.

Despite the recent gains, investors remain wary of making placements in second-tier initial public offerings (IPOs). Purchasers of new issues were disappointed after prices fell in numerous medium-sized companies that made offerings in 1996 and 1997. IPO activity in Mexico remains tepid and the market for second-tier IPOs is barely visible. There were three IPOs in 2005.

Currency policy

Mexico has a floating exchange rate regime.

The floating exchange originated with reforms initiated after the December 1994 peso crash which had followed an unsustainable adherence to a short band. Under the new system, Banco de México now makes no commitment to the level of the peso exchange rate, although it does employ an automatic mechanism to accumulate foreign reserves. It also possesses tools aimed at smoothing out volatility. The Exchange Rate Commission sets policy; it is made up of six members—three each from the Ministry of Finance and Public Credit (Secretaría de Hacienda y Crédito Publico—SHCP) and the central bank, with the SHCP holding the deciding vote.

In August 1996, Banco de México initiated a mechanism to acquire foreign reserves when the peso is strong, without giving the market signals about a target range for the exchange rate. The resulting high levels of reserves, mostly from petroleum revenues, have helped to improve the terms and conditions on debt Mexico places on foreign markets. However, there is concern that the government relies too heavily on oil income in order to build a healthy base of reserves. According to the central bank, international reserves stood at US $75.8 billion in 2007. In May 2003, Banco de México launched a program that sells U.S. dollars via a monthly auction, with the goal of maintaining a stable, but moderate, level of reserves.

From April 1, 1998, through April 1, 2008, the Peso traded around a range varying from $8.46 MXN per US$1.00 on April 21, 1998, to $11.69 MXN per US$1.00 on May 11, 2004, a 10-year peak depreciation of 38.18% between the two reference date extremes before recovering.

After the onset of the US credit crisis that accelerated in October 2008, the Peso had an exchange rate during October 1, 2008, through April 1, 2009 fluctuating from lowest to highest between $10.96 MXN per US$1.00 on October 1, 2008, to $15.42 MXN per US$1.00 on March 9, 2009, a peak depreciation ytd of 28.92% during those six months between the two reference date extremes before recovering.

From the $11.69 rate during 2004's low to the $15.42 rate during 2009's low, the peso depreciated 31.91% in that span covering the US recession coinciding Iraq War of 2003 and 2004 to the US & Global Credit Crisis of 2008.

Some experts including analysts at Goldman Sachs who coined the term BRIC in reference to the growing economies of Brazil, Russia, India, and China for marketing purposes believe that Mexico is going to be the 5th or 6th biggest economy in the world by the year 2050, behind China, United States, India, Brazil, and possibly Russia.

Monetary system

Mexico's monetary policy was revised following the 1994–95 financial crisis, when officials decided that maintaining general price stability was the best way to contribute to the sustained growth of employment and economic activity. As a result, Banco de México has as its primary objective maintaining stability in the purchasing power of the peso. It sets an inflation target, which requires it to establish corresponding quantitative targets for the growth of the monetary base and for the expansion of net domestic credit.

The central bank also monitors the evolution of several economic indicators, such as the exchange rate, differences between observed and projected inflation, the results of surveys on the public and specialists' inflation expectations, revisions on collective employment contracts, producer prices, and the balances of the current and capital accounts.

A debate continues over whether Mexico should switch to a US-style interest rate-targeting system. Government officials in favor of a change say that the new system would give them more control over interest rates, which are becoming more important as consumer credit levels rise.

Until 2008, Mexico used a unique system, amongst the OECD countries, to control inflation in a mechanism known as the *corto* ("shortage") a mechanism that allowed the central bank to influence market interest rates by leaving the banking system short of its daily demand for money by a predetermined amount. If the central bank wanted to push interest rates higher, it increased the *corto*. If it wished to lower interest rates, it decreased the *corto*. Source: BANXICO: in April 2004, the Central Bank began setting a referential overnight interest rate as its monetary policy.

Business regulation

Corruption in Mexico

Petty corruption based on exercise of administrative discretion in matters of zoning and business permits is endemic in Mexico adding about 10% to the cost of consumer goods and services. An April 2012 article in The New York Times reporting payment of bribes to officials throughout Mexico in order to obtain construction permits, information, and other favors resulted in investigations in both the United States and Mexico.

Using relatively recent night light data and electricity consumption in comparison with Gross County Product, the informal sector of the local economy in Veracruz State is shown to have grown during the period of the Fox Administration though the regional government remained PRI. The assumption that the informal economy of Mexico is a constant 30% of total economic activity is not supported at the local level. The small amount of local spatial autocorrelation that was found suggests a few clusters of high and low literacy rates amongst municipios in Veracruz but not enough to warrant including an I-statistic as a regressor. Global spatial autocorrelation is found especially literacy at the macro-regional level which is an area for further research beyond this study.

Improved literacy bolsters both the informal and formal economies in Veracruz indicating policies designed to further literacy are vital for growing the regional economy. While indigenous people are relatively poor, little evidence was found that the informal economy is a higher percentage of total economic activity in a municipio with a high share of indigenous people. While the formal economy might have been expanding relative to the informal economy in 2000, by 2006 this process had been reversed with growing informality. While rural municipios have smaller economies, they are not different than urban municipios in the share of the economy that is informal. Programs in the past that might move economic activity from the informal to the formal sector have not succeeded, suggesting public finance issues such as tax evasion will continue to plague the state with low government revenues.

Trade

World Trade Center in Mexico City	
Exports	US $248.8 billion f.o.b. (2006)
Imports	US $253.1 billion f.o.b. (2006)
Current account	▼ US $400.1 million (2006)
Export partners	US 90.9%, Canada 2.2%, Spain 1.4%, Germany 1.3%, Colombia 0.9% (2006)
Import partners	US 53.4%, China 8%, Japan 5.9% (2005)

Mexico is an export-oriented economy. It is an important trade power as measured by the value of merchandise traded, and the country with the greatest number of free trade agreements. In 2005, Mexico was the world's fifteenth largest merchandise exporter and twelfth largest merchandise importer with a 12% annual percentage increase in overall trade. From 1991 to 2005 Mexican trade increased fivefold. Mexico is the biggest exporter and importer in Latin America; in 2005, Mexico alone exported US $213.7 billion, roughly equivalent to the sum of the exports of Brazil, Argentina, Venezuela, Uruguay, and Paraguay.

By 2009 Mexico ranked once again number 15 on World's leading exporters with US $230 billion (And amongst the top ten excluding Intra-EU countries). Mexican trade is fully integrated with that of its North American partners: close to 90% of Mexican exports and 50% of its imports are traded with the United States and Canada. Nonetheless, NAFTA has not produced trade diversion. While trade with the United States increased 183% from 1993 to 2002, and that with Canada 165%, other trade agreements have shown even more impressive results: trade with Chile increased 285%, with Costa Rica 528% and Honduras 420%. Trade with the European Union increased 105% over the same time period.

Mexican trade facilitation and competitiveness

World Bank suggests that Mexico has the potential to substantially increase trade flows and economic growth through trade facilitation reform. The study examines the poWtential impacts of trade facilitation reforms in four areas: port efficiency, customs administration, information technology, and regulatory environment (including standards).

The study projects overall increments from domestic reforms to be on the order of $31.8 billion, equivalent to 22.4 percent of total Mexican manufacturing exports for 2000–03. On the imports side, the corresponding figures are $17.1 billion and 11.2 percent, respectively. Increases in exports, including textiles, would result primarily from improvements in port efficiency and the regulatory environment. Exports of transport equipment would be expected to increase by the greatest increment from improvements in port efficiency, whereas exports of food and machinery would largely be the result of improvements in the regulatory environment. On the imports side, Mexican improvements in port efficiency would appear to be the most important factor, although for imports of transport equipment, improvements in service sector infrastructure would also be of relative importance.

Present Status of Mexican Economyat Glanse

(1) Currency: Mexical peso12.59 = US$ 1(2010)
(2) Fiscal year: Calendar year
(3) Trade Organizations: APEC, NAFTA, OCED & WORLD BANK
(4) GDP: $2.199 trillion Nominal 15th Rank, $3.508 trillion PPP, 11th Rank
(5) GDP Growth rate: 2.3% in 2015, 2.9% in 2016, 2% in 2017 & 2.3% in 2018
(6) GDP per Capita $10021 (Nominal 69th), $20617 (PPP65th)
(7) GDP by Sector: Agriculture 3.6%, Industry 38.6%, Services 59.8%
(8) Inflation 2.5%
(9) Population: 7.50 crores
(10) Population below poverty 42.3%

(11) Labour force 53million (77% of population)

(12) Labour Force by Sector: Agriculture 13.4%, Industries 25.4% & Services 61.2%

(13) Unemployment: 3.44%

(14) Main Industries: Food & beverage, tobacco, aerospace, chemicals, iron & steel, petroleum's, mining, textiles, clothing, motor vehicles, consumer durables, tourism

External

(15) Exports: $406.5 billion

(16) Export goods: automobiles, electronics, television, computers, mobile phones, LCD, oil & oil products, silver. Fruits, vegetables, cotton, coffee.

(17) Main Export Partners: US 80%, Canada 2.7%, China 1.5% & Brazil 1.2%

(18) Imports: $417.3 billion Import Goods: Metal working machines, steel mills products, agricultural machinery, metals, repairs parts for motor vehicles, aircrafts and aircraft parts, oil production equipments

(19) Main Import Partners: US 49%, China 16.6%, Japan4.4%, South Korea 3.4%.

(20) Trade Deficit: $10.8 billion i.e. 0.49% of GDP Nominal

(21) Public debt: 341 billion (47.9% of GDP)

(22) Fiscal

(23) Revenues: $234.3 billion, Expenses: 261.8 billion, Fiscal deficit: 27.5 billion – 1.25% of GDP

(24) Economic Aid $189.4 million

(25) Foreign Reserves: $179.314 billion

(26) Credit Rating: S & P - A (domestic), BBB+ (Foreign)
T & C – A+ Outlook: Stable
Moody A3 Outlook Stable
Fitch BBB+, Outlook Stable

Critical Observations of Economy of Mexico

(1) Economy of Mexico is the 15th largest economy in nominal terms and 11th by PPP according to the IMF.

(2) Since 1994, crisis administration has improved the country's macroeconomic fundamentals and maintain positive, although rates of growth after a brief period of stagnation.

(3) Mexico was one of the Latin American nations which is most affected by 2008 recession with its GDP contracting by more than 6% in that year.

(4) Economy has had an unprecedented macroeconomy stability which has reduced inflation and interest rates to record low and has increased per capita income. In spite of this, enormous gaps remain between the urban and rural population, the Northern and Southern states and the rich and the poor. Upgragradation of infrastructure, modernization of tax system and labour laws are main issues of Mexico and reduction of income inequality. Tax revenues, all together 19.6% of GDP in 2003 are the lowest among the 34 OCED countries.

(5) Increasing private ownership process was adopted. Recent administration have expanded competition in ports, railways, telecommunications, electricity generation, natural gas distribution and airports with the aim of upgrading infrastructure. Crop production is stagnant at 20 million metric tons.

(6) As an export oriented economy, more than 96% of Mexican trade is under the trade agreement with more than 40 countries including European Union, Japan, Israel and much of Central and South America. The most influential FTA is the North American Trade Agreement (NAFTA) which came into effect in 1994 and was signed in 1992 by the government of America, Canada and Mexico.

(7) President Portfino Diaz brought comprehensive economic growth during the last quarter of 1900s century. The growth was accompanied by foreign investment and European immigration, the development of efficient railroad, network and the exploitation of country's natural resources. Annual economic growth averages 3.3% between 1878 and 1910.

(8) Political repression and fraud, as well as high income inequalitie sexacerbated by the land distribution system in which large lands were owned by a few but worked by millions of underpaid peasants living in precarious conditions, led to the Mexican Revolution in 1910-20. An arm conflict that drastically transformed 20th century under a premise of social democracy. The war itself left harsh toll on the economy and population which decreased over the 11year period between 1910 and 1921. Reconstruction of the country took in the following decade.

(9) The period of 1930-70 was dubbed by economic historians the Mexico Miracle, a period of economic growth that follows the end of the Mexico Revolution and the resumption of capital accumulation during the peace time.

(10) Import Substitution Industralisation (ISI) was adopted which protected and promoted the development of national industries. GDP increased sixth fold during 1940-70.

(11) President Joseph Lopez (1970-82) during whose administration economy soared with the discovery of oil and then crashed when the price of oil were dropped. Interest rates were negative so that Mexico took advantage, borrowed money from abroad and used them for extracting oil and made profit as that time the oil prices were rising resulting in high profits.

(12) Inflation was 139% in 1987 and Mexico made default in debt servicing resulting in bailout package given by the American President Clinton.

(13) Remittance from the abroad from their immigrated labour mostly in America are estimated $ 28.5 billion. Recently Mr. Trump of America has made Immigration laws very stringent under his "American First" Policy. He also is building a protective Wall on the Boarder of Mexico to prevent people entering from there from Mexico and Central American countries. This will result in loss of remittances of Mexico from their immigrated workers. Mexico has protested against this US policy.

(14) Poverty is very high in Mexico. About 42% of population is below poverty line which should be rectified to avoid revolt/ unrest of the Mexican people.

(15) Credit rating by Credit rating companies looks satisfactory and should be maintained all the time.

(16) Mexico has to take bailout package from America which should not be repeated and Debt servicing should be regularly complied with.

(17) Mexican Peso currency is fluctuating widely and is volatile. Depreciations are often of 15%-20%. There is a danger to increase inflation. More precaution should be exercised on this issue.

(18) Being the crude oil exporting country, its economic growth depends upon price fluctuation in crude oil. Country becomes prosperous if oil prices are high and visa a versa. Mexico economy should not be fully dependent on oilexport. This will make its growth stable.

(19) Mexico wall will be built up by USA to restrict the entry of Mexico citizens in USA at the original cost of USD 5.7 billion which now works out to us of 7.80 billion. President Trump wants elicit traffic from Mexico to USA and Mexico citizens entry for work in USA under "First USA" policy. In fact, Mexico citizens have already migrated to USA in large number which has resulted in reducing from employment of USA origin. Citizens prostitution and other elicit traffic the drugs are also to be prohibited. At present boarder military has been employed on Mexico's boarder line to prohibit migration of Mexican citizens.

Chapter - 26

Economy of Venezuela

Introduction of Venezuela Economy at present

Economy of Venezuela is largely dependent on petroleum sector and mining sector. Generally such economies are volatile in the sense that their growth depends upon fluctuation in the prices of petroleum. Venezuela is largely affected today by volatile oil prices and mismanagement of President Mathero in administering the country. Today, financial condition of Venezuela is so bad that people do not get food to eat even with heaps of currency bundle. There is no water and electric supply and people want to leave the country to take shelter in other countries like US. Majority countries have impose trade ban on Venezuela which results in hauling its economy. Still Nicolas Maduro is engaged in strengthing its army and allowing Russia, China and Iran to establish their military bases in Venezuela. Financial condition is so precarious that one usual ice Cream slide costs US$25. Russian and Iran economies are already in reds due to economic sanctions imposed by US and China's financial condition is also not strong due to trade war with US. These countries are not able and willing to help Venezuela in its critical position at present. Financial assistance given by US is not accepted by Maduro and now people and army are going against the President. There will be revolt in the country or war inside the country which will result in heavy caulties.In fact, Chavez who ruled the country from 1999 to 2013 was main cause of deteriorated situation of the country as he was supporter of Russia and always strongly opposed American policy including fixing of quota system agreed with OPEC.

General information of economy of Venezuela prior to the present position

Though the present situation of the country is very bad, the economy of Venezuela is largely based on the petroleum sectorand manufacturing. In 2014, total trade amounted to 48.1% of the country's GDP. Exports accounted for 16.7% of GDP and petroleum products accounted for about 95% of those exports. Venezuela is the sixth largest member of OPEC by oil production.

Since the 1920s, Venezuela has been a rentier state, offering oil as its main export. From the 1950s to the early 1980s, the Venezuelan economy experienced a steady growth that attracted many immigrants, with the nation enjoying the highest standard of living in Latin America. During the collapse of oil prices in the 1980s, the economy contracted the monetary sign, commenced a progressive devaluation and inflation skyrocketed to reach peaks of 84% in 1868 and 99% in 1996, three years prior to Hugo Chavez taking office. The nation, however, has experienced hyperinflation since 2015 far exceeding the oil price collapse of the 1990s.

Venezuela manufactures and exports heavy industry products such as steel, aluminum and cement. Production is concentrated around Ciudad Guayana, near the Guri DAm, one of the largest dams in the world and the provider of about three-quarters of Venezuela's electricity. Other notable manufacturing includes electronics and automobiles as well as beverages and foodstuffs. Agriculture in Venezuela accounts for approximately 4.4% of GDP, 7.3% of the labor force and at least one-fourth of Venezuela's land area. Venezuela exports rice, corn, fish, tropical fruit, coffee, pork and beef. The country is not self-sufficient in most areas of agriculture.

In spite of strained relations between the two countries, the Unites States has been Venezuela's most important trading partner. American exports to Venezuela have included machinery, agricultural products, medical instruments and cars. Venezuela is one of the top four suppliers of foreign oil to the United States. About 500 American companies are represented in Venezuela.According to Central Bank of Venezuela, between 1998 and 2008 the government received around 325 billion USD through oil production and exports in general. According to the International Agency (as of August 2015), the production of 2.4 million barrels per day supplied 500,000 barrels to the United States.

Since the Bolivarian Revolution half-dismantled its PDVSA oil giant corporation in 2002 by firing most of its 20,000-strong dissident professional human capital and imposed stringent currency controls in 2003 in an attempt to prevent capital flight, there has been a steady decline in oil production and exports and a series of stern currency devaluations, disrupting the economy. Further yet, price controls,expropriation of numerous farmlands and various industries, among other disputable government policies including a near-total freeze on any access to foreign currency at reasonable "official" exchange rates, have resulted in severe shortages in Venezuela and steep price rises of all common goods, including food, water, household products, spare parts, tools and medical supplies; forcing many manufacturers to either cut production or close down, with many ultimately abandoning the country as has been the case with several technological firms and most automobile makers. In 2015, Venezuela had over 100% inflation, the highest in the world and the highest in the country's history at that time. According to independent sources, the rate increased to 4,000% in 2017 with Venezuela spiraling into hyperinflation while the population poverty rate was between 76% and 87%. On 14 November 2017, credit rating agencies declared that Venezuela was in default with its debt payments, with Standards & Poor's categorizing Venezuela as being in "selective default". (S.D.)

History

1922–1959

After oil was discovered in Venezuela in 1922 during the Maracaibo strike, Venezuela's dictator Juan Vicente Gomez allowed American oil companies to write Venezuela's petroleum law. In 1943, Standard oil of New Jersey accepted a new agreement in Venezuela based on the 50–50 principle, described as "a landmark event". Even more favorable terms were negotiated in 1945, after a coup brought to power a left-leaning government that included Juan Pablo Perez Alfonso.

From the 1950s to the early 1980s, the Venezuelan economy, which was buoyed by high oil prices, was one of the strongest and most prosperous in South America. The continuous growth during that period attracted many immigrants.

In 1958, a new government, again including Pérez Alfonso, devised a plan for an international oil cartel that would become OPEC. In 1973, Venezuela voted to nationalize its oil industry outright, effective 1 January 1976, with Petroleos de Venezuela (PDVSA) presiding over a number of holding companies. In subsequent years, Venezuela built a vast refining and marketing system in the United States and Europe.

During Perez Jimenez' dictatorship from 1952 to 1958, Venezuela enjoyed remarkably high GDP growth, so that in the late 1950s Venezuela's real GDP per capita almost reached that of West Germany. In 1950, Venezuela was the world's 4th wealthiest nation per capita. However, Romuio Betancourt (President from 1959 to 1964) inherited from 1958–1959 onward an enormous internal and external debt caused by rampant public spending during the dictatorship. Nevertheless, he managed to balance Venezuela's public budget and initiate an unsuccessful.

1960s–1990s

Agrarian Reform

Buoyed by a strong oil sector in the 1960s and 1970s, Venezuela's governments were able to maintain social harmony by spending fairly large amounts on public programs including health care, education, transport, and food subsidies. Literacy and welfare programs benefited tremendously from these conditions. Because of the oil wealth, Venezuelan workers "enjoyed the highest wages in Latin America". This situation was reversed when oil prices collapsed during the 1980s.

When world oil prices collapsed in the 1980s, the economy contracted and inflation levels (consumer price inflation) rose, remaining between 6 and 12% from 1982 to 1986. The inflation rate peaked in 1989 at 84%, the year the capital city of Caracas suffered from rioting during the Caracazo following the cut of government spending and the opening of markets by President Carlos Andres Perez. After Pérez initiated such liberal economic policies and made Venezuelan markets more free, Venezuela's GDP went from a -8.3% decline in 1989 to growing 4.4% in 1990 and 9.2% in 1991, though wages remained low and unemployment was high among Venezuelans.

Some state that neoliberalism was the cause of Venezuelan economic difficulties, though over reliance on oil prices and a fractured political system without parties agreeing on policies caused many of the problems. By the mid-1990s, Venezuela under President Rafael Caldera saw annual inflation rates of 50–60% from 1993 to 1997 with an exceptional peak in 1996 at 100%. The number of people living in poverty rose from 36% in 1984 to 66% in 1995, with the country suffering a severe banking crisis (Venezyela banking crisis of 1994). In 1998, the economic crisis had grown even worse. Per capita GDP was at the same level as 1963 (after adjusting 1963 dollar to 1998 value), down a third from its 1978 peak; and the purchasing power of the average salary was a third of its 1978 level.

1999–2013

Economic policy of Hugo Chavez government

In 2016, Venezuela had the highest annual inflation in the world (Venezuela is the country colored pink in northern South America)

Hugo Chavez was elected President of Venezuela in December 2018 and took office in February 1999. In 2000, oil prices soared, offering Chávez funds not seen since Venezuela's economic collapse in the 1980s. Chávez then used economic policies that were more social demi social than those of his predecessors, using populist approaches with oil funds that made Venezuela's economy dependent on high oil prices. Chávez also played a leading role within OPEC to reinvigorate the organization and obtain members' adherence to lower quotas designed to drive up the oil price. Ali Rodriquez Araque, the Venezuelan oil minister, gave an announcement in 1999 that his country would respect OPEC production quotas, which marked "a historic turnaround from the nation's traditional pro-US oil policy".

In the first four years of the Chávez presidency, the economy grew at first (1999–2001), then contracted from 2001–2003 to GDP levels similar to 1997. At first, the economic decline was due to low oil prices, but it was fueled by the turmoil of the 2002 coup attempt and the 2002-2003 business strike. Other factors of the decline were an exodus of capital from the country and a reluctance of foreign investors. GDP was 50.0 trillion bolivars in 1998. At the bottom of the recession in 2003, it was 42.4 trillion bolivars (in constant 1998 bolivars).However, GDP rebounded 50.1 trillion bolivars with a calmer political situation in 2004 and rose to 66.1 trillion bolivars in 2007 (both in constant 1998 bolivars).

The government sought international assistance to finance reconstruction after massive flooding and landslides in December 1999 caused an estimated US$15 billion to $20 billion in damage.

The hardest hit sectors in the worst recession years (2002–2003) were construction ("55.9%), petroleum ("26.5%), commerce ("23.6%) and manufacturing ("22.5%). The drop in the petroleum sector was caused by adherence to the OPEC established in 2002 and the virtual cessation of exports during the PdVSAled general strike of 2002–2003. The non-petroleum sector of the economy contracted by 6.5% in 2002. The bolivar, which had been suffering from serious inflation and devaluation relative to international standards since the late 1980s, continued to weaken.

The inflation rate as measured by consumer price index was 35.8% in 1998, falling to a low of 12.5% in 2001 and rising to 31.1% in 2003. Historically, the highest yearly inflation was 100% in 1996. In an attempt to support the bolivar, bolster the government's declining level of international reserves and mitigate the adverse impact from the oil industry work stoppage on the financial system, the Ministry of Finance and the central bank suspended foreign exchange trading on 23 January 2003. On 6 February, the government created CADIVI, a currency control board charged with handling foreign exchange procedures. The board set the US$ exchange rate at 1,596 bolivars to the dollar for purchases and 1,600 to the dollar for sales.

The housing market in Venezuela shrunk significantly with developers avoiding Venezuela due to the massive number of companies who have had their property expropriated by the government. According to The Heritage Foundation and The Wall Street Journal, Venezuela had the weakest property rights in the world, scoring only 5.0 on a scale of 100, with expropriation without compensation being common. The shortage of housing is so significant that in 2007 a group of squatters occupied Centro Financiero Confinazas, a cancelled economic center that was supposed to symbolize Venezuela's growing economy.

The Venezuelan economy shrank 5.8% in the first three months of 2010 compared to the same period of 2009 and had the highest inflation rate in Latin America at 30.5%.President Chávez expressed optimism that Venezuela would emerge from recession despite the International Monetary Fund (IMF) forecasts showing that Venezuela would be the only country in the region to remain in recession that year. The IMF qualified the economic recovery of Venezuela as "delayed and weak" in comparison with other countries of the region. Following Chavez's death in early 2013, Venezuela's economy continued to fall into an even greater recession.

2013–present

Crisis in Venezuela and 2013-present economic crisis in Venezuela

According to the misery index in 2013, Venezuela ranked as the top spot globally with the highest misery index score. The International Finance Corporation ranked Venezuela one of the lowest countries for doing business with, ranking it 180 of 185 countries for its *Doing Business 2013* report with protecting investors and taxes being its worst rankings. In early 2013, the bolívar fuerte was devalued due to growing shortages in Venezuela. The shortages included necessities such as toilet paper, milk and flour Shortages also affected healthcare in Venezuela, with the University of Caracus Medical Hospital ceasing to perform surgeries due to the lack of supplies in 2014. The Bolivarian government's policies also made it difficult to import drugs and other medical supplies.Due to such complications, many Venezuelans died avoidable deaths with medical professionals having to use limited resources using methods that were replaced decades ago.

In 2014, Venezuela entered an economic recession having its GDP growth decline to -3.0%. Venezuela was placed at the top of the misery index for the second year in a row. The Economist said Venezuela was "probably the world's worst-managed economy". Citibank believed that "the economy has little prospect of improvement" and that the state of the Venezuelan economy was a "disaster". The Doing Business 2014 report by the International Finance Corporation and the World Bank ranked Venezuela one score lower than the previous year, then 181 out of 185. The Heritage Foundation ranked Venezuela 175th out of 178 countries in economic freedom for 2014, classifying it as a "repressed" economy according to the principles the foundation advocates. According to Foreign Policy, Venezuela was ranked last in the world on its Base Yield Index due to low returns that investors receive when investing in Venezuela. In a 2014 report titled Scaries Places on the Business Frontiers Zurich Financial Services and reported by Bioomberg, Venezuela was ranked as the risking emerging market in the world. Many companies such as Toyata, Ford Motor Co., General Motor CompanyAir Canada, and others slowed or stopped operation due to the lack of hard currency in the country, with Venezuela owing such foreign companies billions of dollars. Venezuela also dismantled CADIVI, a government body in charge of currency exchange. CADIVI was known for holding money from the private sector and was suspected to be corrupt.

Venezuela again topped the misery index according to the World Bank in 2015. The IMF predicted in October 2015 an inflation rate of 159% for the year 2015—the highest rate in Venezuelan history and the highest rate in the world—and that the economy would contract by 10%. According to leaked documents from the Central Bank of Venezuela, the country ended 2015 with an inflation rate of 270% and a shortage rate of goods over 70%.

Venezuelans eating from garbage in late 2015.

President Nicolas Maduro reorganized his economic cabinet in 2016 with the group mainly consisting of leftist Venezuelan academics. According to Bank of America's investment division Merrill Lynch, Maduro's new cabinet was expected to tighten currency and price controls in the country. Alejandro Werner, the head of IMF's Latin American Department, stated that 2015 figures released by the Central Bank of Venezuela were not accurate and that Venezuela's inflation for 2015 was 275%. Other forecast inflation figures by IMF and Bank of America were 720%and 1,000% in 2016, Analysts believed that the Venezuelan government has been manipulating economic statistics, especially since they did not report adequate data since late 2014. According to economist Steve Hanke, the Central Bank of Venezuela delayed the release of statistics and lied about figures much like the Soviet Union did, with Hanke saying that a lie coefficient had to be used to observe Venezuela's economic data.

By 2016, media outlets said that Venezuela was suffering an economic collapse with the IMF estimating a 500% inflation rate and 10% contraction in the GDP. In December 2016, monthly inflation exceeded 50 percent for the 30th consecutive day, meaning the Venezuelan economy was officially experiencing hyperinflation, making it the 57th country to be added to the Hanke-Krus World Hyperinflation Table.

On 25 August 2017, it was reported that new United States sanctions against Venezuela did not ban trading of the country's existing non-government bonds, with the sanctions instead including restrictions intended to block the government's ability to fund itself.

On 26 January 2018, the government ended the protected, subsidized fixed exchange rate mechanism that was highly overvalued as a result of rampant inflation. The National Assembly (led by the opposition) said inflation in 2017 was over 4,000%, a level other independent economists also agreed with. In February, the government launched an oil backed cryptocurrency called the petro.

Bloomberg Café Con Leche Index calculated the price increase for a cup of coffee to have increased by 718% in the 12 weeks before 18 January 2018, an annualized inflation rate of 448,000%. The finance commission of the National Assembly noted in July 2018 that prices were doubling every 28 days with an annualized inflation rate of 25,000%.

The country was heading for a selective default in 2017. In early 2018, the country was in default, meaning it could not pay its lenders.

August 24, 2017 President Trump imposed sanctions on the state debt of Venezuela which ban to make transactions with state debt of Venezuela including the participation in debt restructuring. November 13, 2017 the technical default period ended and Venezuela didn't pay coupons on its dollar

Eurobonds. This caused a cross default on other dollar bonds. November 30 ISDA committee consisting of 15 biggest banks admitted default on state debt obligations what in its turn entailed payments on CDS.

According to Cbonds, nowadays there are 20 international bonds of Venezuela which are recognized in default. The overall amount of defaulted obligations is equal to 36 billion dollars.

Under the tenures of Hugo Chávez and his successor Nicolas Maduro, many businesses abandoned Venezuela. In 1999, there were 13,000 companies in the country. By 2016, less than a third of companies remained in Venezuela, with only 4,000 companies operating in the nation.

Sectors

Petroleum and other resources

Energy policy of Venezuela

A map of world oil reserves according to OPEC, 2013. Venezuela has the world's largest oil reserves.

Venezuela is a major producer of petroleum products, which remain the keystone of the Venezuelan economy. The International Energy Agency shows how Venezuela's oil production has fallen in the last years, producing only 2,300,000 barrels (370,000 m) daily, down from 3.5 million in 1998. However, the oil incomes will double its value in local currency with the recent currency devaluation. Venezuela has large energy subsidies. In 2015, the cost of petrol was just US$0.06 per gallon, costing 23% of government revenues. In February 2016, the government finally decided to raise the price, but only to 6 bolivar (about 60¢ at the official rate of exchange) per litre for premium and just 1 bolivar (10¢) for lower-grade petrol.

A range of other natural resources, including iron ore, coal, baxxide, gold, nickel and diamonds, are in various stages of development and production. In April 2000, Venezuela's president decreed a new mining law and regulations were adopted to encourage greater private sector participation in mineral extraction. During Venezuela's economic crisis, the rate of gold excavated fell 64.1% between February 2013 and February 2014 and iron production dropped 49.8%.

Venezuela mostly utilizes hydropower resources to supply power to the nation's industries, accounting for 57% of total consumption at the end of 2016. However, persistent drought has severely reduced energy production from hydropower resources. The national electricity law is designed to provide a legal framework and to encourage competition and new investment in the sector. After a two-year delay, the government is proceeding with plans to privatize the various state-owned electricity systems under a different scheme than previously envisioned.

Manufacturing

Manufacturing contributed 15% of GDP in 2009. The manufacturing sector is experiencing severe difficulties, amidst lack of investment and accusations of mismanagement. Venezuela manufactures and exports steel, textiles, aluminum transport equipment, apparel, beverages and foodstuff. It produces cement, tires, paper, fertilizer and assembles cars both for domestic and export markets.

In 2014, General Motors Venezolana stopped automotive production after 65 years of service due to a lack of supplies, while the Central Bank of Venezuela announced that the shortage rate of new automobiles was at 100%. By the first half of 2016, only 10 vehicles were manufactured per day in Venezuela with production dropping 86%.

In 2015, estimates showed that Venezuela's industrial production fell about 8% that year alone.

Agriculture

Agriculture in Venezuela

Agriculture in Venezuela accounts for approximately 3% of GDP, 10% of the labor force, and at least a quarter of Venezuela's land area. Venezuela exports rice, corn, fish, tropical fruit, coffee, beef and pork. The country is not self-sufficient in most areas of agriculture. Venezuela imports about two-thirds of its food needs. In 2002, American firms exported $347 million worth of agricultural products, including wheat, corn, soyabean meal, cotton, animal fats, vegetable oil and other items to make Venezuela one of the top two American markets in South America. The United States supplies more than one-third of Venezuela's food imports. Recent government policies have led to problems with food shortages.

Trade

Venezuela is a founding member of the Organization of the Petroleum Exporting Countries (OPEC), the Organization of Gas Exporting Countries (GECF), the Bolivarian Alliance for the Peoples of Our America (ALBA) and the Community of Latin American and Caribbean States (CELAC). Petroleum constitutes 98% of Venezuela's exports with a value of $31.4 billion in 2017. Thanks to petroleum exports, Venezuela usually posts a trade surplus. From 2005, nontraditional (i.e. nonpetroleum) private sector exports have been declining rapidly. By 2015,they constitute 8% of total exports.The United States is Venezuela's leading trade partner. During 2002, the United States exported $4.4 billion in goods to Venezuela, making it the 25th-largest market for the United States Including petroleum products, Venezuela exported $15.1 billion in goods to the United States, making it its 14th-largest source of goods. Venezuela opposes the proposed Free Trade Area of the Americas.

Since 1998, China-Venezuela relations have seen an increasing partnership between the government of the Venezuelan President Hugo Chávez and the People's Republic of China. Sino-Venezuelan trade was less than $500m per year before 1999 and reached $7.5bn in 2009, making China Venezuela's second-largest trade partner and Venezuela China's biggest investment destination in Latin America. Various bilateral deals have seen China invest billions in Venezuela and Venezuela increase exports of oil and other resources to China. China has demanded payment in oil for its exports to Venezuela because of its unwillingness to accept Venezuelan currency and the inability of Venezuela to pay in dollars or gold.

Labor

Under Chávez, Venezuela has also instituted worker-run "co-management" initiatives in which workers' councils play a key role in the management of a plant or factory. In experimental co-managed enterprises, such as the state-owned Alcasa factory, workers develop budgets and elect both managers and departmental delegates who work together with company executives on technical issues related to production.

In November 2010, workers spent a week protesting outside factories in Valera and Valencia following the expropriation of the American bottle-maker Owens-Illinois.

Labor disputes have continued to increase since the financial crisis in 2008. According to the World Economic Forum, Venezuela is ranked as 134th of the 148 countries for economic competitiveness. Many in the private sector attribute these findings to the inflexible labor market.

In recent years, a barrage of pro-worker decrees have been passed. The most significant could be the 2012 labor laws known as the LOTTT. These laws included the virtual ban on dismissal, shorter work week, improved holidays and enhanced maternity benefits. The LOTTT offers job security to most workers after the first month. Employers have reported an absenteeism rate of up to 40% which they blame on the leniency of these labor laws. As expected, employers have been less willing to recruit.

On 17 November 2014, President Maduro issued a decree to increase the minimum salary for all workers by 15%. The decree became effective on 1 December 2014. As part of the May Day celebrations in honor of workers' day, President Maduro announced on 28 April 2015 that the minimum wage would increase 30%; 20% in May and 10% in July, with the newly announced minimum wage for Venezuelans being only about $30 per month at the widely used black market rate.

In September 2017, the National Union of Workers (UNETE) announced that Venezuela had lost 3,345,000 jobs since the election of President Maduro. By December 2017, the number of lost jobs increased by 400,000 to over 3,850,000 lost jobs since the start of Maduro's tenure.

Infrastructure

In the 20th century when Venezuela benefitted from oil sales, infrastructure flourished in Venezuela. However, in recent years Venezuela's public services and infrastructure has suffered, especially utilities such as electricity and water.

Transportation

Venezuela has an extensive road system that was initially created in the 1960s helped aid the oil and aluminum industries. The capital Caracas had a modern subway system designed by the French that was finished in 1995, with the subway tunneling more than 31.6 mi (51 km).

In 1870, Antonio Guzman Blanco helped create Venezuela's railway system.

The Chavez government launched a National Railway Development Plan designed to create 15 railway lines across the country, with 8,500 miles (13,700 km) of track by 2030. The network is being built in cooperation with China Railways, which is also cooperating with Venezuela to create factories for tracks, railway cars and eventually locomotives. However, Venezuela's rail project is being put on hold due to Venezuela not being able to pay the $7.5 billion and owing China Railway nearly $500 million.

Lufthansa said it would stop all flights to Venezuela on 18 June 2016, citing difficulties with currency controls. Other airlines also cut back on flights and required that passengers pay fares in US$.

Energy in Venezuela

The Venezuelan electrical grid is plagued with occasional blackouts in various districts of the country. In 2011, it had so many problems that rations of electricity were put in place to help ease blackouts. On 3 September 2013, 70% of the country plunged into darkness with 14 of 23 states of Venezuela stating they did not have electricity for most of the day.Another power outage on 2 December 2013 left most of Venezuela in the dark again and happened just days before elections.

Energy statistics

  - Electricity – production by source:
  - Fossil fuel: 35.7% (2012 estimates)
  - Hydroelectric 64.3 (2012 estimates.)
  - Nuclear: 0% (2012 estimates.)
  - Other: 0% (2012 estimates.)
- Electricity production: 127.6 billion kWh (2012 estimates.)
- Electricity – consumption: 85.05 billion kWh (2011 estimates.)
- Electricity – exports: 633 million kWh (2009 estimates.)

- Electricity – imports: 260 million kWh (2009 est.)
- Electricity – installed generating capacity: 27.5 million kW (2012 est.)

Statistics

Economy data

The Macroeconomic Stabilization Fund (FIEM) decreased from US$2.59 billion in January 2003 to US$700 million in October, but central bank-held international reserves actually increased from US$11.31 billion in January to US$19.67 billion in October 2003. On the black market, the bolívar fell 28% in 2007 to Bs. 4,750 per US$ and declined to around VEF 5.5 (Bs 5500) per US$ in early 2009.

The economy recovered and grew by 16.8% in 2004. This growth occurred across a wide range of sectors—the oil industry directly provides only a small percentage of employment in the country. International reserves grew to US$27 billion. Polling firm Datanalysis noted that real income in the poorest sectors of society grew by 33% in 2004.

On 7 March 2007, the government announced that the Venezuelan bolívar would be redenominated at a ratio of 1 to 1,000 at the beginning of 2008 and renamed the *bolívar fuerte* ("strong bolivar") to ease accounting and transactions. This was carried out on 1 January 2008, at which time the exchange rate was 2.15 *bolívar fuerte* per US$. The ISO 4217 code for the *bolívar fuerte* is VEF.

Government spending as a percentage of GDP in Venezuela in 2007 was 30%, smaller than other mixed economies such as France (49%) and Sweden (52%). According to official sources from the United Nations, the percentage of people below the national poverty line has decreased during the presidency of Hugo Chavez, from 48.1% in 2002 to 28% in 2008.

With the 2007 rise in oil prices and rising government expenditures, Venezuela's economy grew by 9% in 2007. Oil prices fell starting in July 2008, resulting in a major loss of income. Hit by a global recession, the economy contracted by 2% in the second quarter of 2009, contracting a further 4.5% in the third quarter of 2009. Chavez's response has been that these standards misstate economic fact and that the economy should be measured by socialistic standards. On 17 November, the Central Bank reported that private sector activity declined by 4.5% and that inflation was averaging 26.7%. Compounding such problems is a drought which the government says was caused by EI Nino, resulting in rationing of water and electricity and a short supply of food.

The year 2010 saw Venezuela still in recession as GDP has fallen by 5.8% in the first quarter of 2010. The Central Bank of Venezuela has stated that the recession is due largely "to restricted access to foreign currency for imports, lower internal demand and electricity rationing". The oil sector's performance was also particularly troubling, with oil GDP shrinking by 5%. More importantly, the Central Bank hints at the root cause of the oil contraction, saying that "the bank said it was due to falls in production, "operative problems", maintenance stoppages and the channeling of diesel to run thermal generators during a power crisis". While the public sector of the economy has fallen 2.8%, the private sector has dropped off 6%.

The year 2013 proved to be difficult for Venezuela as shortages of necessities and extreme inflation attacked the nation's economy. Items became so scarce that nearly one quarter of items were not in stock. The bolívar was devalued to 6.3 per US$ in early 2013 taking one third of its value away. However, inflation still continued to rise drastically in the country to the point President Maduro forced stores to sell their items just days before elections. Maduro said that the stores were charging unreasonable prices even though the owners were only charging so much due to the actual devaluation of the bolivar.

In 2014 The Central Bank of Venezuela stopped releasing statistics for the first time in its history as a way to possibly manipulate the image of the economy. Venezuela has also dismantled CADIVI, a government body in charge of currency exchange.

The following table shows the main economic indicators in 1980–2017. Inflation under 5% is in green.[150]

Year	*GDP (in Bil. US$ PPP)*	*GDP per capita (in US$ PPP)*	*GDP growth (real)*	*Inflation rate (in Percent)*	*Unemployment (in Percent)*	*Government debt (in % of GDP))*
1980	117.2	7,838	▼−4.9 %	▲21.4 %	n/a	n/a
1985	▲146.5	▲8,499	▲0.9 %	▲11.4 %	n/a	n/a
1988	▲187.9	▲10,247	▲6.5 %	▲29.5 %	n/a	n/a
1998	▲276.3	▼11,946	▲0.3 %	▲35.8 %	n/a	31.4 %
2006	▲403.7	▲15,031	▲9.9 %	▲13.7 %	▼10.0 %	▼25.7 %
2017	▼380.7	▼12,113	▼−14.0 %	▲1,087.5 %	▲27.1 %	▲34.9 %
2018 (est.)	▼331.0	▼10,399	▼−15.0 %	▲ 13,864.6 %	▲33.4 %	▲162.0 %

Currency black market

According to Dollar Today com, the value of one US dollar in Venezuelan Bolivares fuertes on the black market through time: The currency has lost 90% of its value which happened seven times since 2012, meaning that the currency is worth (as of mid-February 2019) 30,000,000 times less than in August 2012, since it has lost more than 99.99999% of its value Inflation represented by the time it would take for money to lose 90% of its value (301-day rolling average, inverted logarithmic scale).

The parallel exchange rate is what Venezuelans believe the Venezuelan currency is worth compared to the US$. In the first few years of Chávez's office, his newly created social programs required large payments in order to make the desired changes. On 5 February 2003, the government created CADIVI, a currency control board charged with handling foreign exchange procedures. Its creation was to control capital flight by placing limits on individuals and only offering them so much of a foreign currency.This limit to foreign currency led to a creation of a currency black market economy since Venezuelan merchants rely on foreign goods that require payments with reliable foreign currencies. As Venezuela printed more money for their social programs, the bolívar continued to devalue for Venezuelan citizens and merchants since the government held the majority of the more reliable currencies.

As of January 2018, the strongest official exchange rate was 1 US$ to 10 VFF while the free market exchange rate was over 200,000 VEF to 1 US$. Since merchants can only receive so much necessary foreign currency from the government, they must resort to the black market which in turn raises the merchant's prices on.The high rates in the black market make it difficult for businesses to purchase necessary goods since the government often forces these businesses to make price cuts. This leads to businesses selling their goods and making a low profit, such as Venezuelan McDonald's franchises offering a Big Mac meal for only $1.Since businesses make low profits, this leads to shortages since they are unable to import the goods that Venezuela is reliant on. Venezuela's largest food producing company, Empresas, has stated that they may need to suspend some production for nearly the entire year of 2014 since they owe foreign suppliers $463 million. The last report of shortages in Venezuela showed that 22.4% of necessary goods are not in stock. This was the last report by the government since the central bank no longer posts the scarcity index. This has led to speculation that the government is hiding its inability to control the economy which may create doubt about future economic data released.

Socioeconomic indicators

Like most Latin American countries, Venezuela has an unequal distribution of wealth. Although distribution improved when the surplus of rural labor started to diminish and the educational system improved in the middle of the 20th century, equality is far from coinciding with western standards. The rich tend to be very rich and the poor very poor. In 1970, the poorest fifth of the population had 3% of national income while the wealthiest fifth had 54%. For comparison, the United Kingdom 1973 figures were 6.3% and 38.8% and the United States in 1972, 4.5% and 42.8%.

The more recent income distribution data available is for distribution per capita, not per household. The two are not strictly comparable because poor households tend to have more members than rich households, thus per household data tends to show less inequality than the per capita data. The table below shows the available per capita data for recent years from the World Bank.

Poverty in Venezuela increased during the 1980s and early 1990s, but it decreased greatly in the mid to late 1990s. The decreasing trend continued through the Chávez presidency, with the exception of the troubled years 2002 and 2003. Under the Bolivarian government, poverty decreased initially when Venezuela acquired oil funds, though poverty began to increase to its highest level in decades in the 2010s.

Venezuela's extreme poverty rate from 1990 to 2013 Source: INENote: interim presidents excluded and one year delay of data transferred during presidential term changes due to new policies, inaugurations and so on.

Venezuela economic indicators (2017)	
Indicator	%
Real GDP growth	-14.0%
Inflation	1.087.5%
Gross national saving (% of GDP)	12.1%

Foreign trade			
Leading markets 2013	% of total	Leading suppliers	% of total
United States	39.1	United States	31.7
China	14.3	China	16.8
India	12.0	Brazil	9.1
Netherlands Antilles	7.8	Colombia	4.8

Foreign trade			
Major exports	% of total	Major imports	% of total
Oil and gas	90.4	Raw materials and intermediate goods	44.5
Other	9.6	Consumer goods	24.5
		Capital goods	31.0

Social development

In the early 2000s when oil prices soared and offered Chávez funds not seen since the beginning of Venezuela's economic collapse in the 1980s, Chávez's government became "semi-authoritarian and hyper-populist" and consolidated its power over the economy in order to gain control of large amounts of resources. Domestically, Chávez used such oil funds for populist policies, creating the Bolivarian missions, aimed at providing public services to improve economic, cultural and social conditions. From 1999–2009, 60% of government revenues focused on social programs while social investment went from 8.4% of GDP in 1988 to 18.8% in 2008. Despite warnings near the beginning of Chávez's tenure in the early 2000s, Chávez's government continuously overspent in social spending and did not save enough money for any future economic turmoil, which Venezuela faced shortly before and after his death. On the year of Chávez's death, Venezuela was still categorized as having high human development on its Human Development Index in 2013 according to the United Nations Development Programme, although human development began to decline in Venezuela within a year, with the country dropping 10 ranks by 2014.

Poverty and hunger

Although poverty initially declined under Chávez, Venezuela's poverty rate increased to 28% by 2013, with extreme poverty rates increasing 4.4% to 10% according to the Venezuelan government's INE. Estimates of poverty by the United Nations Economic Commission for Latin America and Caribbean (ECLAC) and Luis Pedro Espafia, a sociologist at the Universidad Catolica Andres Bello, showed an increase of poverty in Venezuela. ECLAC showed a 2013 poverty rate of 32% while Pedro España calculated a 2015 rate of 48%. The Venezuelan government estimated that 33% were in poverty in the first half of 2015 and then stopped producing statistics. According to Venezuelan NGO PROVEA, by the end of 2015 there would be the same number of Venezuelans living in poverty as there was in 2000, reversing the advancements against poverty by Chávez. The ENCOVI annual survey by three universities estimated poverty at 48% in 2014, 82% in 2016 and 87% in 2017.

In relation to hunger, under-nutrition, undernourishment and the percentage of children under the age of five who are moderately or severely underweight decreased earlier in Chávez's tenure. However, shortage in Venezuela as a result of price control policies left the majority of Venezuelans without adequate products after his death.

Since the country's economy collapsed in 2014, hunger and malnutrition have become a severe problem.In 2015, close to 45% of Venezuelans said they were unable to afford food at times. In 2018, this figure rose to 79%, one of the highest rates in the world.

According to government figures released in April 2017, 1,446 children under the age of 1 had died in 2016, representing a 30 percent increase in one year. As of August 2017, 31 million people suffered from severe food shortages. The ENCOVI universities survey found that 73% of Venezuelans said they had lost 9 kg (19 lbs) of body weight in 2016 and 64% had lost 11 kg (25 lbs) in 2017.

Extreme poverty and lack of food and medicines has pushed more than three million Venezuelans to leave the country in the recent years.

Education in Venezuela

The total net enrollment ratio in primary education for both sexes increased from 87% in 1999 to 93.9% in 2009.The primary completion rate for both sexes reached 95.1% in 2009 as compared to 80.8% in 1991.The literacy rates of 15- to 24-year-olds in 2007, for men and women, were 98% and 98.8%, respectively. During the Bolivarian, a large percentage of the millions of Venezuelans who left the country were highly educated, resulting in a brain drain in the country.

Since starting in 2003, the free government program Mission Robinson had taught more than 2.3 million people to read and write as of 2012. The program also focused much of its attention on reaching out to geographically isolated and historically excluded members of the population, including indigenous groups and Afro-descendants. In 2008, Francisco Rodríguez of Wesleyan University in Connecticut and Daniel Ortega of IESA stated that there was "little evidence" of "statistically distinguishable effect on Venezuelan illiteracy" during the Chávez administration. The Venezuelan government claimed that it had taught 1.5 million Venezuelans to read, but the study found that "only 1.1m were illiterate to begin with" and that the illiteracy reduction of less than 100,000 can be attributed to adults that were elderly and died.

Health care in Venezuela

Following the Bolivarian Revolution and the establishment of the Bolivarian government, initial healthcare practices were promising with the installation of free healthcare and the assistance received from Cuban medical professionals providing aid. The Bolivarian government's failure to concentrate on healthcare for Venezuelans, the reduction of healthcare spending and government corruption eventually affected medical practices in Venezuela, causing avoidable deaths along with an emigration of medical professionals to other countries.

Venezuela's reliance on imported goods and its complicated exchange rates initiated under Chávez led to increasing shortages during the late-2000s and into the 2010s that affected the availability of medicines and medical equipment in the country. The United Nations reported an increase in the maternal mortality ratio, which increased from 93 per 100,000 in 1990 to 110 per 100,000 in 2013. Following shortages of many medical and common goods in 2014, Venezuelan women have had difficulties accessing contraceptives and were forced to change prescriptions or search several stores and the Internet for their medications. Shortage of antiretroviral medicines to treat HIV/AIDS affected about 50,000 Venezuelans in 2014 as well, potentially causing thousands of Venezuelans with HIV to develop AIDS.

Venezuela is also the only country in Latin America where the incidence of malaria is increasing, allegedly due to illegal mining. In 2013, Venezuela registered the highest number of cases of malaria in the past 50 years, with 300 of 100,000 Venezuelans being infected with the disease.

Technology

In 1990, the number of Internet users was minimal, but 35.63% of Venezuelans were Internet users by 2010. In fact, the number of Internet subscribers has increased six fold.Programs such as the National Technological Literacy Plan, which provides free software and computers to schools, have assisted Venezuela in meeting this goal. However, several experts state that the poor infrastructure in Venezuela had created a poor quality of Internet in Venezuela, which has one of the slowest Internet speeds in the world. The lack of US$ due to the Venezuelan governments currency controls has also damaged Internet services because technological equipment must be imported into Venezuela.

The number of fixed telephone lines per 100 inhabitants was 7.56 in 1990. The number increased to 24.44 in 2010.In 2000, 2,535,966 Venezuelans had landline telephones. By 2009, this had increased to 6,866,626.

The Bolivarian government has also launched an aerospace program in cooperation with the People's Republic of China who built and launched two satellites that are currently in orbit—a communications satellite called Simon Bolivar and a remote sensing satellite called Miranda. In July 2014, President Maduro announced that a third satellite would be built by Chinese–Venezuelan bilateral cooperation.

Present Status of Economy of Venezuela At A Glance

(1) Capital: Caracas

(2) Currency: Boliver Soberano (VES)

(3) Fixed Exchange rate: Bs 66937.50 =US$1

(4) Fiscal year: Calendar Year

(5) Trade Organisations: WTO, OPEC, Unasur, MERCOSUR, ALBA

(6) GDP: GDP (Nominal) $96.3 billion (47th rank -2018),

(7) GDP (PPP) $320.1 billion (47th rank - 2018)

(8) GDP Growth: -6% (2015), -16.5% (2016), -14.5% (2017) and -14.3% (2018) Economy in crisis

(9) GDP per Capita : $3300 (Nominal), $10968 (PPP) - 2017

(10) GDP by Sectors: Agriculture 4.4%, Industries 38.2%, Services 57.4% - 2017

(11) Population: 29.18 million

(12) Population below poverty line 19.7% (2015), 87% (2017)

(13) Labour Force: 14.21 million 48.69% of Population

(14) Labour Force by Occupation: Commercial, Social& personal 31.4%, Commercial, restaurants and hotel 23.4%, Manufacturing industry 1.6%, Construction 9%, Transport, storage and communication 8.7%, Agriculture 6.5%, Finance, Insurance,real estate 6.1% - 2015

(15) Inflation: 65320%- (Hankeassessment, August 2018. 2295981% (An Estimates, February 2019) Country is economically and financially completely ruined.

(16) Unemployment: 34.3% (2015) Govt. has not managed the country efficiently.

(17) Main Industries: Construction Materials, food processing, iron ore mining, steel, aluminum, motor vechicles assembly, real estate, tourism and ecotourism

(18) Ease of doing Business: 188TH (2019)

(19) Foreign Trade

Exports: $32.08 billion (2017), Imports: $ 9.1 billion (2017), Trade Surplus: $22.98 billion

(20) Export Goods: Petroleum, chemicals, agriculture products, and basic manufacturer

(21) Main Export Partners: Us 42%, China 21%, India 19%, Singapore 4.5%, and Spain 1.4%

(22) Import Goods: Food, Clothing, car, technological items, raw materials, machinery equipment, construction material

(23) Main Import Partners: US 38%, China 18%, Mexico 12%, Brazil 5.2% and Colombia 3.5% (2017)

(24) Gross External debt: $100.3 billion (2017) 104.15% of GDP Nominal

(25) Fiscal

(26) Revenues: $ 92.8 billion, Expenses $ 189.7 billion (2017) Deficit $96.90 billion 100.63% of GDP Nominal & 30.27% GDP PPP

(27) Public debt: 38.9% of GDP i.e. $37.69 billion

(28) Foreign Reserves: $ 8.5 billion (June 2018), $ 9.661 billion (2017)

(29) Credit Rating: S & P – SD (Domestic and Foreign) Outlook: Negative. MOODY's– C,Outlook: Stable, FITCH - CC (Domestic), RD (Foreign) Outlook: Negative. Selective Default is a very poor rating given by the Credit Rating agencies rarely to any country. This shows the poor status of the country financially.

Critical Observations on Eonomy of Venezuela

(1) The economy of Venezuela is largely based on the petroleum sector and manufacturing mining.

(2) In 2014, total trade accounted to 48.1% of the country's GDP. Exports accounted for about 16.7% & of GDP and petroleum products accounted for 95% of those products.

(3) It is the sixth largest OPEC by oil production.

(4) In 1950s, Venezuela economy experienced a steady growth that attracted many immigrants with the nations enjoying the highest standard of living in the Latin America.

(5) During the collapse of oil prices in 1980s, economy contracted the monetary sign, commenced a progressive devaluation and inflation skyrocked to reach peak of 84% in 1989 and 99% in 1996 three years prior to Hugo Chavez taking office.

(6) The nation, though was prosperous during Hugo Chavez's time for some period, has experienced hyperinflation since 2015 far exceed the oil price collapse of 1990s. Chavez withdrew gold deposited in Bank of England. But in the present economic crisis, Mathuro was not able to bring gold from Bank of England as he is not recognised President of the country and not supported except China, Russia, Iran and Cuba. As per the agreement of BOE 10 percent of the reserves of exports of oil are kept in the BOE.

(7) In spite of strained relations between the two countries, US has been country's most trading partner with 48% of total exports of Venezuela.

(8) Since the Bolivarian Revolution, the country experienced tremendous firing of labour in 2002.

(9) There was a reduction in oil production and exports and a series of strain currency devaluation disrupting the economy. Price controls, expropriation of numerous farmlands and various industries under the disputable government policies were introduced.

(10) Under the tenure of Hugo Chavez and his successor Nicolas Maduro many businesses abandoned Venezuela. In 1999, out of 13000 companies in Venezuela only 4000 remained.Many foreign companies abandoned the country or slowered their production, labour force was reduced by 25%. There was acute shortage of foodgrains and Venezuelans were eating cabbages in late 2015. One cup of Ice cream has been costing USD 25 in Venezuela.

(11) There was recession only in Venezuela in 2009 and IMF declared that country is not worth doing lowest business.

(12) The government sought international assistance to finance reconstruction after massive flooding and landslides in December

1999 caused an estimated USD 15 billion to USD20 billion in damage.

(13) Present Ruler is NicolasMaduro but during his rule, the country is completely ruined but instead of taking steps to improve the country's conditions, he is engaged with China on research in sky and establishing military base in the Country. No Electricity in the country has stalled production and Venezuela currency has no value at all. Hyperinflation has reached 400% in 2017 and population under poverty rate is 87%. Country has worse condition as it was of Germany after end of World War II. There is no food, water and electricity. People are trying to migrate in nebouring countries but other countries have shut doors for those immigrants.

(14) China trade with the country has risen from USD 500 million to USD 7.5 billion but Venezuela is unable to repay the trade deficit in FCy and Venezuela's currency is not acceptable to China. Almost all countries have stopped to enter into trade with Venezuela.

(15) Almost all Latin American Countries do not recognise Mathoro as the ruler of Venezuela. They recognised Jaun Gaido as the official leader of the country. But Russia, China, Turkey and Cuba are recognising Mathoro as the official leader of Venezuela. Financial and assistance like food, water provided by US are banned by Mathoro who treats US as his main enemy. There is political struggle betweemn Gaido and Mathoro as who should rule the country. In order to set the conditions in order, US may take military action against Venezuela but Russia and China have sent their military troops in Venenzuela in order to fight against US military attack on Venezuela.

(16) It appears that no country is interested in improving the crisis conditions in Venezuela but want to establish supremacy of power on the country. This will led in wosening the situation in Venezuela where urgent solution is required to stop further deterioration of the country.

(17) Latin America has many countries. Most of them have democratic arrangements. Few countries, however, have Communism and dictatorship and they are under the control of Russia and China. Argentina, Mexico, Colmbia, Brazil are democratic countries and are financially srong. In case of any financial difficulties, US assist them to get external debt from IMF/ World Bank. Recently, Argentina was assisted financially by granting loan of USD 57 billion from IMF. But Argentina appears to be attracted to China and wants to install China's military Base in the country which is opposedby US. Argentina has therefore postponed their plan of China's military Base.

(18) Unlike America, Russia and China are not financially strong as they will give financial aid to the country like Venezuela. They can give military support to these countries but not financial support. Financial growth in these countries have been suffering from Sanctions and Trade War imposed by US on these countries. Of course, Cuba has highest sugar production and largest sugar exporter in the world.

Corrective Action to Be Initiated By Venezuela to improve their Present Position

i. Venezuela's two Presidents Chavez and Maduro are in strong opposition with US. Country has military base of Iran, Russia and China. Instead of looking at the country's interest, they are interested in developing strategic military partnership with the Communist countries. Though inflation has reached 4000% and population under poverty has reached 87%, they do not concentrate on improving the country's financial conditions. If the leaders are interested only in their own political ideology, they should be ousted by the country's military and Guido should be made the President of Venezuela.

ii. New President should develop the co-operation with Latin America Countries and US.

iii. He should start international trading with these countries and create Autmosphere and confidence in other countries that Venezuela is a stable country with to do international trading.

iv. Military Bases in Venezuela of Iran, China and Russia should be withdrawn and the relationship with these countries should be kept at minimum level.

v. Efforts should be made for improving credit rating of the country.

vi. Inflation rate and population below poverty rate should be kept lowest. Foodgrains should be imported, financial aid on humanization ground should be accepted and encouraged.

vii. Undue importance to research in sending satellite should be avoided and can be initiated when the country makes good progress.

viii. When there is an economic boom an account of rising petroleum products the country should keep with finds resulted from boom in reserve Emergency fund to be utilised when oil price are dropping in exports.

Part - III
External Debt and Public Sector Loan in Localcurrency of the Different Countries

Debt of any country is divided between (1) External debt in FCY and (2) Public Sector Loan in LCY.

Introduction

When India got independece from the British Raj on midnight 15 August 1947, it was observed that the country was completely ruined by the British Rulers economically and financially and it is required to be erected on all fronts. Agriculture production was lowest, no improvement in land cultivation and agriculture mechanization. There were famines in British raj which killed lacs of people. Millions of people were abruptly killed in epidemics. Raw material was used to manufacture textiles which were sold largely in Indian Market. Thus Indian trade was completely smashed by the Britishers at the cost of the Indians. Britishers gave the worst treatment to India and after the independence, numerous financial and economic issues need to be resolved urgently. Then Prime Minister Mr. Jawarlal Nehru, Home Minister Vallabhbhai Patel and Finance Minister Mr. C. D. Deshmukh were impressed by the five year plan system of Soviet Russian Union that time. Mr. Nehru gave priority to the industrial development to improve financial condition of India. First Five year Plan commenced from 1951 which specified targets to be achieved clearly.

In order to achieve economic growth of the country, large capital and investments were required from the government. It requires foreign investments to be attracted from foreign citizens, Banks and foreign governments. Being closed and foreign exchange control control economy, foreign countries including foreign banks and foreign citizens were not interested in investing their Fcy funds in India, But India is a member of IMF and World Bank and have the Special Drawing rights to its credit. The Government therefore took FCy loans from IMF at low interest rates.

While implementing five year plans, country required to build up infrastructural facilities such as roads, railways, airlines etc. For industrial policy achievement target, the country requires to purchase heavy machinery, erect big factories, give work to the labourers on division of labour principle, purchasing of aeroplanes, defence weapons, advance defence equipments, research in agricultural institutions for improved fertilizers, water supply to the agricultural lands regularly, construction of dams for creation of electricity and establish machinery for generating energy through coal, electricity etc.

Some of the materials is easily available in the local market and can be purchased through LCy payment. Large Lcy funds are required for these purposes. These funds are raised through the Local Market by offering high interest rates to the local institutions/individuals to attract these funds. These funds are taken on short term period (one year or below), medium term period (2 to 5 years period) or long term period (exceeding 5 years period). If the target for short term, medium term and long term periods loans are achieved on time, the debt servicing (repayment of Principal amount of loan and interest thereon) will be done on time and there will be no financially difficulties. However, some projects take longer time than expected because of legal matter or other practical difficulties. In such case, there will be no earnings from such project and funds raised for such project cannot be repaid with interest on time. To repay loan and interest of the previous loan, fresh loan needs to be raised again which result in piling of loan amount. Deficit financing is another method for repayment but that crates inflation and there is a trap that country may face hyperinflation in near future.

In most cases, materials required for implementation of project are to be purchased from abroad with FCy payment. Therefore large capital in form of loans are required to be raised in FCy from foreign institutions, foreign banks or IMF/World Bank. Generally such loans in fcy are granted on short term period. If project cannot be accomplished within that time, there are no earnings to repay the loan and interest. Fresh loan is taken to repay the old loans which piles the loan amount. In case of default of debt servicing after some years, restructuring will be required which is done on very stringent conditions like opening of the countries market to the foreign investors, tightening of the fiscal conditions and restrictions on expending on social welfare facilities. India had to face these difficulties during the initial stages of the economic growth and many times fresh loan was raised for previous outstanding loan servicing. In 1991, a bailout package $1.8 billion was given to India on the condition that Indian market will be opened for foreign institutions and foreign countries. India opened its market accordingly by scrapping licence raj and achieved tremendous economic growth in many fields. India's debt servicing rate came down from 30% in 1991 to 4% recently which is well manageable.

Some countries use the loan granted to any debtor country to dominate the sovereign status of that country. For example, if loan is taken from China at higher interest rate and not repaid, China ruthlessly captures any earning port of that defaulting country as it has done in case of Ceylon to recover its loan servicing. All countries are therefore afraid of China and do not want to involve in the debt trap with China.

International Comparison of Top Developing Debtor Countris - 2015

This shows as that China has external debt $1. 418 trillion which is 13.1% of item GDP, Debt service ratio is 4.7% and short term loans are 64%

In case of Brazil, total external debt is $543 billion which is 31.3% of GDP, Debt servicing ration is 38.1% and short term loan is 9.6%

This shows that Brazil has high debt ratio to GDP and high debt servicing ratio and the country may lead to debt servicing trap.

Turkey, Malaysia, Kazakhstan, Ukraine Romania and Bulgaria have very high GDP ratio to their external debt ranging from 137.4% to 45.2%

Compared with India, India has $ 529 billion external debt. India's debt servicing was 35% in 1991. But after liberalization of Indian economy, it has come down drastically to 4%. Now it is @6% - 8%. GDP ratiois between 17% - 23.4% short term loan. India's key debt indicators, especially external debt to GNI, debt servicing ratio and short term debt to total external debt continue to be comfortable indicating that our external debt is within manageable limits.

Critical Observations of External Debt and Other Indicators of Some Countries

United States: US has external debt $22.284 trillion which is 94% of its GDP $23.40 trillion. It has population of 34 crores. It has 30% of the world's national resources $46 trillion and therefore high external debt to GDP is manageable though it has crossed the limit for external debt by the US law which has resulted in "shut down" several times. Foreign exchange reserves are $121.587 billion which are not comfortable but FDI Stock is $4.084 trillion which is sizable.

U.K. has external debt $ 8.475 trillion with GDP $2.71 trillion which has crossed the dangerous level. It has population of 6.5 crores of which 3.27 crores is labour force i.e. 49.38% of its Population and per capita income is $ 44177- U.K. FDI stock is $361 billion and foreign exchange reserves $ 475 billion which are not so comfortable compared with the external debt.

France has external debt $ 5.690 trillion with GDP $ 2.67 trillion 213% higher than GDP which has crossed dangerous level. Per capita income is $77200- with population 6.443 crores. FDi stock $ 840.5 billion and foreign exchange reserves $153. 8 billion seems adequate.

Netherland has external debt $4.5 trillion with GDP $ 864 billion looks crossing dangerous level with per capita income $26400- and population 3.27 crores.

Luxemburg has external debt $ 3.781 trillion with GDP $ 59.95 billion which is 6307% of GDP which is very high for per capita income $6968000 on account of lower population.

Japan has external debt $ 3.587 trillion which is 74% of GDP 4.82 trillion and per capita income $ 26200 - and population 12.6 crores. Looks stable. FDI stock $252.9 billion and Foreign exchange reserves $ 1.249 trillion are acceptable comfort. Japan' yen currency is, however, very volatile.

China has external debt $ 1.843 trillion with GDP $12.29 trillion which is 15 % of GDP. Per capita income is $1326 and population 140 crores. Per Capita income is inflated which should be $983 for population 140 crores. FDI stock $1.354 trillion and Foreign exchange reserves $ 3.55 trillion ae satisfactory.

Russia has external debt $ 537.458 billion with GDP $ 1.579 trillion which is 40% of GDP. Per capita income is $10068- and population is 15.68 crores. Russia FDI stock $ 361 billion and foreign exchange reserves $475 billion and all other indicators look comfortable.

India has the external debt $ 529billion which is 20% of GDP. GDP works out 2.645 trillion. Per capita income is $2134- Population is 124 crores. India has net FDI stock $ 222 billion and Reserves $391 billion are far better than its lowest foreign exchange reserves in 1990s.

Australia has external debt $ 1.487 trillion which is 97% of GDP$1.5310 trillion and FDI stock $176 billion with foreign exchange reserves $ 51.38 billion with other indicators look comfortable. Population is 25.9 crores.

Argentina has external debt $ 214.9 billion which is 45% of its GDP $475.429 billion. FDI stock $36 billion and foreign exchange reserves $ 55.73 billion are in order. Population is 4.72 crores.Argentina has inflation rate 40.9% and unemployment rate 9.6% which are in red. Argentina has been recently given external loan $57 billion by, Mr.Trump President of US as a bailout package. Argentina had applied for bail-out package to IMF for $30 billion.

Mexico has external debt $930 billion which is 42.5% of its GDP $ 2.199 trillion. Foreign exchange reserves $189.4 billion and FDI stock $179.314 billion. Population 7.10 crores.

Venezuela has external debt $100 billion and foreign exchange reserves only $8.5 billion which are just sufficient for meeting foreign exchange needs of the country for maximum 4 weeks. Credit Rating of Venezuela is very poor as SD (selective default).

For restructuring of external debt, Paris Club and London club make negotiation with creditors. Bank creditors are handled by Paris Club.

Russia, German, Japan, Argentina, German, South African Countries and Venezuela had serious debt servicing issues which were either resolved by bailout package or restructuring. In some cases the external debt was waived known as moratorium. In Second World War, US financed the war but the country like Russia did not repay this war loan which is again a part of Moratorium.

External debt is not bad in itself. It should be properly utilized under the careful and practical planning and projection to achieve the estimated targets on time. India has made tremendous financial growth after independence in August 1947 through external borrowing in the field of agriculture, capital goods factory, self-sufficiency in defence and research in satellite area, textile, industries, banking and insurance and in all other field and its annual growth rate is now about 7.3% and has established itself as the third largest economy after US and China. Agriculture foodgrains production which was 80 million metric tons in 1965 has been increased to 277 million metric tons through advanced cultivation, improved fertilizers and using medicine to kill the pesticides on the crops. Manufacturing of motor cars, Scooters, textile factories producing high quality cloth are some of these growth indicators.

Pakistan has always assumed India as their enemy and wants to defeat India in the war. In fact, Pakistan was miserably defeated by India in 1965 and again 1971 and again in Kargill War. It is not taking care of its economy and its financial conditions are seriously deteriorated. It has no longer foreign exchange reserves to cover its imports for more than 2weeks. Its military is dominating the civic government elected by the people of Pakistan in so called democratic process. Pakistan Army is supporting terrorists financially and with military equipments. It encourages terrorists to attack constantly Indian borders and Afghanistan borders. This has resulted in Indian army constantly safeguarding its Jummu-Kasmir borders from all sides. Pakistan is always supported by China and it has given large amount of loans to Pakistan. Pakistan may at any time be caught by the debt trap of China.

Since there was no other way, Pakistan Present Prime Minister Mr. Imran Khan applied for a Loan of $12 billion as a bailout package to IMF. There were extensive negotiations between Pakistan government and IMF. IMF ultimately approved the loan of $6 billion to Pakistan with following stringent conditions:

(1) Pakistan should keep exchange rate for Pakistani rupee freely convertible. At present, Pak Rupee has been deteriorated. Pak Rs.140 =US$1. Economists in Pakistan are afraid that with floating rate, it will touch to Rs.200=US$1. There is at present unmanageable inflation which will tremendously increase.

(2) Public Spending and Welfare expenditure should be drastically reduced. This will created public unrest.

(3) Taxes should be levied to raise state income by PR 200 billion. This will become unbearable to the Pakistani people.

In order to come out of this situation (if that is Pakistani government and Military rulers sincerely desire so),

(1) Pakistan should stop encouraging terrorism in its country and all terrorist group active in Pakistan should be banned as all countries in the world want Pakistan to do and should punish them ruthlessly. For that purpose, Kashmir issue should not be made as a prestigious issue by Pakistan and it should agree that Kashmir is the integral part of India.

(2) It should not treat India as its enemy but as a friend and resume trade with India.
(3) It should stop immediately attacks on India by terrorists.
(4) Military rule should abandon their dominance over civil government and allow the government to rule the country peacefully with implementation of economic reforms that are essential for the country's development.
(5) It should stop taking loans at high interest rates to avoid in falling in the China's debt trap and should acquire confidence of the various countries who will do financial business with it for its economic development.
(6) Present loan $6 billion should be fully utilized for the purpose it was taken and it should not be misused.
(7) All conditions stipulated by IMF should be strictly complied with. Of course, IMF will closely monitor compliance of the conditions by Pakistan fully all the times and will impose the penalty for non-accomplice at any time.

General cautions to be ensured about External debt

(1) All countries should take external loan essentially for capital development.
(2) Country should ensure that loan amount is fully utilized strictly for the purpose it is taken
(3) Projects for which should be completed within the timeframe of Project to void enhancement of project cost and project completion period.
(4) Planning should be effective and critical path of the project should be completed within the projected time/period.
(5) Country should ensure that debt servicing ratio should not be so high that to pay interest on loan, fresh loan needs to be taken from the international financial institutions.
(6) Returns on completed projects should be high enough to discharge the liability of the debt servicing.
(7) In 1991, India implemented liberal financial policy. India's debt servicing before 1991 was 30% p.a. which came to 4% p.a. which is now manageable. Countries incurring high debt like US, UK, Australia and others should ensurethat their debt servicing should always be manageable and they should avoid unnecessary expenditure on defence, star wars and unnecessary public welfare measures.

Public Debt

As mentioned above, public debts are taken by the country for their progress. If used productivity, it will yield comfortable returns to meet servicing. Generally, such loans should not exceed 40% of GDP.

Following is the observations of some countries.

India 70% of GDP which works out to $ 2 trillion. Such loans are in LCy but with high rate of interest usually @8% p.a. Therefore earning of investment from such loans should minimum exceed 10 p.a. for ease of economy.

US has 130% of GDP as its public loan which works out to $26.08 trillion. This is very high and US should curtail its exoabarent expenses.

China has reasonable ratio of public debt i.e. 16.1% of GDP.

Russia has high ratio of 138.9% of GDP for Public debt and it should ensure productivity of such loans to avoid debt trap.

France has 96.8% of GDP as its Public debt which is high and should be curtailed.

German has 64.13% of GDP as public loan which looks comfortable.

Australia is within the limit of 42.3% of GDP in public loan while Argentina has public loan which is 97.7% i.e. $ 464 billion which is quite panful.

Mexico is comfortable with public debt of 341 billon but under figure for population below poverty line is 42.37% which is worrying.

Venezuela has big crisis and its economy has completely collapsed with inflation of 2200% andunemployment @14.3% with public loan 138.9% of GDP. Recovery can be possible if the Maduro will drastically change his political ideology in the interest of the nation and should improve its relationship with US for economic and financial improvement at the earliest.

Additional information on external debts of countries:

(1) As per Quarterly external debt report of World Bank, There was invasion of Mexico by France after the government of Benito Juarez suspended interest payments on its external debt in 1861. Another was blockade of Venezuelan ports by the fleets of Germany, Italy and United Kingdom in 1902-03 to force the Venezuelan government to pay its foreign debt to their nationals. This prompted the Drago-PorterConvention of 1907., which established the universal principle that States may not use force in order to collect claims arising from the sovereign debt of a State held by their nationals.(Benedek, 2007)

(2) The UK also suspended the convertibility of the pound; this forced its foreign creditors to use resources obtained from UK debt repayments in purchase of goods or assets within the pound area.

(3) In the decision, Republic of Argentina v. Waltover, Inc; 1992 under which issuing bonds was considered a ‘commercial activity”.

(4) In all these schemes, creditors should choose between a "debt reduction option", which applied the appropriate debt cancellation rates and rescheduled the remaining debt, including ODAcredits, or other options that reduced the debt burden by extending the repayment period and reducing interest rates.

(5) For instance, the Paris Club obliged Pakistan and Ukraine to obtain a level of debt relief from private creditors' equivalent the Club's concessions.

(6) Conditionality (especially that involving structural reforms) by the IMF and World Bank has, in fact, followed some additional goals, such as redefining national development choices according the creditors views and interest (Akyuz, 2005). Some IMF reports have acknowledged that there are "legitimate concerns that in many instances structural conditionality may have gone beyond what can be justified in relation to the intended purpose of conditionality in safeguarding Fund resources" IMF, 2001; 27). Moreover, a report by the Independent Evaluation Office of IMF stresses that 'the crisis should not be used as an opportunity to seek long term agenda of reforms with detailed timetables just because leverage is high, even though such reforms may be beneficial to long term economic efficiency (IMF, 20013a: 50).

(7) Success in associating commercial creditors has been limited, and some of them have initiated litigation against HIPCsto obtain full debt repayment.

(8) In the Greek debt restructuring in 2012, for instance, commercial banks holding Greek bonds were represented by the Institute of International Finance, whose members include banks, insurance companies, asset managers, sovereign wealth funds, pension funds, central banks and development banks.

(9) In 1997, the IMF launched the Supplemental Reserves Facility to help countries cope with "large short-term financing need resulting from a sudden and disruptive loss of market confidence reflected in pressure on the capital account and the member'sreserves" (IMF, 1997). Subsequently, countries meeting pre-established eligibility criteria could have rapid access to short term precautionary credit lines. The Contingent Credit Line was made available in 1999, followed by the Reserve Augumentation Line in 2006 and Short-term Liquidity Facility (SLF) in 2008, immediately after the collapse of Lehman Brothers. As potential users did not apply to this precautionary financing, the IMF had to propose new credit lines to finally receive a number of requests:the Flexible Credit Line (FCL) in 2009 and Precautionary Credit Line (PCL)in 2010 – with larger access, longer repayment periods and more

flexibility, and without ex-post conditionality. Colombia, Mexico and Poland applied for the IMF's FCL, and the Former Yugoslav Republic of Macedonia and Morocco for the IMF's PCL.

(10) The new legislation did not totally override the Chambery principle, but added a "safe harbour" provision for litigation claims where the aggregate purchase price was at least $500,000-

External Private Debt

External private debtwas historically quite limited. Thus it attracted little attention from oversight bodies. Moreover, those bodies tended to be influenced by free market advocates, who opposed government intervention in growing private external liabilities on the grounds that such liabilities resulted from the actions of so-called "rational agents" with respect to private saving and investment decisions, and therefore would not lead to financial distress. However, experience, particularly in the aftermath of the global financial crisis, when high external private debt became main driver of public sector debt crises, has challenged the validity of such an argument.

Policymakers should therefore not be too keen about the overall lower level of public debt in many developing countries; rather, they should be wary of the significant risks to financial stability associated with the increasing ratios of private external debt to GIN. This includes rising levels of private external borrowing by non-financial corporations, primarily for purposes of financial operations via the offshore issuance of debt securities over the past few years. This is compound by exchange-rate risks and the danger of sudden reversals of capital flows, for example in the wake of normalization of US interest rates, and/or volatile commodity prices. Hence, a rapid expansion of private external debt could be followed by debt crises and a rapid increase of public external debts. Indeed, following Latin Amercan debt crisis in the 1980s, a large share of external debt owed by the private sectorwas transferred to the public sector. Similarly, during the built-up to the Asian finamcial crisis of 1997, a significant proportion of the debt incurred in the region was in the form of bank loans to private borrowers that were de facto nationalized after the onset of the crisis.

The structure of external debt has also evolved significantly on the creditors' side in most developing countries, until the 1870s, and sometimes in subsequent decades, a large proportion of long-term external debt was owed to official creditors mostly on a bilateral basis. This was the cause, in particular, for developing countries whose economic links with their former metropolitan centres had remained strong.Commercial banks were reluctant to lend to less developing countries. In the early 1970s, in all developing regions other than Latin America, external debt owed to official creditors outpaced that owed to private creditors. In 1967, 67% of African external debt was owed to bilateral or multilaternal official creditors; in West Asia this share was 92 per cent, climbing to 93 per cent in South Asia. By contrast, 70 per cent of Latin American debt and almost half that of South-East Asia was contracted with private creditors.

Throughout the 1970s, developing countries' external debt rose sharply. Their total long-term external debt increase from 13 per cent of their GNI in 1970 to 21 per cent in 1980, due primarly to a surge in their debt owed to private creditors.

After 1987, the stock of debt owed by borrowing developing countries to private creditors declined from the peak of 24 per cent of their GNI in 1987 to 9 per cent in 2011. This was due to the booms during the period. Even when governments have not engaged in foreign borrowing during the boom period, they are frequently forced to absorb bad private debts. Thus, external debt crises are also public sector crises.

Sovereign Debt Issues

Throughout the nineteenth century, debt restructuring were bilateral matter, dealt with exclusively between the debtor and creditor. Crisis resolution was not always swift or smooth, but mutual self-interest helped the parties to reach agreement. In general, domestic currency devaluation was not an option, since debt instrument frequently included gold clauses, which obliged the Debtor State to make payments in gold, or equivalent thereof. Creditors, on the other hand, were in weak bargaining position at a time when the respect for sovereign immunity was stronger than it was today. Creditor lacked an effective means to coordinate their claims.

This changed after First World War., when sovereign debt was new dynamic in the context of German defaultson reparation payment. US took the lead in designing ways to settle German First World War reparation debt without taking the latter's total economic collapse and political disintegration, through the 1924 Dawes Plan and its successor, the 1929 Young Plan.

The substantial shift from syndicated bank loans to external bond financing over the past two decades has significantly increased the complexity of debt structuring. Thousands of bondholders with diverse interest can face divergent regulatory constraints, and bond series can be issued in different jurisdiction. Usually, informal negotiation takes place in committees where different groups of bondholders are represented. The debtor country eventually proposes bond swaps with lower face values, longer maturities and/or lower interest rates. Other basic characteristics of the bond may also be altered; new bond may be denominated in a different currency, be subject to different jurisdiction, and incorporate new clauses, such as collective action clauses (CACs). Bondholders then vote for or against accepting the swaps.

The Role of Contingent Liabilities in Sovereign Debt

Problem of contingent liability is recent and growing area of concern. Contingent sovereign liabilities refer mostly to third party debt guarantees, granted either explicitly through a formal undertaking, or implicitly through informal or semi-informal arrangements that signal to the creditor the sovereign's awareness and implicit approval of a transaction. Another, even less formally acknowledged form of contingent liability of a sovereign arises from its role as lender of last resort during debt crises.

INDEX

C

D

E

G

O

P

Q

R

S

W

Y

Z